TCL/TK
IN A NUTSHELL

A Desktop Quick Reference

TCL/TK
IN A NUTSHELL

A Desktop Quick Reference

Paul Raines & Jeff Tranter

O'REILLY®

Beijing · Cambridge · Farnham · Köln · Paris · Sebastopol · Taipei · Tokyo

Tcl/Tk in a Nutshell

by Paul Raines and Jeff Tranter

Copyright © 1999 O'Reilly & Associates, Inc. All rights reserved.
Printed in the United States of America.

Published by O'Reilly & Associates, Inc., 101 Morris Street, Sebastopol, CA 95472.

Editor: Andy Oram

Production Editor: Madeleine Newell

Printing History:

> March 1999:   First Edition.

ISBN: 1-56592-433-9   [8/99]

In memory of my father, William B. Raines

—Paul Raines

Table of Contents

Preface

This book is about Tcl, the scripting language developed by John Ousterhout. Tcl stands for *tool command language* and was originally designed as a simple scripting language interpreter that could be embedded inside applications written in the C language. With the addition of the Tk graphical toolkit and a host of other language extensions supporting such features as graphics, relational databases, and object-oriented programming, Tcl has become a popular programming language for developing applications in its own right. The freely available Tcl language interpreter runs on many computer platforms, including most Unix-compatible systems, Microsoft Windows, and Apple Macintosh.

Tcl/Tk in a Nutshell is a quick reference for the basic commands of Tcl, Tk, and several other popular Tcl language extensions. As with other books in O'Reilly's "In a Nutshell" series, this book is geared toward users who know what they want to do but just can't remember the right command or option. For subtle details, you will sometimes want to consult the official Tcl reference documentation, but for most tasks you should find the answer you need in this volume. We hope that this guide will become an invaluable desktop reference for the Tcl user.

Conventions

This desktop quick reference uses the following typographic conventions:

Italic
> Used for commands, methods, functions, programs, and options. All terms shown in italic are typed literally. Italic is also used for filenames and URLs, and to highlight terms under discussion.

`Constant width`
> Used for code in program listings and for data structures and values to be entered exactly as shown. Also used for special variables, global variables, options showing resource and class names, and subwidget names.

Constant width italic

Used to show arguments, options, and variables that should be replaced with user-supplied values.

[ ]

Surround optional elements in a description of syntax. Note that square braces are also a commonly used Tcl language construct and appear in some Tcl program examples, in which case they are part of the Tcl code.

|

Used in syntax descriptions to separate items for which only one alternative may be chosen at a time.

...

Indicates that the preceding item may be repeated as many times as desired.

 The owl symbol is used to designate a note.

 The turkey symbol is used to designate a warning.

Contact O'Reilly & Associates

We have tested and verified all of the information in this book to the best of our ability, but you may find that features have changed (or even that we have made mistakes!). Please let us know about any errors you find, as well as your suggestions for future editions, by writing to us at the following address:

O'Reilly & Associates, Inc.
101 Morris Street
Sebastopol, CA 95472
1-800-998-9938 (in the U.S. or Canada)
1-707-829-0515 (international/local)
1-707-829-0104 (FAX)

You can also send us messages electronically. To be put on a mailing list or request a catalog, send email to:

info@oreilly.com

To ask technical questions or comment on the book, send email to:

bookquestions@oreilly.com

About This Book

When Jeff Tranter first started with Tcl sometime around 1992, he felt the need for a simple language quick-reference card to help jog his memory when programming. He created a simple one-page cheat sheet that listed all of the Tcl language commands. In the spirit of freely sharing with other users, he uploaded his quick reference to one of the Tcl archive sites.

Some time later, Paul Raines created a nice quick reference for the commands provided by the Tk toolkit. Again, initially this was one double-sized page in length.

Inspired by the excellent *Perl 5 Pocket Reference* by Johan Vromans (published by O'Reilly & Associates), Paul combined the Tcl and Tk references into a small booklet of about 40 half-size pages, and made it freely available on the Internet. The current version is now over 80 pages in length and can also be purchased from O'Reilly as the *Tcl/Tk Pocket Reference*.

After finishing O'Reilly's first book on Tcl/Tk, *Tcl/Tk Tools* (by Mark Harrison et al.), O'Reilly editor Andy Oram thought about doing a Tcl reference book. So he approached us about expanding our work into a full-blown reference on Tcl, Tk, and all of the popular language extensions. Thus, the one-page Tcl cheat sheet that Jeff created for his own use has now grown into a 450-page book. We hope that you are happy with the result and find it a useful reference.

Acknowledgments

A motivational speaker once said that the formula for a successful manager was to give your people the tools they need to do the job and stay out of their way. Our editor, Andy Oram, did a great job of keeping us on track but generally staying out of our way. As the first Nutshell book to use SGML text-processing tools developed in-house, *Tcl/Tk in a Nutshell* had some teething pains but we were able to get the job done with help from the O'Reilly tools group.

Special thanks go to the reviewers of the first draft of this book: Allan Brighton, De Clarke, Robert Gray, Cameron Laird, Don Libes, Michael McLennan, Wayne Miller, Tom Poindexter, and Mark Roseman. Their many useful comments helped make this a better book.

One of the reviewers, Tom Poindexter, went beyond the call of duty. He suggested that we add a chapter on Tcl programming hints, and even volunteered to write it for us.

Paul would like to thank his wife, Deborah, for her understanding and patience when he disappeared into "computerland."

Jeff would like to thank his family—Veronica, Jennifer, and Jason—for bearing with him while he wrote yet another book, taking more than his share of time on the computer.

CHAPTER 1

Introduction

This chapter presents a brief history of and an introduction to the Tcl language and describes how this book is organized.

What Is Tcl?

In the early 1980s John Ousterhout, then at the University of California at Berkeley, was working with a group that developed hardware design tools. They found that they kept inventing a new scripting language with each new tool they developed. It was always added as an afterthought and poorly implemented. John decided to create a general-purpose scripting language that could be reused when developing new tools. He called the language Tcl, for tool command language, made it freely available for download, and presented it at the Winter 1990 USENIX conference. It soon became popular, with an estimated 50 Tcl applications written or in development one year later.

One of the attendees at Ousterhout's presentation, Don Libes, saw the applicability of Tcl to a problem he was working on. Within a few weeks he developed the first version of Expect, which became the first killer application for Tcl, driving many people to install Tcl who might have otherwise ignored it.

Ousterhout's philosophy is to embed a scripting language inside applications. Combining the advantages of a compiled language like C (portability, speed, access to operating system functions) with those of a scripting language (ease of learning, runtime evaluation, no compilation) gives an overall reduction in development time and opportunities for creating small, reliable, and reusable software components. An application with an embedded Tcl interpreter can be extended and customized by the end user in countless ways.

The Tcl interpreter has a well-defined interface and is typically built as an object library, making it easy to extend the basic language with new commands. Tcl can also be used as a prototyping language. An application can be written entirely in

Tcl, and once the design is proven, critical portions can be rewritten in C for performance reasons.

A year later, at the Winter USENIX conference, Ousterhout presented Tk, a graphical toolkit for Tcl that made it easy to write applications for the X11 windowing system. It also supported the *send* command, a simple yet powerful way to allow Tk applications to communicate with each other.

Since then, with dozens of Tcl extensions, many of them designed to solve problems related to specific domains such as graphics and relational databases, the Tcl programming environment has become even more powerful. Today, Tcl runs on Unix, Macintosh, and Windows platforms, and even inside a web browser. It has a huge installed base of users and applications, both free and commercial. As Tcl approaches its tenth anniversary, it is poised to continue its growth in popularity.

Structure of This Book

Following this brief introduction, Chapter 2 covers the core features of the Tcl language itself. Chapter 3 covers Tk, the graphical user interface (GUI) toolkit that is probably the most popular Tcl extension. Chapter 4 covers the C-language application programming interface for Tcl, and Chapter 5 does the same for Tk.

Each language extension chapter follows a similar format: after a brief introduction, any special global and environment variables are described, followed by a logically grouped summary of the commands. The heart of each chapter is an alphabetical summary of each command that lists the options in detail. Short programming examples are provided for the more complex commands.

Chapter 6 covers Expect, the first popular application to be built using Tcl. Chapter 7 is on [incr Tcl], which adds object-oriented programming features to Tcl. Chapter 8 covers [incr Tk], a framework for object-oriented graphical widgets built using [incr Tcl].

Chapter 9 covers Tix, a Tk extension that adds powerful graphical widgets. Chapter 10 is on TclX, also known as Extended Tcl, a number of extensions that make Tcl more suited to general-purpose programming. Chapter 11 is on BLT, which provides a number of useful new commands for producing graphs, managing data, and performing other graphics-related functions.

Tcl has good support for relational databases. Chapter 12 and Chapter 13 cover the Tcl extensions for the popular Oracle and Sybase relational databases, and Chapter 14 describes Tclodbc, which supports the Microsoft Windows ODBC database protocol.

Chapter 15, *Hints and Tips for the Tcl Programmer*, by Tom Poindexter, departs from the style of the rest of the book somewhat by presenting a collection of tips for using Tcl effectively, commonly made errors, and suggestions on programming style.

The Appendix, *Tcl Resources*, lists further resources on Tcl, both in print and on the Internet. The index cross-references the material in the book, including every Tcl command described in the text.

CHAPTER 2

Tcl Core Commands

This chapter summarizes the features and commands of the core Tcl language, which was developed by John Ousterhout. The chapter is based on Tcl Version 8.0; a few features are not part of Tcl per se, but are included in the Tcl shell and most Tcl applications, so are included here and noted with (*tclsh*).

Overview

The Tcl interpreter has a simple syntax, making it suitable as an interactive command language and allowing it to be reasonably small and fast.

Tcl programs consist of *commands*. Commands consist of a command name, optionally followed by arguments separated by whitespace. Commands are separated by newline or semicolon characters. All commands return a value. The user can create new commands (usually called *procs*), which operate just like built-in commands.

Within commands, the language supports several additional language constructs. *Double quotation marks* are used to group characters, possibly containing whitespace, into one word. *Curly braces* group arguments. They can cross lines and be nested, and no further substitutions are performed within them. *Square brackets* perform command substitution. The text within the brackets is evaluated as a Tcl command and replaced with the result. The *dollar sign* is used to perform variable substitution and supports both scalar and array variables. C language–style backslash escape codes support special characters, such as newline. The *pound sign* or hash mark (#) is the null command, acting as a comment.

In Tcl, all data is represented as strings. Strings often take one of three forms. *Lists* are strings consisting of whitespace-separated values. Using curly braces, list elements can in turn be other lists. Tcl provides several utility commands for manipulating lists. Numeric *expressions* support variables and essentially the same operators and precedence rules as the C language. Strings often represent *commands*, the most common use being as arguments to control structure commands such as *if* and *proc*.

Basic Language Features

; or `newline`
> Statement separator

\
> Statement continuation if last character in line

#
> Comment (null command)

var
> Simple variable

var(index)
> Associative array variable

var(i,j,...)
> Multidimensional array variable

$var
> Variable substitution (also ${*var*})

[*command*]
> Command substitution

char
> Backslash substitution (see "Backslash Substitutions," later in this chapter)

"*string*"
> Quoting with variable substitution

{*string*}
> Quoting with no substitution (deferred substitution)

The only data type in Tcl is a string. However, some commands interpret arguments as numbers or boolean values. Here are some examples:

Integer
> 123 0xff 0377

Floating point
> 2.1 3. 6e4 7.91e+16

Boolean
> true false 0 1 yes no

Command-Line Options

The standard Tcl shell program *tclsh* accepts a command line of the form:

> *tclsh* [*fileName*] [*arg*...]

where *fileName* is an optional file from which to read Tcl commands. With no *fileName* argument, *tclsh* runs interactively using standard input and output.

The filename and any additional arguments are stored in the Tcl variables argc, argv, and argv0 (see the section "Special Variables").

Environment Variables

The following environment variables are used by the Tcl interpreter:

HOME
> Used by commands such as *cd*, *filename*, and *glob* to determine the user's home directory

PATH
> Used by *exec* to find executable programs

TCLLIBPATH
> A Tcl list of directories to search when autoloading Tcl commands

TCL_LIBRARY
> The location of the directory containing Tcl library scripts

Special Variables

The following global variables have special meaning to the Tcl interpreter:

argc
> Number of command-line arguments, not including the name of the script file (*tclsh*)

argv
> List containing command-line arguments (*tclsh*)

argv0
> Filename being interpreted, or name by which script was invoked (*tclsh*)

env
> Array in which each element name is an environment variable

errorCode
> Error code information from last Tcl error

errorInfo
> Describes the stack trace of the last Tcl error

`tcl_interactive`
Set to 1 if running interactively, 0 otherwise (*tclsh*)

`tcl_library`
Location of standard Tcl libraries

`tcl_pkgPath`
List of directories where packages are normally installed

`tcl_patchLevel`
Current patch level of Tcl interpreter

`tcl_platform`
Array with elements `byteOrder`, `machine`, `osVersion`, `platform`, and `os`

`tcl_precision`
Number of significant digits to retain when converting floating-point numbers to strings (default 12)

`tcl_prompt1`
Primary prompt (*tclsh*)

`tcl_prompt2`
Secondary prompt for incomplete commands (*tclsh*)

`tcl_rcFileName`
The name of a user-specific startup file

`tcl_traceCompile`
Controls tracing of bytecode compilation; 0 for no output, 1 for summary, and 2 for detailed

`tcl_traceExec`
Controls tracing of bytecode execution; 0 for no output, 1 for summary, and 2 for detailed

`tcl_version`
Current version of Tcl interpreter

Backslash Substitutions

The following backslash substitutions are valid in words making up Tcl commands, except inside braces:

\a
Audible alert (0x07)

\b
Backspace (0x08)

\f
Form feed (0x0C)

\n
> Newline (0x0A)

\r
> Carriage return (0x0D)

\t
> Horizontal tab (0x09)

\v
> Vertical tab (0x0B)

\space
> Space (0x20)

\newline
> Newline (0x0A)

\ddd
> Octal value (*d* = 0–7)

\xd...
> Hexadecimal value (*d* = 0–9, a–f)

\c
> Replace \c with character *c*

\\
> A backslash

Operators and Math Functions

The *expr* command recognizes the following operators, in decreasing order of precedence:

+ - ~ !
> Unary plus and minus, bitwise NOT, logical NOT

* / %
> Multiply, divide, remainder

+ -
> Add, subtract

<< >>
> Bitwise shift left, bitwise shift right

< > <= >=
> Boolean comparison for less than, greater than, less than or equal, greater than or equal

== !=
> Boolean test for equality, inequality

&
> Bitwise AND

^
> Bitwise exclusive OR

|
> Bitwise inclusive OR

&&
> Logical AND

| |
> Logical OR

x?y:z
> If $x \neq 0$, then y, else z

All operators support integers. All except ^, %, <<, >>, &, ^, and | support floating-point values. Boolean operators can also be used for string operands, in which case string comparison will be used. This will occur if any of the operands are not valid numbers. The &&, | |, and ?: operators have lazy evaluation, as in C, in which evaluation stops if the outcome can be determined.

The *expr* command also recognizes the following math functions:

abs(*arg*)
> Absolute value of *arg*

acos(*arg*)
> Arc cosine of *arg*

asin(*arg*)
> Arc sine of *arg*

atan(*arg*)
> Arc tangent of *arg*

atan2(*x, y*)
> Arc tangent of x/y

ceil(*arg*)
> Rounds *arg* up to the nearest integer

cos(*arg*)
> Cosine of *arg*

cosh(*arg*)
> Hyperbolic cosine of *arg*

double(*arg*)
> Floating-point value of *arg*

exp(*arg*)
> *e* to the power of *arg*

```
floor(arg)
```
Round *arg* down to the nearest integer

```
fmod(x, y)
```
Remainder of x/y

```
hypot(x, y)
```
sqrt($x^*x + y^*y$)

```
int(arg)
```
arg as integer by truncating

```
log(arg)
```
Natural logarithm of *arg*

```
log10(arg)
```
Base 10 logarithm of *arg*

```
pow(x, y)
```
x raised to the exponent *y*

```
rand()
```
Random floating-point number ≥ 0 and < 1

```
round(arg)
```
arg as integer by rounding

```
sin(arg)
```
Sine of *arg*

```
sinh(arg)
```
Hyperbolic sine of *arg*

```
sqrt(arg)
```
Square root of *arg*

```
srand(arg)
```
Seeds random number generator using integer value *arg*

```
tan(arg)
```
Tangent of *arg*

```
tanh(arg)
```
Hyperbolic tangent of *arg*

Regular Expressions

Several Tcl commands, including *regexp*, support the use of regular expressions:

regex| regex
> Match either expression.

regex *
> Match zero or more of *regex*.

regex+

   Match one or more of *regex*.

regex?

   Match zero or one of *regex*.

.

   Any single character except newline.

^

   Match beginning of string.

$

   Match end of string.

c

   Match character *c*.

c

   Match character *c*.

[*abc*]

   Match any character in set *abc*.

[^*abc*]

   Match characters not in set *abc*.

[*a-z*]

   Match range of characters *a* through *z*.

[^*a-z*]

   Match characters not in range *a* through *z*.

(*regex*)

   Group expressions.

Pattern Globbing

Many Tcl commands, most notably *glob*, support filename globbing using the following forms:

?

   Match any single character.

*

   Match zero or more characters.

[*abc*]

   Match characters in set *abc*.

[*a-z*]

   Match range of characters *a* through *z*.

\c
> Match character *c*.

{a,b,...}
> Match any of strings *a*, *b*, etc.

~
> Home directory (for *glob* command).

~user
> Match home directory of *user* (for *glob* command).

For the *glob* command, a period at the beginning of a file's name or just after "/" must be matched explicitly and all "/" characters must be matched explicitly.

Predefined I/O Channel Identifiers

The following predefined I/O channel names can be used with commands that perform input or output over channels (e.g., *gets*):

stdin
> Standard input

stdout
> Standard output

stderr
> Standard error output

Group Listing of Commands

This section briefly lists all Tcl commands, grouped logically by function.

Control Statements

break	Abort innermost containing loop command.
case	Obsolete, see *switch*.
continue	Skip to next iteration of innermost containing loop command.
exit	Terminate process.
for	Loop based on an expression.
foreach	Loop over each element of a list.
if	Conditional evaluation.
return	Return from procedure.
switch	Evaluation based on pattern match.
while	Loop based on a condition being true.

File Manipulation

file atime	Return file access time.
file mtime	Return file modification time.
file attributes	Set or get platform-dependent file attributes.
file copy	Make copy of a file or directory.
file delete	Remove file or directory.
file dirname	Return directory portion of pathname.
file executable	Return 1 if file is executable, 0 otherwise.
file exists	Return 1 if file exists, 0 otherwise.
file isdirectory	Return 1 if file is a directory, 0 otherwise.
file isfile	Return 1 if file is a regular file, 0 otherwise.
file owned	Return 1 if file is owned by current user, 0 otherwise.
file readable	Return 1 if file is readable by current user, 0 otherwise.
file writable	Return 1 if file is writable by current user, 0 otherwise.
file extension	Return characters after and including last period.
file join	Combine arguments with path separator to form pathname.
file mkdir	Create a directory.
file nativename	Return platform-specific filename.
file pathtype	Return type of path: `absolute`, `relative`, or `volumerelative`.
file readlink	Return value of symbolic link.
file rename	Rename file, moving if necessary.
file rootname	Return characters before last period in pathname.
file size	Return file size in bytes.
file split	Split pathname into separate elements.
file stat	Store file information in an array variable.
file lstat	Same as *file stat*, but return information for target of symbolic links.
file tail	Return characters in name after last file separator.
file type	Return type of file: `file`, `directory`, `characterSpecial`, `blockSpecial`, `fifo`, `link`, or `socket`.
file volume	Return list of mounted volumes or drive letters.

Tcl Interpreter Information

info args	Return information on procedure arguments.
info body	Return body of procedure.
info cmdcount	Return count of commands invoked by interpreter.
info commands	Return list of Tcl commands.
info complete	Return 1 if command is complete.
info default	Return default procedure argument.
info exists	Return 1 if variable exists.
info globals	Return list of global variables.
info hostname	Return machine hostname.
info level	Return procedure stack level or stack arguments.
info library	Return name of library directory.
info loaded	Return list of loaded packages.

info locals	Return list of local variables.
info nameofexecutable	Return name of application.
info patchlevel	Return Tcl patch level.
info procs	Return list of Tcl procedures.
info script	Return name of file being evaluated.
info sharedlibextension	Return file extension for shared libraries.
info tclversion	Return Tcl version.
info vars	Return list of local and global variables.

Lists

concat	Concatenate (join) lists into a new list.
join	Join lists into a string.
lappend	Append elements to list.
lindex	Retrieve element from list.
linsert	Insert element into list.
list	Create a list.
llength	Number of elements in list.
lrange	Return sequential range of elements from list.
lreplace	Replace elements in list.
lsearch	Search list for element.
lsort	Sort elements of list.
split	Split a string into a list.

Arrays

array anymore	Return 1 if more array elements left during search.
array donesearch	Terminate array search.
array exists	Return 1 if array exists.
array get	Return list of array element names and values.
array names	Return list of array element names.
array nextelement	Return name of next element during search.
array set	Set array values.
array size	Return number of elements in array.
array startsearch	Initialize array search operation.
parray	Print array.

Strings

append	Append values to variable.
binary	Insert and extract fields from binary strings.
format	*printf( )*-style string formatting.
regexp	Regular expression pattern matching.
regsub	Regular expression string substitution.
scan	*sscanf( )*-style string parsing.
string compare	Lexical string comparison.
string first	Search for first occurrence of substring.
string index	Return character from string.

string last	Search for last occurrence of substring.
string length	Return number of characters in string.
string match	Compare strings using shell glob pattern matching.
string range	Return range of characters from string.
string tolower	Convert to lowercase.
string toupper	Convert to uppercase.
string trim	Remove leading and trailing characters.
string trimleft	Remove leading characters.
string trimright	Remove trailing characters.
string wordend	Return end position of word in string.
string wordstart	Return start position of word in string.
subst	Backslash, command, variable substitutions.

Input/Output

close	Close channel.
eof	Check for end of file.
fblocked	Return 1 if last operation exhausted available input.
fconfigure	Set or get I/O options.
fcopy	Copy from one channel to another.
fileevent	Set file event handler.
flush	Flush buffered output.
gets	Read line of input.
open	Open channel.
puts	Write to channel.
read	Read from channel.
seek	Set the access position.
socket	Open network connection.
tell	Get access position.

System Interaction

cd	Change working directory.
clock	Time functions.
exec	Invoke subprocesses.
glob	Filename pattern matching.
pid	Return process IDs.
pwd	Return current working directory.

Command History

history	Same as history info.
history add	Add command to history list.
history change	Change command in history list.
history clear	Clear history list.
history event	Return event.
history info	Return formatted history list.
history keep	Get or set size of history list.

| *history nextid* | Return next event number. |
| *history redo* | Execute command from history list. |

The *tclsh* program also supports the following *csh*-style history commands:

!!	Repeat last command.
`!event`	Repeat command, matching a number or name.
`^old^new`	Repeat command, substituting occurrences of regular expression *old* with *new*.

Multiple Interpreters

interp alias	Create, delete, or return definition of an interpreter alias.
interp aliases	Return list of command aliases.
interp create	Create slave interpreter.
interp delete	Delete slave interpreters.
interp eval	Evaluate command using slave interpreter.
interp exists	Test if slave interpreter exists.
interp expose	Make hidden command visible to slave interpreter.
interp hidden	Return list of hidden commands.
interp hide	Hide exposed command.
interp invokehidden	Invoke hidden command.
interp issafe	Return 1 if interpreter is safe.
interp marktrusted	Mark interpreter as trusted.
interp share	Share I/O channel between interpreters.
interp slaves	Return list of slave interpreters.
interp target	Return list describing target interpreter for an alias.
interp transfer	Move I/O channel to another interpreter.

Packages

package forget	Remove information about package from interpreter.
package ifneeded	Tell interpreter how to load a package.
package names	Return list of available packages.
package provide	Indicate that package is present in interpreter.
package require	Indicate that package is needed.
package unknown	Supply command to load packages when not found.
package vcompare	Compare package version numbers.
package versions	Return list of package versions available.
package vsatisfies	Return package version compatibility information.
pkg_mkIndex	Build index for automatic loading of packages.

Miscellaneous Commands

after	Execute a command after a time delay.
auto_execok	Return path of executable.
auto_load	Autoload Tcl command.
auto_mkindex	Generate *tclIndex* file.
auto_reset	Reset autoloading cache.

bgerror	Process background errors.
catch	Evaluate script and trap exceptional returns.
error	Generate an error.
eval	Evaluate a Tcl script.
expr	Evaluate an expression.
global	Access global variables.
incr	Increment the value of a variable.
load	Load machine code and initialize new commands.
namespace	Create and manipulate contexts for commands and variables.
proc	Create a Tcl procedure.
rename	Rename or delete a command.
set	Read and write variables.
source	Evaluate a file or resource as a Tcl script.
time	Time the execution of a script.
trace	Trace variable access.
unknown	Handle attempts to use nonexistent commands.
unset	Delete variables.
update	Process pending events and idle callbacks.
uplevel	Execute a script in a different stack frame.
upvar	Create link to variable in a different stack frame.
variable	Create and initialize a namespace variable.
vwait	Process events until a variable is written.

Alphabetical Summary of Commands

This section describes all Tcl commands, listed in alphabetical order.

---

after

after `options`...

Delay execution of the current program or schedule another command to be executed sometime in the future.

after `ms`

Delay execution of current program for *ms* milliseconds.

after `ms` `script`...

Return immediately but schedule the given list of command script arguments to be executed *ms* milliseconds in the future and return an identifier that can be used for *after cancel*.

after cancel `id`

Cancel a previous *after* command using the identifier `id` returned previously.

after cancel `script`...

Cancel a previously set *after* command by specifying the command script arguments originally used in the command.

---

after idle `script`...

Schedule a command script to be executed when the event loop is idle.

after info [`id`]

If no `id` is specified, return a list of currently scheduled *after* commands. With an `id`, return a list consisting of the command and the time of the specified idle or timer event.

append

append varName [`value`...]

Append the specified values to variable `varName` The variable need not already exist.

array

array option `arrayName` [`arg`...]

Provide functions to manipulate array variables.

array anymore `arrayName searchId`

Return 1 if there are more elements left in an array search, or 0 if all elements have been returned. Accepts an array name and a search ID obtained from a previous call to *array startsearch*.

array donesearch `arrayName searchId`

Terminate an array search. Accepts an array name and a search ID obtained from a previous call to *array startsearch*.

array exists `arrayName`

Return 1 if an array variable with the given name exists; otherwise, return 0.

array get `arrayName` [`pattern`]

Return a list containing pairs of elements consisting of array names and values. If `pattern` is specified, only the elements that match the glob `pattern` are included; otherwise, all are returned.

array names `arrayName` [`pattern`]

Return a list consisting of the names of array elements whose names match the glob `pattern` (or all elements if `pattern` is omitted).

array nextelement `arrayName searchId`

Given an array name and a search ID from a previous call to *array startsearch*, return the name of the next element. Return an empty string if all elements have already been returned.

array set `arrayName list`

Set values of array elements. The list should consist of pairs of words specifying element names and values.

array size `arrayName`

Return the number of elements in the array, or 0 if `arrayName` is not the name of an array.

array startsearch `arrayName`

Starts an array search, returning an identifier that can be used for subsequent *array nextelement*, *donesearch*, and *anymore* commands.

auto_execok

auto_execok `execFile`

If an executable file named `execFile` is found in the user's path, return the full pathname; otherwise, return 0.

auto_load

auto_load `command`

Attempt to load a definition for command `command` by searching `$auto_path` and `$env(TCLLIBPATH)` for a *tclIndex* file that will inform the interpreter where it can find `command`'s definition.

auto_mkindex

auto_mkindex `directory pattern...`

Generate a *tclIndex* file from all files in `directory` that match the given glob patterns.

auto_reset

auto_reset

Discard cached information used by *auto_execok* and *auto_load*.

bgerror

bgerror `message`

A user-defined procedure that is called if an error occurs during background processing. Passed the error message string as its argument.

binary

binary `options...`

Convert data between Tcl string format and machine-dependent binary representation.

binary format `formatString` [`args...`]

Return a binary string in a format defined by `formatString` with data taken from `args`. The format string consists of zero or more field codes, each followed by an optional integer count. The field codes are listed here:

a	Chars (null padding)	A	Chars (space padding)
b	Binary (low-to-high)	B	Binary (high-to-low)
h	Hex (low-to-high)	H	Hex (high-to-low)
c	8-bit int	s	16-bit int (little-endian)
S	16-bit int (big-endian)	i	32-bit int (little-endian)
I	32-bit int (big-endian)	f	Float
d	Double	x	Nulls
X	Backspace	@	Absolute position

binary scan `string` `formatString` [`varName...`]

Parse a binary string according to the format defined in `formatString` and place the results in the specified variable names. Return the number of variables that were set. The format string is the same as for *binary format* except for the following:

a	Chars (no stripping)
A	Chars (stripping)
x	Skip forward

Example

```
set i 1234
set j 3.14
set s hello
set str [binary format ida5 $i $j $s]
binary scan $str ida5 i j s
```

break

break

Cause a loop command, such as *for*, *foreach*, or *while*, to break out of the innermost loop and abort execution.

case

Obsolete; see the *switch* command.

catch

catch `script` [`varName`]

Evaluate `script` using the Tcl interpreter, suspending normal error handling if errors occur. Return a number indicating the Tcl interpreter error code, or 0 if there were no errors. If `varName` is specified, store the return value of the `script` in the named variable.

cd

cd [*dirName*]

Set the current working directory to *dirname*. If no directory name is specified, change to the home directory. Returns an empty string.

clock

clock options...

Perform time-related functions.

clock clicks

Return system time as a high-resolution, system-dependent number.

clock format clockValue [*-format* string] [*-gmt* boolean]

Format time in human-readable format. ClockValue is a time value as returned by *clock seconds*, *clock scan*, or the *-atime*, *-mtime*, or *-ctime* options of the *file* command. The optional format string indicates how the string should be formatted, using the symbols described below. The optional *-gmt* argument takes a boolean argument: if true, the time is formatted using Greenwich Mean Time; otherwise, the local time zone is used.

%%	%	%a	Weekday (abbr.)
%A	Weekday (full)	%b	Month (abbr.)
%B	Month (full)	%c	Local date and time
%d	Day (01–31)	%H	Hour (00–23)
%h	Hour (00–12)	%j	Day (001–366)
%m	Month (01–12)	%M	Minute (00–59)
%p	A.M./P.M.	%S	Seconds (00–59)
%U	Week (01–52)	%w	Weekday (0–6)
%x	Local date	%X	Local time
%y	Year (00–99)	%Y	Year (full)
%Z	Time zone		

clock scan dateString [*-base* clockVal] [*-gmt* boolean]

Parse dateString as a date and time, returning an integer clock value (the reverse of *clock format*). If the optional *-base* argument is used, clockVal is used to specify the date to be used for the resulting time value. If the boolean *-gmt* argument is true, assume that time is specified in Greenwich Mean Time.

clock seconds

Return the current time, in seconds, using a system-dependent format.

close

close channelId

Close a previously opened I/O channel, specified by channel identifier channelId. Returns an empty string.

concat

concat [*arg...*]

Treating each argument as a list, concatenate all arguments and return the resulting list.

continue

continue

Cause a loop command, such as *for*, *foreach*, or *while*, to break out of the innermost loop and resume execution with the next iteration.

eof

eof *channelId*

Return a boolean value indicating if an end-of-file condition occurred during the most recent input operation on *channelId*.

error

error *message* [*info*] [*code*]

Generate a Tcl error. Return *message* as the optional error string to the calling application. Optional string *info* is stored in global variable errorInfo, and *code* is stored in errorCode.

eval

eval *arg...*

Treating each argument as a list, concatenate arguments and evaluate the resulting list as a Tcl command, returning the result of the command.

exec

exec [*options*] *arg* [*tag...*]

Execute arguments as one or more shell commands. Return standard output from the last command in the pipeline.

Options

-keepnewline
  Keep trailing newline at end of command pipeline's output.

- -

  Marks end of options (useful for commands that may start with a dash).

Command arguments can include these special symbols:

		Separate commands in pipeline.
	&	Pipe standard out and standard error.
< *fileName*	Use *fileName* as standard input for command.
<@ *fileId*	Use *fileId* (from open command) as standard input.
<< *value*	Pass immediate value as standard input.
> *fileName*	Redirect standard output to file.
2> *fileName*	Redirect standard error to file.
>& *fileName*	Redirect standard error and standard output to file.
>> *fileName*	Append standard output to file.
2>> *fileName*	Append standard error to file.
>>& *fileName*	Append standard error and standard output to file.
>@ *fileId*	Redirect standard output to *fileId*.
2>@ *fileId*	Redirect standard error to *fileId*.
>&@ *fileId*	Redirect standard error and standard output to *fileId*.

exit

exit [*returnCode*]

Terminate the application using the specified return code (default is 0).

expr

expr arg...

Concatenate the command arguments, evaluate them as an expression, and return the result.

fblocked

fblocked channelId

Return 1 if last input operation on *channelId* exhausted available input; otherwise, return 0.

fconfigure

fconfigure options

Perform operations on an I/O channel.

fconfigure channelId

Return current settings for *channelId* as a list of name-value pairs.

fconfigure channelId name

Return current setting of *name* for channel *channelId*.

fconfigure channelId name value...

Set one or more channel options for *channelId*.

Options

The command accepts the following standard options (other options are specific to certain types of I/O channels):

-blocking `boolean`
> Set blocking or nonblocking I/O.

-buffering `mode`
> Set I/O buffering mode to `full`, `line`, or `none`.

-buffersize `size`
> Set size of I/O buffer, in bytes.

-eofchar `char`
> Set character to indicate end of file (disable with empty string).

-eofchar `{inChar outChar}`
> Set input and output end-of-file characters.

-translation `mode`
> Set end-of-line translation to `auto`, `binary`, `cr`, `lf`, or `crlf`.

-translation `{inMode outMode}`
> Set input and output line translation mode.

Tcl Core Commands

---

fcopy

fcopy `inchan outchan` [*-size* `size`] [*-command* `callback`]

Copy data from I/O channel `inchan` to channel `outchan`. Continue copying until end of file is reached on the input channel or the maximum number of bytes has been transferred. Return the number of bytes written to `outchan`.

Options

-size `size`
> Specify maximum number of bytes to transfer (default is to copy until end of file is reached on the input channel).

-command `callback`
> Change behavior of *fcopy* to run in the background. When copying is complete, the command `callback` will be invoked with an argument list consisting of the number of bytes written and an optional error string.

---

file

file `option name` [*arg...*]

This command provides operations for reading and writing attributes of files. *Option* is one of the options described below. *Name* is a filename, which can use tilde (˜) expansion.

file atime name

Return time that file was last accessed, in POSIX format (seconds since the start of the epoch).

file attributes name
file attributes name [option]
file attributes name [option value...]

Set or get platform-dependent file attributes. The first form returns attributes as a list of name-value pairs. The second form returns the value of the named attribute. The third form sets one or more named attributes.

file copy [-force] [– –] source target
file copy [-force] [– –] source... targetDir

Make a copy of a file or copy files to a directory.

Options

-force
    Overwrite existing files.

– –

    Marks end of options.

file delete [-force] [– –] pathname...

Delete one or more files indicated by pathname.

Options

-force
    Overwrite existing files.

– –

    Marks end of options.

file dirname name

Return directory portion of path name.

file executable name

Return 1 if file name is executable by current user, 0 otherwise.

file exists name

Return 1 if file name exists and current user has search permissions for directories leading to it, 0 otherwise.

file extension name

Return characters after and including last period. If there is no period in name, return empty string.

file isdirectory name

Return 1 if file name is a directory, 0 otherwise.

file isfile name

Return 1 if file *name* is a regular file, 0 otherwise.

file join name...

Combine arguments using path separator to form a file pathname.

file lstat name varName

Same as *stat*, but return information for the target of a symbolic link rather than the link itself.

file mkdir dir...

Create one or more directories, creating full path if necessary.

file mtime name

Return time that file was last modified, in POSIX format (seconds since the start of the epoch).

file nativename name

Return platform-specific form of file *name*.

file owned name

Return 1 if file is owned by current user, 0 otherwise.

file pathtype name

Return type of file or directory *name* as one of `absolute`, `relative`, or `volumerelative` (e.g., `C:filename`).

file readable name

Return 1 if file is readable by the current user, 0 otherwise.

file readlink name

Return name of file to which symbolic link points, or an error if *name* is not a symbolic link.

file rename [-force] [- -] source target
file rename [-force] [- -] source [source...] targetDir

Rename one or more files. Target destination can be in a different directory.

file rootname name

Return characters before the last period in path *name*, or *name* if last component does not contain a period.

file size name

Return file size in bytes.

file split name

Split path *name* into a list of separate pathname elements, discarding path separators.

file stat name varName

Store file information in an array variable. The array element names are as shown below, with numeric values corresponding to the result from the *stat* system call. Returns an empty string.

atime	Time of last access
ctime	Time of last change
dev	Device number
gid	Group ID of owner
ino	Inode number
mode	Protection
mtime	Time of last modification
nlink	Number of hard links
size	Total size in bytes
type	Device type
uid	User ID of owner

file tail name

Return characters in *name* after the last directory separator, or *name* if it contains no separators.

file type name

Return a string indicating the type of file *name*: file, directory, characterSpecial, blockSpecial, fifo, link, or socket.

file volume

Return a list of the currently mounted volumes or drive letters.

file writable name

Return 1 if file is writable by current user, 0 otherwise.

---

fileevent

fileevent channelId readable [script]
fileevent channelId writable [script]

Set up an event handler to execute *script* when an I/O channel becomes readable or writable. *ChannelId* is an I/O channel identifier from a previous call to *open* or *socket*. If *script* is omitted, returns the current script for the *channelId*. If *script* is specified, returns an empty string.

---

flush

flush channelId

Flush output that has been buffered for I/O channel *channelId*, which must have been opened for writing. Returns an empty string.

---

for

for start test next body

Implement a loop construct, similar to the *for* loop in C.

start   Command string, executed once at beginning
test   Expression string, for loop test
next   Command string, executed at end of each iteration
body   Command string, executed in each loop iteration

The interpreter executes start once. Then it evaluates the expression test; if the result is zero, it returns an empty string. If non-zero, it executes body, then next, and repeats the loop starting with test again.

Example

```
for {set i 0} {$i < 100} {incr i} {
    puts $i
}
```

foreach

foreach varname list body
foreach varlist1 list1 [varlist2 list2...] body

Execute a loop that iterates over each element of a list. In the first form, variable varname is repeatedly assigned the value of each element in list list, and the expression body is evaluated. In the second form, there can be pairs of lists of loop variables (varlistN) and lists (listN). In each iteration of the loop the variables in varlistN are assigned to the next values of the corresponding list.

Example

```
foreach i {1 2 3 4 5 6 7 8 9 10} {
    puts $i
}
```

format

format formatString [arg...]

Format a string using ANSI *sprintf()*-style formatString and arguments. Returns the formatted string. The format string placeholders have the form:

```
%[argpos$][flag][width][.prec][h|l]char
```

where argpos, width, and prec are integers and possible values for char are as follows:

d	Signed integer	u	Unsigned integer
i	Signed integer (n, 0n, or 0xn)	o	Unsigned octal
x	Unsigned hex	X	Unsigned HEX
c	Int to char	s	String

f	Float (fixed)	e	Float (0e0)
E	Float (0E0)	g	Auto float (f or e)
G	Auto float (F or E)	%	Percent sign

Possible values for *flag* are as follows:

−	Left justified	+	Always signed
0	Zero padding	space	Space padding
#	Alternate output format		

Example

```
set i 12
set j 1.2
puts [format "%4d %5.3f" $i $j]
  12 1.200
puts [format "%04X %5.3e" $i $j]
000C 1.200e+00
```

gets

> *gets* channelId [varName]

Read characters from I/O channel *channelId* until end-of-line character or end of file is reached. Assign the resulting string (without end-of-line character) to variable *varName* and return the number of characters read. If *varName* is omitted, return the string that was read.

glob

> *glob* [options] pattern...

Return a list of files that match the given glob patterns.

Options

-nocomplain
> Prevents an error from occurring if there are no matches; an empty string is returned instead.

− −
> Marks the end of options.

global

> *global* varname...

Declare given names as global variables. Meaningful only inside a procedure.

history

> *history* [option] [arg...]

Perform operations using the history list, a list of recently executed commands. Command events can be indicated using a number or a string that matches the command itself.

history

The same as *history info*.

history add `command` [*exec*]

Add command to history list, optionally executing it.

history change `newValue` [*event*]

Change command in history list to `newValue`. If `event` is not specified, use current event.

history clear

Clear the history list and reset event numbers.

history event [*event*]

Return an event. Default is event –1.

history info [*count*]

Return formatted list of history commands and event numbers. Return the last `count` events, or all if `count` is not specified.

history keep [*count*]

Change the maximum size of the history list to `count`. If `count` is omitted, return the current history size limit.

history nextid

Return the next event number.

history redo [*event*]

Execute a command from the history list. If event not specified, uses event –1.

Tcl Core
Commands

---

if

if `expr1` [*then*] `body1` [*elseif* `expr2` [*then*] `body2`...] [*else*] [`bodyN`]

Execute a conditional expression. If boolean expression `expr1` is true, evaluate `body1`. Otherwise, test optional additional expressions and execute the matching body. The optional *else* keyword is followed by a command body that is executed if no previous conditional expressions were true. The keywords *then* and *else* are optional.

Example

```
if {$x < 0} {
    set y 1
} elseif {$x == 0} {
    set y 2
} else {
    set y 3
}
```

incr

incr varName [*increment*]

Increment the variable *varName*. The optional *increment* specifies the value to be added to the variable; it defaults to 1. The new value is returned.

info

info option [*arg...*]

Return information about the Tcl interpreter.

info args procname

Return a list of the argument names to procedure *procname*.

info body procname

Return the body of procedure *procname*.

info cmdcount

Return total count of commands invoked by the interpreter.

info commands [*pattern*]

Return a list of Tcl commands (built-in and procedures) matching *pattern*. Return all commands if *pattern* is omitted.

info complete command

Return 1 if *command* is complete (i.e., no unmatched quotes, braces, etc.).

info default procname arg varname

Return 1 if argument *arg* of procedure *procname* has a default argument value, otherwise 0. If there is a default value, it is placed in variable *varname*.

info exists varName

Return 1 if local or global variable *varName* exists.

info globals [*pattern*]

Return a list of global variables matching *pattern*. Return all variable names if *pattern* is omitted.

info hostname

Return system hostname.

info level [*number*]

If *number* is not specified, return a number indicating the current procedure stack level, or 0 for global level. With *number*, return a list containing the name and arguments for the procedure at the specified stack level.

info library

Return the name of the standard Tcl library directory; the same as global variable `tcl_library`.

info loaded [`interp`]

Return a list of the currently loaded packages for interpreter `interp` (default is for all interpreters; use empty string for current interpreter).

info locals [`pattern`]

Return list of local variables, including procedure arguments, that match `pattern` (default is all).

info nameofexecutable

Return full name of file from which application was invoked.

info patchlevel

Return Tcl patch level; same as global variable `tcl_patchLevel`.

info procs [`pattern`]

Return list of Tcl procedures matching `pattern`, or all procedures if `pattern` is omitted.

info script

Return name of Tcl file being evaluated.

info sharedlibextension

Return the platform-dependent file extension used for shared libraries, or an empty string if shared libraries are not supported.

info tclversion

Return Tcl version; same as global variable `tcl_version`.

info vars [`pattern`]

Return a list of local and global variables matching `pattern`, or all variables if `pattern` is omitted.

Tcl Core Commands

interp

interp option [`arg...`]

Manage Tcl interpreters. A *master* Tcl interpreter can create a new interpreter, called a *slave*, which coexists with the master. Each interpreter has its own namespace for commands, procedures, and global variables. Using *aliases*, a command in a slave interpreter can cause a command to be invoked in the master or another slave interpreter. *Safe* interpreters can be created that may be used for executing untrusted code because all potentially dangerous commands have been disabled by making them *hidden*.

interp alias `srcPath srcCmd`

Return a list containing the target command and arguments for the alias named `srcCmd` in interpreter specified by `srcPath`.

interp alias `srcPath srcCmd` {}

Delete the alias named `srcCmd` from the interpreter specified by `srcPath`.

interp alias `srcPath srcCmd targetPath targetCmd` [`arg...`]

Create an alias between two slave Tcl interpreters. The source command is named `srcCmd` in interpreter `srcPath` and is placed in interpreter `target-Path` as command `targetCmd`. Additional arguments to be appended to `targetCmd` can be specified.

interp aliases [`path`]

Return a list of the command aliases defined in interpreter `path`.

interp create [*-safe*] [*- -*] [`path`]

Create a slave interpreter using the specified `path`.

Options

-safe
> Creates a safe interpreter.

- -

> Marks the end of options.

interp delete [`path...`]

Delete slave interpreters specified using zero or more pathnames.

interp eval `path arg...`

Concatenate arguments and evaluate them as a command using the slave interpreter specified by `path`. Return result of command.

interp exists `path`

Return 1 if the slave interpreter with name `path` exists; otherwise, return 0.

interp expose `path hiddenName` [`exposedCmdName`]

Make the hidden command `hiddenName` visible to a slave interpreter path with name `exposedCmdName`.

interp hidden `path`

Return a list containing the hidden commands in interpreter `path`.

interp hide `path exposedCmdName` [`hiddenCmdName`]

Make the exposed command `exposedCmdName` a hidden command in interpreter `path` with name `hiddenCmdName` (default name is same as exposed name).

interp invokehidden `path` [-*global* `hiddenCmdName` [*arg*...]

Invoke the hidden command `hiddenCmdName` in interpreter `path` with specified arguments. With *-global*, invoke command at global level (default is current level).

interp issafe [`path`]

Return 1 if the interpreter specified by `path` is a safe interpreter.

interp marktrusted `path`

Mark the interpreter `path` as a trusted interpreter.

interp share `srcPath channelId destPath`

Share the I/O channel `channelId` between interpreters `srcPath` and `destPath`.

interp slaves [`path`]

Return a list of the slave interpreters associated with interpreter `path` (default is the invoking interpreter).

interp target `path alias`

Return a list describing the target interpreter for an `alias`.

interp transfer `srcPath channelId destPath`

Move the I/O channel `channelId` from `srcPath` to interpreter `destPath`.

Slave interpreter names are commands that also accept these options:

`slave` *aliases*
`slave` *alias* `srcCmd`
`slave` *alias* `srcCmd` {}
`slave` *alias* `srcCmd targetCmd` [*arg*...]
`slave` *eval arg*...
`slave` *expose* `hiddenName`
`slave` *hide* `exposedCmdName`
`slave` *hidden*
`slave` *invokehidden* [-*global* `hiddenName`] [*arg*...]
`slave` *issafe*
`slave` *marktrusted*

join

join `list` [`joinString`]

Concatenate the elements of list `list` and return the resulting string. Optionally separate the elements using `joinString`, which defaults to a single space.

lappend

lappend varName [*value*...]

Append the *value* arguments to the list contained in variable *varName*, interpreting each value as a list element. Works in place, making it relatively efficient. If *varName* does not exist, it is created.

lindex

lindex list index

Return item number *index* from list *list*. *Index* starts at zero, and can be the string "end" to return the last item.

linsert

linsert list index element...

Insert elements into *list* starting at the specified *index*. An index of 0 inserts at the beginning, and the string "end" inserts at the end. Returns the resulting list.

list

list [*arg*...]

Return a list containing the given arguments.

llength

llength list

Return the number of elements in list *list*.

load

load fileName [*packageName*] [*interp*]

Loads a binary file containing new Tcl commands. *fileName* is the filename to load (i.e., shared library or DLL), and *packageName* is the name of a package, used to compute the name of init procedure. *interp* is the pathname of the interpreter into which to load the file (default is invoking interpreter).

lrange

lrange list first last

Return a list consisting of elements from *list* having indices *first* through *last*. Indices start at zero, and can also be the string "end".

lreplace

lreplace list first last [*element...*]

Replace elements of *list* having indices *first* through *last* with the given elements and return the resulting list. If no new elements are supplied, list elements are deleted.

lsearch

lsearch [*mode*] *list pattern*

Search *list* for an element that matches *pattern*. If found, return the index of the matching element; otherwise, return –1. The type of search is defined by one of the following mode options:

-exact   Use exact matching.
-glob   Use glob pattern matching (default).
-regexp   Use regular expression matching.

lsort

lsort [*options*] *list*

Sort the elements of list *list* and return the resulting list.

Options

-ascii
> Sort by ASCII collation order (default).

-dictionary
> Sort using dictionary order (case insensitive, compare numbers as integers).

-integer
> Compare elements as integer numbers.

-real
> Compare elements as floating-point numbers.

-command command
> Compare using a command that must return <0, 0, or >0.

-increasing
> Sort in increasing order (default).

-decreasing
> Sort in decreasing order.

-index index
> Sort a list of lists based on the values with index *index* in each sublist.

namespace

namespace [`option`] [`arg...`]

Create and manipulate contexts for commands and variables.

namespace children [`namespace`] [`pattern`]

Return a list of child namespaces that belong to the namespace matching `pattern`. If `pattern` is omitted, return all namespaces. If `namespace` is omitted, return children of the current namespace.

namespace code `script`

Accept a command `script` and return it wrapped such that the resulting script can be evaluated from any namespace, but will execute in the current namespace in which the *namespace code* command was invoked.

namespace current

Return the fully qualified name of the current namespace.

namespace delete [`namespace...`]

Delete the given namespaces and all associated variables, procedures, and child namespaces.

namespace eval `namespace arg...`

Evaluate the arguments in the context of the specified `namespace`.

namespace export [*-clear*] [`pattern...`]

Export commands matching one or more patterns from the current namespace. With the *-clear* option, first reset any previous exports. With no option or patterns, return the current export list.

namespace forget [`pattern...`]

Remove previously exported commands matching one or more patterns from a namespace.

namespace import [*-force*] [`pattern...`]

Import commands matching one or more fully qualified patterns. Option *-force* allows imported commands to replace existing commands.

namespace inscope `namespace arg...`

Evaluate arguments in the context of `namespace`.

namespace origin `command`

Return the fully qualified name of the imported command `command`.

namespace parent [`namespace`]

Return the fully qualified name of the parent for namespace `namespace`. Return the parent of the current namespace if the argument is omitted.

namespace qualifiers `string`

Return the leading namespace qualifiers from `string`, which refers to a namespace name.

namespace tail `string`

Return the simple name at the end of `string`, which refers to a namespace name.

namespace which [*-command* | *-variable*] `name`

Return the fully qualified name of *name*. Option *-command* looks up name as a command (default), and option *-variable* looks up name as a variable.

open

open `fileName` [`access`] [`permissions`]

Open the specified file, device, or command pipeline using an access specifier (described in the following list). Return a channel identifier that can be used in subsequent I/O commands. *FileName* can be a string corresponding to a regular file. If the first character is "|", open a command pipeline (can be open for read or write). *FileName* can also be a device name for a serial port (platform dependent). When creating a new file, optionally specify the access permissions to be given to the file in conjunction with the process's file creation mask (default is read and write access for all).

Access specifiers:

r	Open for reading; file must already exist (default).
r+	Open for read and write; file must already exist.
w	Open for write; create new file if needed.
w+	Open for read and write; create new file if needed.
a	Open existing file for write, appending to end.
a+	Open for read and write, appending to end.

Alternate (POSIX) form for access (must specify one of the first three):

RDONLY	Open for reading.
WRONLY	Open for writing.
RDWR	Open for read and write.

You can add one or more of the following (as a list):

APPEND	Open file for append.
CREAT	Create file if it does not exist.
EXCL	Report error if file does already exist.
NOCTTY	For terminals, do not become controlling terminal for process.
NONBLOCK	Open in nonblocking mode.
TRUNC	Truncate file to zero length.

package

package [options]

Manage the loading and version control of Tcl packages.

package forget package

Remove package *package* from the current interpreter.

package ifneeded package version [script]

Indicate that version *version* of package *package* will be loaded when *script* is executed. If *script* is omitted, return the current script.

package names

Return a list of the names of packages that have been indicated using a *package provide* or *package ifneeded* command.

package provide package [version]

Indicate that version *version* of package *package* is present in interpreter. With no *version* argument, return the version of the package.

package require [-exact] package [version]

Load a package into the interpreter. *Version* indicates the version that is desired; any package with the same major number will be loaded. *-exact* indicates that exactly the specified version should be loaded.

package unknown [command]

Supply a command to be executed if the interpreter is unable to load a package. With no *command* argument, return the current *package unknown* command.

package vcompare version1 version2

Compare two package version numbers. Return −1 if *version1* is earlier than *version2*, 0 if equal, or 1 if newer.

package versions package

Return a list of the versions of *package* that have been registered by *package ifneeded* commands.

package vsatisfies version1 version2

Return 1 if scripts written for version *version2* work with *version1*.

pid

pid [fileId]

Return a list of process IDs for the commands invoked by the command pipeline associated with *fileId*. With no *fileId*, return the current process's ID.

pkg_mkIndex

pkg_mkIndex `dir pattern...`

Create an index file for autoloading packages. `Dir` is the directory containing the files. Supply one or more glob patterns to match the files in the directory to be indexed for autoloading.

proc

proc `name arglist body`

Create a new Tcl procedure called `name`. The commands in `body` will be executed when the command is invoked. `Arglist` is a list describing the formal arguments. Each element can be a variable name, or a list containing a variable name and its default value. Returns an empty string.

If the last argument has the special variable name `args`, it is set to a list of the remaining arguments passed to the procedure, which can vary in number.

Example

```
proc myCommand { i j {k 0} } {
    puts "This is my command"
    return $k
}
```

puts

puts [*-nonewline*] [`channelId`] `string`

Output a string of characters to the I/O channel specified using `channelId`. If `channelId` is omitted, uses standard output. Option *-nonewline* suppresses the newline character normally appended when printing.

pwd

pwd

Return the pathname of the current working directory.

read

read [*-nonewline*] `channelId` [`numBytes`]

Read characters from the I/O channel `channelId`. Read the number of bytes specified by `numBytes`, or if omitted, read all characters until end of file. With option *-nonewline*, discard the last character in the file if it is a newline. Returns the characters read.

regexp

regexp [*options*] *exp string* [*matchVar*] [*subMatchVar*...]

Return 1 if regular expression *exp* matches string *string*; otherwise, return 0. If specified, *matchVar* will contain the portion of string that matched, whereas *subMatchVar* variables will contain strings matching parenthesized expressions in *exp*.

Options

-nocase

>Ignore case in pattern matching.

-indices

>Rather than storing strings in *subMatchVar*, store the indices of the first and last matching characters as a list.

– –

>Marks the end of options.

Example

```
regexp {^[0-9]+$} 123
1
regexp {^[0-9]+$} abc
0
```

regsub

regsub [*options*] *exp string subSpec varName*

Match regular expression *exp* against string *string*, making replacements defined by *subSpec*, and store the result in variable *varName*.

Options

-all

>Replace all matching expressions in the string.

-nocase

>Ignore case in pattern matching.

– –

>Marks the end of options.

Example

```
regsub {[0-9]} a1b2c3 {#} result
set result
a#b2c3
regsub -all< {[0-9]} a1b2c3 {#} result
set result
a#b#c#
```

rename

rename oldName newName

Rename the command *oldName* to have the new name *newName*. Delete *oldName* if *newName* is an empty string.

return

return [-code code] [-errorinfo info] [-errorcode code] [string]

Return from a procedure, top-level command, or source command. Return *string* as the return value (default is an empty string).

Options

-code

Return an error code, one of the strings "ok", "error", "return", "break", or "continue", or an integer value.

-errorinfo

Return an initial stack trace for the *errorInfo* variable.

-errorcode

Return a value for the *errorCode* variable.

scan

scan string format varName...

Parse fields from the string *string* according to the ANSI C *scanf()*-style format *format* and place results in the specified variables. Return the number of conversions, or −1 if unable to match any fields. Format placeholders have the form %[*][*width*]*char*, where * discards the field, *width* is an integer, and possible values of *char* are as follows:

d	Decimal	o	Octal
x	Hex	c	Char to int
e	Float	f	Float
g	Float	s	String (no whitespace)
[*chars*]	Chars in given range	[^*chars*]	Chars not in given range

seek

seek channelId offset [origin]

Set position for random access to I/O channel *channelId*. Specify starting byte position using integer value *offset* relative to *origin*, which must be one of the following:

start	Offset bytes from start of the file (default).
current	Offset bytes from the current position (positive or negative).
end	Offset bytes relative to the end of file (positive or negative).

set

set varName [*value*]

Set the value of variable *varName* to *value* and return the value. If *value* is omitted, return the current value of *varName*.

socket

socket [*options*] *host port*

Create a client-side connection to a socket using the specified host and port number. Return a channel identifier that can be used for subsequent I/O commands.

Options

-myaddr addr
> Specify domain name or IP address of client interface.

-myport port
> Specify port number to use for client side of connection.

-async
> Connect asynchronously.

socket -server command [*option*] *port*

Create the server side of a socket using the specified port number. When a client connects, invoke *command*.

Option

-myaddr addr
> Specify domain name or IP address of server interface.

source

source fileName

Read file *fileName* and pass it to the current interpreter for evaluation. Return the return value of last command executed in file.

source -rsrc resourceName [*fileName*]
source -rsrcid resourceId [*fileName*]

On the Macintosh platform only, source the script using the text resource with the given name or resource identifier.

split

split string [*splitChars*]

Split a string into a list. Elements are split if separated by any of the characters in list *splitChars* (default is whitespace). Returns the resulting list.

string

stringoption arg...

Perform string operations on one or more strings, based on the value of *option*. String indices start at 0.

string compare `string1 string2`

Compare strings lexicographically. Return −1 if `string1` is less than `string2`, 0 if equal, or 1 if greater.

string first `string1 string2`

Return the index of the first occurrence of `string1` in `string2`, or −1 if no match.

string index `string charIndex`

Return the character in `string` that has index `charIndex`. Return empty string if `charIndex` is out of range.

string last `string1 string2`

Return the index of the last occurrence of `string1` in `string2`, or −1 if no match.

string length `string`

Return the length of `string` in characters.

string match `pattern string`

Return 1 if `string` matches glob pattern `pattern`; otherwise, return 0.

string range `string first last`

Return substring of `string` consisting of characters from index `first` through `last`. `Last` can be the string "end".

string tolower `string`

Return `string` converted to lowercase.

string toupper `string`

Return `string` converted to uppercase.

string trim `string` [`chars`]

Return `string` with leading and trailing characters from the set `chars` removed (default is whitespace characters).

string trimleft `string` [`chars`]

Return `string` with leading characters from the set `chars` removed (default is whitespace characters).

string trimright `string` [`chars`]

Return `string` with trailing characters from the set `chars` removed (default is whitespace characters).

string wordend `string index`

Return index of first character after word in **`string`** that occurs at character position **`index`**.

string wordstart `string index`

Return index of first character of word in **`string`** that occurs at character position **`index`**.

---

subst

subst [`options`] `string`

Perform variable, command, and backslash substitutions on **`string`** and return result.

Options

-nobackslashes
: Do not perform backslash substitution.

-nocommands
: Do not perform command substitution.

-novariables
: Do not perform variable substitution.

---

switch

switch [`options`] `string pattern body` [`pattern body`...]
switch [`options`] `string` {`pattern body` [`pattern body`...]}

Match **`string`** against each pattern argument. If a match is found, evaluate the corresponding **`body`** and return result. **`Pattern`** can be "default" to match anything. **`Body`** can be "-" to fall through to the next pattern.

Options

-exact
: Use exact matching (default).

-glob
: Use glob matching.

-regexp
: Use regular expression matching.

- -
: Marks the end of options.

Example

```
switch $tcl_platform(platform) {
    windows   {puts "Running on Windows"}
    unix      {puts "Running on Unix"}
    macintosh {puts "Running on Macintosh"}
    default   {puts "Running on unknown platform"}
}
```

---

tell

tell channelId

Return the current access position of I/O channel *channelId* as a decimal number, or −1 if the channel does not support random access.

time

time script [count]

Execute the command *script* and return a string indicating the average elapsed time required. The command is run *count* times (default is 1) and the result is averaged.

trace

trace option [arg...]

Trace variable accesses by executing a user-defined command whenever the variable is read, written, or unset.

trace variable name ops command

Trace operations on variable *name*. Operations are specified by one or more of the characters **r** (read), **w** (write), or **u** (unset). When the operation occurs, execute *command*.

trace vdelete name ops command.

Delete a trace previously set on a variable.

trace vinfo name

Return a list describing the traces currently set on variable *name*.

unknown

unknown cmdName [arg...]

This command is invoked by the Tcl interpreter if a program attempts to perform a nonexistent command. The user can redefine the default implementation of *unknown* defined in the Tcl system startup file.

unset

unset name...

Remove one or more variables specified by *name*.

update

update [*idletasks*]

Call the event handler loop until all pending events have been processed. The *idletasks* option specifies only to update idle callbacks.

uplevel

uplevel [`level`] `arg`...

Concatenate arguments and evaluate them in the stack frame context indicated by `level`, where `level` is either a number indicating the number of levels up the stack relative to the current level or a number preceded by "#", indicating an absolute level. The default level is 1.

upvar

upvar [`level`] `otherVar myVar`...

Make local variable `myVar` become an alias for variable `otherVar` in the stack frame indicated by `level`, where `level` is either a number indicating the number of levels up the stack relative to the current level or a number preceded by "#", indicating an absolute level. The default level is 1.

variable

variable [`name value`...] `name` [`value`]

Create one or more variables in the current namespace and assign them the given values.

vwait

vwait `varName`

Call the event handler to process events and block until the value of variable `varName` changes.

while

while `test body`

A loop construct that repeatedly evaluates expression `test`; if it returns a true value, it executes `body`.

Example

```
set i 1
while {$i <= 10} {
    puts $i
    incr i
}
```

CHAPTER 3

Tk Core Commands

Tk is the most popular extension to the Tcl language. John Ousterhout, the author of Tcl itself, wrote the Tk extension soon after releasing Tcl to the public. Tk is available at *http://www.scriptics.com*. This chapter covers Version 8.0.

Tk adds many new commands to the Tcl interpreter for writing graphical user interface (GUI) applications. Commands are available to create and lay out several different types of windows, called *widgets*, bind Tcl scripts to window system events, create and manipulate graphical images, and interact with the window manager and server.

Tk scripting provides an excellent tool for quickly prototyping GUI applications. Programs that take many hundreds of lines of Xlib or Motif C code can typically be done in less than a hundred lines of Tk. Also, no compilation is necessary and almost all aspects can be dynamically reconfigured during runtime. Using the powerful I/O commands of Tcl, it is also easy to add graphical interfaces on top of existing command-line applications.

The Tk extension can be loaded into a running Tcl interpreter by using the command:

```
package require Tk
```

on systems supporting dynamic loading. Typically, one runs the program *wish*, which starts a Tcl interpreter with the Tk extension already loaded.

Example

The following Tcl code demonstrates the use of most of the major widget commands and several of the non-widget commands. The resulting interface is shown in Figure 3-1.

```
wm withdraw .
set w [toplevel .t]
wm title .t {Tk Code Example}
set m [menu $w.menubar -tearoff 0]
$m add cascade -label File -menu [menu $m.file]
$m.file add command -label Quit -command exit
$m add cascade -label Help -menu [menu $m.help]
$m.help add command -label Index -command {puts Sorry}
$w configure -menu $m

set f [frame $w.f1]
pack [label $f.label -text {A label}] -side left
pack [entry $f.entry] -side left -fill x -expand true
$f.entry insert 0 {This is an entry}
pack $f -fill x -padx 2 -pady 2

set f [frame $w.f2]
pack [frame $f.rg -relief groove -bd 3] -side left -fill x -expand true
pack [label $f.rg.lbl -text Radiobuttons:] -side left
pack [radiobutton $f.rg.b1 -text Tea -variable choice -value 1] \
        -side left
pack [radiobutton $f.rg.b2 -text Coffee -variable choice -value 0] \
        -side left
pack [frame $f.cg -relief groove -bd 3] -side left -fill x -expand true
pack [label $f.cg.lbl -text Checkbuttons:] -side left
pack [checkbutton $f.cg.b1 -text Cream] -side left
pack [checkbutton $f.cg.b2 -text Sugar] -side left
pack $f -fill x -padx 2 -pady 2

set f [frame $w.f3]
pack [label $f.lbl -text Scale:] -side left
pack [label $f.val -textvariable scaleval -width 4] -side left
pack [scale $f.scl -variable scaleval -orient horizontal -from 0 \
        -to 10 -showvalue false] -side left -fill x -expand true
pack $f -fill x -padx 2 -pady 2

set f [frame $w.f4 -relief groove -bd 3]
pack [frame $f.lf] -side left -fill both -padx 3 -pady 3
pack [listbox $f.lf.lb -yscrollcommand "$f.lf.sb set" -height 4] \
    -side left -fill both -expand true
pack [scrollbar $f.lf.sb -command "$f.lf.lb yview"] \
    -side left -fill y
$f.lf.lb insert end {Line 1 of listbox} {Line 2 of listbox}
pack [frame $f.tf] -side left -fill both -expand true -padx 3 -pady 3
grid columnconfigure $f.tf 0 -weight 1
grid rowconfigure $f.tf 0 -weight 1
grid [text $f.tf.tx -yscrollcommand "$f.tf.sy set" -height 4 -width 25 \
    -xscrollcommand "$f.tf.sx set"] -column 0 -row 0 -sticky nsew
grid [scrollbar $f.tf.sy -command "$f.tf.tx yview"] \
    -column 1 -row 0 -sticky ns
grid [scrollbar $f.tf.sx -command "$f.tf.tx xview" -orient horizontal] \
    -column 0 -row 1 -sticky ew
$f.tf.tx insert end {This is a text widget}
pack $f -fill both -expand true -padx 2 -pady 2

set f [frame $w.f5]
button $f.b1 -text Apply -default active -command {puts $scaleval}
button $f.b2 -text Reset -default normal -command {set scaleval 0}
button $f.b3 -text Quit -default normal -command exit
pack $f.b1 $f.b2 $f.b3 -padx 10 -side left
pack $f -pady 2
```

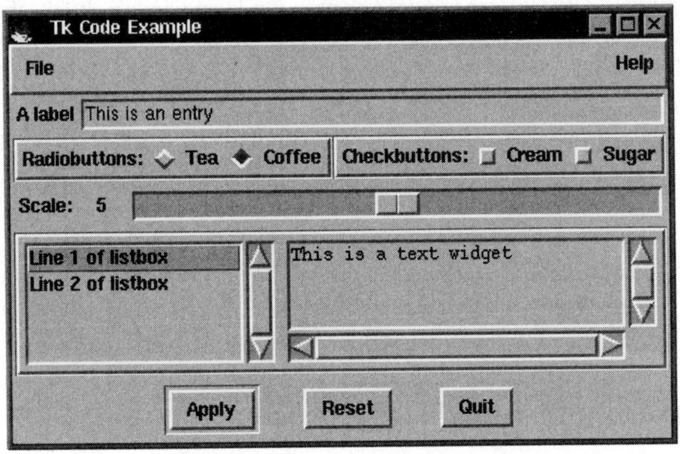

Figure 3-1: Resulting interface from sample Tk code

Command-Line Options

The *wish* program has the following command-line format:

wish [cmdfile] [options] [– –] [arg arg...]]

Its behavior is identical to the *tclsh* program in the handling of the cmdfile and arg arguments. In addition, the following options are available:

-colormap new
> Specify that the root window should have a new colormap rather than the default colormap of the screen.

-display display
> For the X Window System, the display (and screen) on which to display the root window.

-geometry geometry
> Geometry to use for the root window in standard X Window System geometry format. It will be stored in the geometry global variable.

-name name
> Specify the title for the root window and the name of the interpreter for *send* commands.

-sync
> Execute all X Window System commands synchronously. This option makes sure that all errors are reported immediately, but slows down execution.

-use id
> Instead of the root window being a top-level window, it is embedded in the window whose system identifier is *id* (as returned by *winfo id* command).

-visual visual
> Visual class to use for the root window. *Visual* must be direct-color, grayscale, pseudocolor, staticcolor, staticgray, or truecolor.

− −

> Denote end of *wish* options. Additional arguments are passed to the script's argv global variable. Normally, all arguments are scanned for matches to the above options.

Environment Variable

The following environment variable is used by Tk:

TK_LIBRARY   Directory containing Tk scripts and other files needed by Tk at runtime.

Special Variables

The following global variables are defined by the Tk extension:

tk_library   Directory containing the standard Tk script library.
tk_patchLevel   Current patch level of Tk extension.
tk_strictMotif   When non-zero, Tk tries to adhere to Motif look and feel.
tk_version   Current version of Tk extension.

Group Listing of Tk Commands

This section briefly lists all Tk commands, grouped logically by function.

Widgets

button   Create a button widget.
canvas   Create a canvas widget.
checkbutton   Create a checkbutton widget.
entry   Create an entry widget.
frame   Create a frame widget.
label   Create a label widget.
listbox   Create a listbox widget.
menu   Create a menu widget.
menubutton   Create a menubutton widget.
message   Create a message widget.
radiobutton   Create a radiobutton widget.
scale   Create a scale widget.

scrollbar	Create a scrollbar widget.
text	Create a text widget.
toplevel	Create a top-level widget.

Geometry Management

grid	Lay out widgets on a grid.
pack	Lay out widgets by packing them along borders.
place	Lay out widgets using explicit placement.

Event Handling

bind	Bind window events to Tcl scripts.
bindtags	Control the precedence order of event bindings.
event	Generate window events and define virtual events.

Focus

focus	Give a window the keyboard focus.
grab	Set focus grabs on windows.
tk_focusNext	Get the next window in the focus order.
tk_focusPrev	Get the previous window in the focus order.
tk_focusFollowsMouse	Arrange for the focus to follow the mouse pointer.

Dialogs

tk_chooseColor	Pop up a dialog for choosing a color.
tk_dialog	Pop up a message dialog with arbitrary buttons.
tk_getOpenFile	Pop up a dialog for choosing an existing file.
tk_getSaveFile	Pop up a dialog for choosing any filename.
tk_messageBox	Pop up a message dialog with predefined buttons.

Miscellaneous

bell	Ring the window system's bell.
clipboard	Manipulate the window system's clipboard.
destroy	Destroy a widget.
font	Create and delete named fonts.
image	Create and manipulate images.
lower	Lower a window in the stacking order.
option	Manipulate the Tk option database.
raise	Raise a window in the stacking order.
selection	Manipulate selection ownership and handling.
send	Evaluate a command in another interpreter.
tk	Access Tk's internal state.
tkwait	Pause program until a defined change occurs.
tk_bisque	Set default color palette to old bisque scheme.
tk_optionMenu	Create an Option menu.

tk_pop-up	Post a popup menu.
tk_setPalette	Change the Tk color scheme.
winfo	Get information on various window properties.
wm	Communicate with the window manager.

Widget Overview

All Tk widgets are created by a Tcl command of the same name as the widget. These widget creation commands have the form:

   widgetCmd pathName [*option value...*]

where *widgetCmd* is the name of the widget type desired (e.g., *button* or *listbox*) and *pathName* is the pathname for the new widget. The return value for the command is *pathName*.

A widget's pathname consists of a *child name* appended to the pathname of its parent widget using a "." character. The child name is an arbitrary string that excludes the "." character and is unique among its siblings, the other widget children of its parent. The pathname for the Tk main (or root) window is simply a single dot (i.e., "."); its immediate children begin with a dot, and each additional level of a child widget appears after an additional dot. This scheme is analogous to file pathnames in the Unix file system, where the "/" character is used as a directory name separator. For example, the pathname of a frame widget named `frame1` whose parent is the main window would have the pathname `.frame1`. A button widget named `button1` who is a child of `frame1` would have the pathname `.frame1.button1`. Almost all Tk commands require the full pathname for arguments that specify a widget.

When a new widget is created with the pathname *pathName*, a new Tcl command is also defined with the same name. Invoking this command allows one to manipulate the widget in various ways depending on the arguments passed. The first argument to the widget's command is referred to as the *widget method* and selects the action to be taken by the widget. Additional arguments to the widget's command may be allowed or required, depending on the method. The methods available to each widget type are described in the "Widget Commands" section, later in this chapter.

The optional *option-value* pair arguments to the widget creation command allow one to set the value of the widget's supported configuration options. All widgets support the *configure* and *cget* methods to change and query their configuration options after creation.

The *configure* method has the form:

   pathName configure [*option* [*value* [*option value...*]]]

If one or more option-value pairs are specified, the given options are set to the given values. If no option-value pairs are specified, the command returns a list with an element for each supported widget option. Each element itself is a list of five items describing an option. These items are the option itself, its database name, its class name, its default value, and its current value. For example, the list for *-activebackground* might look like this: `{-activebackground active-Background Foreground #ececec blue}`. If only the first *option* argument is specified, just the five-item list describing that option is returned.

The *cget* command has the form:

> `pathName` *cget* `option`

and simply returns the current setting of the option *option*.

The configuration options available differ depending on the widget type. Many options are supported by all or several of the widget types. These standard options are described in the next section. Which standard options a widget type supports and the options that are specific to a particular widget type are described in the "Widget Commands" section .

For distance and coordinate options that take values in screen units, the valid format is a floating-point number followed by an optional one-character suffix: c for centimeters, i for inches, m for millimeters, p for printer's points ($1/72$ inch), or no character for pixels. Commands that return values for screen distances and coordinates do so in pixels, unless otherwise stated.

Standard Widget Options

Each of the following entries lists the option or options used in Tk, the name in the window system's resource database for the option, the associated class name in the resource database, and a description of the option.

-activebackground color   (activeBackground, Foreground)
> Background color of widget when it is active.

-activeborderwidth width   (activeBorderWidth, BorderWidth)
> Width, in screen units, of widget's border when it is active.

-activeforeground color   (activeForeground, Background)
> Foreground color of widget when it is active.

-anchor anchorPos   (anchor, Anchor)
> How information is positioned inside widget. Valid *anchorPos* values are n, ne, e, se, s, sw, w, nw, and center.

-background color   (background, Background)
-bg color
> Background color of widget in normal state.

-bitmap bitmap   (bitmap, Bitmap)
> A bitmap image to display in the widget in place of a textual label. Valid *bitmap* values are the special sequence @*filename*, specifying a file from which to read the bitmap data or one of the built-in bitmaps: error, gray12, gray25, gray50, gray75, hourglass, info, questhead, question, or warning. On the Macintosh, the following bitmaps are available: document, stationery, edition, application, accessory, folder, pfolder, trash, floppy, ramdisk, cdrom, preferences, querydoc, stop, note, and caution.

-borderwidth `width`   (borderWidth, BorderWidth)
-bd `width`

> Width, in screen units, of widget's border in its normal state.

-cursor `cursor`   (cursor, Cursor)

> Cursor to display when mouse pointer is inside the widget's borders. The `cursor` argument may take the following forms:

> `name` [`fgColor` [`bgColor`]]

>> *Name* is the name of a cursor font as defined in the X Window System *cursorfont.h* include file (e.g., `cross` and `left_ptr`). If *fgColor* and *bgColor* are specified, they give the foreground and background colors for the cursor, respectively. If *bgColor* is omitted, the background will be transparent. If neither is specified, the defaults will be black and white, respectively.

> `@`*sourceName* `maskName fgColor bgColor*

>> *Sourcename* and *maskName* are the names of files describing bitmaps for the cursor's source bits and mask. *Fgcolor* and *bgColor* indicate the foreground and background colors, respectively, for the cursor. This form is invalid on Macintosh and Windows platforms.

> `@`*sourceName* `fgColor`

>> *sourceName* is the name of a file describing a bitmap for the cursor's source bits. *fgColor* is the foreground color for the cursor. This form is invalid on Macintosh and Windows platforms.

-disabledforeground `color`   (disabledForeground,
                                                    DisabledForeground)

> Foreground color of widget when it is disabled.

-exportselection `boolean`   (exportSelection, ExportSelection)

> Whether a selection in the widget should also be made the X Window System selection.

-font `font`   (font, Font)

> Font to use when drawing text inside the widget.

-foreground `color`   (foreground, Foreground)
-fg `color`

> Foreground color of widget in its normal state.

-highlightbackground `color`   (highlightBackground,
                                                    HighlightBackground)

> Color of the rectangle drawn around the widget when it does not have the input focus.

-highlightcolor `color`   (highlightColor, HighlightColor)

> Color of the rectangle drawn around the widget when it has the input focus.

-highlightthickness `width`   (highlightThickness,
                                                    HighlightThickness)

> Width, in screen units, of highlighted rectangle drawn around widget when it has the input focus.

-image imageName   (image, Image)
>   Name of image to display in the widget in place of its textual label (see the *image* command).

-insertbackground color   (insertBackground, Foreground)
>   Color to use for the background of the area covered by the insertion cursor.

-insertborderwidth width   (insertBorderWidth, BorderWidth)
>   Width, in screen units, of the border to draw around the insertion cursor.

-insertofftime milliseconds   (insertOffTime, OffTime)
>   Time the insertion cursor should remain "off" in each blink cycle.

-insertontime milliseconds   (insertOnTime, OnTime)
>   Time the insertion cursor should remain "on" in each blink cycle.

-insertwidth width   (insertWidth, InsertWidth)
>   Width, in screen units, of the insertion cursor.

-jump boolean   (jump, Jump)
>   Whether to notify slider controls (e.g., scrollbars) connected to the widget to delay making updates until mouse button is released.

-justify alignment   (justify, Justify)
>   How multiple lines of text are justified. Valid *alignment* values are left, center, or right.

-orient orientation   (orient, Orient)
>   The orientation in which the widget should be laid out. Valid *orientation* values are vertical or horizontal.

-padx width   (padX, Pad)
>   Extra space, in screen units, to request for padding the widget's top and bottom sides.

-pady height   (padY, Pad)
>   Extra space, in screen units, to request for padding the widget's left and right sides.

-relief effect   (relief, Relief)
>   3D effect desired for the widget's border. Valid *effect* values are flat, groove, raised, ridge, or sunken.

-repeatdelay milliseconds   (repeatDelay, RepeatDelay)
>   Time a button or key must be held down before it begins to autorepeat.

-repeatinterval milliseconds   (repeatInterval, RepeatInterval)
>   Time between autorepeats once action has begun.

-selectbackground color   (selectBackground, Foreground)
>   Background color to use when displaying selected items or text.

-selectborderwidth `width`   (`selectBorderWidth, BorderWidth`)
    Width, in screen units, of border to draw around selected items or text.

-selectforeground `color`   (`selectForeground, Background`)
    Foreground color to use when displaying selected items or text.

-setgrid `boolean`   (`setGrid, SetGrid`)
    Whether the widget controls the resizing grid for its top-level window. See the
    wm grid command for details.

-takefocus `focusType`   (`takeFocus, TakeFocus`)
    If 0 or 1, signals that the widget should never or always take the focus. If
    empty, Tk decides. Otherwise, evaluates argument as script with widget name
    appended as argument. Returned value must be 0, 1, or empty.

-text `string`   (`text, Text`)
    Text string to be displayed inside the widget.

-textvariable `variable`   (`textVariable, Variable`)
    Variable whose value is a text string to be displayed inside the widget.

-troughcolor `color`   (`troughColor, Background`)
    Color to use for the rectangular trough areas in widget.

-underline `index`   (`underline, Underline`)
    Integer index of a character to underline in the widget.

-wraplength `length`   (`wrapLength, WrapLength`)
    Maximum line length, in screen units, for word wrapping.

-xscrollcommand `cmdPrefix`   (`xScrollCommand, ScrollCommand`)
    Prefix for a command used to communicate with an associated horizontal
    scrollbar. Typically `scrollbar set`, where `scrollbar` is the pathname of
    a horizontal scrollbar widget.

-yscrollcommand `cmdPrefix`   (`yScrollCommand, ScrollCommand`)
    Prefix for a command used to communicate with an associated vertical scroll-
    bar. Typically `scrollbar set`, where `scrollbar` is the pathname of a ver-
    tical scrollbar widget.

Widget Commands

This section describes each Tk widget type and the options and methods the widget supports. Only the names of the standard options supported by the widget are
listed. Refer to the "Standard Widget Options" section earlier in this chapter for
option definitions.

---

button

    button `pathName` [`option value`...]

    The *button* command creates a new button widget named `pathName`.

Standard Options

-activebackground	*-activeforeground*	*-anchor*
-background	*-bitmap*	*-borderwidth*
-cursor	*-disabledforeground*	*-font*
-foreground	*-highlightbackground*	*-highlightcolor*
-highlightthickness	*-image*	*-justify*
-padx	*-pady*	*-relief*
-takefocus	*-text*	*-textvariable*
-underline	*-wraplength*	

Widget-Specific Options

-command `tclCommand`   (command, Command)
> Command to be evaluated when button is invoked.

-default `state`   (default, Default)
> State for the default ring, a platform-dependent border drawn around the
> button to indicate it is the default button. Must be `normal` (button is not
> the default), `active` (button is the default), or `disabled` (no ring is
> drawn).

-height `height`   (height, Height)
> Desired height, in lines for text content or in screen units for images and
> bitmaps.

-state `state`   (state, State)
> State of the button. *State* must be `normal`, `active`, or `disabled`.

-width `width`   (width, Width)
> Desired width, in characters, for text content, or in screen units, for
> images and bitmaps.

Methods

`pathName` *flash*
> Flash button by alternating between active and normal colors.

`pathName` *invoke*
> Invoke the Tcl command associated with the button and return its result.
> An empty string is returned if there is no command associated with the
> button. This command is ignored if the button's state is `disabled`.

---

canvas

> *canvas* `pathName` [*option value...*]

The *canvas* command creates a new canvas widget named `pathName`. The
canvas widget provides a drawing area for displaying a number of graphic
items, including arcs, bitmaps, images, lines, ovals, polygons, rectangles, text,
and windows (other widgets). Methods exist to draw, manipulate, and bind
events to items.

Standard Options

-background	*-borderwidth*	*-cursor*
-highlightbackground	*-highlightcolor*	*-highlightthickness*
-insertbackground	*-insertborderwidth*	*-insertofftime*
-insertontime	*-insertwidth*	*-relief*
-selectbackground	*-selectborderwidth*	*-selectforeground*
-takefocus	*-xscrollcommand*	*-yscrollcommand*

Widget-Specific Options

-closeenough `float`   (closeEnough, CloseEnough)

How close the mouse cursor must be to an item to be considered inside it. Default is `1.0`.

-confine `boolean`   (confine, Confine)

Whether the view can be set outside the region defined by *-scrollregion*. Default is `true`.

-height `height`   (height, Height)

Desired height, in screen units, that the canvas should request from its geometry manager.

-scrollregion `region`   (scrollRegion, ScrollRegion)

Boundary for scrolling in the canvas as a list of four coordinates describing the left, top, right, and bottom coordinates of a rectangular region in screen units.

-width `width`   (width, Width)

Width, in screen units, that the canvas should request from its geometry manager.

-xscrollincrement `increment`   (xScrollIncrement, ScrollIncrement)

Increment, in screen units, for horizontal scrolling. If not set or equal to zero or less, defaults to one-tenth of the visible width of the canvas.

-yscrollincrement `increment`   (yScrollIncrement, ScrollIncrement)

Increment, in screen units, for vertical scrolling. If not set or equal to zero or less, defaults to one-tenth of the visible height of the canvas.

Item IDs and Tags

An item in a canvas widget is identified either by its unique ID or by an associated tag. A unique ID (an integer number) is assigned to each item when it is created. The ID assigned to an item cannot be changed.

Multiple tags may be associated with an item. A tag is just a string of characters that can take any form except that of an integer. For instance, "squares" and "arc32" are valid, but "32" is not. The same tag can be associated with multiple items.

Two special tag names are reserved. The tag `all` is implicitly associated with every item in the canvas. The tag `current` is associated with the topmost item whose drawn area is underneath the mouse cursor. If the mouse cursor is not in the canvas widget or over an item, no item has the `current` tag.

The canvas appends the ID of each item when created to its display list. This list defines the stacking order, with items later in the display list obscuring those that are earlier in the display list. Canvas methods exist to manipulate the order of items in the display list. However, window items are always drawn on top of other items. The normal *raise* and *lower* Tk commands control the stacking order of overlapping window items.

Unless otherwise stated, the token *tagOrId* is used in the method descriptions below to indicate that either an item ID or tag is accepted. If a tag specifies multiple items and the method operates only on a single item, the first (lowest) item in the display list suitable for the operation is used.

Coordinates

Coordinates and distances are specified in screen units as described in the "Widget Overview" section. Larger y-coordinates refer to points lower on the screen; larger x-coordinates refer to points farther to the right.

Text Indices

Text items support the notion of an *index* for identifying particular character positions within the item. A decimal number indicates the position of the desired character within the item, with 0 referring to the first character. Special *index* values are as follows:

`end`	The character just after the last one in the item
`insert`	The character just after the insertion cursor
`sel.first`	The first selected character in the item
`sel.last`	The last selected character in the item
`@x,y`	The character closest to coordinates *x,y*

Item Event Binding

Binding events to canvas items using the *bind* method works in a similar manner to binding events to widgets with the Tk *bind* command. However, only events related to the mouse and keyboard or virtual events can be bound to canvas items. Enter and Leave events for an item are triggered when it becomes the `current` item or ceases to be the `current` item. Other mouse-related events are directed to the `current` item, if any. Keyboard-related events are directed to the item that has the keyboard focus as set by the canvas *focus* method. If a virtual event is used in a binding, it can be triggered only if the underlying "real" event is mouse related or keyboard related.

When multiple bindings match a particular event, all of the matching bindings are invoked. This can happen when an item is associated with two tags and both tags have bindings for the same event. A binding associated with the `all` tag is invoked first, followed by only one binding for each of the item's tags, followed by any binding associated with the item's ID. If there are multiple matching bindings for a single tag, the most specific binding is invoked. A *continue* command in a binding script terminates just that binding. A *break* command terminates the script for that binding and skips any remaining bindings for the event. Any bindings made to the canvas widget using the *bind* command are invoked after any matching item bindings.

Methods

pathName addtag tag searchSpec [*arg arg...*]

Associate *tag* with each item in the canvas selected by the contraints of *searchSpec*. *Searchspec* and *args* may take any of the following forms:

above *tagOrId*

Select the item just after (above) the one identified by *tagOrId* in the display list. If *tagOrId* denotes more than one item, the last (topmost) item is used.

all

Select all items in the canvas.

below *tagOrId*

Select the item just before (below) the one identified by *tagOrId* in the display list. If *tagOrId* denotes more than one item, the first (lowest) item is used.

closest *x y* [*halo* [*start*]]

Select the item closest to coordinates *x*, *y*. If more than one item is at the same closest distance, the last one (topmost) in the display list is selected. If *halo* is specified, any item closer than *halo* to the point is considered to be close enough. The *start* argument may be used to cycle through all the closest items. This form will select the topmost closest item that is below *start* (a tag or ID) in the display list; if no such item exists, the selection behaves as if the *start* argument were not given.

enclosed *x1 y1 x2 y2*

Select all the items completely inside the rectangular region given by *x1,y1* on the top left and *x2,y2* on the bottom right.

overlapping *x1 y1 x2 y2*

Select all the items that overlap or are fully enclosed within the rectangular region given by *x1,y1* on the top-left corner and *x2,y2* on the bottom-right corner.

withtag *tagOrId*

Select all the items identified by *tagOrId*.

pathName bbox tagOrId [*tagOrId...*]

Return a coordinate list of the form {*x1 y1 x2 y2*} giving an approximate bounding box enclosing all the items named by the *tagOrId* arguments.

pathName bind tagOrId [*sequence* [*script*]]

Associate *script* with all the items identified by *tagOrId* such that whenever the event sequence given by *sequence* occurs for one of the items, the script will be evaluated. If the *script* argument is not given, the current associated script is returned. If the *sequence* is also not given, a list of all the sequences for which bindings have been defined for *tagName* is returned. See the "Item Event Binding" section for more details.

pathName canvasx screenx [*gridspacing*]
Return the canvas x-coordinate that is displayed at the location of window x-coordinate *screenx*. If *gridspacing* is specified, the canvas coordinate is rounded to the nearest multiple of gridspacing units.

pathName canvasy screeny [*gridspacing*]
Return the canvas y-coordinate that is displayed at the location of window y-coordinate *screeny*. If *gridspacing* is specified, the canvas coordinate is rounded to the nearest multiple of gridspacing units.

pathName coords tagOrId [*x0 y0...*]
If no coordinates are specified, a list of the current coordinates for the item named by *tagOrId* is returned. If coordinates are specified, the item is moved to the specified coordinates. If *tagOrId* refers to multiple items, the first one in the display list is used.

pathName create type x y [*x y...*] [*option value...*]
Create a new canvas item of type *type* and return the assigned ID. See the following subsections on individual item types for the exact syntax of this method.

pathName dchars tagOrId first [*last*]
For each item identified by *tagOrId* that supports text operations, delete the characters in the range *first* through *last*, inclusive.

pathName delete tagOrId [*tagOrId...*]
Delete each item named by *tagOrId*.

pathName dtag tagOrId [*tagToDelete*]
For each item identified by *tagOrId*, delete the tag *tagToDelete* from the list of those associated with the item. If *tagToDelete* is omitted, it defaults to *tagOrId*.

pathName find searchSpec [*arg arg...*]
Return a list of IDs for all items selected by the constraint *searchSpec*. See the *addtag* method for possible values for *searchSpec*.

pathName focus tagOrId
Set the keyboard focus for the canvas widget to the first item in the display list identified by *tagOrId* that supports the insertion cursor. If *tagOrId* is an empty string, the focus is cleared so that no item has it. If *tagOrId* is omitted, the method returns the ID for the item that currently has the focus, or an empty string if no item has the focus.

pathName gettags tagOrId
Return a list of tags associated with the first item in the display list identified by *tagOrId*.

pathName *icursor* `tagOrId` `index`

Set the position of the insertion cursor to just before the character at `index` for all items identified by `tagOrId` that support text operations.

pathName *index* `tagOrId` `index`

Return the numerical index position of `index` within the first item in the display list identified by `tagOrId` that supports text operations. This value is guaranteed to lie between 0 and the number of characters within the item.

pathName *insert* `tagOrId` `beforeThis` `string`

Insert `string` just before the character at index `beforeThis` in all items identified by `tagOrId` that support text operations.

pathName *itemcget* `tagOrId` `option`

Return the current value of `option` for the first item in the display list identified by `tagOrId`. `Option` may have any of the values accepted by the *create* method when the item was created.

pathName *itemconfigure* `tagOrId` [`option` [`value` [`option value`...]]]

Query or modify the configuration options for the items identified by `tagOrId` in the same manner as the general widget *configure* method. For queries, only results for the first item in the display identified by `tagOrId` are returned. The options and values are the same as those accepted by the *create* method when the items were created.

pathName *lower* `tagOrId` [`belowThis`]

Move all of the items identified by `tagOrId` to a new position in the display list just before the first item in the display list identified by `belowThis`, maintaining relative order.

pathName *move* `tagOrId` `xAmount` `yAmount`

Move each of the items identified by `tagOrId` in the canvas by adding `xAmount` to the x-coordinate and `yAmount` to the y-coordinate of each point associated with the item.

pathName *postscript* [`option` `value`...]

Return a PostScript representation for printing all or part of the canvas. The following options are supported:

-channel `channel`

The generated PostScript will be written to the channel `channel` (already opened), and the method will return an empty string.

-colormap `varName`

`VarName` is an array in which each element maps a color name to PostScript code that sets a particular color value. If this option is not specified or no color entry is found, Tk uses the standard X11 RGB color intensities.

-colormode `mode`

How to output color information. `Mode` must be `color` for full color, `gray` for grayscale equivalents, or `mono` for black and white.

-file `fileName`

The generated PostScript will be written to file `fileName` and the method will return an empty string.

-fontmap `varName`

`VarName` is an array in which each element maps a Tk font name to a two-element list consisting of a PostScript font name and point size. If this option is not specified or no font entry is found, Tk makes its best guess.

-height `size`

Height of the area of the canvas to print. Defaults to the height of the canvas window. This is *not* the height of the printed page.

-pageanchor `anchor`

`Anchor` specifies which cardinal point of the printed area of the canvas should appear over the positioning point on the page (see *-pagex* and *-pagey*). Must be n, nw, w, sw, s, se, e, ne, or center (the default).

-pageheight `size`

Specifies that the PostScript should be scaled equally in both x and y so that the printed area is `size` high on the page.

-pagewidth `size`

Specifies that the PostScript should be scaled equally in both x and y so that the printed area is `size` wide on the page. Overrides *-page-height* setting.

-pagex `position`

The x-coordinate of the positioning point on the PostScript page. Defaults to page center.

-pagey `position`

The y-coordinate of the positioning point on the PostScript page. Defaults to page center.

-rotate `boolean`

Whether the printed area is to be rotated 90 degrees (i.e., landscape).

-width `size`

Width of the area of the canvas to print. Defaults to the full width of the canvas. This is *not* the width of the printed page.

-x `position`

The x-coordinate of the left edge of the area in the canvas that is to be printed. Defaults to left edge set by the canvas *-scrollregion* option.

-y `position`

The y-coordinate of the top edge of the area in the canvas that is to be printed. Defaults to top edge set by the canvas *-scrollregion* option.

pathName raise tagOrId [*aboveThis*]

Move all of the items identified by *tagOrId* to a new position in the display list just after the last item in the display list identified by *aboveThis*, maintaining relative order.

pathName scale tagOrId xOrigin yOrigin xScale yScale

Rescale all of the items identified by *tagOrId* in canvas coordinate space. For each of the points defining each item, the x-coordinate is adjusted to change the distance from *xOrigin* by a factor of *xScale*. Similarly, each y-coordinate is adjusted to change the distance from *yOrigin* by a factor of *yScale*.

pathName scan dragto x y

Scroll the widget's view horizontally and vertically. The distance scrolled is equal to 10 times the difference between this command's *x* and *y* arguments and the *x* and *y* arguments to the last *scan mark* command for the widget.

pathName scan mark x y

Record *x* and *y* as anchors for a following *scan dragto* method call.

pathName select adjust tagOrId index

If the selection is currently owned by an item identified by *tagOrId*, locate the end of the selection nearest to *index*, adjust that end to be at *index*, and make the other end of the selection the anchor point. If the selection is not currently owned by an item identified by *tagOrId*, this method behaves the same as the *select to* widget method.

pathName select clear

Clear the selection if it is owned by any non-window item in the canvas.

pathName select from tagOrId index

Set the selection anchor point to be just before the character given by *index* in the first item identified by *tagOrId* that supports selection.

pathName select item

Return the ID of the item, if any, that owns the selection in the canvas.

pathName select to tagOrId index

For the first item identified by *tagOrId* that supports selection, set the selection to consist of those characters between the anchor point and *index*. If no anchor point has been set, it defaults to *index*. The new selection will always include the character given by *index*; it will include the character given by the anchor point only if it exists and is less than or equal to *index*.

pathName type tagOrId

Return the item type of the first item in the display list identified by *tagOrId*.

pathName xview

Return a two-element list describing the currently visible horizontal region of the canvas. The elements are real numbers representing the fractional distance that the view's left and right edges extend into the horizontal span of the widget as described by the *-scrollregion* option.

pathName xview moveto `fraction`
> Adjust the visible region of the canvas so that the point indicated by `fraction` along the widget's horizontal span appears at the region's left edge.

pathName xview scroll `number` `what`
> Shift the visible region of the canvas horizontally by `number`. If `what` is `units`, then `number` is in units of the *-xscrollincrement* option. If `what` is `pages`, then `number` is in units of nine-tenths the visible region's width.

pathName yview
> Return a two-element list describing the currently visible vertical region of the canvas. The elements are real numbers representing the fractional distance that the view's top and bottom edges extend into the vertical span of the widget as described by the *-scrollregion* option.

pathName yview moveto `fraction`
> Adjust the visible region of the canvas so that the point indicated by `fraction` along the canvas's vertical span appears at the region's top edge.

pathName yview scroll `number` `what`
> Shift the visible region of the canvas vertically by `number`. If `what` is `units`, then `number` is in units of the *-yscrollincrement* option. If `what` is `pages`, then `number` is in units of nine-tenths the visible region's height.

Arc Items

An arc is a section of an oval delimited by two angles (see *-start* and *-extent*) and can be displayed in one of several ways (see *-style*). Arcs are created with a widget method of the following form:

pathName create arc x1 y1 x2 y2 [`option value option value...`]

The arguments *x1,y1* and *x2,y2* define the top-left and bottom-right corners of a rectangular region enclosing the oval that defines the arc.

-extent `degrees`
> Angle that the arc's range should extend, measured counterclockwise from the starting angle.

-fill `color`
> Color used for filled region of the arc.

-outline `color`
> Color used to draw the arc's outline.

-outlinestipple bitmap
>Stipple pattern used to draw the arc's outline.

-start degrees
>Starting angle of the arc, as measured counterclockwise from the three o'clock position.

-stipple bitmap
>Stipple pattern used for filled region of the arc.

-style type
>How to draw the arc. *Type* may be pieslice (the default), chord, or arc. A pieslice is a region defined by the arc with two lines connecting the ends to the center of the implied oval. A chord is a region defined by the arc with the two ends connected by a line. An arc is simply the curve of the arc alone.

-tags tagList
>List of tags to associate with the item. Replaces any existing list.

-width outlineWidth
>Width of the outline to be drawn around the arc's region.

Bitmap Items

Bitmap items display two-color images on the canvas. They are created with a widget method of the following form:

pathName create bitmap x y [option value option value...]

The arguments *x* and *y* give the coordinates of a point used to position the bitmap on the canvas (see *-anchor*).

-anchor anchorPos
>Which cardinal point on the bitmap should line up over the positioning point of the item. *AnchorPos* must be n, nw, w, sw, s, se, e, ne, or center (the default).

-background color
>Color to use for each of the bitmap pixels whose value is 0.

-bitmap bitmap
>Bitmap to display in the item.

-foreground color
>Color to use for each of the bitmap pixels whose value is 1. Default is black.

-tags tagList
>List of tags to associate with the item. Replaces any existing list.

Image Items

Image items are used to display Tk images in the canvas. They are created with a widget method of the following form:

pathName *create image* *x* *y* [option value option value...]

The arguments *x* and *y* give the coordinates of a point used to position the image on the canvas (see *-anchor*).

-anchor anchorPos
> Which cardinal point on the image should line up over the positioning point of the item. *AnchorPos* must be n, nw, w, sw, s, se, e, ne, or center (the default).

-image imageName
> Name of image to display in the item.

-tags tagList
> List of tags to associate with the item. Replaces any existing list.

Line Items

Line items display one or more connected line segments or curves on the canvas. They are created with a widget method of the following form:

pathName *create line* *x1 y1 . . . xn yn* [option value option value...]

The arguments *x1* through *yn* give the coordinates for a series of two or more points that describe a series of connected line segments.

-arrow where
> Where to draw arrowheads. *Where* may be none (the default), first, last, or both.

-arrowshape shape
> How to draw the arrowheads. *Shape* is a three-element list indicating the distance from neck to tip, from tip to trailing points, and from trailing points to nearest outside edge of the line.

-capstyle style
> How caps are drawn at endpoints of line. *Style* may be butt (the default), projecting, or round.

-fill color
> Color to use for drawing the line.

-joinstyle style
> How joints are drawn. *Style* may be bevel, miter (the default), or round.

-smooth boolean
> Whether the line should be drawn as a curve using parabolic splines.

-splinesteps number
> Number of line segments with which to approximate each spline when smoothing.

-stipple bitmap
> Stipple pattern to use when drawing the line.

-tags tagList
> List of tags to associate with the item. Replaces any existing list.

-width lineWidth
> Width of the line. Defaults to 1.0.

Oval Items

Oval items display circular or oval shapes on the canvas. They are created with a widget method of the following form:

pathName create oval x1 y1 x2 y2 [option value option value...]

The arguments *x1,y1* and *x2,y2* define the top-left and bottom-right corners of a rectangular region enclosing the oval. The oval will include the top and left edges of the rectangle but not the lower or right edges.

-fill color
> Color used for filled region of the oval.

-outline color
> Color used for drawing oval's outline.

-stipple bitmap
> Stipple pattern used for filled region of oval.

-tags tagList
> List of tags to associate with the item. Replaces any existing list.

-width outlineWidth
> Width of the oval's outline. Defaults to 1.0.

Polygon Items

Polygon items display multisided or curved regions on the canvas. They are created with a widget method of the following form:

pathName create polygon x1 y1... xn yn [option value option value...]

The arguments *x1* through *yn* specify the coordinates for three or more points that define a closed polygon. If the first and last points are not the same, a line is drawn between them.

-fill color
> Color used to fill the area of the polygon.

-outline color
> Color used to draw the polygon's outline.

-smooth boolean
> Whether the polygon should be drawn with a curved perimeter using parabolic splines.

-splinesteps number
> Number of line segments with which to approximate for each spline when smoothing.

-stipple bitmap
> Stipple pattern used to fill the area of the polygon.

-tags tagList
> List of tags to associate with the item. Replaces any existing list.

-width outlineWidth
> Width of the polygon's outline. Defaults to 1.0.

Rectangle Items

Rectangle items display rectangular shapes on the canvas. They are created with a widget method of the following form:

pathName create rectangle x1 y1 x2 y2 [option value option value...]

The arguments *x1,y1* and *x2,y2* define the top-left and bottom-right corners of the rectangle (the region of the rectangle will include its upper and left edges but not its lower or right edges).

-fill color
> Color used to fill the area of the rectangle.

-outline color
> Color used to draw the rectangle's outline.

-stipple bitmap
> Stipple pattern used to fill the area of the rectangle.

-tags tagList
> List of tags to associate with the item. Replaces any existing list.

-width outlineWidth
> Width of the rectangle's outline. Defaults to 1.0.

Text Items

Text items display one or more lines of characters on the canvas. They are created with a widget method of the following form:

pathName create text x y [option value option value...]

The arguments *x* and *y* specify the coordinates of a point used to position the text on the display.

-anchor anchorPos
> Which cardinal point of the text bounding region should line up over the positioning point of the item. *AnchorPos* must be n, nw, w, sw, s, se, e, ne, or center (the default).

-fill `color`

    Color to use for drawing the text characters.

-font `fontName`

    Font for drawing text characters.

-justify `how`

    How to justify the text within its bounding region. *How* may be `left` (the default), `right`, or `center`.

-stipple `bitmap`

    Stipple pattern for drawing text characters.

-tags `tagList`

    List of tags to associate with the item. Replaces any existing list.

-text `string`

    Characters to be displayed in the text item.

-width `lineLength`

    Maximum length (using coordinate units) for a line of text. If 0, text is broken only on newline characters. Otherwise, lines are broken on any whitespace.

Window Items

Window items display other windows (i.e., Tk widgets) on the canvas. They are created with a widget method of the following form:

pathName *create window* `x` `y` [`option value option value...`]

The arguments `x` and `y` specify the coordinates of a point used to position the window on the display. A window item always obscures any graphics that overlap it, regardless of their order in the display list.

-anchor `anchorPos`

    Which cardinal point of the window should line up over the positioning point of the item. *AnchorPos* must be `n`, `nw`, `w`, `sw`, `s`, `se`, `e`, `ne`, or `center` (the default).

-height `pixels`

    Height to assign to item's window.

-tags `tagList`

    List of tags to associate with the item. Replaces any existing list.

-width `pixels`

    Width to assign to item's window.

-window `pathName`

    Window to associate with the item, which must be a descendant of the canvas widget.

checkbutton

checkbutton pathName [*option value*...]

The *checkbutton* command creates a new checkbutton widget named *path-Name*.

Standard Options

-activebackground	*-activeforeground*	*-anchor*
-background	*-bitmap*	*-borderwidth*
-cursor	*-disabledforeground*	*-font*
-foreground	*-highlightbackground*	*-highlightcolor*
-highlightthickness	*-image*	*-justify*
-padx	*-pady*	*-relief*
-takefocus	*-text*	*-textvariable*
-underline	*-wraplength*	

Widget-Specific Options

-command tclCommand   (command, Command)
  Command to be evaluated when button is invoked.

-height height   (height, Height)
  Desired height, in lines for text content or in screen units for images and bitmaps.

-indicatoron boolean   (indicatorOn, IndicatorOn)
  Whether the indicator should be drawn. If false, the *-relief* option is ignored, and the widget's relief is sunken if selected and raised if not.

-offvalue value   (offValue, Value)
  Value to store in associated variable when button is not selected.

-onvalue value   (onValue, Value)
  Value to store in associated variable when button is selected.

-selectcolor color   (selectColor, Background)
  Background color to use for indicator when button is selected (at all times for Windows). If *-indicatoron* is false, the color is used for the background of the entire widget when it is selected.

-selectimage image   (selectImage, SelectImage)
  Image to display instead of normal image when button is selected. This option is ignored if *-image* option has not been set.

-state state   (state, State)
  State of the checkbutton. *State* must be normal, active, or disabled.

-variable varName   (variable, Variable)
  Name of global variable (defaults to last element of *pathName*) to set to indicate whether the checkbutton is selected.

-width width   (width, Width)
>   Desired width, in characters for text content or in screen units for images
>   and bitmaps.

Methods

pathName deselect
>   Deselect the checkbutton and set its associated variable to the value of its
>   *-offvalue* option.

pathName flash
>   Flash the button by alternating between active and normal colors.

pathName invoke
>   Toggle the selection state, invoke the Tcl command associated with the
>   button, and return its result. An empty string is returned if there is no
>   command associated with the button. This command is ignored if the
>   button's state is `disabled`.

pathName select
>   Select the checkbutton and set its associated variable to the value of the
>   *-onvalue* option.

pathName
>   Toggle the selection state of the checkbutton and set its associated vari-
>   able appropriately.

---

entry

entry pathName [option value...]

The *entry* command creates a new entry widget named *pathName*. An entry
is a widget that displays a one-line text string that can be edited.

Standard Options

-background	*-borderwidth*	*-cursor*
-exportselection	*-font*	*-foreground*
-highlightbackground	*-highlightcolor*	*-highlightthickness*
-insertbackground	*-insertborderwidth*	*-insertofftime*
-insertontime	*-insertwidth*	*-justify*
-relief	*-selectbackground*	*-selectborderwidth*
-selectforeground	*-setgrid*	*-takefocus*
-xscrollcommand		

Widget-Specific Options

-show char   (show, Show)
>   Character to show instead of actual characters typed. Useful for password
>   entries.

-state state   (state, State)
>   State for the entry. *State* must be `normal` or `disabled`.

-width width   (width, Width)

> Desired width in characters. If zero or less, the width is made large enough to hold current text.

Text Indices

Several entry widget methods support the notion of an *index* for identifying particular positions within the line of text. Valid index values are as follows:

number	Character as a numerical index (starting from 0)
anchor	Anchor point for the selection
end	Character just after the last one in the entry's string
insert	Character just after the insertion cursor
sel.first	First character in the selection, if in entry
sel.last	Character just after last one in selection, if in entry
@*x*	Character at x-coordinate *x* in entry

Methods

pathName bbox index

> Return a list of four numbers giving coordinates of upper-left corner (relative to the widget) and width and height of character at *index*.

pathName delete first [*last*]

> Delete range of characters starting at *first* up to, but not including, *last*. If *last* is omitted, only the character at *first* is deleted.

pathName get

> Return the entry's current string.

pathName icursor index

> Place the insertion cursor just before the character at *index*.

pathName index index

> Return the numerical index corresponding to position *index*.

pathName insert index string

> Insert *string* just before the position indicated by *index*.

pathName scan dragto x

> Scroll the widget's view horizontally. The distance scrolled is equal to 10 times the difference between this command's *x* argument and the *x* argument to the last *scan mark* command for the widget.

pathName scan mark x

> Record *x* as the anchor for a following *scan dragto* method call.

pathName selection adjust index

> Locate the end of the selection nearest to *index*, adjust that end of the selection to be at *index*, and make the other end of the selection the selection anchor point. If no current selection exists, the selection is created to encompass the characters between *index* and the current anchor point, inclusive.

pathName selection clear

Clear the selection if it is owned by this widget.

pathName selection from `index`

Set the selection anchor point to just before the character at `index`.

pathName selection present

Return 1 if any characters in entry are currently selected, 0 otherwise.

pathName selection range `start end`

Set the selection to include characters starting at `start` up to, but not including, the character at `end`.

pathName selection to `index`

If `index` is before the anchor point, set the selection to the character range from `index` up to just before the anchor point. If `index` is after the anchor point, set the selection to the character range from the anchor point up to just before `index`.

pathName xview

Return a two-element list describing the currently visible horizontal region of the entry. The elements are real numbers representing the fractional distance that the view's top and bottom edges extend into the vertical span of the widget.

pathName xview `index`

Adjust the visible region of the entry so the character at `index` is at the left edge of the view.

pathName xview moveto `fraction`

Adjust the visible region of the entry so that the point indicated by `fraction` along the widget's horizontal span appears at the region's left edge.

pathName xview scroll `number what`

Shift the visible region of the entry horizontally by `number`. If `what` is `units`, then `number` is in units of the characters. If `what` is `pages`, then `number` is in units of the visible region's width.

frame

frame `pathName` [`option value`...]

The *frame* command creates a new frame widget named `pathName`. The main purpose of a frame widget is to serve as a container for laying out other widgets using one of Tk's geometry managers.

Standard Options

-borderwidth	*-cursor*	*-highlightbackground*
-highlightcolor	*-highlightthickness*	*-relief*
-takefocus		

Widget-Specific Options

-background color   (background, Background)
> Same as standard option, but may be the empty string to display no background or border.

-class name   (class, Class)
> Class to use when querying the option database and for bindings. May not be changed with *configure*.

-colormap colormap   (colormap, Colormap)
> Colormap to use for window. *Colormap* may be either new, in which case a new colormap is created, or the name of another window, in which case that window's colormap is used. The default is to use the colormap of its parent. May not be changed with *configure*.

-container boolean   (container, Container)
> Whether the window will be used as a container in which to embed some other application. May not be changed with *configure*.

-height height   (height, Height)
> Desired height, in screen units, for the window.

-visual visual   (visual, Visual)
> Visual class to use for the window. *Visual* must be directcolor, grayscale, pseudocolor, staticcolor, staticgray, or true-color.

-width width   (width, Width)
> Desired width, in screen units, for the window.

---

label

> *label pathName* [*option value...*]

The *label* command creates a new label widget named *pathName*.

Standard Options

-anchor	*-background*	*-bitmap*
-borderwidth	*-cursor*	*-font*
-foreground	*-highlightbackground*	*-highlightcolor*
-highlightthickness	*-image*	*-justify*
-padx	*-pady*	*-relief*
-takefocus	*-text*	*-textvariable*
-underline	*-wraplength*	

Widget-Specific Options

-height height   (height, Height)
> Desired height, in lines, for text content or in screen units for images or bitmaps. If not set, widget is autosized.

-width width   (width, Width)
> Desired width, in characters, for text content or in screen units for images or bitmaps. If not set, widget is autosized.

listbox

> *listbox pathName [option value...]*

The *listbox* command creates a new listbox widget named *pathName*. A listbox is a widget that displays a list of strings, one per line. When first created, a new listbox has no elements. Elements can be added, deleted, and selected using methods described here.

Many listbox methods take index arguments to identify elements. Listbox indices are numbered starting at 0. Special index values are active, anchor, end, and @x, y.

Standard Options

-background	*-borderwidth*	*-cursor*
-exportselection	*-font*	*-foreground*
-highlightbackground	*-highlightcolor*	*-highlightthickness*
-relief	*-selectbackground*	*-selectborderwidth*
-selectforeground	*-setgrid*	*-takefocus*
-xscrollcommand	*-yscrollcommand*	

Widget-Specific Options

-height height   (height, Height)
> Desired height of listbox in lines. If zero or less, the height is made just large enough to hold all lines.

-selectmode mode   (selectMode, SelectMode)
> Specifies one of several styles understood by the default listbox bindings for manipulation of the element selection. Supported styles are single, browse, multiple, and extended. Any arbitrary string is allowed, but the programmer must extend the bindings to support it.

-width width   (width, Width)
> Desired width of listbox in characters. If zero or less, the width is made just large enough to hold the longest element.

Methods

pathName active index
> Set the active element to the one at *index*.

pathName bbox index
> Return a list of numbers in the format {x y width height} describing the bounding box around the text of element at *index*.

pathName curselection
> Return a list of indices of all elements currently selected.

pathName delete index1 [*index2*]

 Delete range of elements from *index1* to *index2*. If *index2* is not given, only the element at *index1* is deleted.

pathName get index1 [*index2*]

 Return as a list the elements from *index1* to *index2*. If *index2* is not given, only the element at *index1* is returned.

pathName index index

 Return the numeric index of the element at *index*.

pathName insert index [*string...*]

 Insert given *strings* as new elements just before element at *index*. If *index* is specified as end, the new elements are appended at the end of the list.

pathName nearest y

 Return the index of the element nearest to y-coordinate *y*.

pathName scan dragto x y

 Scroll the widget's view horizontally and vertically. The distance scrolled is equal to 10 times the difference between this command's *x* and *y* arguments and the *x* and *y* arguments to the last *scan mark* command for the widget.

pathName scan mark x y

 Record *x* and *y* as anchors for a following *scan dragto* method call.

pathName see index

 Adjust the view in the listbox so that the element at *index* is visible.

pathName selection anchor index

 Set the anchor for selection dragging to the element at *index* (or closest to it).

pathName selection clear first [*last*]

 Deselect any selected elements between *first* and *last*, inclusive.

pathName selection includes index

 Return 1 if the element at *index* is selected, 0 otherwise.

pathName selection set first [*last*]

 Select all elements between *first* and *last*, inclusive.

pathName size

 Return the total number of elements in the listbox.

pathName xview

 Return a two-element list describing the currently visible horizontal region of the listbox. The elements are real numbers representing the fractional distance that the view's left and right edges extend into the horizontal span of the widget.

pathName xview index

Adjust the visible region of the listbox so that the character position *index* is at the left edge of the view.

pathName xview moveto *fraction*

Adjust the visible region of the listbox so that the point indicated by *fraction* along the widget's horizontal span appears at the region's left edge.

pathName xview scroll number what

Shift the visible region of the listbox horizontally by *number*. If *what* is units, then *number* is in units of characters. If *what* is pages, then *number* is in units of the visible region's width.

pathName yview

Return a two-element list describing the currently visible vertical region of the listbox. The elements are real numbers representing the fractional distance that the view's top and bottom edges extend into the vertical span of the widget.

pathName yview index

Adjust the visible region of the listbox so that the element given by *index* is at the top of the view.

pathName yview moveto *fraction*

Adjust the visible region of the listbox so that the point indicated by *fraction* along the widget's vertical span appears at the region's top edge.

pathName yview scroll number what

Shift the visible region of the listbox vertically by *number*. If *what* is units, then *number* is in units of text lines. If *what* is pages, then *number* is in units of the visible region's height.

Selection Modes

The behavior of the default bindings for a listbox is determined by the value of the *-selectmode* option. If the selection mode is single or browse, only a single element in the list may be selected at one time. Clicking button 1 on an element selects it and deselects any other element. In browse mode, it is possible to drag the selection.

If the selection mode is multiple or extended, then multiple elements may be selected at once, including discontiguous ranges. In multiple mode, clicking button 1 on an element alternately selects and deselects it. In extended mode, pressing button 1 on an element selects it, makes that element the new anchor element, and deselects all other elements. Dragging the mouse button then extends the selection with respect to the anchor element.

menu

menu pathName [`option value...`]

The *menu* command creates a new menu widget named pathName. A menu is a top-level window that displays a collection of one-line entries arranged in one or more columns. Several different types of menu entries exist and can be combined in a single menu.

Standard Options

-activebackground	*-activeborderwidth*	*-activeforeground*
-background	*-borderwidth*	*-cursor*
-disabledforeground	*-font*	*-foreground*
-relief	*-takefocus*	

Widget-Specific Options

-postcommand `command`   (`postCommand`, `Command`)
> Command to evaluate each time the menu is posted.

-selectcolor `color`   (`selectColor`, `Background`)
> Color to display in the indicator when menu entries of type `checkbutton` or `radiobutton` are selected.

-tearoff `boolean`   (`tearOff`, `TearOff`)
> Whether the menu should include a tear-off entry at the top.

-tearoffcommand `command`   (`tearOffCommand`, `TearOffCommand`)
> Command to evaluate whenever menu is torn off. The menu widget's name and the name of the window for the torn-off menu are appended as the last two arguments.

-title `string`   (`title`, `Title`)
> String to use as a title for the window created when the menu is torn off.

-type `type`   (`type`, `Type`)
> Menu's type. `Type` must be `menubar`, `tearoff`, or `normal`. Can only be set at menu's creation.

Entry Indices

Several menu widget methods support the notion of an `index` for identifying a particular entry position within the menu. Indices have the following form:

`number`
> The entry numerically, where 0 is the topmost entry.

`active`
> The entry that is currently active.

`end`
> The bottommost entry in the menu.

last
>Same as end.

none
>Indicates "no entry at all." Used mainly with *activate* method to make no entry active.

@y
>The entry closest to y-coordinate *y* in the menu's window.

pattern
>The first entry from the top with a label that matches pattern *pattern* (see Tcl command *string match* for rules).

Special Menubar Menus

Any menu can be made into a menubar for a top-level window (see the *toplevel* widget). Certain specially named menus that are children of a menubar will be treated in a system-specific manner. For a menubar named .menubar, on the Macintosh, the special menus would be .menubar.apple and .menubar.help; on Windows, the special menu would be .menubar.system; on X Window System, the special menu would be .menubar.help.

On the Macintosh, items in the .menubar.apple will make up the first items of the Apple menu, and items in the .menubar.help are appended to the standard Help menu on the right of the menubar whenever the window containing the menubar is in front. Under Windows, items in the .menubar.system menu are appended to the system menu for the window containing the menubar. On X Windows, when the last menu entry in .menubar is a cascade entry with submenu .menubar.help, it is right-justified on the menubar.

Methods

pathName activate index
>Redisplay the entry at *index* in its active colors. If *index* is none, the menu will end up with no active entry.

pathName add type [option value [option value...]]
>Add a new entry of type *type* to the bottom of the menu, configured with the given options. The possible values for *type* are cascade, checkbutton, command, radiobutton, or separator. Possible options are:

>*-activebackground color*
>>Background color for entry when active. Not available for separator or tear-off entries.

>*-activeforeground color*
>>Foreground color for entry when active. Not available for separator or tear-off entries.

-accelerator `string`

String to display at right side of menu entry (usually to show accelerator keystroke). Not available for separator or tear-off entries.

-background `color`

Background color for entry when it is in the normal state. Not available for separator or tear-off entries.

-bitmap `bitmap`

Bitmap to display in menu instead of textual label. Overrides *-label*. Not available for separator or tear-off entries.

-columnbreak `boolean`

Whether entry should start a new column in the menu.

-command `tclCommand`

Command to evaluate when menu entry is invoked. Not available for separator or tear-off entries.

-font `font`

Font to use when drawing label and accelerator for entry. Not available for separator or tear-off entries.

-foreground `color`

Foreground color for entry when in the normal state. Not available for separator or tear-off entries.

-hidemargin `boolean`

Whether standard margins should be drawn for menu entry.

-image `imageName`

Name of image to display in menu instead of textual label. This option overrides *-label* and *-bitmap*. Not available for separator or tear-off entries.

-indicatoron `boolean`

Whether indicator should be displayed. Available only for checkbutton and radiobutton entries.

-label `string`

String to display as identifying label of entry. Not available for separator or tear-off entries.

-menu `menuName`

Pathname of submenu associated with entry. Available for cascade entries only.

-offvalue `value`

Value to store in entry's associated variable when it is deselected. Available only for checkbutton entries.

-onvalue `value`

Value to store in entry's associated variable when it is selected. Available only for checkbutton entries.

-selectcolor `color`

> Color to display in the indicator when entry is selected. Available only for checkbutton and radiobutton entries.

-selectimage `image`

> Image to display in entry when it is selected in place of the one specified with *-image*. Available only for checkbutton and radiobutton entries.

-state `state`

> State of the menu entry. `State` must be `normal`, `active`, or `disabled`.

-underline `integer`

> Integer index of character to underline in entry's label. Not available for separator or tear-off entries.

-value `value`

> Value to store in the entry's associated variable when selected. Available only for radiobutton entries.

-variable `varName`

> Global variable to associate with entry. Available only for checkbutton and radiobutton entries.

pathName clone `newPathName` [`cloneType`]

> Make a clone of the menu with name `newPathName`. The clone will have type `cloneType` (one of `normal`, `menubar`, or `tearoff`). Changes in configuration of the original are automatically reflected in the clone. Any cascade menus pointed to are also cloned. Clones are destroyed when the original is destroyed.

pathName delete `index1` [`index2`]

> Delete all menu entries between `index1` and `index2`, inclusive. If `index2` is not given, only entry at `index1` is deleted.

pathName entrycget `index option`

> Return the current value of configuration option `option` for entry at `index`. See the *add* method for available options.

pathName entryconfigure `index` [`option` [`value` [`option value`...]]]

> Query or modify the configuration options for the menu entry at `index` in the same manner as the general widget *configure* method. See the *add* method for available options.

pathName index `index`

> Return the numerical index corresponding to `index` (or none if `index` is none).

pathName insert `index type` [`option value` [`option value`...]]

> Same as *add* method except that it inserts the new entry just before the entry at `index`. It is not possible to insert new entries before the tear-off entry, if the menu has one.

pathName *invoke* `index`

Invoke the action appropriate to the entry type of the menu entry at `index` if it is not disabled.

pathName *post* `x y`

Arrange for the menu to be displayed at root-window coordinates `x` and `y` (possibly adjusted to make sure the entire menu is visible on the screen). If a script has been given to the *-postcommand* option, it is evaluated first and the results returned. If an error occurs in the script, the menu is not posted.

pathName *postcascade* `index`

If entry at `index` is a cascade entry, the submenu associated with it is posted. Any other currently posted submenu is unposted.

pathName *type* `index`

Return the type of menu entry at `index`.

pathName *unpost*

Unmap menu's window so it is no longer displayed. Does not work on Windows or Macintosh.

pathName *yposition* `index`

Return the y-coordinate of the topmost pixel of the entry at `index` within the menu window.

menubutton

menubutton `pathName` [`option value...`]

The *menubutton* command creates a new menubutton widget named *path-Name*.

Standard Options

-activebackground	*-activeforeground*	*-anchor*
-background	*-bitmap*	*-borderwidth*
-cursor	*-disabledforeground*	*-font*
-foreground	*-highlightbackground*	*-highlightcolor*
-highlightthickness	*-image*	*-justify*
-padx	*-pady*	*-relief*
-takefocus	*-text*	*-textvariable*
-underline	*-wraplength*	

Widget-Specific Options

-direction `direction`   (direction, Height)

Where menu should pop up in relation to button. Valid `direction` values are `above`, `below`, `right`, `left`, or `flush` (directly over button).

-height `height`   (height, Height)

Desired height, in lines, for text content or in screen units for images and bitmaps.

-indicatoron boolean   (indicatorOn, IndicatorOn)
> If true, a small indicator is drawn on the button's right side and the default bindings will treat the widget as an option menubutton.

-menu pathName   (menu, menuName)
> Name of menu widget to post when button is invoked.

-state state   (state, State)
> State of menubutton. *State* must be normal, active, or disabled.

-width width   (width, Width)
> Desired width, in characters for text content, or in screen units for images and bitmaps.

---

message

> *message pathName [option value...]*

The *message* command creates a new message widget named *pathName*.

Standard Options

-anchor	*-background*	*-borderwidth*
-cursor	*-font*	*-foreground*
-highlightbackground	*-highlightcolor*	*-highlightthickness*
-justify	*-padx*	*-pady*
-relief	*-takefocus*	*-text*
-textvariable		

Widget-Specific Options

-aspect integer   (aspect, Aspect)
> Ratio of the text's width to its height on a scale from 0 to 100. The ratio is used to choose the line length for word wrapping.

-width width   (width, Width)
> Desired line length in characters. If greater than zero, overrides *-aspect* option.

---

radiobutton

> *radiobutton pathName [option value...]*

The *radiobutton* command creates a new radiobutton widget named **path-Name**.

Standard Options

-activebackground	*-activeforeground*	*-anchor*
-background	*-bitmap*	*-borderwidth*
-cursor	*-disabledforeground*	*-font*
-foreground	*-highlightbackground*	*-highlightcolor*
-highlightthickness	*-image*	*-justify*
-padx	*-pady*	*-relief*

Widget-Specific Options

-command `tclCommand`   (command, Command)
>   Command to be evaluated when button is invoked.

-height `height`   (height, Height)
>   Desired height, in lines for text content or in screen units for images and bitmaps.

-indicatoron `boolean`   (indicatorOn, IndicatorOn)
>   Whether the indicator should be drawn. If `false`, the *-relief* option is ignored and the widget's relief is sunken if selected and raised if not.

-selectcolor `color`   (selectColor, Background)
>   Background color to use for indicator when button is selected (at all times for Windows). If *indicatorOn* is false, the color is used for the background of the entire widget when it is selected.

-selectimage `imageName`   (selectImage, SelectImage)
>   Name of image to display instead of normal image when button is selected. This option is ignored if the *-image* option has not been set.

-state `state`   (state, State)
>   State of the radiobutton. `State` must be *normal, active,* or *disabled.*

-value `value`   (value, Value)
>   Value to store in associated variable when button is selected.

-variable `varName`   (variable, Variable)
>   Name of global variable (defaults to last element of `pathName`) to set to indicate whether the radiobutton is selected.

-width `width`   (width, Width)
>   Desired width in characters for text content or screen units for image and bitmap.

Methods

`pathName` *deselect*
>   Deselect the radiobutton and set the value of its associated variable to an empty string.

`pathName` *flash*
>   Flash the button by alternating between active and normal colors.

`pathName` *invoke*
>   Select the button, invoke the Tcl command associated with the button, and return its result. An empty string is returned if there is no command associated with the button. This command is ignored if the button's state is *disabled.*

Tk Core
Commands

pathName select

Select the radiobutton and set its associated variable to the value of the
-value option.

scale

scale pathName [option value...]

The *scale* command creates a new scale widget named *pathName*. A scale is
a widget that displays a rectangular trough and a small slider. The position of
the slider selects a particular real value.

Standard Options

-activebackground	*-background*	*-borderwidth*
-cursor	*-font*	*-foreground*
-highlightbackground	*-highlightcolor*	*-highlightthickness*
-orient	*-relief*	*-repeatdelay*
-repeatinterval	*-takefocus*	*-troughcolor*

Widget-Specific Options

-bigincrement value   (bigIncrement, BigIncrement)
Real number for "large" increments of the scale. Default (or if set to 0) is
one-tenth the range of the scale.

-command tclCommand   (command, Command)
Command to invoke whenever the scale's value is changed. The scale's
new value will be appended as an argument.

-digits integer   (digits, Digits)
How many significant digits should be retained when converting scale's
value to a string. If *integer* is zero or less, Tk chooses the smallest
value that guarantees each position is unique.

-from value   (from, From)
Real value limit for the left or top end of the scale.

-label string   (label, Label)
Text string to label the scale. Label is displayed just to the right of the top
end of vertical scales and just to the left of horizontal scales.

-length size   (length, Length)
Desired long dimension, in screen units, for the scale.

-resolution value   (resolution, Resolution)
Real value specifying the resolution of the scale. Defaults to 1 (i.e., the
scale's value will be integral).

-showvalue boolean   (showValue, ShowValue)
Whether the current value of the scale is displayed.

-sliderlength size   (sliderLength, SliderLength)
Size of the slider, in screen units, along the long dimension.

-sliderrelief `relief`   (sliderRelief, SliderRelief)
> The relief to use for drawing the slider.

-state `state`   (state, State)
> State of the scale. `State` must be `normal`, `active`, or `disabled`.

-tickinterval `value`   (tickInterval, TickInterval)
> Real value specifying spacing between numerical tick marks displayed below or to the left of the slider. If 0, no tick marks will be displayed.

-to `value`   (to, To)
> Real value corresponding to the right or bottom end of the scale.

-variable `varName`   (variable, Variable)
> Name of global variable to associate with the scale. Changes to either the variable or the scale will automatically update the value of the other.

-width `size`   (width, Width)
> Desired narrow dimension, in screen units, of the scale's trough.

Methods

pathName coords [`value`]
> Return the x- and y-coordinates (as a two-element list) of the point along the centerline of the trough corresponding to `value`. If `value` is not given, the scale's current value is used.

pathName get [`x y`]
> Return the current value of the scale if `x` and `y` are not given. Otherwise, return the value corresponding to the point on the scale closest to coordinates `x` and `y` within the widget.

pathName identify `x y`
> Return the name of the part of the scale that lies under the coordinates given by `x` and `y`. The name will be one of `slider`, `trough1` (above or to the left of the slider), or `trough2` (below or to the right of the slider). If the point is not within the widget, an empty string is returned.

pathName set `value`
> Change the current value of the scale to `value` and update the slider's position.

---

scrollbar

scrollbar `pathName` [`option value...`]

The *scrollbar* command creates a new scrollbar widget named `pathName`.

Standard Options

-activebackground	*-background*	*-borderwidth*
-cursor	*-highlightbackground*	*-highlightcolor*
-highlightthickness	*-jump*	*-orient*
-relief	*-repeatdelay*	*-repeatinterval*
-takefocus	*-troughcolor*	

Widget-Specific Options

-activerelief relief   (activeRelief, ActiveRelief)
>   Relief type to use when scrollbar is active.

-command string   (command, Command)
>   Prefix of Tcl command to invoke to change view in widget associated
>   with the scrollbar. See "Scrolling Methods," later in this section.

-elementborderwidth width   (elementBorderWidth, BorderWidth)
>   Width of borders drawn around internal elements of scrollbar.

-width width   (width, Width)
>   Desired narrow dimension, in screen units, for the scrollbar.

Scrollbar Elements

arrow1	Top (or left) arrow
trough1	Region between slider and arrow1
slider	Rectangle indicating visible region
trough2	Region between slider and arrow2
arrow2	Bottom (or right) arrow

Methods

pathName activate [element]
>   Mark element indicated by *element* as active. If not given, return name
>   of current element, or an empty string if no element is active.

pathName delta deltaX deltaY
>   Return a real number indicating the change in the scrollbar setting that
>   will result if the slider moves *deltaX* pixels to the right and *deltaY*
>   pixels to the left. The arguments may be zero or negative.

pathName fraction x y
>   Return real number between 0 and 1 indicating the fractional position of
>   coordinates *x y* (in pixels relative to the widget) along the scrollbar.

pathName get
>   Return a list containing the most recent arguments to the *set* method.

pathName identify x y
>   Return the name of the element at point *x y* (in pixels relative to the
>   widget) in the scrollbar. Return an empty string if the point is not inside
>   the scrollbar.

pathName set first last
>   Usually invoked by associated widget to inform the scrollbar about its
>   current view. Arguments *first* and *last* are real numbers between 0
>   and 1 describing the viewable range in the widget within the widget.

Scrolling Methods

When the user interacts with the scrollbar, for example, by dragging the slider,
the scrollbar notifies the associated widget that it must change its view. The
scrollbar makes the notification by evaluating a Tcl command generated by
appending action-specific arguments to the value of the scrollbar's *-command*

option. The possible forms of the resulting command are described next. In each case, *prefix* is the value of the *-command* option, which usually has a form like *pathName xview* or *pathName yview*, where *pathName* is the associated widget pathname.

prefix *moveto fraction*
> Tells associated widget to adjust its view so that the point indicated by *fraction* appears at the beginning of the widget's visible region. A value of 0.333 means the visible region should begin one-third of the way through the widget's span.

prefix *scroll number units*
> Tell associated widget to adjust its view by *number* units. The meaning of *units* is widget specific.

prefix *scroll number pages*
> Tell associated widget to adjust its view by *number* pages. The meaning of *pages* is widget specific.

text

> *text pathName* [*option value...*]

The *text* command creates a new text widget named *pathName*. A text widget displays one or more lines of text and allows that text to be edited. Several options exist to change the text's style (fonts, color, justification, etc.). Tags can be assigned to regions of text to allow different styles to be applied. The text widget also allows the embedding of images and other windows. Floating marks can be set to keep track of special points in the text.

Standard Options

-background	*-borderwidth*	*-cursor*
-exportselection	*-font*	*-foreground*
-highlightbackground	*-highlightcolor*	*-highlightthickness*
-insertbackground	*-insertborderwidth*	*-insertofftime*
-insertontime	*-insertwidth*	*-padx*
-pady	*-relief*	*-selectbackground*
-selectborderwidth	*-selectforeground*	*-setgrid*
-takefocus	*-xscrollcommand*	*-yscrollcommand*

Widget-Specific Options

-height   (height, Height)
> Desired height for the window, in characters.

-spacing1   (spacing1, Spacing1)
> Space to add above each line of text. If the line wraps, the space is added above the first displayed line only.

-spacing2   (spacing2, Spacing2)
> Space to add between the lines that display a long, wrapped line of text.

-spacing3 (spacing3, Spacing3)

> Space to add below each line of text. If the line wraps, the space is added below the last displayed line only.

-state (state, State)

> State of the text widget. *State* must be normal or disabled. If the text is disabled, no insertions or deletions are allowed.

-tabs (tabs, Tabs)

> List of screen distances giving the positions for tab stops. Each position may optionally be followed in the next list element by one of left (the default), right, center, or numeric (align on decimal point), which specifies how to justify text relative to the tab stop. If a line contains more tabs than defined tab stops, the last tab stop is used for the additional tabs. Example: {2c left 4c 6c center}

-width (width, Width)

> Desired width for window, in characters.

-wrap (wrap, Wrap)

> How to handle lines of text longer than the window width. Allowed values are none for no wrapping, char for line breaking on any character, or word for breaking only on word boundaries.

Text Indices

Several text widget methods support the notion of an *index* for identifying particular positions within the text. Indices have the syntax:

base [*modifier* [*modifier*...]]

where the base gives the starting point and the optional modifiers adjust the index from the starting point. Possible values for *base* are as follows:

line.char

> The *char*th character on line *line*. Lines are numbered starting at 1, characters starting at 0. If *char* is end, it refers to the newline character that ends the line.

@x,y

> The character that covers the pixel whose coordinates within the text's window are *x* and *y*.

end

> The end of the text (the character just after the last newline).

mark

> The character just after the mark whose name is *mark*.

tag.first

> The first character in the text range tagged with *tag*.

tag.last

> The character just after the last one in the text range tagged with *tag*.

pathName
> The position of the embedded window *pathName*.

imageName
> The position of the embedded image *imageName*.

The *modifier* arguments may take the following form:

+ *count* chars
> Adjust the index forward by *count* characters.

- *count* chars
> Adjust the index backward by *count* characters.

+ *count* lines
> Adjust the index forward by *count* lines, retaining the same character position within the line.

- *count* lines
> Adjust the index backward by *count* lines, retaining the same character position within the line.

linestart
> Adjust the index to refer to the first character on the line.

lineend
> Adjust the index to refer to the last character on the line (the newline).

wordstart
> Adjust the index to refer to the first character of the word containing the index. A word consists of any number of adjacent characters that are letters, digits, or underscores, or a single character that is not one of these and is not whitespace.

wordend
> Adjust the index to refer to the character just after the last one of the word containing the index.

Several widget methods operate on a range of text defined by the arguments *index1* and *index2*. This range includes all characters from *index1* up to, but not including, the character at *index2*. If *index2* is not given, the range consists only of the character at *index1*.

Tags

A tag is a textual string that is associated with one or more ranges of characters. Tags are used in methods to change the character's style (fonts, color, etc.), bind events to the characters, and manage the selection. Since an individual character may have any number of tags associated with it, a priority list of tags is maintained to resolve conflicts in style. When a tag is created, it is given highest priority. The *tag raise* and *tag lower* methods can be used to change a tag's priority.

The special tag `sel` exists when the *-exportselection* option for the text widget is `true`. This tag is used to manipulate the current selection. Whenever characters are tagged with `sel`, the text widget will claim ownership of the selection and return those characters when the selection is retrieved. When the selection is claimed by another window or application, the `sel` tag is removed from all characters in the text.

Marks

A mark is a textual string associated with a single position (a gap between characters). If the characters around a mark are deleted, the mark will still remain; it will just have new neighbors. Each mark has a gravity, either `left` or `right` (the default). The gravity specifies what happens when new text is inserted at the mark. With left gravity, the mark will end up to the left of the new text. With right gravity, the mark will end up to the right of new text.

Two marks are defined automatically and cannot be deleted. The `insert` mark represents the position of the insertion cursor; the insertion cursor will automatically be drawn at this point whenever the text widget has the input focus. The `current` mark is associated with the character closest to the mouse and is adjusted automatically to track the mouse motion (except during dragging).

Tag Event Binding

Binding events to tagged characters using the *tag bind* method works in a manner similar to binding events to widgets with the Tk *bind* command. However, only events related to the mouse and keyboard or virtual events can be bound to text tags. If a virtual event is used in a binding, it can be triggered only if the underlying "real" event is mouse related or keyboard related.

When multiple bindings for a character match a particular event, all of the matching bindings are invoked. This can happen when a character is associated with two tags and both tags have bindings for the same event. One binding is invoked for each tag in order from lowest to highest priority. If there are multiple matching bindings for a single tag, only the most specific binding is invoked. A *continue* command in a binding script terminates just that binding. A *break* command terminates the script for that binding and skips any remaining bindings for the event. Any bindings made to the text widget using the *bind* command are invoked after any matching tag bindings.

Methods

pathName bbox index
> Return a list of four numbers giving the x- and y-coordinates of the upper-left corner (relative to the widget) and the width and height of the visible area occupied by the character at *index*. If the character is not visible, an empty list is returned.

pathName compare index1 op index2
> Compare the two indices with relational operator *op* and return 1 if the relationship is satisfied, 0 if it isn't. *Op* may be <, <=, ==, >=, >, or !=.

pathName debug [*boolean*]

> Whether to turn on internal consistency checks in the B-tree code for all text widgets. Return current setting if *boolean* is not given.

pathName delete index1 index2

> Delete all characters (including embedded windows and images) from the given text range. The final newline in the text cannot be deleted.

pathName dlineinfo index

> Return a list of five numbers giving the x- and y-coordinates of the upper-left corner (relative to the widget) and the width and height of the area occupied by the line at *index*. The fifth element is the position of the baseline for the line as measured from the top of the area. If the line is not visible, an empty list is returned.

pathName dump [*switches*] *index1* [*index2*]

> Return detailed information on the text widget contents in the given text range. Information is returned in the following format:
>
> *key1 value1 index1 key2 value2 index2...*
>
> The possible *key* values are text, mark, tagon, tagoff, and window. The corresponding *value* is the text string, mark name, tag name, or window name. The *index* information is the index of the start of the text, the mark, the tag transition, or the window. One or more of the following switches are allowed:
>
> *-all* Include information for all element types. This is the default.
>
> *-command tclCommand*
>
> > Instead of returning information, invoke *tclCommand* on each element, appending the *key*, *value*, and *index* as arguments.
>
> *-mark*
>
> > Include information on marks in the dump.
>
> *-tag*
>
> > Include information on tags in the dump.
>
> *-text*
>
> > Include information on text in the dump. Will not span newlines, marks, or tag transitions.
>
> *-window*
>
> > Include information on windows in the dump.

pathName get index1 [*index2*]

> Return characters from given text range.

pathName image cget index option

> Return the value of configuration option *option* for the embedded image at *index*.

pathName image configure index [*option* [*value* [*option value*...]]]
> Query or modify the configuration options for an embedded image in the same manner as the general widget *configure* method. Supported options are as follows:

> *-align where*
>> How to align the image on the line in which it is displayed. *Where* may be `top` (align the top of the image with the top of the line), `bottom` (bottom with bottom), `center` (center the image on the line), or `baseline` (align the bottom of the image with the baseline of the line).

> *-image imageName*
>> Name of image to display.

> *-name imageName*
>> Name by which image can be referenced in the text widget (defaults to name of image set with *-image*).

> *-padx pixels*
>> Amount of extra space to leave on each side of the image.

> *-pady pixels*
>> Amount of extra space to leave on the top and bottom of the image.

pathName image create index [*option value*...]
> Create an embedded image at position *index* configured with the given options and return a unique identifier that may be used as an index to refer to the image.

pathName image names
> Return a list of the names of all embedded images in the text widget.

pathName index index
> Return the position corresponding to *index* in the form *line.char*.

pathName insert index chars [*tagList* [*chars* [*tagList*...]]]
> Insert the string *chars* just before the character at *index*. If *tagList* is given, it is a list of tags to be associated with the inserted text. Otherwise, any tags associated with both of the characters before and after *index* are associated with the inserted text. If multiple *chars-tagList* argument pairs are given, they are inserted in order as if by separate *insert* method calls.

pathName mark gravity markName [*direction*]
> Set the gravity for mark *markName* to *direction* (either `left` or `right`). If *direction* is not specified, returns current setting for the mark.

pathName mark names
> Return a list of the names of all marks currently set in the text widget.

pathName mark next `index`

Return the name of the next mark at or after `index`. If `index` is itself a mark name, that mark name is skipped as well as those marks at the same position that come before it in the *dump* list. Return an empty string if no marks appear after `index`.

pathName mark previous `index`

Return the name of the next mark at or before `index`. If `index` is itself a mark name, that mark name is skipped as well as those marks at the same position that come after it in the *dump* list. Return an empty string if no marks appear before `index`.

pathName mark set markName `index`

Set a mark named *markName* just before the character at `index`.

pathName mark unset markName [*markName*...]

Remove the marks corresponding to each of the *markName* arguments.

pathName scan dragto `x` `y`

Scroll the widget's view horizontally and vertically. The distance scrolled is equal to 10 times the difference between this command's `x` and `y` arguments and the `x` and `y` arguments to the last *scan mark* command for the widget.

pathName scan mark `x` `y`

Record `x` and `y` as anchors for a following *scan dragto* method call.

pathName search [`switches`] `pattern index` [`stopIndex`]

Search the text for a range of characters that match `pattern` starting at position `index`. If a match is found, the index of the first character of the match is returned. Otherwise, an empty list is returned. If `stopIndex` is given, the search will not go past that index. Possible switches are:

-forward

Search forward through the text. This is the default.

-backward

Search backward through the text, finding matching text closest to `index` whose first character is before `index`.

-exact

The characters in the matching range must be identical to those in `pattern`.

-regexp

Treats `pattern` as a regular expression (see the *regexp* command).

-nocase

Ignore case differences in matching.

-count varName

Store number of characters in matching range in the variable *var-Name*.

-- Terminate further processing of switches so that pattern may begin with a hyphen.

pathName see index
Adjust the view in the window if needed so that the character at *index* is completely visible.

pathName tag add tagName index1 [*index2* [*index1* [*index2*...]]]
Associate the tag *tagName* with the characters in each given text range.

pathName tag bind tagName [*sequence* [*script*]]
Associate *script* with tag *tagName* such that whenever the event sequence given by *sequence* occurs for a character tagged with *tag-Name*, the script will be evaluated. See "Tag Event Binding," earlier in this chapter. If the *script* argument is not given, the current associated script is returned. If the *sequence* is also not given, a list of all the sequences for which bindings have been defined for *tagOrId* is returned.

pathName tag cget tagName option
Return the value of configuration option *option* for the tag *tagName*.

pathName tag configure tagName [*option* [*value* [*option value*...]]]
Query or modify the configuration options for tag *tagName* in the same manner as the general widget *configure* method. Tag options are used to change the displayed style of characters marked with the tag. Options that change the line style (margins, spacing, justification) take effect only if the first character of the line is associated with the tag. The following options are available:

-background color
Background color for drawing characters.

-bgstipple bitmap
Bitmap to use as stipple pattern for character background.

-borderwidth pixels
Width of a 3D border to draw around background.

-fgstipple bitmap
Bitmap to use as stipple pattern for character foreground.

-font fontName
Font to use for drawing characters.

-foreground color
Foreground color for drawing characters.

-justify justify
How to align lines in the window when the first character of the line is associated with the tag. Must be left, right, or center.

-lmargin1 pixels
How much to indent lines. If the line wraps, this indent applies only to the first displayed line.

-lmargin2 `pixels`

How much to indent lines that follow the first one in a long, wrapped line.

-offset `pixels`

Amount to vertically offset the baseline of characters from the baseline. Useful for superscripts and subscripts.

-overstrike `boolean`

Whether to draw a horizontal line through the middle of the characters.

-relief `relief`

3D relief to use for drawing background border.

-rmargin `pixels`

How much to indent all displayed lines of a line of text from the right edge of the window.

-spacing1 `pixels`

Space to add above each line of text. If the line wraps, the space is added above the first displayed line only.

-spacing2 `pixels`

Space to add between the lines that display a long, wrapped line of text.

-spacing3 `pixels`

Space to add below each line of text. If the line wraps, the space is added below the last displayed line only.

-tabs `tabList`

Tab stops for a line of text (see the *-tabs* option in "Widget-Specific Options," earlier in this section).

-underline `boolean`

Whether to draw an underline beneath characters.

-wrap `mode`

How the line of text should be wrapped. Must be one of none, char, or word.

pathName *tag delete* `tagName` [`tagName...`]

Delete all tag information for each of the tags identified by the `tagName` arguments.

pathName *tag lower* `tagName` [`belowThis`]

Change the priority of tag `tagName` such that it is lower in priority than tag `belowThis`. If `belowThis` is not given, the tag is changed to have lowest priority.

pathName *tag names* [`index`]

Return a list of the names of all tags associated with the character at position `index`. If `index` is not given, a list of all tags that exist in the text is returned.

pathName tag nextrange tagName index1 [index2]

Return starting and ending index of the next range of characters associated with tag *tagName* in which the first character of the range is no earlier than position *index1* and no later than just before position *index2* (or end if not given).

pathName tag prevrange tagName index1 [index2]

Return starting and ending index of the next range of characters associated with tag *tagName* in which the first character of the range is before position *index1* and no earlier than position *index2* (or 1.0 if not given).

pathName tag raise tagName [aboveThis]

Change the priority of tag *tagName* such that it is higher in priority than tag *aboveThis*. If *aboveThis* is not given, the tag is changed to have highest priority.

pathName tag ranges tagName

Return a list of all ranges of text that have been tagged with *tagName*.

pathName tag remove tagName index1 [index2 [index1 [index2...]]]

Remove tag *tagName* from those tags associated with the characters in the given text ranges.

pathName window cget index option

Return the value of configuration option *option* for the window identified by *index*.

pathName window configure index [option [value [option value...]]]

Query or modify the configuration options for the window identified by *index* in the same manner as the general widget *configure* method. The following options are available:

-align where

How to align the window on the line in which it is displayed. *Where* may be top (align the top of the window with the top of the line), bottom (bottom with bottom), center (center the window on the line), or baseline (align the bottom of the window with the baseline of the line).

-create script

As an alternative to the *-window* option, specifies a script to evaluate when a window is first displayed on screen. *Script* must return the name of the window to display. If the window is ever destroyed, *script* will be evaluated again the next time the text widget requires the window to be displayed.

-padx pixels

Amount of extra space to leave on each side of the window.

-pady pixels

Amount of extra space to leave on the top and bottom of the window.

-stretch `boolean`

> Whether window should be stretched vertically to fill the height of its line.

-window `pathName`

> Pathname of the window to embed in the text widget.

`pathName` *window create* `index` [`option value`...]

> Create an embedded window at position `index` configured with the given options.

`pathName` *window names*

> Return a list of the names of all windows currently embedded in the text widget.

`pathName` *xview*

> Return a two-element list describing the currently visible horizontal region of the widget. The elements are real numbers representing the fractional distance that the view's left and right edges extend into the horizontal span of the widget.

`pathName` *xview moveto* `fraction`

> Adjust the visible region of the widget so' that the point indicated by `fraction` along the widget's horizontal span appears at the region's left edge.

`pathName` *xview scroll* `number` `what`

> Shift the visible region of the widget horizontally by `number`. If `what` is `units`, then `number` is in units of characters. If `what` is `pages`, then `number` is in units of the visible region's width.

`pathName` *yview*

> Return a two-element list describing the currently visible vertical region of the widget. The elements are real numbers representing the fractional distance that the view's top and bottom edges extend into the vertical span of the widget.

`pathName` *yview -pickplace* `index`

> Adjust the visible region of the widget so position `index` is visible at the top edge of the view. If *-pickplace* is specified, the widget chooses where `index` appears in the view to cause the least possible screen movement necessary to make the position visible. This method is made obsolete by the *see* method.

`pathName` *yview moveto* `fraction`

> Adjust the visible region of the widget so that the point indicated by `fraction` along the widget's vertical span appears at the region's top edge.

`pathName` *yview scroll* `number` `what`

> Shift the visible region of the widget vertically by `number`. If `what` is `units`, then `number` is in units of text lines. If `what` is `pages`, then `number` is in units of the visible region's height.

toplevel

toplevel pathName [*option value...*]

The *toplevel* command creates a new top-level widget named pathName. It is similar to a frame widget, but its actual window system parent is the root window of the screen rather than the hierarchical parent from its pathname.

Standard Options

-borderwidth   *-cursor*   *-highlightbackground*
-highlightcolor   *-highlightthickness* *-relief*
-takefocus

Widget-Specific Options

-background color   (background, Background)
> Same as standard option, but may be the empty string to display no background or border.

-class name   (class, Class)
> Class to use when querying the option database and for bindings. May not be changed with *configure*.

-colormap colormap   (colormap, Colormap)
> Colormap to use for window. Colormap may be either new, in which case a new colormap is created, or the name of another window, in which case that window's colormap is used. The default is to use the colormap of its screen. May not be changed with *configure*.

-container boolean   (container, Container)
> Whether the window will be used as a container in which to embed some other application. May not be changed with the *configure* method.

-height height   (height, Height)
> Desired height, in screen units, for the window.

-menu pathName   (menu, Menu)
> Menu widget to be used as a menubar.

-screen screen
> Screen on which to place the new window. May not be changed with the *configure* method.

-use windowId   (use, Use)
> Used for embedding. WindowId is the ID of a window to be the parent of top-level widget instead of the root window. May not be changed with the *configure* method.

-visual visual   (visual, Visual)
> Visual class to use for the window. Visual must be directcolor, grayscale, pseudocolor, staticcolor, staticgray, or truecolor.

-width width   (width, Width)
> Desired width, in screen units, for the window.

Utility Commands

This section describes the commands in the Tk extension that do not create widgets. These commands include those needed to bind to window system events, control the layout of widgets, interact with the window manager, and several other miscellaneous GUI-related operations.

bell

bell [*-displayof* `window`]

Ring the bell on the display of `window`. If `window` is not given, the bell is rung on the display of the main window.

bind

bind `tag` [`sequence` [[+] `script`]]

Set or query event bindings. If all three arguments are specified, the Tcl script `script` will be evaluated whenever the event specified by the pattern `sequence` occurs in the windows identified by `tag`. If `script` is prefixed by the character "+", it is appended to any existing script bound to `tag` for `sequence`. Otherwise, any current script is replaced. If `script` is an empty string, any current binding to the event is destroyed.

If no `script` is specified, the script currently bound to `tag` for `sequence` is returned. If only `tag` is given, a list of all the sequences for which there exist bindings for `tag` is returned.

Binding Tags

The windows to which a binding applies are selected by the `tag` argument. If `tag` begins with the "`.`" character, it must be a pathname for a window; otherwise, it can be an arbitrary string. Each window has an associated list of tags that can be manipulated with the *bindtags* command. The default tags for a newly created window, in priority order, are as follows:

- The pathname of the window itself (e.g., `.main.text`). Binding to this tag will bind the sequence to that window only, unless the window is top-level.

- The pathname of the top-level window containing the window (e.g., "`.`"). Binding to this tag will bind the sequence to all windows contained by the top-level window.

- The widget class of the window (e.g., `Text`). Binding to this tag will bind the sequence to all windows of that class. This is how the default bindings for all widgets are set up in the standard Tk script library.

- The special value `all`. Binding to this tag will bind the sequence to all windows in the application.

Event Patterns

The *sequence* argument consists of a sequence of one or more event patterns. If multiple patterns are concatenated without whitespace, the binding requires the matched events to happen in the order of events given. When *script* is given, the *sequence* argument may also be a list of valid sequences, in which case each sequence is bound to the same script separately.

Event patterns in a sequence take one of three forms. The simplest form is a single printable ASCII character, such as a or [, with the exclusion of the space character and the character <. This form of an event pattern matches a KeyPress event for the given character.

The second form of pattern is used to specify a user-defined, named virtual event. It has the following syntax:

    <<name>>

Name is an arbitrary string surrounded by double angle brackets. See the *event* command. Bindings on a virtual event can be created before the virtual event is defined. If the definition of a virtual event is later changed, all windows bound to that virtual event will respond immediately to the new definition.

The third form has the following syntax:

    <modifier-modifier-type-detail>

Surrounded by a single pair of angle brackets is a pattern of zero or more modifiers, an event type, and an extra piece of information (the detail), which can identify a particular button or keysym. All the fields are optional, except that at least one of *type* and *detail* must be present. The fields can be separated by either whitespace or dashes.

Possible values for the *modifier* elements are as follows:

Control	Shift	Lock
Button1 or B1	Button2 or B2	Button3 or B3
Button4 or B4	Button5 or B5	Mod1 or M1
Mod2 or M2	Mod3 or M3	Mod4 or M4
Mod5 or M5	Meta or M	Alt
Double	Triple	

Most of these indicate a key or mouse button that must be pressed in addition to the action specified by *type* and *detail*. The Double and Triple modifiers are a convenience for specifying repeated events with the addition of a time and space requirement on the sequence.

For a binding to match a given event, the modifiers in the event must include all of those specified in the event pattern. An event may also contain additional modifiers not specified in the binding. For example, if button 1 is pressed while the Shift and Control keys are down, the pattern <Control-Button-1> will match the event, but <Mod1-Button-1> will not. If no modifiers are specified, any combination of modifiers may be present in the event.

The *type* element may take any of the following values corresponding to the standard X Window System event types:

ButtonPress or Button	ButtonRelease	Circulate
Colormap	Configure	Destroy
Enter	Deactivate	Expose
FocusIn	FocusOut	Gravity
KeyPress or Key	KeyRelease	Leave
Map	Motion	Property
Reparent	Unmap	Visibility
Activate		

The allowed values for the *detail* element depend on the preceding *type* element. For ButtonPress and ButtonRelease, the possible values are 1 through 5, identifying the number of the mouse button. For KeyPress and KeyRelease, the possible values are any valid X Window System keysym. This includes all alphanumeric ASCII characters (e.g., a and 8) and descriptions for other characters (e.g., comma for the comma character). The actual keysyms available will depend on your operating system and hardware. On most Unix systems, the keysyms are listed in the include file */usr/include/X11/keysymdef.h*.

As a special shortcut, the *type* element may be omitted when a *detail* is specified. For *detail* values 1 through 5, the type defaults to Button-Press. For any other valid keysym value, the type defaults to KeyPress.

Binding Script and Substitutions

Whenever the given event sequence occurs, the *script* argument to *bind* will be evaluated at global scope in the same interpreter in which the *bind* was executed. If an error occurs in executing the script for a binding, the *bgerror* mechanism is used to report the error.

The script is passed through a substitution phase before being executed. Occurrences of the % character followed by a second character will be replaced by a value dependent on the second character, when valid. The substitution will always be properly escaped or surrounded with braces to maintain a valid Tcl command. The possible substitutions are as follows:

%% Replaced with a single percent sign.

%# The number of the last client request (the *serial* field from the event).

%a The *above* field from the event as a hexadecimal number. Valid only for Configure events.

%b The number of the button that was pressed or released. Valid only for ButtonPress and ButtonRelease events.

%c The *count* field from the event. Valid only for Expose events.

%d The *detail* field from the event. Valid only for Enter, Leave, FocusIn, and FocusOut events. Will be one of the following:

```
NotifyAncestor              NotifyDetailNone
NotifyInferior              NotifyNonlinear
NotifyNonlinearVirtual      NotifyPointer
NotifyPointerRoot           NotifyVirtual
```

%f   The *focus* field from the event (0 or 1). Valid only for `Enter` and `Leave` events.

%h   The *height* field from the event. Valid only for `Configure` and `Expose` events.

%k   The *keycode* field from the event. Valid only for `KeyPress` and `Key-Release` events.

%m   The *mode* field from the event. Valid only for `Enter`, `Leave`, `FocusIn`, and `FocusOut` events. The value will be `NotifyNormal`, `Notify-Grab`, `NotifyUngrab`, or `NotifyWhileGrabbed`.

%o   The *override_redirect* field from the event. Valid only for `Map`, `Reparent`, and `Configure` events.

%p   The *place* field from the event. Valid only for `Circulate` events. The value will be `PlaceOnTop` or `PlaceOnBottom`.

%s   The *state* field from the event. For `ButtonPress`, `ButtonRelease`, `Enter`, `Leave`, `KeyPress`, `KeyRelease`, and `Motion` events, a decimal string is substituted. For `Visibility`, the value will be `VisibilityUnobscured`, `VisibilityPartiallyObscured`, or `VisibilityFullyObscured`.

%t   The *time* field from the event. Valid only for events that contain a *time* field.

%w   The *width* field from the event. Valid only for `Configure` and `Expose` events.

%x   The *x* field from the event. Valid only for events containing a *x* field.

%y   The *y* field from the event. Valid only for events containing a *y* field.

%A   Substitutes the ASCII character corresponding to the event (or the empty string if there is none). Valid only for `KeyPress` and `KeyRelease` events.

%B   The *border_width* field from the event. Valid only for `Configure` events.

%E   The *send_event* field from the event.

%K   The keysym corresponding to the event as a textual string. Valid only for `KeyPress` and `KeyRelease` events.

%N   The keysym corresponding to the event as a decimal number. Valid only for `KeyPress` and `KeyRelease` events.

%R The *root* window identifier from the event. Valid only for events containing a *root* field.

%S The *subwindow* window identifier from the event. Valid only for events containing a *subwindow* field.

%T The *type* field from the event.

%W The pathname of the window for which the event was reported.

%X The *x_root* field from the event. This is the x-coordinate in the root (or virtual root) window. Valid only for `ButtonPress`, `ButtonRelease`, `KeyPress`, `KeyRelease`, and `Motion` events.

%Y The *y_root* field from the event. This is the y-coordinate in the root (or virtual root) window. Valid only for `ButtonPress`, `ButtonRelease`, `KeyPress`, `KeyRelease`, and `Motion` events.

Multiple Matches

It is possible for an event to match several bindings. If the bindings are associated with different *tag*s, each of them will be executed in the order of the tags as set by *bindtags*. The *continue* and *break* commands can be used inside a binding to control processing of the matching scripts. The *continue* command terminates the current script and continues on to the next tag's script. The *break* command terminates the current script and does not invoke the scripts for the following tags.

If more than one binding matches a particular event and each has the same *tag*, the script for the most specific binding is evaluated. The following tests are applied, in order, to determine which of several matching sequences is more specific:

1. An event pattern that specifies a specific button or key is more specific than one that doesn't.

2. A longer sequence (in terms of number of events matched) is more specific than a shorter sequence.

3. If the modifiers specified in one pattern are a subset of the modifiers in another pattern, the pattern with more modifiers is more specific.

4. A virtual event whose physical pattern matches the sequence is less specific than the same physical pattern that is not associated with a virtual event.

5. Given a sequence that matches two or more virtual events, one of the virtual events will be chosen, but the order is undefined.

If there are two (or more) virtual events bound to the same tag that are both triggered by the same sequence, only one of the virtual events will be triggered. Which one is chosen is undefined.

Multievent Sequences and Ignored Events

If a *sequence* contains multiple event patterns, its script is executed whenever the events leading up to and including the current event match the order of events given in the sequence. For example, if button 1 is clicked repeatedly, the sequence <Double-ButtonPress-1> will match each button press but the first. Extraneous events that occur in the middle of an event sequence will prevent a match only if they are KeyPress or ButtonPress events not in the sequence. Extraneous modifier key presses are ignored, however. When several Motion events occur in a row, only the last one is considered for matching binding sequences.

bindtags

bindtags window [tagList]

With no *tagList* argument, the current list of binding tags associated with window *window* is returned. Otherwise, the current list is replaced with the list of tags given by *tagList*. If *tagList* is the empty list, the tag list is reset to the default as described in the "Binding Tags" section of the *bind* command.

clipboard

clipboard operation [arg arg...]

Clear or append to the contents of the Tk clipboard for later retrieval using the *selection* command. The following operations are defined:

clipboard append [-*displayof* window] [-*format* format] [-*type* type] [--]
    data
    Append data to the clipboard on *window*'s display. type specifies the form in which the selection is to be returned as an atom name such as STRING or FILE_NAME (see the *Inter-Client Communication Conventions Manual*). The default is STRING.

    When compatibility with a non-Tk clipboard requester is needed, the *format* argument can be used to specify the representation that should be used to transmit the selection. Format defaults to STRING, which transmits the selection as 8-bit ASCII characters.

clipboard clear [-*displayof* window]
    Claim ownership of the clipboard on *window*'s display (defaults to ".") and remove any previous contents.

destroy

destroy window [window...]

Destroy the windows given by the *window* arguments as well as all their descendants. The windows are destroyed in the order given. If an error occurs in destroying a window, the command aborts without destroying the remaining windows. It is not an error if *window* does not exist.

event

event operation [*arg arg...*]

The *event* command provides several facilities for dealing with window system events, such as defining virtual events and synthesizing events. The following operations are defined:

event add <<*virtual*>> *sequence* [*sequence...*]
> Add the given event *sequences* to those associated with the virtual event *virtual*. The virtual event will trigger whenever any one of the given *sequences* occurs. See the *bind* command for allowed *sequence* values.

event delete <<*virtual*>> [*sequence* [*sequence...*]]
> Delete the given event *sequences* from those associated with the virtual event *virtual*. If no *sequence* is given, all sequences associated with the virtual event are removed.

event generate window sequence [*option value...*]
> Generate an event for window *window* and arrange for it to be processed just as if it had come from the window system. *Window* may be a window pathname or an identifier (as returned by *winfo id*), as long as it is in the current application. The *sequence* argument describes the event to generate. It may have any of the forms allowed for the *sequence* argument to the *bind* command, except that it must consist of a single event pattern (e.g., <Shift-Button-2> or <<Paste>>).

> The event generated can be further described with the optional option-value pairs. In the descriptions of these options that follow, the [%char] at the beginning identifies the corresponding *bind* command substitution. The available options are as follows:

> *-above window*
>> [%a] The *above* field for the event, either as a window or integer window ID.

> *-borderwidth size*
>> [%B] The *border_width* field for the event as a screen distance.

> *-button number*
>> [%b] The *detail* field for a ButtonPress or ButtonRelease event.

> *-count integer*
>> [%c] The *count* field for the event.

> *-detail detail*
>> [%d] The *detail* field for the event.

> *-focus boolean*
>> [%f] The *focus* field for the event.

-height `size`
> [%h] The *height* field for the event as a screen distance.

-keycode `integer`
> [%k] The *keycode* field for the event.

-keysym `name`
> [%K] The *keysym* field for the event.

-mode `notify`
> [%m] The *mode* field for the event.

-override `boolean`
> [%o] The *override_redirect* field for the event.

-place `where`
> [%p] The *place* field for the event.

-root `window`
> [%R] The *root* field for the event as a window pathname or integer window ID.

-rootx `coord`
> [%X] The *x_root* field for the event as a screen distance.

-rooty `coord`
> [%Y] The *y_root* field for the event as a screen distance.

-sendevent `boolean`
> [%E] The *send_event* field for the event.

-serial `integer`
> [%#] The *serial* field for the event.

-state `state`
> [%s] The *state* field for the event.

-subwindow `window`
> [%S] The *subwindow* field for the event as a window pathname or an integer window ID.

-time `integer`
> [%t] The *time* field for the event.

-width `size`
> [%w] The *width* field for the event as a screen distance.

-when `when`
> Determines when the event will be processed. *When* must have one of the following values:
>
> now
>> Process the event immediately before the *event* command returns. This is the default.
>
> tail
>> Place the event at the end of Tcl's event queue.

---

head
> Place the event at the front of Tcl's event queue.

mark
> Place the event at the front of Tcl's event queue but behind any other events already queued with -*when* mark.

-*x coord*
> [%x] The *x* field for the event as a screen distance.

-*y coord*
> [%y] The *y* field for the event as a screen distance.

event info [<<virtual>>]
> If the <<virtual>> argument is omitted, a list of all currently defined virtual events is returned. Otherwise, the return value is the list of event sequences currently associated with virtual event *virtual*.

focus

focus [[option] window]

tk_focusFollowsMouse
tk_focusNext window
tk_focusPrev window

Manage the Tk input focus. At any given time, one window on each display is given the focus so that key press and key release events for the display are sent to that window. Tk remembers the last window in each top-level window to receive the focus. When the window manager gives the focus to a top-level window, Tk automatically redirects it to the remembered window.

Focus within a Tk top-level window uses an *explicit* focus model by default (i.e., moving the mouse within a top-level window does not change the focus). The model can be changed to *implicit* (focus changes to a window whenever the mouse enters it) by calling the *tk_focusFollowsMouse* procedure.

The Tcl procedures *tk_focusNext* and *tk_focusPrev* implement a focus order among the windows of a top-level window. They return the next and previous windows after *window* in the focus order that accepts the focus (see the -*takefocus* widget configuration option). The focus order is determined by the structure of the window hierarchy and by the stacking order of the windows among siblings.

The *focus* command can take the following forms:

focus [-*displayof window*]
> Return the pathname of the focus window on the display containing *window*. If not given, *window* defaults to the root window.

focus window
> If the application currently has the input focus for *window*'s display, the focus is given to *window*. Otherwise, *window* is made the remembered focus window for its top-level window.

focus -force `window`

Set the focus of `window`'s display to `window` even if the application doesn't currently have the input focus for the display.

focus -lastfor `window`

Return the pathname of the window to most recently own the input focus among all windows in the same top-level window as `window` (i.e., the remembered window). If no window currently present in that top level has ever had the input focus, the name of the top-level window is returned.

font

font operation [`arg arg`...]

The *font* command provides several facilities for defining named fonts and inspecting their attributes. If the window system does not have a font that matches the requested attributes, Tk makes a best guess. The following operations are supported:

font actual `font` [*-displayof* `window`] [`option`]

Return information on the actual attributes that are obtained when `font` is used on `window`'s display. If `option` is specified, only the value of that attribute is returned. Otherwise, a list of all attributes and their values is returned.

font configure `fontName` [`option` [`value` [`option value`...]]]

Query or modify the desired attributes for the named font `fontName` in the same manner as the general widget *configure* method. The available attribute options are as follows:

-family `name`

The case-insensitive font family name. The families `Courier`, `Times`, and `Helvetica` are guaranteed to be supported on all platforms.

-size `size`

The desired size for the font in points (or pixels if `size` is negative).

-weight `weight`

The thickness of the characters in the font. `Weight` may be `normal` (the default) or `bold`.

-slant `slant`

How characters in the font are slanted away from the vertical. `Slant` may be `roman` (the default) or `italic`.

-underline `boolean`

Whether characters in font should be underlined. Default is `false`.

-overstrike `boolean`

Whether a horizontal line is drawn through the middle of the characters of the font. Default is `false`.

font create [*fontName*] [*option value...*]]]

Create a new named font. *FontName* specifies the name for the font; if it is omitted, Tk generates a unique name of the form font*x*, where *x* is an integer. Either way, the name of the font is then returned. See the *font configure* command for options.

font delete fontName [*fontName...*]

Delete the specified named fonts. A named font will not actually be deleted until all widgets using the font release it. If a deleted named font is later recreated with another call to *font create*, the widgets will redisplay themselves using the new attributes of that font.

font families [*-displayof window*]

Return a list of all font families that exist on *window*'s display.

font measure font [*-displayof window*] *text*

Return total width in pixels that the string *text* would use in the given *font* when displayed in *window*.

font metrics font [*-displayof window*] [*option*]

Return information about the metrics for *font* when it is used on *window*'s display. If *option* is specified, returns only the value of that metric. Otherwise, returns a list of all metrics and their values. The available metrics are as follows:

-ascent

Amount in pixels that the tallest letter sticks above the baseline, plus any extra blank space added by the font's designer.

-descent

Amount in pixels that any letter sticks down below the baseline, plus any extra blank space added by the font's designer.

-linespace

How far apart vertically, in pixels, two lines of text using the font should be placed so there is no overlap.

-fixed

1 if this is a fixed-width font, or 0 if it is a proportionally spaced font.

font names

Return a list of all the named fonts currently defined.

Font Description

The following formats are allowed as a font description anywhere *font* is specified as an argument in the previous *font* commands and for the *-font* option to widgets:

fontName

A named font created with the *font create* command.

systemfont

The platform-specific name of a font as interpreted by the window system.

family [*size*] [*style* [*style*...]]

A Tcl list whose first element is the desired font *family* followed optionally by the desired *size* and zero or more of the following *style* arguments: normal or bold, roman or italic, underline, and overstrike.

X-font names (XLFD)

An X11-format font name of the form *-foundry-family-weight-slant-setwidth-addstyle-pixel-point-resx-resy-spacing-width-charset-encoding*. The "*" character can be used to skip individual fields or at the end to skip remaining fields.

option value [*option value*...]

A Tcl list of option-value pairs as would be given to the *font create* command.

---

grab

grab operation [*arg arg*...]

The *grab* command implements simple pointer and keyboard grabs. Tk restricts all pointer events to the grab window and its descendants (which may include top-level windows). Pointer events outside the grab window's tree are reported as events to the grab window. No window entry or window exit events are reported to the grab window. A grab applies only to the display of the grab window.

Two types of grabs are possible: local and global. A local grab, the default, affects only the grabbing application, so events are reported normally to other applications on the display. A global grab blocks events to all other applications on the display so that only the specified subtree of the grabbing application will receive pointer events.

The *grab* command can take the following forms:

grab [*-global*] *window*

Same as *grab set*.

grab current [*window*]

Return the name of the application's current grab window on *window*'s display, or an empty string if there is no such window. If *window* is not given, a list of all windows grabbed by this application for all displays is returned.

grab release window

Release the grab on *window* if there is one.

grab set [*-global*] `window`
> Set a grab on `window`. If *-global* is specified, the grab will be global. Any other grab by the application on `window`'s display is released.

grab status `window`
> Return none, `local`, or `global` to describe the grab currently set on `window`.

---

grid

grid operation [`arg arg...`]

Communicate with the grid geometry manager that arranges widgets in rows and columns inside of another window called the master window. The *grid* command can take the following forms:

grid `slave` [`slave...`] [`options`]
> Same as *grid configure*.

grid bbox `master` [`column row` [`column2 row2`]]
> With no arguments, the bounding box of grid is returned consisting of a list of four integers: the pixel offset within the master window of the top-left corner of the grid (x and y) and the pixel width and height of the grid. If just `column` and `row` are specified, only the bounding box for that cell is returned. If `column2` and `row2` are also specified, the bounding box spanning the rows and columns indicated is returned.

grid columnconfigure `master index` [`option value...`]
> Query or set the column properties of the `index` column in geometry master `master`. If options are provided, `index` may be a list of column positions. Valid options are as follows:

-minsize `size`
> Minimum width, in screen units, permitted for column.

-pad `amount`
> Number of screen units in padding to add to the left and right of the widest window in column.

-weight `integer`
> Relative weight for apportioning any extra space among columns. A weight of 0 indicates that the column will not deviate from its requested size. A column whose weight is 2 will grow at twice the rate as a column of weight 1.

grid configure `slave` [`slave...`] [`options`]
> Configure how given slave windows should be managed by their grid geometry master. `Slave` can be a pathname of a window to manage or one of the special relative-placement characters –, x, or ^. Supported options are as follows:

-column n

Insert the slave *slave* in the *n*th column (starting from 0). If not specified, the slave is placed in the column just to the right of the previously placed slave, or column 0 if it is the first slave. For each **x** that immediately precedes a *slave*, a column is skipped.

-columnspan n

Arrange for the slave to span *n* columns in the grid. The default is 1 unless the *slave* is followed by a "−" character in the slave list. The columnspan is incremented by one for each immediately following "−" character.

-in master

Insert the slaves in master window given by *master*. The master window must either be the slave's parent (the default) or a descendant of the slave's parent.

-ipadx amount

How much horizontal internal padding, in screen units, to add to the side of the slaves.

-ipady amount

How much vertical internal padding, in screen units, to add to the top and bottom of the slaves.

-padx amount

How much horizontal external padding, in screen units, to add to the side of the slaves.

-pady amount

How much vertical external padding, in screen units, to add to the top and bottom of the slaves.

-row n

Insert the slave in the *n*th row (starting from 0). If not specified, the slave is placed on the same row as the last placed slave, or the first unoccupied row for the first slave.

-rowspan n

Arrange for the slave to span *n* rows in the grid. The default is one row. If the next *grid* command contains "^" characters instead of window pathnames that line up with the columns of this slave, the rowspan of this slave is extended by one.

-sticky sides

How the slave should be positioned and stretched within its cell. *Sides* is a string containing zero or more of the characters n, s, e, or w. Each letter refers to a side to which the slave will stick. If both n and s (or e and w) are specified, the slave will be stretched to fill the cell's height (or width). The default is the empty string, which causes the slave to be centered within its cell at its requested size.

grid forget `slave` [`slave...`]

Remove each of the `slave`s from the grid of its master and unmap their windows. The grid configuration options for each `slave` are forgotten.

grid info `slave`

Return the current configuration state of the slave `slave` in the same option-value form given to *grid configure*. The first two elements will be *-in* `master`.

grid location `master x y`

Return the column and row numbers at locations `x` and `y` (in screen units) inside `master`'s grid. For locations above or to the left of the grid, a –1 is returned.

grid propagate `master` [`boolean`]

Set or query whether propagation has been enabled for `master`. Propagation is enabled by default. If disabled, the master window will not be resized to adjust to the size of its slaves.

grid rowconfigure `master index` [`option value...`]

Query or set the row properties of the `index` row in geometry master `master`. If options are provided, `index` may be a list of row positions. Valid options are as follows:

-minsize `size`

Minimum height, in screen units, permitted for row.

-pad `amount`

Number of screen units in padding to add to the top and bottom of the tallest window in row.

-weight `integer`

Relative weight for apportioning any extra space among rows. A weight of 0 indicates that the row will not deviate from its requested size. A row whose weight is 2 will grow twice as fast as a row of weight 1.

grid remove `slave` [`slave...`]

Remove each of the `slave`s from the grid of its master and unmap their windows. The grid configuration options for each `slave` are remembered as defaults for the next time they are managed by the same master.

grid size `master`

Return the size of the grid (in columns, then rows) for `master`.

grid slaves `master` [*-row* `row`] [*-column* `column`]

If no options are supplied, a list of all the slaves in `master` is returned. The options specify that the list should include only the slaves in row `row` and/or column `column`.

image

image `operation` [`arg arg`...]

Create and manipulate image objects. The *image* command can take the following forms:

image create `type` [`name`] [`option value`...]

Create a new image of type `type` and return its name. The currently supported image types are `bitmap` and `photo`. The option-value pairs valid for these types are described in the individual sections that follow. The name returned will be *name* if given; otherwise, Tk picks a unique name of the form `imageN`. If an image already exists by the given *name*, it is replaced with the new image and any instances of that image will be redisplayed.

A new Tcl command is created with the image's name. This command supports the *cget* and *configure* operation for changing and querying the image's configuration options in the same manner as for widgets.

image delete `image` [`image`...]

Delete each of the given images. If a widget is using an instance of an image, it won't actually be deleted until all of the instances are released. Existing instances will redisplay as empty areas. If a deleted image is recreated, the existing instances will use the new image.

image height `image`

Return the height, in pixels, of the image *image*.

image names

Return a list of all existing images.

image type `image`

Return the type of the image *image*.

image types

Return a list of supported image types.

image width `image`

Return the width, in pixels, of image *image*.

Bitmap Images

A bitmap image is represented by a background color, a foreground color, and two X11-format bitmaps, called the source and the mask. Each of the bitmaps specifies a rectangular array of 0's and 1's representing a pixel in the image. The two bitmaps must have the same dimensions. For pixels for which the mask is 0, the image displays nothing, producing a transparent effect. For other pixels, the image displays the foreground color if the corresponding source pixel is 1 and the background color if the corresponding source pixel is 0. Bitmaps support the following options:

-background color

    Background color for the image. An empty value will make the background pixels transparent.

-data string

    Contents of the source bitmap as a string.

-file fileName

    Name of a file from which to read source bitmap contents.

-foreground color

    Foreground color for the image.

-maskdata string

    Contents of the mask bitmap as a string.

-maskfile fileName

    Name of a file from which to read mask bitmap contents.

Photo Images

A photo image can have pixels of any color. Only GIF and PPM/PGM (Portable Pixmap/Portable Graymap) formats are supported in standard Tk, but an interface exists to add additional image file formats easily. Pixels of a photo image are transparent in regions where no image data has been supplied. Photo images support the following options:

-data string

    Contents of the image as a string.

-format format

    The graphic format of the data. In standard Tk, *format* must be either GIF or PPM.

-file fileName

    Name of a file from which to read the image data.

-gamma value

    Specifies that the colors allocated should be corrected for a nonlinear display with the gamma exponent *value*.

-height size

    Height of the image in pixels. A value of 0 (the default) allows the image to expand or shrink vertically.

-palette paletteSpec

    Specifies number of colors to use from the colormap for the image. *PaletteSpec* may be either a single decimal number, specifying the number of shades of gray to use, or three decimal numbers separated by slashes, specifying the number of shades of red, green, and blue to use.

-width size

    Width of the image in pixels. A value of 0 (the default) allows the image to expand or shrink horizontally.

In addition to the *cget* and *configure* operation, the command created with the image's name supports the following operations:

imageName *blank*
>   Set the entire image to have no data so it will be displayed as transparent.

imageName *copy* **sourceImage** [*option value...*]
>   Copy a region from the image *sourceImage* to the image *imageName* according to the following options:

>   *-from x1 y1* [*x2 y2*]
>>   The top-left and bottom-right coordinates of rectangular region to copy from the source image. If this option is not given, the default is the whole image. If *x2* and *y2* are omitted, they default to the bottom-right corner of the source image.

>   *-shrink*
>>   Reduce the size of the destination image, if necessary, so the region being copied into it is at the bottom-right corner.

>   *-subsample x* [*y*]
>>   Reduce the copied source region in size by using only every *x*th pixel in the x direction and every *y*th pixel in the y direction. If *y* is not given, it defaults to the value for *x*. If negative values are given, the image is flipped about that axis.

>   *-to x1 y1* [*x2 y2*]
>>   The top-left and bottom-right coordinates of the rectangular region in the destination image where the source region should be copied. If *x2* and *y2* are omitted, the default is (*x1,y1*) plus the size of the source region (after subsampling or zooming). If *x2* and *y2* are specified, the source region will be tiled as necessary to fill the region. If the *-to* option is not given, *imageName*'s data is set to the source region.

>   *-zoom x* [*y*]
>>   Magnify the copied source region by a factor of *x* in the x direction and *y* in the y direction. If *y* is not given, it defaults to the value of *x*.

imageName *get x y*
>   Return a list of three integers, ranging from 0 to 255, representing the RGB color of the pixel at coordinates (*x,y*).

imageName *put* **data** [*-to x1 y1* [*x2 y2*]]
>   Set the pixels in *imageName* to the colors specified in **data**, a 2D array of colors. Each color may be specified by name (e.g., **red**) or in RGB hexadecimal form (e.g., **#4576c0**). The *-to* option specifies the region in *imageName* affected. If only *x1* and *y1* are given, the area affected has its top-left corner at (*x1, y1*) and is the same size as **data**. If *x2* and *y2* are given, they define the bottom-right corner of the region affected and the colors in **data** are tiled as necessary to fill the region.

imageName read [*fileName* [*option value...*]

> Read image data from the file *fileName* into the image according to the following options:

> *-format format*
>> Graphic format of image data in *fileName*.

> *-from x1 y1* [*x2 y2*]
>> The top-left and bottom-right coordinates of rectangular region in image file data to be copied into *imageName*. If *x2* and *y2* are omitted, they default to the bottom right of the image in the file. If the *-from* option is not specified, the whole image in the file is copied.

> *-shrink*
>> Reduce the size of *imageName*, if necessary, so the region into which the image file data is copied is at the bottom-right corner of *imageName*.

> *-to x y*
>> The top-left coordinates of the region of *imageName* into which the data from *fileName* is to be copied. The default is (0,0).

imageName redither

> Recalculate the dithered image in each window where *imageName* is displayed. Useful when the image data has been supplied in pieces.

imageName write [*fileName* [*option value...*]

> Write image data from *imageName* to the file *fileName* according to the following options:

> *-format format*
>> Graphic format to use in writing data to *fileName*.

> *-from x1 y1* [*x2 y2*]
>> The top-left and bottom-right coordinates of rectangular region in *imageName* to write to *fileName*. If *x2* and *y2* are omitted, they default to the bottom right of the image. If the *-from* option is not specified, the whole image is written to the file.

Tk Core
Commands

lower

lower window [*belowThis*]

Change the *window*'s position in the stacking order. If *belowThis* is specified, it must be a sibling of *window* or a descendant of a sibling of *window*. In this case, *window* is placed in the stacking order just below *belowThis* (or its ancestor that is a sibling of *window*). If *belowThis* is not given, *window* is placed below all its siblings in the stacking order.

option

option operation [*arg arg...*]

Add or retrieve window options to or from the Tk option database. The following forms of the *option* command are supported:

option add `pattern value` [`priority`]

Add a new option specified by `pattern` to the database with value `value`. `Pattern` consists of names and/or classes separated by asterisks or dots, in the usual X resource format. `Priority`, if given, indicates the priority level for the option (see "Option Priorities"). The default priority is `interactive`.

option clear

Clear all options from the database. The default options (from the RESOURCE_MANAGER property or the *.Xdefaults* file) will be reloaded into the database the next time the option database is modified.

option get `window name class`

Return the value of the option specified for `window` under `name` and `class` with the highest priority. If there are several matching entries at the same priority level, the most recently entered entry is returned. An empty string is returned if no match is found.

option readfile `fileName` [`priority`]

Add all the options specified in the file `fileName` with the proper X resource format to the Tk option database. If `priority` is specified, it indicates the priority level for the options added (see "Option Priorities"). The default priority is `interactive`.

Option Priorities

The `priority` arguments to the *option* command can be either an integer between 0 (lowest priority) and 100 (highest priority), inclusive, or one of the following strings:

widgetDefault

Same as 20. Used for default values hardcoded into widgets.

startupFile

Same as 40. Used for options specified in application-specific startup files.

userDefault

Same as 60. Used for options specified in the resource database of the X server or user-specific startup files.

interactive

Same as 80. Used for options specified interactively after the application starts running.

pack

pack operation [*arg arg...*]

Communicate with the packer, a geometry manager that arranges widgets around the edges of another window called the master window. The *pack* command can take the following forms:

pack slave [*slave...*] [*options*]
> Same as *pack configure*.

pack configure slave [*slave...*] [*options*]
> Pack the given *slave* windows into their master. Valid options are as follows:

-after other
> Insert slaves into the window *other*'s master just after *other* in the packing order.

-anchor anchorPos
> Where to position each slave in its parcel. Valid *anchorPos* values are n, ne, e, se, s, sw, w, nw, and center (the default).

-before other
> Insert slaves into the window *other*'s master just before *other* in the packing order.

-expand boolean
> Whether the slaves should be expanded to consume extra space in their master.

-fill direction
> What direction the slaves should stretch if their parcel is larger than the slave's requested dimensions. *Direction* must be none (do not stretch slave), x (stretch the slave horizontally to fill parcel's width), y (stretch the slave vertically to fill parcel's height), or both (stretch the slave both horizontally and vertically).

-in master
> Insert the slaves at the end of the packing order for master window *master*. A slave's master must either be the slave's parent (the default) or a descendant of the slave's parent.

-ipadx size
> How much horizontal internal padding, in screen units, to leave on each side of the slaves.

-ipady size
> How much vertical internal padding, in screen units, to leave on the top and bottom of the slaves.

-padx size
> How much horizontal external padding, in screen units, to leave on each side of the slaves.

-pady size

How much vertical external padding, in screen units, to leave on the top and bottom of the slaves.

-side side

Which side of the master to pack the slaves against. Must be `left`, `right`, `top` (the default), or `bottom`.

If no *-in*, *-after*, or *-before* option is specified, each slave is appended to the end of the packing list for its parent unless already packed in another master. A previously packed slave retains the previous values for any unspecified options.

pack forget slave [*slave...*]

Remove each given *slave* from the packing order for its master and unmap its window.

pack info slave

Return the current configuration state of the slave *slave* in the same option-value form given to *pack configure*. The first two elements will be *-in master*.

pack propagate master [*boolean*]

Set or query whether propagation has been enabled for *master*. Propagation is enabled by default. If disabled, the master window will not be resized to adjust to the size of its slaves.

pack slaves master

Return a list of all slaves in the packing order for *master*.

place

place operation [*arg arg...*]

Communicate with the placer, which provides simple fixed placement geometry management of slave windows inside another window called the master. The *place* command can take the following forms:

place slave [*slave...*] [*options*]

Same as *place configure*.

place configure slave [*slave...*] [*options*]

Place the given *slave* windows into their master. Valid options are as follows:

-in master

Pathname of window relative to which *slave* is to be placed. *Master* must be either *slave*'s parent (the default) or a descendant of *slave*'s parent. Also, *slave* and *master* must be descendants of the same top-level window.

-x location

> The x-coordinate within the master of the anchor point for *slave* in screen units.

-relx location

> The x-coordinate within the master of the anchor point for *slave* as a relative distance along the master's width. A value of 0.0 corresponds to the left edge of the master and 1.0 to the right edge. *Location* need not be in the range 0.0–1.0. If both *-x* and *-relx* are specified, their values are summed.

-y location

> The y-coordinate within the master of the anchor point for *slave* in screen units.

-rely location

> The y-coordinate within the master of the anchor point for *slave* as a relative distance along the master's height. A value of 0.0 corresponds to the top edge of the master and 1.0 to the bottom edge. *Location* need not be in the range 0.0–1.0. If both *-y* and *-rely* are specified, their values are summed.

-anchor anchorPos

> Which point of *slave* is to be positioned at the location selected by the *-x*, *-y*, *-relx*, and *-rely* options. Valid *anchorPos* values are n, ne, e, se, s, sw, w, nw, and center. The default is nw.

-width size

> Width for *slave* in screen units.

-relwidth size

> Width for *slave* as a ratio to the width of the master. For instance, a *size* of 0.5 means *slave* will be half as wide as the master. If both *-width* and *-relwidth* are specified, their values are summed.

-height size

> Height for *slave* in screen units.

-relheight size

> Height for *slave* as a ratio to the height of the master. A *size* of 0.5 means *slave* will be half as high as the master. If both *-height* and *-relheight* are specified, their values are summed.

-bordermode mode

> How the master's borders are treated in placement. A value of inside (the default) means that only the area inside the master's border is considered for placement, a value of outside causes the placer to include the area of the borders for placement, and a value of ignore means that only the official X area (includes internal border but no external border) will be used for placement.

place forget slave

> Stop the placer from managing the placement of *slave* and unmap *slave* from the display.

place info `slave`

Return the current configuration state of the slave `slave` in the same option-value form given to *place configure.*

place slaves `master`

Return a list of all slave windows placed in `master`.

raise

raise `window` [`aboveThis`]

Change the `window`'s position in the stacking order. If `aboveThis` is specified, it must be a sibling of `window` or a descendant of a sibling of `window`. In this case, `window` is placed in the stacking order just above `aboveThis` (or the ancestor if this is a sibling of `window`). If `aboveThis` is not given, `window` is placed above all its siblings in the stacking order.

selection

selection `operation` [`arg arg`...]

The *selection* command provides a Tcl interface to the X selection mechanism as described in the X *Inter-Client Communication Conventions Manual* (ICCCM). For the commands that follow, `selection` specifies the X selection and should be an atom name such as PRIMARY (the default) or CLIPBOARD. A selection is display specific. If the display is not specified with the *-displayof* option, it defaults to the display of the "." window. The *selection* command can take the following forms:

selection clear [*-displayof* `window`] [*-selection* `selection`]

If `selection` exists anywhere on the display of `window`, clear it so that no window owns the selection.

selection get [*-displayof* `window`] [*-selection* `selection`] [*-type* `type`]

Retrieve the value of `selection` from the display of `window` and return it in the form specified by `type`. *Type* must be a valid atom name as described in the ICCCM and defaults to STRING.

selection handle [*-displayof* `window`] [*-type* `type`] [*-format* `format`] `window` `command`

Arrange for `command` to be evaluated whenever `selection` is owned by `window` and an attempt is made to retrieve it in the form given by `type` (defaults to STRING).

`Command` will be executed as a Tcl command with two additional numbers appended as arguments: `offset` and `maxBytes`. The command should return a value consisting of at most `maxBytes` of the selection starting at position `offset`. If exactly `maxBytes` is returned, `command` will be invoked again until it eventually returns a result shorter than `maxBytes`.

The *format* argument is for compatibility with non-Tk selection requesters and specifies the representation that should be used to transmit the selection. The default is STRING.

selection own [*-displayof window*] [*-selection selection*]
    Return the pathname of the window in the application that owns *selection* on *window*'s display.

selection own [*-command command*] [*-selection selection*] *window*
    Make *window* the new owner of *selection* on *window*'s display. If *command* is specified, it is a Tcl script that will be evaluated when ownership of *selection* is taken away from *window*.

---

send

send [*options*] *app command* [*arg arg*...]

Arrange for *command* (concatenated with any given *args*) to be evaluated in the application named by *app* and return the result or error from the evaluation. *App* may be the name of any application (as returned by the *tk appname* command) whose main window is on the same display as the sender's main window (unless the *-displayof* option is given). This command is not supported under Windows or Macintosh platforms. Possible options are:

-async
    Forces the *send* command to complete immediately without waiting for *command* to complete in target application. This option is ignored if the target is in the same process as the sender.

-displayof window
    Specifies that the target application's main window is on *window*'s display.

--
    Terminates option processing in case *app* starts with a "-" character.

Security

For security reasons, the *send* mechanism will work only if the control mechanism being used by the X server has *xhost*-style access control enabled and the list of enabled hosts is empty. This means applications cannot connect to the server unless they use some more secure form of authorization, such as *xauth*. The send mechanism can be turned off (both sending and receiving) by removing the *send* command using *rename send {}*. Communication can be reenabled by invoking the *tk appname* command.

---

tk

tk operation [*arg arg*...]

The *tk* command provides access to miscellaneous elements of Tk's internal state. The following operations are defined:

tk appname `newName`

> Change the name of the application to `newName`. If the name `newName` is already in use, a suffix of the form #2 or #3 is appended to make the name unique. If `newName` is not given, the application's current name is returned. As a general rule, the application name should not begin with a capital letter, as that form is reserved for class names. If sends have been disabled by deleting the *send* command, this command will reenable them and recreate the *send* command.

tk scaling [*-displayof* `window`] [`number`]

> Set the scaling factor for conversion between physical units (e.g., points or inches) and pixels. `Number` is a floating-point value that specifies the number of pixels per point ($1/72$ inch) on `window`'s display. If `window` is not given, it defaults to the main window. If `number` is omitted, the current scaling factor is returned.

tkwait

tkwait `operation name`

Wait for a variable to change, a window to be destroyed, or a window's visibility state to change. While waiting, events are processed in the normal fashion. If an event handler invokes *tkwait* again, the nested call to *tkwait* must complete before the outer call can complete. Possible forms of the *tkwait* command are as follows:

tkwait variable `varName`

> Wait for the global variable `varName` to be modified.

tkwait visibility `window`

> Wait for a change in the visibility state of window `window`.

tkwait window `window`

> Wait for window `window` to be destroyed.

tk_

tk_bisque

tk_chooseColor [`option value...`]

tk_dialog `topw title text bitmap default string` [`string...`]

tk_focusNext `window`

tk_focusPrev `window`

tk_focusFollowsMouse `window`

tk_getOpenFile [`option value...`]

tk_getSaveFile [`option value...`]

tk_messageBox [`option value...`]

tk_optionMenu `window varName value` [`value...`]

tk_popup menu *x y* [*entry*]

tk_setPalette color

tk_setPalette name color [name color...]

Each of these commands is a Tcl procedure defined at runtime in the Tk script library. The *tk_bisque* procedure sets the default color scheme to the light brown ("bisque") scheme used by Tk 3.6 and earlier versions. The *tk_setPalette* procedure called with a single argument color sets the default color scheme to a computed one based on color as the default background color. The *tk_setPalette* can be called with one or more name-color pairs to set specific colors for the default color scheme. The possible values for name are:

activeBackground	activeForeground
background	disabledForeground
foreground	highlightBackground
highlightColor	insertBackground
selectColor	selectBackground
selectForeground	troughColor

The *tk_getOpenFile* procedure posts a modal dialog for choosing an existing filename. The *tk_getSaveFile* procedure does the same but does not require the chosen file to exist. In fact, if an existing file is chosen, a separate dialog box prompts for confirmation. Both procedures return the full pathname of the chosen file, or the empty string if the user cancels the operation. The available options for these procedures are as follows:

-defaultextension extension
> A string that will be appended to the chosen file if it lacks an extension. The default is an empty string. This option is ignored on the Macintosh.

-filetypes filePatternList
> The possible file types for the *File types* listbox in the dialog (if it exists). *FilePatternList* is a list of file patterns; each pattern is a two- or three-element list. The first element is a string describing the type (e.g., {Text files}), and the second element is a list of extensions that match this type (e.g., {.txt .log} or the special asterisk character to match all extensions. The empty string is a valid extension that means files with no extension. The third element is required only on the Macintosh and is the appropriate Macintosh file type identifier (e.g., TEXT). This element is ignored on Windows and Unix. Any file patterns with the same first element are merged in the *File types* listbox.

-initialdir directory
> The files in directory should be displayed when the dialog pops up. The default is the current working directory.

-initialfile fileName
> Filename to be displayed in the dialog as a default choice when it pops up.

-parent `window`

> Make `window` the logical parent of the dialog and position the dialog on top of it.

-title `title`

> Text to appear in window manager's titlebar for the dialog.

The *tk_messageBox* procedure pops up a message dialog window with buttons and waits for a user response. The symbolic name of the selected button is returned. The following options are supported:

-default `name`

> Make the button with symbolic name `name` the default button. See *-type* for valid names. If the dialog has only one button, it is made the default automatically. Otherwise, if this option is not specified, no button is made the default.

-icon `iconImage`

> Icon to display in the dialog. `IconImage` must be `error`, `info`, `question`, or `warning`. The default is to display no icon.

-message `string`

> Message to display in this dialog.

-parent `window`

> Make `window` the logical parent of the dialog and position the dialog on top of it.

-title `title`

> Text to appear in window manager's titlebar for the dialog.

-type `type`

> The set of buttons to be displayed. The following values are possible for `type`:

> `abortretryignore`
>> Display three buttons with names Abort, Retry, and Ignore.

> `ok` Display one button with the name OK.

> `okcancel`
>> Display two buttons with names OK and Cancel.

> `retrycancel`
>> Display two buttons with names Retry and Cancel.

> `yesno`
>> Display two buttons with names Yes and No.

> `yesnocancel`
>> Display three buttons with names Yes, No, and Cancel.

The *tk_dialog* is an older, more configurable version of a message box dialog. A message and a row of buttons are presented to the user. The numerical index of the button chosen is returned. The arguments are as follows:

topw
> Name of top-level window for dialog to use. Any existing window by this name is destroyed.

title
> Text to appear in window manager's titlebar for the dialog.

text
> Message to appear in top portion of the dialog.

bitmap
> If nonempty, a bitmap to display to the left of message text.

default
> Index of button that is to be the default button. The default is 0, which is the first, leftmost button. If *default* is less than zero, there will be no default button.

string
> There will be one button for each *string* argument, where *string* specifies the text for the button.

The *tk_optionMenu* procedure creates an option menubutton whose name is *window*, along with an associated menu. Invoking the menubutton will pop up the associated menu with an entry for each of the *value* arguments. The current choice will be stored in the global variable *varName* and be displayed as the label of the menubutton. The procedure returns immediately with a value of the name of the associated menu.

The *tk_popup* procedure posts pop-up menu *menu* at the root coordinate position *x,y*. If *entry* is omitted, the menu's upper-left corner is positioned at the given point. Otherwise, *entry* gives the index of a menu entry in *menu* to position over the given point.

The *tk_focusNext*, *tk_focusPrev*, and *tk_focusFollowsMouse* procedures are described in the listing for the *focus* command earlier in this chapter.

winfo

winfo operation [*arg arg*...]

The *winfo* command provides information about the windows managed by Tk. The following operations are supported:

winfo atom [*-displayof window name*]
> Return as a decimal string the identifier for the atom named *name* on *window*'s display.

winfo atomname [*-displayof* `window id`]
> Return the textual name of the atom on `window`'s display whose integer identifier is `id`.

winfo cells `window`
> Return the number of cells in the colormap of `window`.

winfo children `window`
> Return a list of the pathnames of all children of `window`, in stacking order.

winfo class `window`
> Return the class name for `window`.

winfo colormapfull `window`
> Return 1 if the colormap for `window` is known to be full (the last attempt to allocate a new color failed and this application has not freed any), 0 otherwise.

winfo containing [*-displayof* `window`] `rootX rootY`
> Return the pathname of the window containing the point `rootX` and `rootY` in the root window of `window`'s display. If multiple windows contain the point, children are given higher priority than parents. Among siblings, the highest one in the stacking order has priority.

winfo depth `window`
> Return the depth of `window` (number of bits per pixel).

winfo exists `window`
> Return 1 if a window named `window` exists, 0 otherwise.

winfo fpixels `window size`
> Return as a floating-point value the number of pixels in `window` corresponding to the distance `size` in screen units.

winfo geometry `window`
> Return the geometry for `window` in the X geometry specification form `widthxheight+x+y`, where dimensions are in pixels.

winfo height `window`
> Return `window`'s height in pixels. A new window's height is 1 pixel until it is actually mapped.

winfo id `window`
> Return the hexadecimal, platform-specific identifier for `window`.

winfo interps [*-displayof* `window`]
> Return a list of the names of all Tk-based applications currently registered on `window`'s display.

winfo ismapped `window`
> Return 1 if `window` is currently mapped, 0 otherwise.

winfo manager `window`

    Return the name of the geometry manager currently responsible for `win-dow` (e.g., `pack`, `place`, or `canvas`).

winfo name `window`

    Return `window`'s name within its parent. The command *winfo name* will return the name of the application.

winfo parent `window`

    Return the pathname of `window`'s parent, or an empty string if `window` is the main window.

winfo pathname [*-displayof* `window`] `id`

    Return the pathname of the window whose X identifier on `window`'s display is `id`.

winfo pixels `window size`

    Return the number of pixels (rounded to the nearest integer) in `window` corresponding to the distance `size` in screen units.

winfo pointerx `window`

    Return the pointer's x-coordinate measured in pixels on the screen's root window. If the mouse pointer is not on the same screen as `window`, return −1.

winfo pointerxy `window`

    Return the pointer's y-coordinate measured in pixels on the screen's root window. If the mouse pointer is not on the same screen as `window`, return −1.

winfo pointery `window`

    Return the pointer's y-coordinate measured in pixels on the screen's root window. If the mouse pointer is not on the same screen as `window`, return −1.

winfo reqheight `window`

    Return `window`'s requested height in pixels.

winfo reqwidth `window`

    Return `window`'s requested width in pixels.

winfo rgb `window color`

    Return a three-element list of the red, green, and blue intensities corresponding to `color` in `window`.

winfo rootx `window`

    Return the x-coordinate of the upper-left corner of `window` (including its border) in the root window of its screen.

winfo rooty `window`

    Return the y-coordinate of the upper-left corner of `window` (including its border) in the root window of its screen.

winfo screen window
> Return the name of the screen associated with *window* in the form *displayName.screenIndex*.

winfo screencells window
> Return number of cells in the default colormap for *window*'s screen.

winfo screendepth window
> Return the depth (bits per pixel) of the root window of *window*'s screen.

winfo screenheight window
> Return the height of *window*'s screen in pixels.

winfo screenmmheight window
> Return the height of *window*'s screen in millimeters.

winfo screenmmwidth window
> Return the width of *window*'s screen in millimeters.

winfo screenvisual window
> Return the default visual class for *window*'s screen. The result will be `directcolor`, `grayscale`, `pseudocolor`, `staticcolor`, `staticgray`, or `truecolor`.

winfo screenwidth window
> Return the width of *window*'s screen in pixels.

winfo server window
> Return information about the server for *window*'s display. For X servers, the string has the form `XmajorRminor vendor vendorVersion`.

winfo toplevel window
> Return the pathname of the top-level window containing *window*.

winfo viewable window
> Return 1 if *window* and all its ancestors up through the nearest top-level window are mapped, 0 otherwise.

winfo visual window
> Return the visual class for *window*. The result will be `directcolor`, `grayscale`, `pseudocolor`, `staticcolor`, `staticgray`, or `truecolor`.

winfo visualid window
> Return the X identifier for the visual of *window*.

winfo visualsavailable window [includeids]
> Return the list of visuals available for *window*'s screen. Each element consists of a visual class (see *winfo visual* for possible values) and an integer depth. If *includeids* is specified, the X identifier for each visual is also provided.

winfo vrootheight window
> Return the height of the virtual root window associated with *window*. If there is no virtual root, the height of *window*'s screen is returned.

winfo vrootwidth window
> Return the width of the virtual root window associated with *window*. If there is no virtual root, the width of *window*'s screen is returned.

winfo vrootx window
> Return the x-offset of the virtual root window relative to the root window of *window*'s screen.

winfo vrooty window
> Return the y-offset of the virtual root window relative to the root window of *window*'s screen.

winfo width window
> Return *window*'s height in pixels. A new window's width is 1 pixel until it is actually mapped.

winfo x window
> Return the x-coordinate of the upper-left corner of *window* (including any border) in its parent.

winfo y window
> Return the y-coordinate of the upper-left corner of *window* (including any border) in its parent.

wm

wm operation window [arg arg...]

The *wm* command communicates with the window manager to control such things as window titles, geometry, and state. All window managers are different and may not honor all of Tk's requests. The possible operations are:

wm aspect window [minNumber minDenom maxNumer maxDenom]
> Request that the window manager enforce a range of acceptable aspect ratios for *window*. The aspect ratio of *window* (width/length) must lie between *minNumber/minDenom* and *maxNumer/maxDenom*. If all the aspect arguments are specified as empty strings, any existing constraint is removed. If the aspect arguments are omitted, the current values are returned as a Tcl list, which will be empty if there is no constraint.

wm client window [name]
> Store in *window*'s WM_CLIENT_MACHINE property the value *name*, which should be the name of the host on which the application is running. If *name* is not given, the last name set for *window* is returned. If *name* is the empty string, the WM_CLIENT_MACHINE property for *window* is deleted.

wm colormapwindows window [windowList]
> Store in *window*'s WM_COLORMAP_WINDOWS property the value *windowList*, which should be a complete list of the internal window pathnames within *window* whose colormaps differ from their parents. If *windowList* is not given, the current setting is returned.

wm command `window` [`cmdLine`]

Store in `window`'s WM_COMMAND property the value `cmdLine`, which should be a proper list containing the words of the command used to invoke the application. If `cmdLine` is not given, the last value set for `window` is returned. If `cmdLine` is the empty string, the WM_COMMAND property for `window` is deleted.

wm deiconify `window`

Request that the window manager display `window` in normal (non-iconified) form.

wm focusmodel `window` [`model`]

Set the focus model for `window` to `model`, which must be `active` or `passive` (the default). If `model` is omitted, the current model is returned. An `active` focus model means that the window will claim the input focus for itself or its descendants, even at times when the focus is currently in some other application. A `passive` model means that `window` will never explicitly claim the focus for itself but will let the window manager give it focus at appropriate times. Tk's *focus* command assumes a passive model.

wm frame `window`

If `window` has been reparented by the window manager into a decorative frame, return the platform-specific window identifier for the outermost frame that contains `window`. Otherwise, return the identifier for `window`.

wm geometry `window` [`newGeometry`]

Set the geometry for `window` to `newGeometry`, an X geometry specification in the form `widthxheight+x+y`. If `window` is gridded, units for `width` and `height` are in grid units; otherwise, they are specified in pixels. If `newGeometry` is the empty string, the window will revert to the size requested internally by its widgets. If `newGeometry` is omitted, `window`'s current geometry is returned.

wm grid `window` [`baseWidth baseHeight widthInc heightInc`]

Request that window be managed as a gridded window. `BaseWidth` and `baseHeight` specify the number of grid units that the current requested size of `window` represents. `WidthInc` and `heightInc` specify the number of pixels in each horizontal and vertical grid unit. Specifying all values as empty strings turns off gridded management for `window`. If the arguments are omitted, their current values are returned (or an empty string if `window` is not gridded).

wm group `window` [`pathName`]

Add `window` to the group of related windows led by window `pathName`. The window manager may use this information to unmap the entire group of windows when the leader window is iconified. If `pathName` is the empty string, `window` is removed from any group with which it is associated. If it is omitted, `window`'s group leader is returned (or the empty string if `window` is not part of a group).

wm iconbitmap window [bitmap]

Request that the window manager display *bitmap* in *window*'s icon. If *bitmap* is the empty string, any current bitmap registered is canceled. If it is omitted, the current bitmap registered, if any, is returned.

wm iconify window

Arrange for *window* to be iconified.

wm iconmask window [bitmap]

Request that the window manager use *bitmap* as a mask in *window*'s icon in conjunction with the bitmap set with the *iconbitmap* operation. If *bitmap* is the empty string, any current bitmap mask is canceled. If it is omitted, the current bitmap mask, if any, is returned.

wm iconname window [newName]

Request that the window manger use *newName* for the title of *window*'s icon. If *newName* is omitted, the current setting, if any, is returned.

wm iconposition window [x y]

Request that the window manager use coordinates *x y* on the root window as the location to place *window*'s icon. If the coordinates are specified as empty strings, any current request is canceled. If they are not given, the current setting, if any, is returned.

wm iconwindow window [pathName]

Request that the window manager use window *pathName* as *window*'s icon. If *pathName* is the empty string, any current icon window request is canceled. If it is omitted, the current icon window, if any, is returned. Button press events are disabled for *pathName* while it is an icon window so that the window manager can own those events.

wm maxsize window [width height]

Request that the window manager restrict *window*'s dimensions to be less than or equal to *width* and *height*. If *window* is gridded, the dimensions are in grid units; otherwise, they are in pixels. If the *width* and *height* are not given, the current setting is returned. The default setting is the dimensions of the screen.

wm minsize window [width height]

Request that the window manager restrict *window*'s dimensions to be greater than or equal to *width* and *height*. If *window* is gridded, the dimensions are in grid units; otherwise, they are in pixels. If the *width* and *height* are not given, the current setting is returned.

wm overrideredirect window [boolean]

Set the override-redirect flag for *window* if *boolean* is true; unset it otherwise. Setting the override-redirect flag causes the window to be ignored by the window manager. If *boolean* is not given, the current setting is returned.

wm positionfrom window [who]

Set the position source of *window* to *who*, either program or user, which tells the window manager whether *window*'s position was set by the program or user, respectively. If *who* is the empty string, the current position source is canceled. If *who* is not given, the current setting is returned. Tk will automatically set the position source to user when a *wm geometry* command is invoked, unless the source has been explicitly set to program.

wm protocol window [*name* [*command*]]

Set or query window manager protocols for *window*. *Name* is the name of an atom for a window manager protocol, such as WM_DELETE_WIN-DOW or WM_SAVE_YOURSELF. If *command* is specified, it is made the handler for the given protocol and will be invoked whenever the window manager sends a message to the application for that protocol on *window*. If *command* is the empty string, any current handler is canceled. If *command* is not given, the current associated command for *name* is returned. If *name* is not given, a list of all protocols for which handlers are currently defined for *window* is returned. Tk always sets up a default handler for the WM_DELETE_WINDOW protocol, which simply destroys the window.

wm resizeable window [*widthBool heightBool*]

Whether *window* should be resizeable along its width and height according to the boolean values *widthBool* and *heightBool*. By default, windows are resizeable in both dimensions. If the boolean arguments are omitted, the current setting is returned.

wm sizefrom window [*who*]

Set the size source of *window* to *who*, either program or user, which tells the window manager whether *window*'s size was set by the program or user, respectively. If *who* is the empty string, the current size source is canceled. If *who* is not given, the current setting is returned.

wm state window

Return the current state of *window*: one of normal, iconic, withdrawn, or icon. The value icon refers to a window that is being displayed as an icon (using the *wm iconwindow* command).

wm title window [*string*]

Request that the window manager use *string* as the title for *window* if it has a titlebar. If *string* is not given, the current setting is returned.

wm transient window [*master*]

Request that the window manager treat *window* as a transient window (e.g a pull-down menu) belonging to the window *master*. If *master* is an empty string, *window* is treated as no longer transient. If it is omitted, the command returns *window*'s current master, or an empty string if *window* is not transient.

wm withdraw window

Withdraw *window* from the screen. The window is unmapped and forgotten about by the window manager.

CHAPTER 4

The Tcl C Interface

This chapter presents a summary of the Tcl C-language interface. Everything described here is defined in the header file *tcl.h*, part of the Tcl distribution. For clarity, ANSI C function prototypes are shown here, although the actual header file supports non-ANSI compilers.

To avoid name conflicts, all functions are prefixed with `Tcl_` and constants are prefixed with `TCL_`.

See the full Tcl reference documentation for the most detailed and up-to-date information. C interfaces are typically found in Section 3 of the Tcl manpages.

Constants

The following constants contain Tcl interpreter version information:

`TCL_MAJOR_VERSION`
    Tcl major version number (e.g., 8)

`TCL_MINOR_VERSION`
    Tcl minor version number (e.g., 0)

`TCL_RELEASE_LEVEL`
    Release level: 0 for alpha, 1 for beta, 2 for final/patch

`TCL_RELEASE_SERIAL`
    Version number that changes with each patch (e.g., 2)

`TCL_VERSION`
    Tcl version as a string (e.g., "8.0")

TCL_PATCH_LEVEL
Tcl version and patch level as a string (e.g., "8.0p2")

The following constants contain completion codes for Tcl command procedures:

TCL_OK
Normal command completion

TCL_ERROR
Unrecoverable error occurred

TCL_RETURN
return command invoked

TCL_BREAK
break command invoked

TCL_CONTINUE
continue command invoked

Data Types

The more commonly used Tcl data structures are listed here:

ClientData
Application-defined data that can be stored by interpreter

Tcl_AsyncHandler
Token used to refer to asynchronous event handlers

Tcl_Channel
A Tcl I/O channel

Tcl_ChannelProc
Function implementing operations on an I/O channel

Tcl_ChannelType
Pointers to functions implementing operations on an I/O channel

Tcl_CloseProc
Type of procedure used by close and delete handlers

Tcl_CmdDeleteProc
Type of procedure called when Tcl command is deleted

Tcl_CmdInfo
Structure containing information about a Tcl command

Tcl_CmdProc
Type of procedure used to implement a Tcl command

Tcl_Command
Token used to refer to Tcl command procedures

Tcl_DString
Structure used for Tcl dynamic strings

Tcl_Event
Data structure used by Tcl event queue

Tcl_EventCheckProc
Type of procedure for checking event queue

Tcl_EventDeleteProc
Type of procedure to invoke for delete events

Tcl_EventSetupProc
Type of procedure to invoke for prepare events

Tcl_ExitProc
Type of procedure to invoke before exiting application

Tcl_FileProc
Type of procedure to invoke for file handler

Tcl_FreeProc
Type of procedure for freeing storage

Tcl_HashEntry
Tcl hash table entry

Tcl_HashTable
Structure for Tcl hash table

Tcl_Interp
Structure defining a Tcl interpreter

Tcl_InterpDeleteProc
Procedure to call when interpreter is deleted

Tcl_Obj
Dual-ported object type for Tcl values

Tcl_ObjCmdProc
Type of procedure used to implement a Tcl command

Tcl_ObjType
Structure for representing type of Tcl object

Tcl_RegExp
Compiled regular expression

Tcl_Time
Data structure to represent time intervals

Tcl_Trace
Token for command trace

Tcl_VarTraceProc
Type of procedure to call for command tracing

Group Listing of Functions

Note that a few of these routines are implemented as macros for the sake of efficiency, but logically they behave the same as functions.

Tcl Objects

Tcl_Obj *Tcl_NewObj()

Tcl_Obj *Tcl_DuplicateObj(Tcl_Obj *objPtr)

void Tcl_IncrRefCount(Tcl_Obj *objPtr)

void Tcl_DecrRefCount(Tcl_Obj *objPtr)

int Tcl_IsShared(Tcl_Obj *objPtr)

void Tcl_InvalidateStringRep(Tcl_Obj *objPtr)

Tcl_Obj *Tcl_NewBooleanObj(int boolValue)

void Tcl_SetBooleanObj(Tcl_Obj *objPtr, int boolValue)

int Tcl_GetBooleanFromObj(Tcl_Interp *interp, Tcl_Obj *objPtr, int *boolPtr)

Tcl_Obj *Tcl_NewDoubleObj(double doubleValue)

void Tcl_SetDoubleObj(Tcl_Obj *objPtr, double doubleValue)

int Tcl_GetDoubleFromObj(Tcl_Interp *interp, Tcl_Obj *objPtr, double *doublePtr)

Tcl_Obj *Tcl_NewIntObj(int intValue)

Tcl_Obj *Tcl_NewLongObj(long longValue)

void Tcl_SetIntObj(Tcl_Obj *objPtr, int intValue)

void Tcl_SetLongObj(Tcl_Obj *objPtr, long longValue)

int Tcl_GetIntFromObj(Tcl_Interp *interp, Tcl_Obj *objPtr, int *intPtr)

int Tcl_GetLongFromObj(Tcl_Interp *interp, Tcl_Obj *objPtr, long *longPtr)

int Tcl_ListObjAppendList(Tcl_Interp *interp, Tcl_Obj *listPtr, Tcl_Obj *elemListPtr)

int Tcl_ListObjAppendElement(Tcl_Interp *interp, Tcl_Obj *listPtr, Tcl_Obj *objPtr)

Tcl_Obj *Tcl_NewListObj(int objc, Tcl_Obj *cont objv[])

void Tcl_SetListObj(Tcl_Obj *objPtr, int objc, Tcl_Obj *const objv[])

int Tcl_ListObjGetElements(Tcl_Interp *interp, Tcl_Obj *listPtr, int *objcPtr,
     Tcl_Obj ***objvPtr)

int Tcl_ListObjIndex(Tcl_Interp *interp, Tcl_Obj *listPtr, int index,
     Tcl_Obj **objPtrPtr)

int Tcl_ListObjLength(Tcl_Interp *interp, Tcl_Obj *listPtr, int *intPtr)

int Tcl_ListObjReplace(Tcl_Interp *interp, Tcl_Obj *listPtr, int first, int count,
     int objc, Tcl_Obj *const objv[])

void Tcl_RegisterObjType(Tcl_ObjType *typePtr)

Tcl_ObjType *Tcl_GetObjType(char *typeName)

int Tcl_AppendAllObjTypes(Tcl_Interp *interp, Tcl_Obj *objPtr)

int Tcl_ConvertToType(Tcl_Interp *interp, Tcl_Obj *objPtr, Tcl_ObjType *typePtr)

Tcl_Obj *Tcl_NewStringObj(char *bytes, int length)

void Tcl_SetStringObj(Tcl_Obj *objPtr, char *bytes, int length) char *Tcl_GetStringFromObj(Tcl_Obj *objPtr, int *lengthPtr)

void Tcl_AppendToObj(Tcl_Obj *objPtr, char *bytes, int length)

void Tcl_AppendStringsToObj(Tcl_Obj *interp, ...)

void Tcl_SetObjLength(Tcl_Obj *objPtr, int length)

Tcl_Obj *Tcl_ConcatObj(int objc, Tcl_Obj *const objv[])

Interpreters and Script Evaluation

Tcl_Interp *Tcl_CreateInterp(void)

void Tcl_DeleteInterp(Tcl_Interp *interp)

int Tcl_InterpDeleted(Tcl_Interp *interp)

int Tcl_Eval(Tcl_Interp *interp, char *string)

int Tcl_EvalObj(Tcl_Interp *interp, Tcl_Obj *objPtr)

int Tcl_EvalFile(Tcl_Interp *interp, char *fileName)

int Tcl_GlobalEval(Tcl_Interp *interp, char *command)

int Tcl_GlobalEvalObj(Tcl_Interp *interp, Tcl_Obj *objPtr)

int Tcl_VarEval(Tcl_Interp *interp, ...)

int Tcl_RecordAndEval(Tcl_Interp *interp, char *cmd, int flags)

int Tcl_RecordAndEvalObj(Tcl_Interp *interp, Tcl_Obj *cmdPtr, int flags)

void Tcl_AllowExceptions(Tcl_Interp *interp)

Tcl_AsyncHandler Tcl_AsyncCreate(Tcl_AsyncProc *proc, ClientData clientData)

void Tcl_AsyncMark(Tcl_AsyncHandler async)

int Tcl_AsyncInvoke(Tcl_Interp *interp, int code)

void Tcl_AsyncDelete(Tcl_AsyncHandler async)

int Tcl_AsyncReady(void)

void Tcl_CallWhenDeleted(Tcl_Interp *interp, Tcl_InterpDeleteProc *proc,
    ClientData clientData)

void Tcl_DontCallWhenDeleted(Tcl_Interp *interp, Tcl_InterpDeleteProc *proc,
    ClientData clientData)

int Tcl_IsSafe(Tcl_Interp *interp)

int Tcl_MakeSafe(Tcl_Interp *interp)

Tcl_Interp *Tcl_CreateSlave(Tcl_Interp *interp, char *slaveName, int isSafe)

Tcl_Interp *Tcl_GetSlave(Tcl_Interp *interp, char *slaveName)

Tcl_Interp *Tcl_GetMaster(Tcl_Interp *interp)

int Tcl_GetInterpPath(Tcl_Interp *askInterp, Tcl_Interp *slaveInterp)

int Tcl_CreateAlias(Tcl_Interp *slave, char *slaveCmd, Tcl_Interp *target,
    char *targetCmd, int argc, char **argv)

int Tcl_CreateAliasObj(Tcl_Interp *slave, char *slaveCmd, Tcl_Interp *target,
    char *targetCmd, int objc, Tcl_Obj *const objv[])

int Tcl_GetAlias(Tcl_Interp *interp, char *slaveCmd, Tcl_Interp **targetInterpPtr,
    char **targetCmdPtr, int *argcPtr, char ***argvPtr)

int Tcl_GetAliasObj(Tcl_Interp *interp, char *slaveCmd, Tcl_Interp **targetInterpPtr,
    char **targetCmdPtr, int *objcPtr, Tcl_Obj ***objv)

int Tcl_ExposeCommand(Tcl_Interp *interp, char *hiddenCmdToken,
    char *cmdName)

int Tcl_HideCommand(Tcl_Interp *interp, char *cmdName,
    char *hiddenCmdToken)

int Tcl_DoOneEvent(int flags)

void Tcl_DoWhenIdle(Tcl_IdleProc *proc, ClientData clientData)

void Tcl_CancelIdleCall(Tcl_IdleProc *idleProc, ClientData clientData)

void Tcl_Exit(int status)

void Tcl_Finalize(void)

void Tcl_CreateExitHandler(Tcl_ExitProc *proc, ClientData clientData)

void Tcl_DeleteExitHandler(Tcl_ExitProc *proc, ClientData clientData)

int Tcl_SetRecursionLimit(Tcl_Interp *interp, int depth)

void Tcl_StaticPackage(Tcl_Interp *interp, char *pkgName,
    Tcl_PackageInitProc *initProc, Tcl_PackageInitProc *safeInitProc)

Creating New Tcl Commands

Tcl_Command Tcl_CreateCommand(Tcl_Interp *interp, char *cmdName,
    Tcl_CmdProc *proc, ClientData clientData, Tcl_CmdDeleteProc *deleteProc)

Tcl_Command Tcl_CreateObjCommand(Tcl_Interp *interp, char *cmdName,
    Tcl_ObjCmdProc *proc, ClientData clientData,
    Tcl_CmdDeleteProc *deleteProc)

int Tcl_DeleteCommand(Tcl_Interp *interp, char *cmdName)

int Tcl_DeleteCommandFromToken(Tcl_Interp *interp, Tcl_Command command)

void Tcl_SetResult(Tcl_Interp *interp, char *string, Tcl_FreeProc *freeProc)

void Tcl_AppendResult(Tcl_Interp *interp, ...)

void Tcl_AppendElement(Tcl_Interp *interp, char *string)

void Tcl_ResetResult(Tcl_Interp *interp)

int Tcl_GetCommandInfo(Tcl_Interp *interp, char *cmdName,
    Tcl_CmdInfo *infoPtr)

int Tcl_SetCommandInfo(Tcl_Interp *interp, char *cmdName, Tcl_CmdInfo *infoPtr)

char *Tcl_GetCommandName(Tcl_Interp *interp, Tcl_Command command)

void Tcl_SetObjResult(Tcl_Interp *interp, Tcl_Obj *resultObjPtr)

Tcl_Obj *Tcl_GetObjResult(Tcl_Interp *interp)

void Tcl_FreeResult(Tcl_Interp *interp)

char *Tcl_GetStringResult(Tcl_Interp *interp)

Initialization and Packages

int Tcl_AppInit(Tcl_Interp *interp)

int Tcl_Init(Tcl_Interp *interp)

Parsing

int Tcl_GetInt(Tcl_Interp *interp, char *string, int *intPtr)

int Tcl_GetDouble(Tcl_Interp *interp, char *string, double *doublePtr)

int Tcl_GetBoolean(Tcl_Interp *interp, char *string, int *boolPtr)

int Tcl_ExprString(Tcl_Interp *interp, char *string)

int Tcl_ExprLong(Tcl_Interp *interp, char *string, long *ptr)

int Tcl_ExprDouble(Tcl_Interp *interp, char *string, double *ptr)

int Tcl_ExprBoolean(Tcl_Interp *interp, char *string, int *ptr)

int Tcl_SplitList(Tcl_Interp *interp, char *list, int *argcPtr, char ***argvPtr)

char *Tcl_Merge(int argc, char **argv)

char Tcl_Backslash(const char *src, int *readPtr)

void Tcl_CreateMathFunc(Tcl_Interp *interp, char *name, int numArgs,
    Tcl_ValueType *argTypes, Tcl_MathProc *proc,
    ClientData clientData)

int Tcl_ExprLongObj(Tcl_Interp *interp, Tcl_Obj *objPtr, long *ptr)

int Tcl_ExprDoubleObj(Tcl_Interp *interp, Tcl_Obj *objPtr, double *ptr)

int Tcl_ExprBooleanObj(Tcl_Interp *interp, Tcl_Obj *objPtr, int *ptr)

int Tcl_ExprObj(Tcl_Interp *interp, Tcl_Obj *objPtr, Tcl_Obj **resultPtrPtr)

int Tcl_GetIndexFromObj(Tcl_Interp *interp, Tcl_Obj *objPtr, char **tablePtr,
    char *msg, int flags, int *indexPtr)

void Tcl_PrintDouble(Tcl_Interp *interp, double value, char *dst)

int Tcl_ScanCountedElement(const char *string, int length, int *flagPtr)

int Tcl_ScanElement(const char *string, int *flagPtr)

int Tcl_ConvertCountedElement(const char *src, int length, char *dst, int flags)

int Tcl_ConvertElement(const char *src, char *dst, int flags)

Exceptions

void Tcl_AddErrorInfo (Tcl_Interp *interp, char *message)

void Tcl_AddObjErrorInfo(Tcl_Interp *interp, char *message, int length)

void Tcl_SetErrorCode(Tcl_Interp *arg1, ...)

void Tcl_SetObjErrorCode(Tcl_Interp *interp, Tcl_Obj *errorObjPtr)

void Tcl_BackgroundError(Tcl_Interp *interp)

void Tcl_WrongNumArgs(Tcl_Interp *interp, int objc, Tcl_Obj *const objv[],
    char *message)

Accessing Tcl Variables

char *Tcl_SetVar(Tcl_Interp *interp, char *varName, char *newValue, int flags)

char *Tcl_SetVar2(Tcl_Interp *interp, char *part1, char *part2, char *newValue,
    int flags)

char *Tcl_GetVar(Tcl_Interp *interp, char *varName, int flags) char *Tcl_GetVar2(Tcl_Interp *interp, char *part1, char *part2, int flags)

int Tcl_UnsetVar(Tcl_Interp *interp, char *varName, int flags)

int Tcl_UnsetVar2(Tcl_Interp *interp, char *part1, char *part2, int flags)

int Tcl_LinkVar(Tcl_Interp *interp, char *varName, char *addr, int type)

void Tcl_UnlinkVar(Tcl_Interp *interp, char *varName)

void Tcl_UpdateLinkedVar(Tcl_Interp *interp, char *varName)

int Tcl_TraceVar(Tcl_Interp *interp, char *varName, int flags,
    Tcl_VarTraceProc *proc, ClientData clientData)

int Tcl_TraceVar2(Tcl_Interp *interp, char *part1, char *part2, int flags,
    Tcl_VarTraceProc *proc, ClientData clientData)

void Tcl_UntraceVar(Tcl_Interp *interp, char *varName, int flags,
    Tcl_VarTraceProc *proc, ClientData clientData)

void Tcl_UntraceVar2(Tcl_Interp *interp, char *part1, char *part2, int flags,
    Tcl_VarTraceProc *proc, ClientData clientData)

ClientData Tcl_VarTraceInfo(Tcl_Interp *interp, char *varName, int flags,
    Tcl_VarTraceProc *procPtr, ClientData prevClientData)

ClientData Tcl_VarTraceInfo2(Tcl_Interp *interp, char *part1, char *part2, int flags,
    Tcl_VarTraceProc *procPtr, ClientData prevClientData)

Tcl_Obj *Tcl_ObjGetVar2(Tcl_Interp *interp, Tcl_Obj *part1Ptr, Tcl_Obj *part2Ptr,
    int flags)

Tcl_Obj *Tcl_ObjSetVar2(Tcl_Interp *interp, Tcl_Obj *part1Ptr, Tcl_Obj *part2Ptr,
    Tcl_Obj *newValuePtr, int flags)

int Tcl_UpVar(Tcl_Interp *interp, char *frameName, char *varName,
    char *localName, int flags)

int Tcl_UpVar2(Tcl_Interp *interp, char *frameName, char *part1, char *part2,
    char *localName, int flags)

Hash Tables

void Tcl_InitHashTable(Tcl_HashTable *tablePtr, int keyType)

void Tcl_DeleteHashTable(Tcl_HashTable *tablePtr)

Tcl_HashEntry *Tcl_CreateHashEntry(Tcl_hashTable *tablePtr, char *key,
    int *newPtr)

Tcl_HashEntry *Tcl_FindHashEntry(Tcl_HashTable *tablePtr, char *key)

void Tcl_DeleteHashEntry(Tcl_HashEntry *entryPtr)

ClientData Tcl_GetHashValue(Tcl_HashEntry *entryPtr)

void Tcl_SetHashValue(Tcl_HashEntry *entryPtr, Clientdata value)

char *Tcl_GetHashKey(Tcl_HashEntry *entryPtr)

Tcl_HashEntry *Tcl_FirstHashEntry(Tcl_HashTable *tablePtr,
    Tcl_HashSearch *searchPtr)

Tcl_HashEntry *Tcl_NextHashEntry(Tcl_HashSearch *searchPtr)

char *Tcl_HashStats(Tcl_HashTable *tablePtr)

ClientData Tcl_GetAssocData(Tcl_Interp *interp, char *name,
    Tcl_InterpDeleteProc **procPtr)
void Tcl_SetAssocData(Tcl_Interp *interp, char *name, Tcl_InterpDeleteProc *proc,
    ClientData clientData)
void Tcl_DeleteAssocData(Tcl_Interp *interp, char *name)

String Utilities

void Tcl_DStringInit(Tcl_DString *dsPtr)
char *Tcl_DStringAppend(Tcl_DString *dsPtr, const char *string, int length)
char *Tcl_DStringAppendElement(Tcl_DString *dsPtr, const char *string)
void Tcl_DStringStartSublist(Tcl_DString *dsPtr)
void Tcl_DStringEndSublist(Tcl_DString *dsPtr)
int Tcl_DStringLength(Tcl_DString *dsPtr)
char *Tcl_DStringValue(Tcl_DString *dsPtr)
void Tcl_DStringSetLength(Tcl_DString *dsPtr, int length)
void Tcl_DStringFree(Tcl_DString *dsPtr)
void Tcl_DStringResult(Tcl_Interp *interp, Tcl_DString *dsPtr)
void Tcl_DStringGetResult(Tcl_Interp *interp, Tcl_DString *dsPtr)
int Tcl_CommandComplete(char *cmd)
int Tcl_StringMatch(char *string, char *pattern)
int Tcl_RegExpMatch(Tcl_Interp *interp, char *string, char *pattern)
Tcl_RegExp Tcl_RegExpCompile(Tcl_Interp *interp, char *string)
int Tcl_RegExpExec(Tcl_Interp *interp, Tcl_RegExp regexp, char *string, char *start)
void Tcl_RegExpRange(Tcl_RegExp regexp, int index, char **startPtr, char **endPtr)
char *Tcl_Concat(int argc, char **argv)

POSIX Utilities

char *Tcl_TildeSubst(Tcl_Interp *interp, char *name, Tcl_DString *resultPtr)
char *Tcl_PosixError(Tcl_Interp *interp)
char *Tcl_ErrnoId(void)
char *Tcl_SignalId(int sig)
char *Tcl_SignalMsg(int sig)
void Tcl_DetachPids(int numPids, Tcl_Pid *pidPtr)
void Tcl_ReapDetachedProcs(void)
void Tcl_SetErrno(int err)
int Tcl_GetErrno(void)

Input/Output

Tcl_Channel Tcl_OpenCommandChannel(Tcl_Interp *interp, int argc, char **argv, int flags)

Tcl_Channel Tcl_CreateChannel(Tcl_ChannelType *typePtr, char *chanName, ClientData instanceData, int mask)

ClientData Tcl_GetChannelInstanceData(Tcl_Channel chan)

Tcl_ChannelType *Tcl_GetChannelType(Tcl_Channel chan)

char *Tcl_GetChannelName(Tcl_Channel chan)

int Tcl_GetChannelHandle(Tcl_Channel chan, int direction, ClientData *handlePtr)

int Tcl_GetChannelFlags(Tcl_Channel channel)

void Tcl_SetDefaultTranslation(TclChannel channel, Tcl_EolTranslation transMode)

int Tcl_GetChannelBufferSize(Tcl_Channel chan)

void Tcl_SetChannelBufferSize(Tcl_Channel chan, int sz)

void Tcl_NotifyChannel(Tcl_Channel channel, int mask)

int Tcl_BadChannelOption(Tcl_Interp *interp, char *optionName, char *optionList)

void Tcl_CreateChannelHandler(Tcl_Channel chan, int mask, Tcl_ChannelProc *proc, ClientData clientData)

void Tcl_DeleteChannelHandler(Tcl_Channel chan, Tcl_ChannelProc *proc, ClientData clientData)

void Tcl_CreateCloseHandler(Tcl_Channel chan, Tcl_CloseProc *proc, ClientData clientData)

void Tcl_DeleteCloseHandler(Tcl_Channel chan, Tcl_CloseProc *proc, ClientData clientData)

int Tcl_GetOpenFile(Tcl_Interp *interp, char *string, int write, int checkUsage, ClientData *filePtr)

Tcl_Channel Tcl_GetStdChannel(int type)

void Tcl_SetStdChannel(Tcl_Channel channel, int type)

Tcl_Channel Tcl_OpenFileChannel(Tcl_Interp *interp, char *fileName, char *modeString, int permissions)

Tcl_Channel Tcl_MakeFileChannel(ClientData handle, int mode)

Tcl_Channel Tcl_GetChannel(Tcl_Interp *interp, char *chanName, int *modePtr)

void Tcl_RegisterChannel(Tcl_Interp *interp, Tcl_Channel chan)

int Tcl_UnregisterChannel(Tcl_Interp *interp, Tcl_Channel chan)

int Tcl_Close(Tcl_Interp *interp, Tcl_Channel chan)

int Tcl_Read(Tcl_Channel chan, char *bufPtr, int toRead)

int Tcl_Gets(Tcl_Channel chan, Tcl_DString *dsPtr)

int Tcl_GetsObj(Tcl_Channel chan, Tcl_Obj *objPtr)

int Tcl_Write(Tcl_Channel chan, char *s, int slen)

int Tcl_Flush(Tcl_Channel chan)

int Tcl_Seek(Tcl_Channel chan, int offset, int mode)

int Tcl_Tell(Tcl_Channel chan)

int Tcl_GetChannelOption(Tcl_Interp *interp, Tcl_Channel chan,
    char *optionName, Tcl_DString *dsPtr)

int Tcl_SetChannelOption(Tcl_Interp *interp, Tcl_Channel chan, char *optionName,
    char *newValue)

int Tcl_Eof(Tcl_Channel chan)

int Tcl_InputBlocked(Tcl_Channel chan)

int Tcl_InputBuffered(Tcl_Channel chan)

Tcl_Channel Tcl_OpenTcpClient(Tcl_Interp *interp, int port, char *address,
    char *myaddr, int myport, int async)

Tcl_Channel Tcl_MakeTcpClientChannel(ClientData tcpSocket)

Tcl_Channel Tcl_OpenTcpServer(Tcl_Interp *interp, int port, char *host,
    Tcl_TcpAcceptProc *acceptProc, ClientData callbackData)

int Tcl_Ungets(Tcl_Channel chan, char *str, int len, int atHead)

int Tcl_GetChannelMode(Tcl_Channel chan)

Notifier and Events

void Tcl_CreateEventSource(Tcl_EventSetupProc *setupProc,
    Tcl_EventCheckProc *checkProc, ClientData clientData)

void Tcl_DeleteEventSource(Tcl_EventSetupProc *setupProc,
    Tcl_EventCheckProc *checkProc, ClientData clientData)

void Tcl_SetMaxBlockTime(Tcl_Time *timePtr)

void Tcl_QueueEvent(Tcl_Event *evPtr, Tcl_QueuePosition position)

void Tcl_DeleteEvents(Tcl_EventDeleteProc *proc, ClientData clientData)

int Tcl_WaitForEvent(Tcl_Time *timePtr)

void Tcl_SetTimer(Tcl_Time *timePtr)

int Tcl_ServiceAll(void)

int Tcl_ServiceEvent(int flags)

int Tcl_GetServiceMode(void)

int Tcl_SetServiceMode(int mode)

Miscellaneous

char *Tcl_Alloc(int size)

void Tcl_Free(char *ptr)

char *Tcl_Realloc(char *ptr, int size)

void Tcl_CreateFileHandler(int fd, int mask, Tcl_FileProc *proc,
    ClientData clientData)

void Tcl_DeleteFileHandler(int fd)

Tcl_TimerToken Tcl_CreateTimerHandler(int milliseconds, Tcl_TimerProc *proc,
    ClientData clientData)

void Tcl_DeleteTimerHandler(Tcl_TimerToken token)

Tcl_Trace Tcl_CreateTrace(Tcl_Interp *interp, int level, Tcl_CmdTraceProc *proc, ClientData clientData)

void Tcl_DeleteTrace(Tcl_Interp *interp, Tcl_Trace trace)

void Tcl_FindExecutable(char *argv0)

int Tcl_PkgProvide(Tcl_Interp *interp, char *name, char *version)

char *Tcl_PkgRequire(Tcl_Interp *interp, char *name, char *version, int exact)

void Tcl_Preserve(ClientData data)

void Tcl_Release(ClientData clientData)

void Tcl_EventuallyFree(ClientData clientData, Tcl_FreeProc *freeProc)

void Tcl_Sleep(int ms)

void Tcl_SplitPath(char *path, int *argcPtr, char ***argvPtr)

char *Tcl_JoinPath(int argc, char **argv, Tcl_DString *resultPtr)

Tcl_PathType Tcl_GetPathType(char *path)

void Tcl_Main(int argc, char **argv, Tcl_AppInitProc *appInitProc

char *Tcl_TranslateFileName(Tcl_Interp *interp, char *name, Tcl_DString *bufferPtr)

Alphabetical Summary of Functions

void Tcl_AddErrorInfo (Tcl_Interp *interp, char *message)

void Tcl_AddObjErrorInfo(Tcl_Interp *interp, char *message, int length)

char *Tcl_Alloc(int size)

void Tcl_AllowExceptions(Tcl_Interp *interp)

int Tcl_AppInit(Tcl_Interp *interp)

int Tcl_AppendAllObjTypes(Tcl_Interp *interp, Tcl_Obj *objPtr)

void Tcl_AppendElement(Tcl_Interp *interp, char *string)

void Tcl_AppendResult(Tcl_Interp *interp, ...)

void Tcl_AppendStringsToObj(Tcl_Obj *interp, ...)

void Tcl_AppendToObj(Tcl_Obj *objPtr, char *bytes, int length)

Tcl_AsyncHandler Tcl_AsyncCreate(Tcl_AsyncProc *proc, ClientData clientData)

void Tcl_AsyncDelete(Tcl_AsyncHandler async)

int Tcl_AsyncInvoke(Tcl_Interp *interp, int code)

void Tcl_AsyncMark(Tcl_AsyncHandler async)

int Tcl_AsyncReady(void)

void Tcl_BackgroundError(Tcl_Interp *interp)

char Tcl_Backslash(const char *src, int *readPtr)

int Tcl_BadChannelOption(Tcl_Interp *interp, char *optionName, char *optionList)

void Tcl_CallWhenDeleted(Tcl_Interp *interp, Tcl_InterpDeleteProc *proc, ClientData clientData)

void Tcl_CancelIdleCall(Tcl_IdleProc *idleProc, ClientData clientData)

int Tcl_Close(Tcl_Interp *interp, Tcl_Channel chan)

int Tcl_CommandComplete(char *cmd)

Tcl_Obj *Tcl_ConcatObj(int objc, Tcl_Obj *const objv[])

char *Tcl_Concat(int argc, char **argv)

int Tcl_ConvertCountedElement(const char *src, int length, char *dst, int flags)

int Tcl_ConvertElement(const char *src, char *dst, int flags)

int Tcl_ConvertToType(Tcl_Interp *interp, Tcl_Obj *objPtr, Tcl_ObjType *typePtr)

int Tcl_CreateAliasObj(Tcl_Interp *slave, char *slaveCmd, Tcl_Interp *target,
    char *targetCmd, int objc, Tcl_Obj *const objv[])

int Tcl_CreateAlias(Tcl_Interp *slave, char *slaveCmd, Tcl_Interp *target,
    char *targetCmd, int argc, char **argv)

void Tcl_CreateChannelHandler(Tcl_Channel chan, int mask,
    Tcl_ChannelProc *proc, ClientData clientData)

Tcl_Channel Tcl_CreateChannel(Tcl_ChannelType *typePtr, char *chanName,
    ClientData instanceData, int mask)

void Tcl_CreateCloseHandler(Tcl_Channel chan, Tcl_CloseProc *proc,
    ClientData clientData)

Tcl_Command Tcl_CreateCommand(Tcl_Interp *interp, char *cmdName,
    Tcl_CmdProc *proc, ClientData clientData, Tcl_CmdDeleteProc *deleteProc)

void Tcl_CreateEventSource(Tcl_EventSetupProc *setupProc,
    Tcl_EventCheckProc *checkProc, ClientData clientData)

void Tcl_CreateExitHandler(Tcl_ExitProc *proc, ClientData clientData)

void Tcl_CreateFileHandler(int fd, int mask, Tcl_FileProc *proc,
    ClientData clientData)

Tcl_HashEntry *Tcl_CreateHashEntry(Tcl_hashTable *tablePtr, char *key,
    int *newPtr)

Tcl_Interp *Tcl_CreateInterp(void)

void Tcl_CreateMathFunc(Tcl_Interp *interp, char *name, int numArgs,
    Tcl_ValueType *argTypes, Tcl_MathProc *proc, ClientData clientData)

Tcl_Command Tcl_CreateObjCommand(Tcl_Interp *interp, char *cmdName,
    Tcl_ObjCmdProc *proc, ClientData clientData,
    Tcl_CmdDeleteProc *deleteProc)

Tcl_Interp *Tcl_CreateSlave(Tcl_Interp *interp, char *slaveName, int isSafe)

Tcl_TimerToken Tcl_CreateTimerHandler(int milliseconds, Tcl_TimerProc *proc,
    ClientData clientData)

Tcl_Trace Tcl_CreateTrace(Tcl_Interp *interp, int level, Tcl_CmdTraceProc *proc,
    ClientData clientData)

char *Tcl_DStringAppendElement(Tcl_DString *dsPtr, const char *string)

char *Tcl_DStringAppend(Tcl_DString *dsPtr, const char *string, int length)

void Tcl_DStringEndSublist(Tcl_DString *dsPtr)

void Tcl_DStringFree(Tcl_DString *dsPtr)

void Tcl_DStringGetResult(Tcl_Interp *interp, Tcl_DString *dsPtr)

void Tcl_DStringInit(Tcl_DString *dsPtr)

int Tcl_DStringLength(Tcl_DString *dsPtr)

void Tcl_DStringResult(Tcl_Interp *interp, Tcl_DString *dsPtr) void Tcl_DStringSetLength(Tcl_DString *dsPtr, int length)

void Tcl_DStringStartSublist(Tcl_DString *dsPtr)

char *Tcl_DStringValue(Tcl_DString *dsPtr)

void Tcl_DecrRefCount(Tcl_Obj *objPtr)

void Tcl_DeleteAssocData(Tcl_Interp *interp, char *name)

void Tcl_DeleteChannelHandler(Tcl_Channel chan, Tcl_ChannelProc *proc,
    ClientData clientData)

void Tcl_DeleteCloseHandler(Tcl_Channel chan, Tcl_CloseProc *proc,
    ClientData clientData)

int Tcl_DeleteCommandFromToken(Tcl_Interp *interp, Tcl_Command command)

int Tcl_DeleteCommand(Tcl_Interp *interp, char *cmdName)

void Tcl_DeleteEventSource(Tcl_EventSetupProc *setupProc,
    Tcl_EventCheckProc *checkProc, ClientData clientData)

void Tcl_DeleteEvents(Tcl_EventDeleteProc *proc, ClientData clientData)

void Tcl_DeleteExitHandler(Tcl_ExitProc *proc, ClientData clientData)

void Tcl_DeleteFileHandler(int fd)

void Tcl_DeleteHashEntry(Tcl_HashEntry *entryPtr)

void Tcl_DeleteHashTable(Tcl_HashTable *tablePtr)

void Tcl_DeleteInterp(Tcl_Interp *interp)

void Tcl_DeleteTimerHandler(Tcl_TimerToken token)

void Tcl_DeleteTrace(Tcl_Interp *interp, Tcl_Trace trace)

void Tcl_DetachPids(int numPids, Tcl_Pid *pidPtr)

int Tcl_DoOneEvent(int flags)

void Tcl_DoWhenIdle(Tcl_IdleProc *proc, ClientData clientData)

void Tcl_DontCallWhenDeleted(Tcl_Interp *interp, Tcl_InterpDeleteProc *proc,
    ClientData clientData)

Tcl_Obj *Tcl_DuplicateObj(Tcl_Obj *objPtr)

int Tcl_Eof(Tcl_Channel chan)

char *Tcl_ErrnoId(void)

int Tcl_EvalFile(Tcl_Interp *interp, char *fileName)

int Tcl_EvalObj(Tcl_Interp *interp, Tcl_Obj *objPtr)

int Tcl_Eval(Tcl_Interp *interp, char *string)

void Tcl_EventuallyFree(ClientData clientData, Tcl_FreeProc *freeProc)

void Tcl_Exit(int status)

int Tcl_ExposeCommand(Tcl_Interp *interp, char *hiddenCmdToken,
    char *cmdName)

int Tcl_ExprBooleanObj(Tcl_Interp *interp, Tcl_Obj *objPtr, int *ptr)

int Tcl_ExprBoolean(Tcl_Interp *interp, char *string, int *ptr)

int Tcl_ExprDoubleObj(Tcl_Interp *interp, Tcl_Obj *objPtr, double *ptr)

int Tcl_ExprDouble(Tcl_Interp *interp, char *string, double *ptr)

int Tcl_ExprLongObj(Tcl_Interp *interp, Tcl_Obj *objPtr, long *ptr)

int Tcl_ExprLong(Tcl_Interp *interp, char *string, long *ptr) int Tcl_ExprObj(Tcl_Interp *interp, Tcl_Obj *objPtr, Tcl_Obj **resultPtrPtr)

int Tcl_ExprString(Tcl_Interp *interp, char *string)

void Tcl_Finalize(void)

void Tcl_FindExecutable(char *argv0)

Tcl_HashEntry *Tcl_FindHashEntry(Tcl_HashTable *tablePtr, char *key)

Tcl_HashEntry *Tcl_FirstHashEntry(Tcl_HashTable *tablePtr,
    Tcl_HashSearch *searchPtr)

int Tcl_Flush(Tcl_Channel chan)

void Tcl_FreeResult(Tcl_Interp *interp)

void Tcl_Free(char *ptr)

int Tcl_GetAliasObj(Tcl_Interp *interp, char *slaveCmd, Tcl_Interp **targetInterpPtr,
    char **targetCmdPtr, int *objcPtr, Tcl_Obj ***objv)

int Tcl_GetAlias(Tcl_Interp *interp, char *slaveCmd, Tcl_Interp **targetInterpPtr,
    char **targetCmdPtr, int *argcPtr, char ***argvPtr)

ClientData Tcl_GetAssocData(Tcl_Interp *interp, char *name,
    Tcl_InterpDeleteProc **procPtr)

int Tcl_GetBooleanFromObj(Tcl_Interp *interp, Tcl_Obj *objPtr, int *boolPtr)

int Tcl_GetBoolean(Tcl_Interp *interp, char *string, int *boolPtr)

int Tcl_GetChannelBufferSize(Tcl_Channel chan)

int Tcl_GetChannelFlags(Tcl_Channel channel)

int Tcl_GetChannelHandle(Tcl_Channel chan, int direction, ClientData *handlePtr)

ClientData Tcl_GetChannelInstanceData(Tcl_Channel chan)

int Tcl_GetChannelMode(Tcl_Channel chan)

char *Tcl_GetChannelName(Tcl_Channel chan)

int Tcl_GetChannelOption(Tcl_Interp *interp, Tcl_Channel chan,
    char *optionName, Tcl_DString *dsPtr)

Tcl_Channel Tcl_GetChannel(Tcl_Interp *interp, char *chanName, int *modePtr)

Tcl_ChannelType *Tcl_GetChannelType(Tcl_Channel chan)

int Tcl_GetCommandInfo(Tcl_Interp *interp, char *cmdName,
    Tcl_CmdInfo *infoPtr)

char *Tcl_GetCommandName(Tcl_Interp *interp, Tcl_Command command)

int Tcl_GetDoubleFromObj(Tcl_Interp *interp, Tcl_Obj *objPtr, double *doublePtr)

int Tcl_GetDouble(Tcl_Interp *interp, char *string, double *doublePtr)

int Tcl_GetErrno(void)

char *Tcl_GetHashKey(Tcl_HashEntry *entryPtr)

ClientData Tcl_GetHashValue(Tcl_HashEntry *entryPtr)

int Tcl_GetIndexFromObj(Tcl_Interp *interp, Tcl_Obj *objPtr, char **tablePtr,
    char *msg, int flags, int *indexPtr)

int Tcl_GetIntFromObj(Tcl_Interp *interp, Tcl_Obj *objPtr, int *intPtr)

int Tcl_GetInt(Tcl_Interp *interp, char *string, int *intPtr)

int Tcl_GetInterpPath(Tcl_Interp *askInterp, Tcl_Interp *slaveInterp)

int Tcl_GetLongFromObj(Tcl_Interp *interp, Tcl_Obj *objPtr, long *longPtr)

Tcl_Interp *Tcl_GetMaster(Tcl_Interp *interp)

Tcl_Obj *Tcl_GetObjResult(Tcl_Interp *interp)

Tcl_ObjType *Tcl_GetObjType(char *typeName)

int Tcl_GetOpenFile(Tcl_Interp *interp, char *string, int write, int checkUsage,
    ClientData *filePtr)

Tcl_PathType Tcl_GetPathType(char *path)

int Tcl_GetServiceMode(void)

Tcl_Interp *Tcl_GetSlave(Tcl_Interp *interp, char *slaveName)

Tcl_Channel Tcl_GetStdChannel(int type)

char *Tcl_GetStringFromObj(Tcl_Obj *objPtr, int *lengthPtr)

char *Tcl_GetStringResult(Tcl_Interp *interp)

char *Tcl_GetVar2(Tcl_Interp *interp, char *part1, char *part2, int flags)

char *Tcl_GetVar(Tcl_Interp *interp, char *varName, int flags)

int Tcl_GetsObj(Tcl_Channel chan, Tcl_Obj *objPtr)

int Tcl_Gets(Tcl_Channel chan, Tcl_DString *dsPtr)

int Tcl_GlobalEvalObj(Tcl_Interp *interp, Tcl_Obj *objPtr)

int Tcl_GlobalEval(Tcl_Interp *interp, char *command)

char *Tcl_HashStats(Tcl_HashTable *tablePtr)

int Tcl_HideCommand(Tcl_Interp *interp, char *cmdName,
    char *hiddenCmdToken)

void Tcl_IncrRefCount(Tcl_Obj *objPtr)

void Tcl_InitHashTable(Tcl_HashTable *tablePtr, int keyType)

int Tcl_Init(Tcl_Interp *interp)

int Tcl_InputBlocked(Tcl_Channel chan)

int Tcl_InputBuffered(Tcl_Channel chan)

int Tcl_InterpDeleted(Tcl_Interp *interp)

void Tcl_InvalidateStringRep(Tcl_Obj *objPtr)

int Tcl_IsSafe(Tcl_Interp *interp)

int Tcl_IsShared(Tcl_Obj *objPtr)

char *Tcl_JoinPath(int argc, char **argv, Tcl_DString *resultPtr)

int Tcl_LinkVar(Tcl_Interp *interp, char *varName, char *addr, int type)

int Tcl_ListObjAppendElement(Tcl_Interp *interp, Tcl_Obj *listPtr, Tcl_Obj *objPtr)

int Tcl_ListObjAppendList(Tcl_Interp *interp, Tcl_Obj *listPtr, Tcl_Obj *elemListPtr)

int Tcl_ListObjGetElements(Tcl_Interp *interp, Tcl_Obj *listPtr, int *objcPtr,
    Tcl_Obj ***objvPtr)

int Tcl_ListObjIndex(Tcl_Interp *interp, Tcl_Obj *listPtr, int index,
    Tcl_Obj **objPtrPtr)

int Tcl_ListObjLength(Tcl_Interp *interp, Tcl_Obj *listPtr, int *intPtr)

int Tcl_ListObjReplace(Tcl_Interp *interp, Tcl_Obj *listPtr, int first, int count,
    int objc, Tcl_Obj *const objv[])

void Tcl_Main(int argc, char **argv, Tcl_AppInitProc *appInitProc

Tcl_Channel Tcl_MakeFileChannel(ClientData handle, int mode)

int Tcl_MakeSafe(Tcl_Interp *interp)

Tcl_Channel Tcl_MakeTcpClientChannel(ClientData tcpSocket)

char *Tcl_Merge(int argc, char **argv)

Tcl_Obj *Tcl_NewBooleanObj(int boolValue)

Tcl_Obj *Tcl_NewDoubleObj(double doubleValue)

Tcl_Obj *Tcl_NewIntObj(int intValue)

Tcl_Obj *Tcl_NewListObj(int objc, Tcl_Obj *cont objv[])

Tcl_Obj *Tcl_NewLongObj(long longValue)

Tcl_Obj *Tcl_NewObj()

Tcl_Obj *Tcl_NewStringObj(char *bytes, int length)

Tcl_HashEntry *Tcl_NextHashEntry(Tcl_HashSearch *searchPtr)

void Tcl_NotifyChannel(Tcl_Channel channel, int mask)

Tcl_Obj *Tcl_ObjGetVar2(Tcl_Interp *interp, Tcl_Obj *part1Ptr, Tcl_Obj *part2Ptr, int flags)

Tcl_Obj *Tcl_ObjSetVar2(Tcl_Interp *interp, Tcl_Obj *part1Ptr, Tcl_Obj *part2Ptr, Tcl_Obj *newValuePtr, int flags)

Tcl_Channel Tcl_OpenCommandChannel(Tcl_Interp *interp, int argc, char **argv, int flags)

Tcl_Channel Tcl_OpenFileChannel(Tcl_Interp *interp, char *fileName, char *modeString, int permissions)

Tcl_Channel Tcl_OpenTcpClient(Tcl_Interp *interp, int port, char *address, char *myaddr, int myport, int async)

Tcl_Channel Tcl_OpenTcpServer(Tcl_Interp *interp, int port, char *host, Tcl_TcpAcceptProc *acceptProc, ClientData callbackData)

int Tcl_PkgProvide(Tcl_Interp *interp, char *name, char *version)

char *Tcl_PkgRequire(Tcl_Interp *interp, char *name, char *version, int exact)

char *Tcl_PosixError(Tcl_Interp *interp)

void Tcl_Preserve(ClientData data)

void Tcl_PrintDouble(Tcl_Interp *interp, double value, char *dst)

void Tcl_QueueEvent(Tcl_Event *evPtr, Tcl_QueuePosition position)

int Tcl_Read(Tcl_Channel chan, char *bufPtr, int toRead)

char *Tcl_Realloc(char *ptr, int size)

void Tcl_ReapDetachedProcs(void)

int Tcl_RecordAndEvalObj(Tcl_Interp *interp, Tcl_Obj *cmdPtr, int flags)

int Tcl_RecordAndEval(Tcl_Interp *interp, char *cmd, int flags)

Tcl_RegExp Tcl_RegExpCompile(Tcl_Interp *interp, char *string)

int Tcl_RegExpExec(Tcl_Interp *interp, Tcl_RegExp regexp, char *string, char *start)

int Tcl_RegExpMatch(Tcl_Interp *interp, char *string, char *pattern)

void Tcl_RegExpRange(Tcl_RegExp regexp, int index, char **startPtr, char **endPtr)

void Tcl_RegisterChannel(Tcl_Interp *interp, Tcl_Channel chan)

void Tcl_RegisterObjType(Tcl_ObjType *typePtr)

void Tcl_Release(ClientData clientData)

void Tcl_ResetResult(Tcl_Interp *interp)

int Tcl_ScanCountedElement(const char *string, int length, int *flagPtr)

int Tcl_ScanElement(const char *string, int *flagPtr)

int Tcl_Seek(Tcl_Channel chan, int offset, int mode)

int Tcl_ServiceAll(void)

int Tcl_ServiceEvent(int flags)

void Tcl_SetAssocData(Tcl_Interp *interp, char *name, Tcl_InterpDeleteProc *proc, ClientData clientData)

void Tcl_SetBooleanObj(Tcl_Obj *objPtr, int boolValue)

void Tcl_SetChannelBufferSize(Tcl_Channel chan, int sz)

int Tcl_SetChannelOption(Tcl_Interp *interp, Tcl_Channel chan, char *optionName, char *newValue)

int Tcl_SetCommandInfo(Tcl_Interp *interp, char *cmdName, Tcl_CmdInfo *infoPtr)

void Tcl_SetDefaultTranslation(TclChannel channel, Tcl_EolTranslation transMode)

void Tcl_SetDoubleObj(Tcl_Obj *objPtr, double doubleValue)

void Tcl_SetErrno(int err)

void Tcl_SetErrorCode(Tcl_Interp *arg1, ...)

void Tcl_SetHashValue(Tcl_HashEntry *entryPtr, Clientdata value)

void Tcl_SetIntObj(Tcl_Obj *objPtr, int intValue)

void Tcl_SetListObj(Tcl_Obj *objPtr, int objc, Tcl_Obj *const objv[])

void Tcl_SetLongObj(Tcl_Obj *objPtr, long longValue)

void Tcl_SetMaxBlockTime(Tcl_Time *timePtr)

void Tcl_SetObjErrorCode(Tcl_Interp *interp, Tcl_Obj *errorObjPtr)

void Tcl_SetObjLength(Tcl_Obj *objPtr, int length)

void Tcl_SetObjResult(Tcl_Interp *interp, Tcl_Obj *resultObjPtr)

int Tcl_SetRecursionLimit(Tcl_Interp *interp, int depth)

void Tcl_SetResult(Tcl_Interp *interp, char *string, Tcl_FreeProc *freeProc)

int Tcl_SetServiceMode(int mode)

void Tcl_SetStdChannel(Tcl_Channel channel, int type)

void Tcl_SetStringObj(Tcl_Obj *objPtr, char *bytes, int length)

void Tcl_SetTimer(Tcl_Time *timePtr)

char *Tcl_SetVar2(Tcl_Interp *interp, char *part1, char *part2, char *newValue, int flags)

char *Tcl_SetVar(Tcl_Interp *interp, char *varName, char *newValue, int flags)

char *Tcl_SignalId(int sig)

char *Tcl_SignalMsg(int sig)

void Tcl_Sleep(int ms)

int Tcl_SplitList(Tcl_Interp *interp, char *list, int *argcPtr, char ***argvPtr)

void Tcl_SplitPath(char *path, int *argcPtr, char ***argvPtr)

void Tcl_StaticPackage(Tcl_Interp *interp, char *pkgName, Tcl_PackageInitProc *initProc, Tcl_PackageInitProc *safeInitProc)

int Tcl_StringMatch(char *string, char *pattern)

int Tcl_Tell(Tcl_Channel chan)

char *Tcl_TildeSubst(Tcl_Interp *interp, char *name, Tcl_DString *resultPtr)

int Tcl_TraceVar2(Tcl_Interp *interp, char *part1, char *part2, int flags,
    Tcl_VarTraceProc *proc, ClientData clientData)

int Tcl_TraceVar(Tcl_Interp *interp, char *varName, int flags,
    Tcl_VarTraceProc *proc, ClientData clientData)

char *Tcl_TranslateFileName(Tcl_Interp *interp, char *name, Tcl_DString *bufferPtr)

int Tcl_Ungets(Tcl_Channel chan, char *str, int len, int atHead)

void Tcl_UnlinkVar(Tcl_Interp *interp, char *varName)

int Tcl_UnregisterChannel(Tcl_Interp *interp, Tcl_Channel chan)

int Tcl_UnsetVar2(Tcl_Interp *interp, char *part1, char *part2, int flags)

int Tcl_UnsetVar(Tcl_Interp *interp, char *varName, int flags)

void Tcl_UntraceVar2(Tcl_Interp *interp, char *part1, char *part2, int flags,
    Tcl_VarTraceProc *proc, ClientData clientData)

void Tcl_UntraceVar(Tcl_Interp *interp, char *varName, int flags,
    Tcl_VarTraceProc *proc, ClientData clientData)

int Tcl_UpVar2(Tcl_Interp *interp, char *frameName, char *part1, char *part2,
    char *localName, int flags)

int Tcl_UpVar(Tcl_Interp *interp, char *frameName, char *varName,
    char *localName, int flags)

void Tcl_UpdateLinkedVar(Tcl_Interp *interp, char *varName)

int Tcl_VarEval(Tcl_Interp *interp, ...)

ClientData Tcl_VarTraceInfo2(Tcl_Interp *interp, char *part1, char *part2, int flags,
    Tcl_VarTraceProc *procPtr, ClientData prevClientData)

ClientData Tcl_VarTraceInfo(Tcl_Interp *interp, char *varName, int flags,
    Tcl_VarTraceProc *procPtr, ClientData prevClientData)

int Tcl_WaitForEvent(Tcl_Time *timePtr)

int Tcl_Write(Tcl_Channel chan, char *s, int slen)

void Tcl_WrongNumArgs(Tcl_Interp *interp, int objc, Tcl_Obj *const objv[],
    char *message)

CHAPTER 5

The Tk C Interface

This chapter presents a summary of the Tk C-language interface. Everything described here is defined in the header file *tk.h*, part of the Tk distribution. For clarity, ANSI C function prototypes are shown here, although the actual header file supports non-ANSI compilers.

To avoid name conflicts, all functions are prefixed with `Tk_` and constants are prefixed with `TK_`. See the full Tk reference documentation for the most detailed and up-to-date information. C interfaces are typically found in Section 3 of the Tk man-pages.

Constants

The following constants contain Tk toolkit version information:

TK_MAJOR_VERSION
> Tk major version number (e.g., 8)

TK_MINOR_VERSION
> Tk minor version number (e.g., 0)

TK_RELEASE_LEVEL
> Release level: 0 for alpha, 1 for beta, 2 for final/patch

TK_RELEASE_SERIAL
> Version number that changes with each patch (e.g., 2)

TK_VERSION
> Tk version as a string (e.g., "8.0")

TK_PATCH_LEVEL
> Tk version and patch level as a string (e.g., "8.0p2")

Data Types

The more commonly used Tk data structures are listed here:

Tk_3DBorder
Token for a three-dimensional window border

Tk_Anchor
Enumerated type describing point by which to anchor an object

Tk_ArgvInfo
Structure used to specify how to handle `argv` options

Tk_BindingTable
Token for a binding table

Tk_Canvas
Token for a canvas object

Tk_CanvasTextInfo
Structure providing information about the selection and insertion cursors

Tk_ConfigSpec
Structure used to specify information for configuring a widget

Tk_Cursor
Token for a cursor

Tk_ErrorHandler
Token for an X protocol error handler

Tk_ErrorProc
Type of procedure used to handle X protocol errors

Tk_EventProc
Type of procedure used to handle events

Tk_Font
Token for a font

Tk_FontMetrics
Data structure describing properties of a font

Tk_GenericProc
Type of procedure used to handle generic X events

Tk_GeomMgr
Structure describing a geometry manager

Tk_GetSelProc
Type of procedure to process the selection

Tk_Image
Token for an image

Tk_ImageChangedProc
　　Type of procedure to invoke when an image changes

Tk_ImageMaster
　　Token for an image master

Tk_ImageType
　　Token for an image instance

Tk_ItemType
　　Structure defining a type of canvas item

Tk_Justify
　　Enumerated type describing a style of justification

Tk_LostSelProc
　　Type of procedure invoked when window loses selection

Tk_PhotoHandle
　　Token for a photo image

Tk_PhotoImageBlock
　　Structure describing a block of pixels in memory

Tk_PhotoImageFormat
　　Structure representing a particular file format for storing images

Tk_RestrictProc
　　Type of procedure used to filter incoming events

Tk_SelectionProc
　　Type of procedure used to return selection

Tk_TextLayout
　　Token for a text layout

Tk_Uid
　　Type used as unique identifiers for strings

Tk_Window
　　Token for a window

Group Listing of Functions

Note that a few of these routines are implemented as macros for the sake of efficiency, but logically they behave the same as functions.

Windows

XSetWindowAttributes *Tk_Attributes(Tk_Window tkwin)

void Tk_ChangeWindowAttributes(Tk_Window tkwin, unsigned long valueMask,
　　XSetWindowAttributes *attsPtr)

XWindowChanges *Tk_Changes(Tk_Window tkwin)

Tk_Uid Tk_Class(Tk_Window tkwin)

void Tk_ConfigureWindow(Tk_Window tkwin, unsigned int valueMask,
    XWindowChanges *valuePtr)

Tk_Window Tk_CoordsToWindow(int rootX, int rootY, Tk_Window tkwin)

Tk_Window Tk_CreateWindowFromPath(Tcl_Interp *interp, Tk_Window tkwin,
    char *pathName, char *screenName)

Tk_Window Tk_CreateWindow(Tcl_Interp *interp, Tk_Window parent,
    char *name, char *screenName)

int Tk_Depth(Tk_Window tkwin)

void Tk_DestroyWindow(Tk_Window tkwin)

char *Tk_DisplayName(Tk_Window tkwin)

Display Tk_Display(Tk_Window tkwin)

void Tk_DrawFocusHighlight(Tk_Window tkwin, GC gc, int width,
    Drawable drawable)

char *Tk_GetAtomName(Tk_Window tkwin, Atom atom)

GC Tk_GetGC(Tk_Window tkwin, unsigned long valueMask, XGCValues *valuePtr)

int Tk_GetNumMainWindows(void)

Tk_Uid Tk_GetOption(Tk_Window tkwin, char *name, char *className)

void Tk_GetRootCoords(Tk_Window tkwin, int *xPtr, int *yPtr)

void Tk_GetVRootGeometry(Tk_Window tkwin, int *xPtr, int *yPtr, int *widthPtr,
    int *heightPtr)

int Tk_Height(Tk_Window tkwin)

Tk_Window Tk_IdToWindow(Display *display, Window window)

Atom Tk_InternAtom(Tk_Window tkwin, char *name)

int Tk_IsContainer(Tk_Window tkwin)

int Tk_IsEmbedded(Tk_Window tkwin)

int Tk_IsMapped(Tk_Window tkwin)

int Tk_IsTopLevel(Tk_Window tkwin)

Tk_Window Tk_MainWindow(Tcl_Interp *interp)

void Tk_MaintainGeometry(Tk_Window slave, Tk_Window master, int x, int y,
    int width, int height)

void Tk_MakeWindowExist(Tk_Window tkwin)

void Tk_MoveToplevelWindow(Tk_Window tkwin, int x, int y)

Tk_Uid Tk_Name(Tk_Window tkwin)

Tk_Window Tk_NameToWindow(Tcl_Interp *interp, char *pathName,
    Tk_Window tkwin)

Tk_Window Tk_Parent(Tk_Window tkwin)

char *Tk_PathName(Tk_Window tkwin)

int Tk_RestackWindow(Tk_Window tkwin, int aboveBelow, Tk_Window other)

int Tk_ScreenNumber(Tk_Window tkwin)

Screen *Tk_Screen(Tk_Window tkwin)

void Tk_SetClass(Tk_Window tkwin, char *className)

void Tk_SetWindowBackground(Tk_Window tkwin, unsigned long pixel)

void Tk_SetWindowBorderPixmap(Tk_Window tkwin, Pixmap pixmap)

void Tk_SetWindowBorder(Tk_Window tkwin, unsigned long pixel)

void Tk_SetWindowBorderWidth(Tk_Window tkwin, int width)

int Tk_StrictMotif(Tk_Window tkwin)

void Tk_Ungrab(Tk_Window tkwin)

void Tk_UnmaintainGeometry(Tk_Window slave, Tk_Window master)

void Tk_UnsetGrid(Tk_Window tkwin)

void Tk_UpdatePointer(Tk_Window tkwin, int x, int y, int state)

Visual *Tk_Visual(Tk_Window tkwin)

int Tk_Width(Tk_Window tkwin)

Window Tk_WindowId(Tk_Window tkwin)

int Tk_X(Tk_Window tkwin)

int Tk_Y(Tk_Window tkwin)

Configuring Widgets

int Tk_ConfigureInfo(Tcl_Interp *interp, Tk_Window tkwin, Tk_ConfigSpec *specs, char *widgRec, char *argvName, int flags)

int Tk_ConfigureValue(Tcl_Interp *interp, Tk_Window tkwin, Tk_ConfigSpec *specs, char *widgRec, char *argvName, int flags)

int Tk_ConfigureWidget(Tcl_Interp *interp, Tk_Window tkwin, Tk_ConfigSpec *specs, int argc, char **argv, char *widgRec, int flags)

void Tk_FreeOptions(Tk_ConfigSpec *specs, char *widgRec, Display *display, int needFlags)

int Tk_Offset(type, field)

Bitmaps and Photo Images

void Tk_CreateImageType(Tk_ImageType *typePtr)

void Tk_CreatePhotoImageFormat(Tk_PhotoImageFormat *formatPtr)

int Tk_DefineBitmap(Tcl_Interp *interp, Tk_Uid name, char *source, int width, int height)

void Tk_DeleteImage(Tcl_Interp *interp, char *name)

Tk_PhotoHandle Tk_FindPhoto(Tcl_Interp *interp, char *imageName)

void Tk_FreeBitmap(Display *display, Pixmap bitmap)

void Tk_FreeImage(Tk_Image image)

void Tk_FreePixmap(Display *display, Pixmap pixmap)

Pixmap Tk_GetBitmapFromData(Tcl_Interp *interp, Tk_Window tkwin, char *source, int width, int height)

Pixmap Tk_GetBitmap(Tcl_Interp *interp, Tk_Window tkwin, Tk_Uid string)

ClientData Tk_GetImageMasterData(Tcl_Interp *interp, char *name, Tk_ImageType **typePtrPtr)

Tk_Image Tk_GetImage(Tcl_Interp *interp, Tk_Window tkwin, char *name,
    Tk_ImageChangedProc *changeProc, ClientData clientData)

void Tk_ImageChanged(Tk_ImageMaster master, int x, int y, int width, int height,
    int imageWidth, int imageHeight)

char *Tk_NameOfBitmap(Display *display, Pixmap bitmap)

char *Tk_NameOfImage(Tk_ImageMaster imageMaster)

void Tk_PhotoBlank(Tk_PhotoHandle handle)

void Tk_PhotoExpand(Tk_PhotoHandle handle, int width, int height)

int Tk_PhotoGetImage(Tk_PhotoHandle handle, Tk_PhotoImageBlock *blockPtr)

void Tk_PhotoGetSize(Tk_PhotoHandle handle, int *widthPtr, int *heightPtr)

void Tk_PhotoPutBlock(Tk_PhotoHandle handle, Tk_PhotoImageBlock *blockPtr,
    int x, int y, int width, int height)

void Tk_PhotoPutZoomedBlock(Tk_PhotoHandle handle,
    Tk_PhotoImageBlock *blockPtr, int x, int y, int width, int height, int zoomX,
    int zoomY, int subsampleX, int subsampleY)

void Tk_PhotoSetSize(Tk_PhotoHandle handle, int width, int height)

void Tk_RedrawImage(Tk_Image image, int imageX, int imageY, int width,
    int height, Drawable drawable, int drawableX, int drawableY)

void Tk_SetWindowBackgroundPixmap(Tk_Window tkwin, Pixmap pixmap)

void Tk_SizeOfBitmap(Display *display, Pixmap bitmap, int *widthPtr,
    int *heightPtr)

void Tk_SizeOfImage(Tk_Image image, int *widthPtr, int *heightPtr)

Events

void Tk_BindEvent(Tk_BindingTable bindingTable, XEvent *eventPtr,
    Tk_Window tkwin, int numObjects, ClientData *objectPtr)

Tk_BindingTable Tk_CreateBindingTable(Tcl_Interp *interp)

unsigned long Tk_CreateBinding(Tcl_Interp *interp,
    Tk_BindingTable bindingTable, ClientData object, *eventString,
    char *command, int append)

void Tk_CreateEventHandler(Tk_Window token, unsigned long mask,
    Tk_EventProc *proc, ClientData clientData)

void Tk_CreateGenericHandler(Tk_GenericProc *proc, ClientData clientData)

void Tk_DeleteAllBindings(Tk_BindingTable bindingTable, ClientData object)

void Tk_DeleteBindingTable(Tk_BindingTable bindingTable)

int Tk_DeleteBinding(Tcl_Interp *interp, Tk_BindingTable bindingTable,
    ClientData object, char *eventString)

void Tk_DeleteEventHandler(Tk_Window token, unsigned long mask,
    Tk_EventProc *proc, ClientData clientData)

void Tk_DeleteGenericHandler(Tk_GenericProc *proc, ClientData clientData)

void Tk_GetAllBindings(Tcl_Interp *interp, Tk_BindingTable bindingTable,
    ClientData object)

char *Tk_GetBinding(Tcl_Interp *interp, Tk_BindingTable bindingTable,
    ClientData object, char *eventString)

void Tk_HandleEvent(XEvent *eventPtr)

void Tk_MainLoop(void)

void Tk_QueueWindowEvent(XEvent *eventPtr, Tcl_QueuePosition position)

Tk_RestrictProc *Tk_RestrictEvents(Tk_RestrictProc *proc, ClientData arg,
    ClientData *prevArgPtr)

Displaying Widgets

GC Tk_3DBorderGC(Tk_Window tkwin, Tk_3DBorder border, int which)

void Tk_3DHorizontalBevel(Tk_Window tkwin, Drawable drawable,
    Tk_3DBorder border, int x, int y, int width, int height, int leftIn, int rightIn,
    int topBevel, int relief)

void Tk_3DVerticalBevel(Tk_Window tkwin, Drawable drawable,
    Tk_3DBorder border, int x, int y, int width, int height, int leftBevel, int relief)

void Tk_Draw3DPolygon(Tk_Window tkwin, Drawable drawable,
    Tk_3DBorder border, XPoint *pointPtr, int numPoints, int borderWidth,
    int leftRelief)

void Tk_Draw3DRectangle(Tk_Window tkwin, Drawable drawable,
    Tk_3DBorder border, int x, int y, int width, int height, int borderWidth,
    int relief)

void Tk_Fill3DPolygon(Tk_Window tkwin, Drawable drawable,
    Tk_3DBorder border, XPoint *pointPtr, int numPoints, int borderWidth,
    int leftRelief)

void Tk_Fill3DRectangle(Tk_Window tkwin, Drawable drawable,
    Tk_3DBorder border, int x, int y, int width, int height, int borderWidth,
    int relief)

void Tk_Free3DBorder(Tk_3DBorder border)

Tk_3DBorder Tk_Get3DBorder(Tcl_Interp *interp, Tk_Window tkwin,
    Tk_Uid colorName)

char *Tk_NameOf3DBorder(Tk_3DBorder border)

void Tk_SetBackgroundFromBorder(Tk_Window tkwin,
    Tk_3DBorder border)

Canvases

void Tk_CanvasDrawableCoords(Tk_Canvas canvas, double x, double y,
    short *drawableXPtr, short *drawableYPtr)

void Tk_CanvasEventuallyRedraw(Tk_Canvas canvas, int x1, int y1, int x2, int y2)

int Tk_CanvasGetCoord(Tcl_Interp *interp, Tk_Canvas canvas, char *string,
    double *doublePtr)

Tk_CanvasTextInfo *Tk_CanvasGetTextInfo(Tk_Canvas canvas)

int Tk_CanvasPsBitmap(Tcl_Interp *interp, Tk_Canvas canvas, Pixmap bitmap,
    int x, int y, int width, int height)

int Tk_CanvasPsColor(Tcl_Interp *interp, Tk_Canvas canvas, XColor *colorPtr)

int Tk_CanvasPsFont(Tcl_Interp *interp, Tk_Canvas canvas, Tk_Font font)

void Tk_CanvasPsPath(Tcl_Interp *interp, Tk_Canvas canvas, double *coordPtr,
    int numPoints)

int Tk_CanvasPsStipple(Tcl_Interp *interp, Tk_Canvas canvas, Pixmap bitmap)

double Tk_CanvasPsY(Tk_Canvas canvas, double y)

void Tk_CanvasSetStippleOrigin(Tk_Canvas canvas, GC gc)

int Tk_CanvasTagsParseProc(ClientData clientData, Tcl_Interp *interp,
    Tk_Window tkwin, char *value, char *widgRec, int offset)

char *Tk_CanvasTagsPrintProc(ClientData clientData, Tk_Window tkwin,
    char *widgRec, int offset, Tcl_FreeProc **freeProcPtr)

Tk_Window Tk_CanvasTkwin(Tk_Canvas canvas)

void Tk_CanvasWindowCoords(Tk_Canvas canvas, double x, double y,
    short *screenXPtr, short *screenYPtr)

void Tk_CreateItemType(Tk_ItemType *typePtr)

Pixmap Tk_GetPixmap(Display *display, Drawable d, int width, int height,
    int depth)

Text

int Tk_CharBbox(Tk_TextLayout layout, int index, int *xPtr, int *yPtr, int *widthPtr,
    int *heightPtr)

Tk_TextLayout Tk_ComputeTextLayout(Tk_Font font, const char *string,
    int numChars, int wrapLength, Tk_Justify justify, int flags, int *widthPtr,
    int *heightPtr)

int Tk_DistanceToTextLayout(Tk_TextLayout layout, int x, int y)

void Tk_DrawChars(Display *display, Drawable drawable, GC gc, Tk_Font tkfont,
    const char *source, int numChars, int x, int y)

void Tk_DrawTextLayout(Display *display, Drawable drawable, GC gc,
    Tk_TextLayout layout, int x, int y, int firstChar, int lastChar)

Font Tk_FontId(Tk_Font font)

void Tk_FreeFont(Tk_Font)

void Tk_FreeTextLayout(Tk_TextLayout textLayout)

Tk_Font Tk_GetFontFromObj(Tcl_Interp *interp, Tk_Window tkwin,
    Tcl_Obj *objPtr)

void Tk_GetFontMetrics(Tk_Font font, Tk_FontMetrics *fmPtr)

Tk_Font Tk_GetFont(Tcl_Interp *interp, Tk_Window tkwin, const char *string)

int Tk_GetJustify(Tcl_Interp *interp, char *string, Tk_Justify *justifyPtr)

int Tk_IntersectTextLayout(Tk_TextLayout layout, int x, int y, int width, int height)

int Tk_MeasureChars(Tk_Font tkfont, const char *source, int maxChars,
    int maxPixels, int flags, int *lengthPtr)

char *Tk_NameOfFont(Tk_Font font)

char *Tk_NameOfJustify(Tk_Justify justify)

int Tk_PointToChar(Tk_TextLayout layout, int x, int y)

int Tk_PostscriptFontName(Tk_Font tkfont, Tcl_DString *dsPtr)

void Tk_TextLayoutToPostscript(Tcl_Interp *interp, Tk_TextLayout layout)

int Tk_TextWidth(Tk_Font font, const char *string, int numChars)

void Tk_UnderlineChars(Display *display, Drawable drawable, GC gc,
    Tk_Font tkfont, const char *source, int x, int y, int firstChar, int lastChar)

void Tk_UnderlineTextLayout(Display *display, Drawable drawable, GC gc,
    Tk_TextLayout layout, int x, int y, int underline)

The Selection

void Tk_ClearSelection(Tk_Window tkwin, Atom selection)

int Tk_ClipboardAppend(Tcl_Interp *interp, Tk_Window tkwin, Atom target,
    Atom format, char *buffer)

int Tk_ClipboardClear(Tcl_Interp *interp, Tk_Window tkwin)

void Tk_CreateSelHandler(Tk_Window tkwin, Atom selection, Atom target,
    Tk_SelectionProc *proc, ClientData clientData, Atom format)

void Tk_DeleteSelHandler(Tk_Window tkwin, Atom selection, Atom target)

int Tk_GetSelection(Tcl_Interp *interp, Tk_Window tkwin, Atom selection,
    Atom target, Tk_GetSelProc *proc, ClientData clientData)

void Tk_OwnSelection(Tk_Window tkwin, Atom selection, Tk_LostSelProc *proc,
    ClientData clientData)

Geometry Management

void Tk_GeometryRequest(Tk_Window tkwin, int reqWidth, int reqHeight)

int Tk_InternalBorderWidth(Tk_Window tkwin)

void Tk_ManageGeometry(Tk_Window tkwin, Tk_GeomMgr *mgrPtr,
    ClientData clientData)

void Tk_MapWindow(Tk_Window tkwin)

void Tk_MoveResizeWindow(Tk_Window tkwin, int x, int y, int width, int height)

void Tk_MoveWindow(Tk_Window tkwin, int x, int y)

int Tk_ReqHeight(Tk_Window tkwin)

int Tk_ReqWidth(Tk_Window tkwin)

void Tk_ResizeWindow(Tk_Window tkwin, int width, int height)

void Tk_SetGrid(Tk_Window tkwin, int reqWidth, int reqHeight,
    int gridWidth, int gridHeight)

void Tk_SetInternalBorder(Tk_Window tkwin, int width)

void Tk_UnmapWindow(Tk_Window tkwin)

Application Startup and Initialization

int Tk_Init(Tcl_Interp *interp)

void Tk_Main(int argc, char **argv, Tcl_AppInitProc *appInitProc)

int Tk_ParseArgv(Tcl_Interp *interp, Tk_Window tkwin, int *argcPtr, char **argv, Tk_ArgvInfo *argTable, int flags)

int Tk_SafeInit(Tcl_Interp *interp)

char *Tk_SetAppName(Tk_Window tkwin, char *name)

Error Handling

void Tk_DeleteErrorHandler(Tk_ErrorHandler handler)

Tk_ErrorHandler Tk_CreateErrorHandler(Display *display, int errNum, int request, int minorCode, Tk_ErrorProc *errorProc, ClientData clientData)

Color

XColor *Tk_3DBorderColor(Tk_3DBorder border)

Colormap Tk_Colormap(Tk_Window tkwin)

void Tk_FreeColor(XColor *colorPtr)

void Tk_FreeColormap(Display *display, Colormap colormap)

GC Tk_GCForColor(XColor *colorPtr, Drawable drawable)

XColor *Tk_GetColorByValue(Tk_Window tkwin, XColor *colorPtr)

XColor *Tk_GetColor(Tcl_Interp *interp, Tk_Window tkwin, Tk_Uid name)

Colormap Tk_GetColormap(Tcl_Interp *interp, Tk_Window tkwin, char *string)

char *Tk_NameOfColor(XColor *colorPtr)

void Tk_PreserveColormap(Display *display, Colormap colormap)

void Tk_SetWindowColormap(Tk_Window tkwin, Colormap colormap)

int Tk_SetWindowVisual(Tk_Window tkwin, Visual *visual, int depth, Colormap colormap)

Cursors

void Tk_DefineCursor(Tk_Window window, Tk_Cursor cursor)

void Tk_FreeCursor(Display *display, Tk_Cursor cursor)

Tk_Cursor Tk_GetCursor(Tcl_Interp *interp, Tk_Window tkwin, Tk_Uid string)

Tk_Cursor Tk_GetCursorFromData(Tcl_Interp *interp, Tk_Window tkwin, char *source, char *mask, int width, int height, int xHot, int yHot, Tk_Uid fg, Tk_Uid bg)

char *Tk_NameOfCursor(Display *display, Tk_Cursor cursor)

void Tk_UndefineCursor(Tk_Window window)

Miscellaneous

void Tk_FreeGC(Display *display, GC gc)

void Tk_FreeXId(Display *display, XID xid)

int Tk_GetAnchor(Tcl_Interp *interp, char *string, Tk_Anchor *anchorPtr)

int Tk_GetCapStyle(Tcl_Interp *interp, char *string, int *capPtr)

Tk_ItemType *Tk_GetItemTypes(void)

int Tk_GetJoinStyle(Tcl_Interp *interp, char *string, int *joinPtr)

int Tk_GetPixels(Tcl_Interp *interp, Tk_Window tkwin, char *string, int *intPtr)

int Tk_GetRelief(Tcl_Interp *interp, char *name, int *reliefPtr)

int Tk_GetScreenMM(Tcl_Interp *interp, Tk_Window tkwin, char *string,
    double *doublePtr)

int Tk_GetScrollInfo(Tcl_Interp *interp, int argc, char **argv, double *dblPtr,
    int *intPtr)

Tk_Uid Tk_GetUid(const char *string)

Visual *Tk_GetVisual(Tcl_Interp *interp, Tk_Window tkwin, char *string,
    int *depthPtr, Colormap *colormapPtr)

int Tk_Grab(Tcl_Interp *interp, Tk_Window tkwin, int grabGlobal)

char *Tk_NameOfAnchor(Tk_Anchor anchor)

char *Tk_NameOfCapStyle(int cap)

char *Tk_NameOfJoinStyle(int join)

char *Tk_NameOfRelief(int relief)

Alphabetical Summary of Functions

XColor *Tk_3DBorderColor(Tk_3DBorder border)

GC Tk_3DBorderGC(Tk_Window tkwin, Tk_3DBorder border, int which)

void Tk_3DHorizontalBevel(Tk_Window tkwin, Drawable drawable,
    Tk_3DBorder border, int x, int y, int width, int height, int leftIn, int rightIn,
    int topBevel, int relief)

void Tk_3DVerticalBevel(Tk_Window tkwin, Drawable drawable,
    Tk_3DBorder border, int x, int y, int width, int height, int leftBevel, int relief)

XSetWindowAttributes *Tk_Attributes(Tk_Window tkwin)

void Tk_BindEvent(Tk_BindingTable bindingTable, XEvent *eventPtr,
    Tk_Window tkwin, int numObjects, ClientData *objectPtr)

void Tk_CanvasDrawableCoords(Tk_Canvas canvas, double x, double y,
    short *drawableXPtr, short *drawableYPtr)

void Tk_CanvasEventuallyRedraw(Tk_Canvas canvas, int x1, int y1, int x2, int y2)

int Tk_CanvasGetCoord(Tcl_Interp *interp, Tk_Canvas canvas, char *string,
    double *doublePtr)

Tk_CanvasTextInfo *Tk_CanvasGetTextInfo(Tk_Canvas canvas)

int Tk_CanvasPsBitmap(Tcl_Interp *interp, Tk_Canvas canvas, Pixmap bitmap,
    int x, int y, int width, int height)

int Tk_CanvasPsColor(Tcl_Interp *interp, Tk_Canvas canvas, XColor *colorPtr)

int Tk_CanvasPsFont(Tcl_Interp *interp, Tk_Canvas canvas, Tk_Font font)

void Tk_CanvasPsPath(Tcl_Interp *interp, Tk_Canvas canvas, double *coordPtr, int numPoints)

int Tk_CanvasPsStipple(Tcl_Interp *interp, Tk_Canvas canvas, Pixmap bitmap)

double Tk_CanvasPsY(Tk_Canvas canvas, double y)

void Tk_CanvasSetStippleOrigin(Tk_Canvas canvas, GC gc)

int Tk_CanvasTagsParseProc(ClientData clientData, Tcl_Interp *interp, Tk_Window tkwin, char *value, char *widgRec, int offset)

char *Tk_CanvasTagsPrintProc(ClientData clientData, Tk_Window tkwin, char *widgRec, int offset, Tcl_FreeProc **freeProcPtr)

Tk_Window Tk_CanvasTkwin(Tk_Canvas canvas)

void Tk_CanvasWindowCoords(Tk_Canvas canvas, double x, double y, short *screenXPtr, short *screenYPtr)

void Tk_ChangeWindowAttributes(Tk_Window tkwin, unsigned long valueMask, XSetWindowAttributes *attsPtr)

XWindowChanges *Tk_Changes(Tk_Window tkwin)

int Tk_CharBbox(Tk_TextLayout layout, int index, int *xPtr, int *yPtr, int *widthPtr, int *heightPtr)

Tk_Uid Tk_Class(Tk_Window tkwin)

void Tk_ClearSelection(Tk_Window tkwin, Atom selection)

int Tk_ClipboardAppend(Tcl_Interp *interp, Tk_Window tkwin, Atom target, Atom format, char *buffer)

int Tk_ClipboardClear(Tcl_Interp *interp, Tk_Window tkwin)

Colormap Tk_Colormap(Tk_Window tkwin)

Tk_TextLayout Tk_ComputeTextLayout(Tk_Font font, const char *string, int numChars, int wrapLength, Tk_Justify justify, int flags, int *widthPtr, int *heightPtr)

int Tk_ConfigureInfo(Tcl_Interp *interp, Tk_Window tkwin, Tk_ConfigSpec *specs, char *widgRec, char *argvName, int flags)

int Tk_ConfigureValue(Tcl_Interp *interp, Tk_Window tkwin, Tk_ConfigSpec *specs, char *widgRec, char *argvName, int flags)

int Tk_ConfigureWidget(Tcl_Interp *interp, Tk_Window tkwin, Tk_ConfigSpec *specs, int argc, char **argv, char *widgRec, int flags)

void Tk_ConfigureWindow(Tk_Window tkwin, unsigned int valueMask, XWindowChanges *valuePtr)

Tk_Window Tk_CoordsToWindow(int rootX, int rootY, Tk_Window tkwin)

unsigned long Tk_CreateBinding(Tcl_Interp *interp, Tk_BindingTable bindingTable, ClientData object, *eventString, char *command, int append)

Tk_BindingTable Tk_CreateBindingTable(Tcl_Interp *interp)

Tk_ErrorHandler Tk_CreateErrorHandler(Display *display, int errNum, int request, int minorCode, Tk_ErrorProc *errorProc, ClientData clientData)

void Tk_CreateEventHandler(Tk_Window token, unsigned long mask,
    Tk_EventProc *proc, ClientData clientData)

void Tk_CreateGenericHandler(Tk_GenericProc *proc, ClientData clientData)

void Tk_CreateImageType(Tk_ImageType *typePtr)

void Tk_CreateItemType(Tk_ItemType *typePtr)

void Tk_CreatePhotoImageFormat(Tk_PhotoImageFormat *formatPtr)

void Tk_CreateSelHandler(Tk_Window tkwin, Atom selection, Atom target,
    Tk_SelectionProc *proc, ClientData clientData, Atom format)

Tk_Window Tk_CreateWindowFromPath(Tcl_Interp *interp, Tk_Window tkwin,
    char *pathName, char *screenName)

Tk_Window Tk_CreateWindow(Tcl_Interp *interp, Tk_Window parent,
    char *name, char *screenName)

int Tk_DefineBitmap(Tcl_Interp *interp, Tk_Uid name, char *source, int width,
    int height)

void Tk_DefineCursor(Tk_Window window, Tk_Cursor cursor)

void Tk_DeleteAllBindings(Tk_BindingTable bindingTable, ClientData object)

void Tk_DeleteBindingTable(Tk_BindingTable bindingTable)

int Tk_DeleteBinding(Tcl_Interp *interp, Tk_BindingTable bindingTable,
    ClientData object, char *eventString)

void Tk_DeleteErrorHandler(Tk_ErrorHandler handler)

void Tk_DeleteEventHandler(Tk_Window token, unsigned long mask,
    Tk_EventProc *proc, ClientData clientData)

void Tk_DeleteGenericHandler(Tk_GenericProc *proc, ClientData clientData)

void Tk_DeleteImage(Tcl_Interp *interp, char *name)

void Tk_DeleteSelHandler(Tk_Window tkwin, Atom selection, Atom target)

int Tk_Depth(Tk_Window tkwin)

void Tk_DestroyWindow(Tk_Window tkwin)

char *Tk_DisplayName(Tk_Window tkwin)

Display Tk_Display(Tk_Window tkwin)

int Tk_DistanceToTextLayout(Tk_TextLayout layout, int x, int y)

void Tk_Draw3DPolygon(Tk_Window tkwin, Drawable drawable,
    Tk_3DBorder border, XPoint *pointPtr, int numPoints, int borderWidth,
    int leftRelief)

void Tk_Draw3DRectangle(Tk_Window tkwin, Drawable drawable,
    Tk_3DBorder border, int x, int y, int width, int height, int borderWidth,
    int relief)

void Tk_DrawChars(Display *display, Drawable drawable, GC gc, Tk_Font tkfont,
    const char *source, int numChars, int x, int y)

void Tk_DrawFocusHighlight(Tk_Window tkwin, GC gc, int width,
    Drawable drawable)

void Tk_DrawTextLayout(Display *display, Drawable drawable, GC gc,
    Tk_TextLayout layout, int x, int y, int firstChar, int lastChar)

void Tk_Fill3DPolygon(Tk_Window tkwin, Drawable drawable,
    Tk_3DBorder border, XPoint *pointPtr, int numPoints, int borderWidth,
    int leftRelief)

void Tk_Fill3DRectangle(Tk_Window tkwin, Drawable drawable,
    Tk_3DBorder border, int x, int y, int width, int height, int borderWidth,
    int relief)

Tk_PhotoHandle Tk_FindPhoto(Tcl_Interp *interp, char *imageName)

Font Tk_FontId(Tk_Font font)

void Tk_Free3DBorder(Tk_3DBorder border)

void Tk_FreeBitmap(Display *display, Pixmap bitmap)

void Tk_FreeColor(XColor *colorPtr)

void Tk_FreeColormap(Display *display, Colormap colormap)

void Tk_FreeCursor(Display *display, Tk_Cursor cursor)

void Tk_FreeFont(Tk_Font)

void Tk_FreeGC(Display *display, GC gc)

void Tk_FreeImage(Tk_Image image)

void Tk_FreeOptions(Tk_ConfigSpec *specs, char *widgRec, Display *display,
    int needFlags)

void Tk_FreePixmap(Display *display, Pixmap pixmap)

void Tk_FreeTextLayout(Tk_TextLayout textLayout)

void Tk_FreeXId(Display *display, XID xid)

GC Tk_GCForColor(XColor *colorPtr, Drawable drawable)

void Tk_GeometryRequest(Tk_Window tkwin, int reqWidth, int reqHeight)

Tk_3DBorder Tk_Get3DBorder(Tcl_Interp *interp, Tk_Window tkwin,
    Tk_Uid colorName)

void Tk_GetAllBindings(Tcl_Interp *interp, Tk_BindingTable bindingTable,
    ClientData object)

int Tk_GetAnchor(Tcl_Interp *interp, char *string, Tk_Anchor *anchorPtr)

char *Tk_GetAtomName(Tk_Window tkwin, Atom atom)

char *Tk_GetBinding(Tcl_Interp *interp, Tk_BindingTable bindingTable,
    ClientData object, char *eventString)

Pixmap Tk_GetBitmapFromData(Tcl_Interp *interp, Tk_Window tkwin,
    char *source, int width, int height)

Pixmap Tk_GetBitmap(Tcl_Interp *interp, Tk_Window tkwin, Tk_Uid string)

int Tk_GetCapStyle(Tcl_Interp *interp, char *string, int *capPtr)

XColor *Tk_GetColorByValue(Tk_Window tkwin, XColor *colorPtr)

XColor *Tk_GetColor(Tcl_Interp *interp, Tk_Window tkwin, Tk_Uid name)

Colormap Tk_GetColormap(Tcl_Interp *interp, Tk_Window tkwin, char *string)

Tk_Cursor Tk_GetCursorFromData(Tcl_Interp *interp, Tk_Window tkwin,
    char *source, char *mask, int width, int height, int xHot, int yHot, Tk_Uid fg,
    Tk_Uid bg)

Tk_Cursor Tk_GetCursor(Tcl_Interp *interp, Tk_Window tkwin, Tk_Uid string)

Tk_Font Tk_GetFontFromObj(Tcl_Interp *interp, Tk_Window tkwin,
    Tcl_Obj *objPtr)

void Tk_GetFontMetrics(Tk_Font font, Tk_FontMetrics *fmPtr)

Tk_Font Tk_GetFont(Tcl_Interp *interp, Tk_Window tkwin, const char *string)

GC Tk_GetGC(Tk_Window tkwin, unsigned long valueMask, XGCValues *valuePtr)

ClientData Tk_GetImageMasterData(Tcl_Interp *interp, char *name,
    Tk_ImageType **typePtrPtr)

Tk_Image Tk_GetImage(Tcl_Interp *interp, Tk_Window tkwin, char *name,
    Tk_ImageChangedProc *changeProc, ClientData clientData)

Tk_ItemType *Tk_GetItemTypes(void)

int Tk_GetJoinStyle(Tcl_Interp *interp, char *string, int *joinPtr)

int Tk_GetJustify(Tcl_Interp *interp, char *string, Tk_Justify *justifyPtr)

int Tk_GetNumMainWindows(void)

Tk_Uid Tk_GetOption(Tk_Window tkwin, char *name, char *className)

int Tk_GetPixels(Tcl_Interp *interp, Tk_Window tkwin, char *string, int *intPtr)

Pixmap Tk_GetPixmap(Display *display, Drawable d, int width, int height,
    int depth)

int Tk_GetRelief(Tcl_Interp *interp, char *name, int *reliefPtr)

void Tk_GetRootCoords(Tk_Window tkwin, int *xPtr, int *yPtr)

int Tk_GetScreenMM(Tcl_Interp *interp, Tk_Window tkwin, char *string,
    double *doublePtr)

int Tk_GetScrollInfo(Tcl_Interp *interp, int argc, char **argv, double *dblPtr,
    int *intPtr)

int Tk_GetSelection(Tcl_Interp *interp, Tk_Window tkwin, Atom selection,
    Atom target, Tk_GetSelProc *proc, ClientData clientData)

Tk_Uid Tk_GetUid(const char *string)

void Tk_GetVRootGeometry(Tk_Window tkwin, int *xPtr, int *yPtr, int *widthPtr,
    int *heightPtr)

Visual *Tk_GetVisual(Tcl_Interp *interp, Tk_Window tkwin, char *string,
    int *depthPtr, Colormap *colormapPtr)

int Tk_Grab(Tcl_Interp *interp, Tk_Window tkwin, int grabGlobal)

void Tk_HandleEvent(XEvent *eventPtr)

int Tk_Height(Tk_Window tkwin)

Tk_Window Tk_IdToWindow(Display *display, Window window)

void Tk_ImageChanged(Tk_ImageMaster master, int x, int y, int width, int height,
    int imageWidth, int imageHeight)

int Tk_Init(Tcl_Interp *interp)

Atom Tk_InternAtom(Tk_Window tkwin, char *name)

int Tk_InternalBorderWidth(Tk_Window tkwin)

int Tk_IntersectTextLayout(Tk_TextLayout layout, int x, int y, int width, int height)

int Tk_IsContainer(Tk_Window tkwin)

int Tk_IsEmbedded(Tk_Window tkwin)

int Tk_IsMapped(Tk_Window tkwin)

int Tk_IsTopLevel(Tk_Window tkwin)

void Tk_MainLoop(void)

Tk_Window Tk_MainWindow(Tcl_Interp *interp)

void Tk_Main(int argc, char **argv, Tcl_AppInitProc *appInitProc)

void Tk_MaintainGeometry(Tk_Window slave, Tk_Window master, int x, int y,
    int width, int height)

void Tk_MakeWindowExist(Tk_Window tkwin)

void Tk_ManageGeometry(Tk_Window tkwin, Tk_GeomMgr *mgrPtr,
    ClientData clientData)

void Tk_MapWindow(Tk_Window tkwin)

int Tk_MeasureChars(Tk_Font tkfont, const char *source, int maxChars,
    int maxPixels, int flags, int *lengthPtr)

void Tk_MoveResizeWindow(Tk_Window tkwin, int x, int y, int width, int height)

void Tk_MoveToplevelWindow(Tk_Window tkwin, int x, int y)

void Tk_MoveWindow(Tk_Window tkwin, int x, int y)

char *Tk_NameOf3DBorder(Tk_3DBorder border)

char *Tk_NameOfAnchor(Tk_Anchor anchor)

char *Tk_NameOfBitmap(Display *display, Pixmap bitmap)

char *Tk_NameOfCapStyle(int cap)

char *Tk_NameOfColor(XColor *colorPtr)

char *Tk_NameOfCursor(Display *display, Tk_Cursor cursor)

char *Tk_NameOfFont(Tk_Font font)

char *Tk_NameOfImage(Tk_ImageMaster imageMaster)

char *Tk_NameOfJoinStyle(int join)

char *Tk_NameOfJustify(Tk_Justify justify)

char *Tk_NameOfRelief(int relief)

Tk_Uid Tk_Name(Tk_Window tkwin)

Tk_Window Tk_NameToWindow(Tcl_Interp *interp, char *pathName,
    Tk_Window tkwin)

int Tk_Offset(type, field)

void Tk_OwnSelection(Tk_Window tkwin, Atom selection, Tk_LostSelProc *proc,
    ClientData clientData)

Tk_Window Tk_Parent(Tk_Window tkwin)

int Tk_ParseArgv(Tcl_Interp *interp, Tk_Window tkwin, int *argcPtr, char **argv,
    Tk_ArgvInfo *argTable, int flags)

char *Tk_PathName(Tk_Window tkwin)

void Tk_PhotoBlank(Tk_PhotoHandle handle)

void Tk_PhotoExpand(Tk_PhotoHandle handle, int width, int height)

int Tk_PhotoGetImage(Tk_PhotoHandle handle, Tk_PhotoImageBlock *blockPtr)

void Tk_PhotoGetSize(Tk_PhotoHandle handle, int *widthPtr, int *heightPtr)

void Tk_PhotoPutBlock(Tk_PhotoHandle handle, Tk_PhotoImageBlock *blockPtr,
    int x, int y, int width, int height)

void Tk_PhotoPutZoomedBlock(Tk_PhotoHandle handle,
    Tk_PhotoImageBlock *blockPtr, int x, int y, int width, int height, int zoomX,
    int zoomY, int subsampleX, int subsampleY)

void Tk_PhotoSetSize(Tk_PhotoHandle handle, int width, int height)

int Tk_PointToChar(Tk_TextLayout layout, int x, int y)

int Tk_PostscriptFontName(Tk_Font tkfont, Tcl_DString *dsPtr)

void Tk_PreserveColormap(Display *display, Colormap colormap)

void Tk_QueueWindowEvent(XEvent *eventPtr, Tcl_QueuePosition position)

void Tk_RedrawImage(Tk_Image image, int imageX, int imageY, int width,
    int height, Drawable drawable, int drawableX, int drawableY)

int Tk_ReqHeight(Tk_Window tkwin)

int Tk_ReqWidth(Tk_Window tkwin)

void Tk_ResizeWindow(Tk_Window tkwin, int width, int height)

int Tk_RestackWindow(Tk_Window tkwin, int aboveBelow, Tk_Window other)

Tk_RestrictProc *Tk_RestrictEvents(Tk_RestrictProc *proc, ClientData arg,
    ClientData *prevArgPtr)

int Tk_SafeInit(Tcl_Interp *interp)

int Tk_ScreenNumber(Tk_Window tkwin)

Screen *Tk_Screen(Tk_Window tkwin)

char *Tk_SetAppName(Tk_Window tkwin, char *name)

void Tk_SetBackgroundFromBorder(Tk_Window tkwin, Tk_3DBorder border)

void Tk_SetClass(Tk_Window tkwin, char *className)

void Tk_SetGrid(Tk_Window tkwin, int reqWidth, int reqHeight, int gridWidth,
    int gridHeight)

void Tk_SetInternalBorder(Tk_Window tkwin, int width)

void Tk_SetWindowBackgroundPixmap(Tk_Window tkwin, Pixmap pixmap)

void Tk_SetWindowBackground(Tk_Window tkwin, unsigned long pixel)

void Tk_SetWindowBorderPixmap(Tk_Window tkwin, Pixmap pixmap)

void Tk_SetWindowBorder(Tk_Window tkwin, unsigned long pixel)

void Tk_SetWindowBorderWidth(Tk_Window tkwin, int width)

void Tk_SetWindowColormap(Tk_Window tkwin, Colormap colormap)

int Tk_SetWindowVisual(Tk_Window tkwin, Visual *visual, int depth,
    Colormap colormap)

void Tk_SizeOfBitmap(Display *display, Pixmap bitmap, int *widthPtr,
    int *heightPtr)

void Tk_SizeOfImage(Tk_Image image, int *widthPtr, int *heightPtr)

int Tk_StrictMotif(Tk_Window tkwin)

void Tk_TextLayoutToPostscript(Tcl_Interp *interp, Tk_TextLayout layout)

int Tk_TextWidth(Tk_Font font, const char *string, int numChars)

void Tk_UndefineCursor(Tk_Window window)

void Tk_UnderlineChars(Display *display, Drawable drawable, GC gc,
    Tk_Font tkfont, const char *source, int x, int y, int firstChar, int lastChar)

void Tk_UnderlineTextLayout(Display *display, Drawable drawable, GC gc,
    Tk_TextLayout layout, int x, int y, int underline)

void Tk_Ungrab(Tk_Window tkwin)

void Tk_UnmaintainGeometry(Tk_Window slave, Tk_Window master)

void Tk_UnmapWindow(Tk_Window tkwin)

void Tk_UnsetGrid(Tk_Window tkwin)

void Tk_UpdatePointer(Tk_Window tkwin, int x, int y, int state)

Visual *Tk_Visual(Tk_Window tkwin)

int Tk_Width(Tk_Window tkwin)

Window Tk_WindowId(Tk_Window tkwin)

int Tk_X(Tk_Window tkwin)

int Tk_Y(Tk_Window tkwin)

CHAPTER 6

Expect

Expect, written by Don Libes, is a tool for communicating with interactive programs. Expect is not part of the core Tcl/Tk package, but can be obtained for free at *http://expect.nist.gov*. This chapter covers Version 5.25.0.

Expect can automate tasks that would normally require a user to interactively communicate with a program. Expect is a Tcl interpreter extended with additional commands. It can be run as the standalone programs *expect* and *expectk* or used with other Tcl language extensions.

Expect was the first major Tcl-based application. This chapter describes the features that Expect adds to the Tcl language.

Overview

You normally run Expect by invoking the program *expect* (or *expectk* if you also want Tk). Expect is a Tcl interpreter with about 40 additional commands. This section briefly describes the most common commands.

The *spawn* command creates a new process that executes a specified program. It creates a connection to that process so that it is accessible by using other Expect commands.

The *send* command passes commands to a process started by *spawn*. It sends strings, just as a user would type if interactively running the spawned program.

The *expect* command is the heart of the Expect program. It compares the output from one or more spawned processes, looking for a match against a string or pattern. If a match is found, it executes Tcl code associated with the pattern. The patterns can be simple strings, glob-style patterns, or regular expressions. Multiple patterns and actions can be specified.

The *interact* command passes control of a spawned process back to the user. This allows the user to connect to the process interactively. For example, an Expect script could log a user on to a remote system, start a text editor, then pass control back to the user. Like *expect*, it performs pattern matching that allows actions to be performed. In our editor example, the script could watch for a pattern that indicated that the text editor program had exited, then pass control back to the Expect script to automatically perform cleanup and log out the user.

The *close* command closes the connection to a spawned process. This is not always needed, as Expect closes all open connections when it exits.

Example

This simple example illustrates logging in to a host using anonymous FTP and then passing control back to the user:

```
set host localhost
set name myname@myhost
spawn ftp $host
expect "Name (*):"
send "anonymous\r"
expect "Password:"
send "$name\r"
expect {
    "ftp>" {
        interact
    }
    "Login failed." {
        exit 1
    }
    timeout {
        exit 1
    }
}
```

Command-Line Options

The *expect* program accepts the following command-line options:

expect [*-v*] [*-d*] [*-D n*] [*-i*] [*-n*] [*-N*] [*-c cmds*] [[*-f* | *-b*] *cmdfile*] [– –] [*args*]

-v
    Display version number and exit.

-d
    Enable diagnostic output.

-D n
    Enable interactive debugger if numeric argument *n* is non-zero.

-i
    Run in interactive mode.

-n

Do not read the user's startup file (`~/.expect.rc`).

-N

Do not read the global startup file (`$exp_library/expect.rc`).

-c cmds

Specify commands to be executed before starting script. The commands can be separated by semicolons. Multiple *-c* options can be specified.

-f

Specify the file from which to read commands.

-b

Same as *-f*, but read the input file one line at a time rather than in its entirety.

cmdfile

The file containing Tcl commands to execute. For standard input use "-".

--

Denote the end of Expect options.

args

Additional arguments to pass to the Tcl program.

The *expectk* program accepts the following command-line options:

expectk [*options*] [*cmdfile*] [*args*]

-version

Display version number and exit.

-Debug n

Enable interactive debugger if numeric argument *n* is non-zero.

-interactive

Run in interactive mode.

-command cmds

Specify commands to be executed before starting script. The commands can be separated by semicolons. Multiple *-command* options can be specified.

-diag

Enable diagnostic output.

-norc

Do not read the user's startup file (`~/.expect.rc`).

-NORC

Do not read the global startup file (`$exp_library/expect.rc`).

-file

Specify the file from which to read commands.

-buffer
> Same as *-file*, but read the input file one line at a time rather than in its entirety.

`cmdfile`
> The file containing Tcl commands to execute. For standard input use "-".

`- -`
> Denote the end of Expect options.

`args`
> Additional arguments to pass to the Tcl program.

Expectk also accepts any of the options supported by the *wish* program.

Environment Variables

The following environment variables are used by the Expect program:

DOTDIR
> Directory in which to look for the user-specific startup file *.expect.rc*. The default is the user's home directory.

EXPECT_DEBUG_INIT
> Initialization command to be executed by the debugger on startup.

EXPECT_PROMPT
> By convention, used by some applications to specify a regular expression that matches the end of the user's login prompt.

Special Variables

The following variables have special meaning to the Expect program.

`spawn_id`
> Spawn descriptor for the current spawned process (can be set).

`user_spawn_id`
> Spawn descriptor for user input.

`tty_spawn_id`
> Spawn descriptor for */dev/tty*.

`any_spawn_id`
> Used in *expect* command to match input on any active spawn descriptor.

`error_spawn_id`
> Spawn descriptor for standard error output.

`argv`
> List containing the command-line arguments.

argc

    The number of elements in `argv`.

argv0

    The name of the script or program being run.

exp_exec_library

    Directory containing architecture-dependent library files.

exp_library

    Directory containing architecture-independent library files.

expect_out

    Array containing output strings collected by the *expect* command (see the description of *expect*, later in this chapter).

expect_out(buffer)

    Matching any previously unmatched output.

expect_out(*n*, string)

    Substring that matched regular expression *n*, where *n* is 1 through 9.

expect_out(0, string)

    String that matched entire pattern.

expect_out(*n* , start)

    Starting index in buffer of regular expression *n*.

expect_out(*n* , end)

    Ending index in buffer of regular expression *n*.

expect_out(spawn_id)

    Spawn ID associated with matching output.

spawn_out(slave, name)

    Name of the pty slave device.

interact_out

    Array containing output strings collected by *interact* command, in the same format as `expect_out`.

send_human

    Controls behavior of *send* with the *-h* option. A list of five numeric elements: (1) interarrival time of characters, (2) interarrival time of word endings, (3) variability parameter, (4) minimum interarrival time, and (5) maximum interarrival time. All times are in decimal seconds.

send_slow

    Controls behavior of *send* with the *-s* option. A list of two numeric elements: (1) number of bytes to send atomically, and (2) number of seconds between sending.

```
stty_init
```
Holds *stty* command settings to be used when initializing a pty for a spawned process.

```
timeout
```
Time, in seconds, before *expect* command will time out. A value of -1 specifies no timeout.

Grouped Summary of Commands

Process Interaction

close	Close connection to a spawned process.
disconnect	Disconnect forked process from terminal.
exp_continue	Continue execution during *expect* command.
expect	Match patterns and perform actions based on process output.
expect_after	Match patterns and specify actions to perform after *expect* command pattern matching.
expect_background	Match patterns and specify actions to perform outside of *expect* command.
expect_before	Match patterns and specify actions to perform before *expect* command pattern matching.
expect_tty	Similar to *expect*, but reads from */dev/tty*.
expect_user	Similar to *expect*, but reads from standard input.
inter_return	Causes an *interact* or *interpreter* command to perform a return in its caller.
interact	Transfer control of a process to the user.
interpreter	Connect user to the Tcl interpreter.
overlay	Execute a new program in place of Expect.
send	Send a string to a spawned process.
send_error	Send a string to standard error output.
send_log	Send a string to the log file.
send_tty	Send a string to */dev/tty*.
send_user	Send a string to standard output.
spawn	Create a new spawned process.
wait	Wait for a spawned process to terminate.

Utility Commands

debug	Start, stop, or return status of the debugger.
exit	Cause Expect to exit.
exp_getpid	Return current process ID.
exp_internal	Enable, disable, or log diagnostic output.
exp_open	Convert spawn ID to Tcl file descriptor.
exp_pid	Return process ID for spawned process.
expect_version	Return, generate an error, or exit based on Expect version.

fork	Create a new process.
log_file	Start or stop logging of session to a file.
log_user	Start or stop logging of spawned process to standard output.
match_max	Set or return size of expect buffer.
parity	Set or return parity generation setting.
remove_nulls	Set or return null character setting.
sleep	Delay execution.
strace	Trace statement execution.
stty	Change terminal mode.
system	Execute shell command.
timestamp	Return a timestamp.
trap	Set or return commands to be executed on receipt of a signal.

Synonyms

To reduce the likelihood of name conflicts with other Tcl extensions, most Expect commands have synonyms that are prefixed with `exp_`.

exp_close	Synonym for *close*
exp_debug	Synonym for *debug*
exp_disconnect	Synonym for *disconnect*
exp_exit	Synonym for *exit*
exp_fork	Synonym for *fork*
exp_inter_return	Synonym for *inter_return*
exp_interact	Synonym for *interact*
exp_interpreter	Synonym for *interpreter*
exp_log_file	Synonym for *log_file*
exp_log_user	Synonym for *log_user*
exp_match_max	Synonym for *match_max*
exp_overlay	Synonym for *overlay*
exp_parity	Synonym for *parity*
exp_remove_nulls	Synonym for *remove_nulls*
exp_send	Synonym for *send*
exp_send_error	Synonym for *send_error*
exp_send_log	Synonym for *send_log*
exp_send_tty	Synonym for *send_tty*
exp_send_user	Synonym for *send_user*
exp_sleep	Synonym for *sleep*
exp_spawn	Synonym for *spawn*
exp_strace	Synonym for *strace*
exp_stty	Synonym for *stty*
exp_system	Synonym for *system*
exp_timestamp	Synonym for *timestamp*
exp_trap	Synonym for *trap*
exp_version	Synonym for *expect_version*
exp_wait	Synonym for *wait*

Alphabetical Summary of Commands

In addition to the following commands, a number of synonyms are provided to prevent name conflicts with other libraries. See the preceding "Synonyms" section.

close

close [*-slave*] [*-onexec* 0 | 1] [*-i spawn_id*]

Close the connection to a spawned process, by default the current process.

Options

-slave
Close the slave pty associated with the spawn ID.

-onexec 0 | 1
With a 0 argument, the spawn ID will be left open in any new processes. If 1, the ID will be closed (the default).

-i spawn_id
Specify the spawn ID of the process to close.

debug

debug [[*-now*] 0 | 1]

Control the Tcl debugger. With no arguments, return 1 if the debugger is running; otherwise, return 0.

An argument of 1 starts the debugger at execution of the next statement. An argument of 0 stops the debugger.

The *-now* option starts the debugger immediately, rather than at the next statement.

disconnect

disconnect

Disconnect a forked process from the terminal. The process continues running in the background with its standard input and output redirected to */dev/null.*

exit

exit [*-onexit* [*handler*]] [*-noexit*] [*status*]

Cause the Expect program to exit. Return the numeric exit status *status* (default is 0).

The *-onexit* option specifies a command to use as the exit handler. By default the current exit handler is used.

The *-noexit* option causes Expect to prepare to exit, calling user-defined and internal exit handlers, but not actually returning control to the operating system.

When the end of a script is reached, an *exit* command is automatically executed.

exp_continue

exp_continue

Within an *expect* command, continues execution rather than returning.

exp_getpid

exp_getpid

Return the process ID of the current process.

exp_internal

exp_internal [*-info*] [*-f file*] `value`

Control output of diagnostic information about data received and pattern matching. Display to standard output is enabled if the numeric `value` parameter is non-zero, and disabled if it is zero.

Output can be sent to a file using the *-f* option and a filename argument.

The *-info* option causes the current status of diagnostic output to be displayed.

exp_open

exp_open [*-leaveopen*] [*-i* `spawn_id`]

Return a Tcl file identifier corresponding to the process opened with spawn ID `spawn_id` (or the current spawn ID, if the *-i* option is not used).

Normally the spawn ID should no longer be used. With the *-leaveopen* option, it is left open for access using Expect commands.

exp_pid

exp_pid [*-i* `spawn_id`]

Return the process ID corresponding to the given spawn ID (by default the current spawn ID).

expect

expect [[*options*] *pat1 body1*] ... [*options*] *patn* [*bodyn*]

Compare output from one or more spawned processes against patterns. If a match is found, execute the associated code body and return.

The *exp_continue* command inside a body causes the *expect* statement to continue execution rather than returning.

Patterns

The pattern can be a string. By default, shell globbing is used, but this can be changed using options listed in the next section. A pattern can also be one of the following special names:

eof
> Matches end of file.

full_buffer
> Matches when maximum number of bytes has been received with no pattern match.

null
> Matches a single ASCII NUL (0) character.

timeout
> Matches when timeout occurs with no pattern matched.

default
> Matches if timeout or eof occur.

Options

-timeout seconds
> Specify amount to wait before timing out.

-i spawn_id_list
> Match against the listed spawn IDs; either a literal list or a global variable name containing the list.

-gl
> Use glob-style pattern matching (default).

-re
> Use regular expression pattern matching.

-ex
> Use exact string pattern matching.

-nocase
> Make matching case-insensitive.

Expect

expect_after

expect_after `options`

Accept the same options as the *expect* command, but return immediately. Patterns and actions are implicitly added to the next *expect* command having the same spawn ID. Matching patterns are executed after those in the *expect* command, in the same context.

Expect tests *expect_before* patterns first, *expect* patterns next, and *expect_after* last. The first successful match gets its action executed. Patterns are tested in the order listed.

expect_background

expect_background `options`

Accept the same options as the *expect* command, but return immediately. Patterns and actions are tested whenever input arrives. Must be used outside of an *expect* command.

expect_before

expect_before `options`

Accept the same options as the *expect* command, but return immediately. Patterns and actions are implicitly added to the next *expect* command having the same spawn ID. Matching patterns are executed before those in the *expect* command, in the same context.

Expect tests *expect_before* patterns first, *expect* patterns next, and *expect_after* last. The first successful match gets its action executed. Patterns are tested in the order listed.

expect_tty

expect_tty `options`

Accept the same options as the *expect* command, but read input from the user using */dev/tty*.

expect_user

expect_user `options`

Accept the same options as the *expect* command, but read input from the user using standard input.

expect_version

expect_version [[-*exit*] version]

Test version of Expect for compatibility. With no arguments, return the version of Expect. With an argument, generate an error if the version of Expect is different from the one specified.

The version parameter is a string in the form major-number.minor-number.patch-level (e.g., 5.24.1). With the -*exit* option, the command also exits if the version of Expect is not the same as specified.

fork

fork

Create a new process that is an exact copy of the current one. Returns 0 to the new process and the new process ID to the parent process. Returns –1 if the new process could not be created.

inter_return

inter_return

Cause a currently active *interact* or *interpreter* command to perform a return in its caller. This differs from *return*. For example, if a procedure called *interact* which then executed the action *inter_return*, the procedure would return to its caller.

interact

interact [[options] string1 body1] ... [[options] stringn [bodyn]]

Pass control of a spawned process to the user. Checks user input against zero or more strings. If a match occurs, the corresponding body is executed.

Patterns

The pattern can be a string. By default, exact string matching is used but can be changed using options listed in the next section. A pattern can also be one of the following special names:

eof
    Matches end of file.

null
    Matches a single ASCII NUL (0) character.

timeout seconds
    Matches when timeout occurs since the last pattern was matched.

Expect

Options

-re

Use regular expression pattern matching.

-ex

Use exact string pattern matching (default).

-indices

Used in conjunction with *-re* to store indices of matching patterns in the *interact_out* array.

-output `spawn_id_list`

Specify a list of spawn IDs to be used for output.

-input `spawn_id_list`

Specify a list of spawn IDs to be used for input.

-iwrite

Cause all matches to set the variable `interact_out(spawn_id)` before performing their associated action.

-reset

Reset the terminal mode to the settings it had before *interact* was executed.

-echo

Send the characters that match the following pattern back to the process that generated them.

-nobuffer

Send characters that match the pattern to the output process immediately as they are read.

-o

Apply any following pattern body pairs against the output of the current process.

-i

Introduce a replacement for the current spawn ID when no other *-input* or *-output* flags are used.

-u `spawn_id`

Cause the currently spawned process to interact with the named process rather than the user.

---

interpreter

interpreter

Cause the user to be interactively prompted for Tcl commands. The *return* and *inter_return* commands can be used to return to the Expect script.

---

log_file

log_file [*options*] [[*-a*] *file*]

Record a transcript of the session to file *file*. With no file argument, stop recording.

Options

-open
> The file parameter is an open Tcl file identifier. The identifier should no longer be used.

-leaveopen
> The file parameter is an open Tcl file identifier. The identifier can continue to be used.

-a
> Log all output, including that suppressed by the *log_user* command.

-noappend
> Truncate existing output file (default is to append).

-info
> Display the current status of transcript recording.

log_user

log_user -info | 0 | 1

Control the logging of *send/expect* dialog to standard output. An argument of 1 enables logging, and 0 disables it. With no arguments or the *-info* option, displays the current setting.

match_max

match_max [*-d*] [*-i spawn_id*] [*size*]

Set the size of the internal *expect* buffer to *size* bytes. With no *size* parameter, returns the current size. The *-d* option makes the specified *size* become the default value (the initial default is 2000). The *-i* option allows setting the buffer size for the given spawn ID rather than the current process.

overlay

overlay [*-# spawn_id...*] *program* [*args*]

Execute program *program* and optional arguments in place of the current Expect program. Spawn IDs can be mapped to file identifiers for the new process by specifying file number and spawn ID pairs.

Example

```
overlay -0 $spawn_id -1 $spawn_id -2 $spawn_id emacs
```

parity

parity [*-d*] [*-i spawn_id*] [*value*]

Control handling of parity bits from the output of the current spawned process. A value of 0 causes parity to be stripped; non-zero values retain parity. With the *-d* option, makes the specified setting the default parity (the initial default is 1). With no *value* parameter, returns the current setting. The *-i* option allows specifying another spawn ID to be used.

remove_nulls

remove_nulls [*-d*] [*-i spawn_id*] [*value*]

Control handling of nulls from the output of the current spawned process. A value of 1 causes null characters to be removed; non-zero values retain null characters. With the *-d* option, makes the specified setting the default value (the initial default is 1). With no *value* parameter, returns the current setting. The *-i* option lets you specify another spawn ID to be used.

send

send [*options*] *string*

Send a string to a spawned process.

Options

--

> Indicate the end of options.

-i spawn_id

> Send the string to the specified spawn ID.

-raw

> Disable the translation of newline to return-newline when sending to the user terminal.

-null num

> Send *num* null characters (one if *num* is omitted).

-break

> Send a break character (applicable only for terminal devices).

-s

> Send output slowly using the settings of the **send_slow** variable.

-h

> Send output, like a human typing, using the settings of the **send_human** variable.

Note that *send* conflicts with the Tk command of the same name. Use *exp_send* instead.

send_error

send_error [options] `string`

Like the *send* command, except output is sent to standard error.

send_log

send_log [– –] `string`

Like the *send* command, except output is sent to the log file opened using the *log_file* command.

send_tty

send_tty [options] `string`

Like the *send* command, except output is sent to */dev/tty*.

send_user

send_user [options] `string`

Like the *send* command, except output is sent to standard output.

sleep

sleep `seconds`

Delay execution of the current program for `seconds` seconds. The parameter is a floating-point number.

spawn

spawn [args] `program` [args]

Create a new process executing `program` and optional arguments `args`. Sets the variable `spawn_id` to the spawn ID for the new process and makes it the default spawn ID. Returns the Unix process ID of the new process, or 0 if the process could not be spawned.

Options

-noecho
   Disable echo of command name and arguments.

-console
   Redirect console output to the spawned process.

-nottycopy
> Skip initialization of spawned process pty to user's tty settings.

-nottyinit
> Skip initialization of spawned process pty to sane values.

-open `fileid`
> Open an existing Tcl file identifier rather than a process. The identifier should no longer be used.

-leaveopen `fileid`
> Open an existing Tcl file identifier rather than a process. The identifier can continue to be used.

-pty
> Open a pty but do not spawn a process.

-ignore `signal`
> Ignore the named signal in the spawned process. More than one *-ignore* option can be specified.

strace

strace [*-info*] [`level`]

Display statements before being executed. Statements are traced as deep as stack level `level`. The *-info* option displays the current trace setting.

stty

stty `args`

Set terminal settings. The arguments take the same form as the *stty* shell command.

system

system `args`

Execute `args` as a shell command, with no redirection and waiting until the command completes.

timestamp

timestamp [`options`]

Return a timestamp. With no arguments, returns the number of seconds since the start of the epoch.

Options

-format `format-string`

> Return time formatted using a format string. The string follows the format of the POSIX *strftime* function, as described below. This command is deprecated; use the Tcl *clock* command instead.

-seconds `source`

> Return a timestamp based on the time `source`, expressed as a number of seconds since the start of the epoch.

-gmt

> Use Greenwitch Mean Time (UTC) rather than the local time zone.

Format Strings

%a	Abbreviated weekday name
%A	Full weekday name
%b	Abbreviated month name
%B	Full month name
%c	Date and time, as in Wed Oct 6 11:45:56 1993
%d	Day of the month (01–31)
%H	Hour (00–23)
%I	Hour (01–12)
%j	Day (001–366)
%m	Month (01–12)
%M	Minute (00–59)
%p	A.M. or P.M.
%S	Second (00–61)
%u	Day (1–7, Monday is first day of week)
%U	Week (00–53, first Sunday is first day of week one)
%V	Week (01–53, ISO 8601 style)
%w	Day (0–6)
%W	Week (00–53, first Monday is first day of week one)
%x	Date and time, as in Wed Oct 6 1993
%X	Time, as in 23:59:59
%y	Year (00–99)
%Y	Year, as in 1993
%Z	Time zone (or nothing if not determinable)
%%	A bare percent sign

Expect

---

trap

trap [`options`] [[`command`] `signal-list`]

Set exception handling behavior. The command `command` will be executed when any of the signals in the list `signal-list` occurs.

The command can be a Tcl command or the special values SIG_IGN (ignore) or SIG_DFL (use default action). The signals can be specified by number or name.

Options

-code
> Use return code of the handler command.

-interp
> Evaluate command using the context active at the time of exception.

-name
> Return signal name of the *trap* command currently being executed.

-max
> Return highest available signal number.

Example

```
trap {send_user "Control-C pressed"} SIGINT
```

---

wait

wait [*-i spawn_id*] [*-nowait*] [*args*]

Wait until a spawned process terminates. By default the current process is waited for; the *-i* option can specify another spawn ID.

The command returns a list of four numbers: (1) the process ID for which to wait, (2) the spawn ID of the process for which to wait, (3) 0 for success or −1 if error occurred, and (4) the return status or error status of the terminating process. Additional optional information may be returned, indicating the reason for termination.

The *-nowait* option causes an immediate return. The process can then terminate later without an explicit *wait* command.

CHAPTER 7

[incr Tcl]

[incr Tcl], written by Michael McLennan, is a Tcl extension that adds support for object-oriented programming. Loosely based on the syntax of C++, it provides support for encapsulating Tcl code into classes that can be instantiated as objects.

[incr Tcl] is not part of the core Tcl/Tk package, but can be obtained for free at *http://www.tcltk.com/itcl*. This chapter covers Version 3.0. [incr Tcl] provides the foundation for [incr Tk], which is discussed in Chapter 8, *[incr Tk]*.

In general, [incr Tcl] is intended to make it easier to develop and maintain large programs written in Tcl and to support Tcl extensions.

Basic Class Definition

An [incr Tcl] class definition takes the form shown here. Each of the commands within the class definition are optional and can be listed in any order. The parameters *args*, *init*, *body*, and *config* are Tcl lists.

```
class className {
    inherit baseClass....
    constructor args [init] body
    destructor body
    method name [args] [body]
    proc name [args] [body]
    variable varName [init] [config]
    common varName [init]
    public command [arg...]
    protected command [arg...]
    private command [arg...]
    set varName [value]
    array option [arg...]
}
```

Special Variables

`itcl::library`
> Name of directory containing library of [incr Tcl] scripts; can be set using ITCL_LIBRARY environment variable

`itcl::patchLevel`
> Current patch level of [incr Tcl]

`itcl::purist`
> When 0, enables backward-compatibility mode for Tk widget access

`itcl::version`
> Current revision level of [incr Tcl]

Group Listing of Commands

Classes

body	Change the body of a class method or procedure.
class	Create a class of objects.
configbody	Change the configuration code for a public variable.
itcl_class	Obsolete; see *class*.

Objects

`className`	Create an object belonging to class `className`.
`objName`	Invoke a method to manipulate object `objName`.
delete	Delete an object, class, or namespace.

Miscellaneous

code	Capture the namespace context for a code fragment.
ensemble	Create or modify a composite command.
find	Search for classes and objects.
itcl_info	Obsolete; see *find*.
local	Create an object local to a procedure.
scope	Capture the namespace context for a variable.

Example

The following example illustrates a small class with several methods and some code to exercise it:

```
class Toaster {
    private variable toastTime 10
    constructor {} {
        puts "Toaster created"
    }
    destructor {
        puts "Toaster destroyed"
```

```
    }
    method getToastTime {} {
        return $toastTime
    }
    method setToastTime {newToastTime} {
        set toastTime $newToastTime
    }
    method toast {} {
        puts "Toaster is toasting..."
        after [expr $toastTime*1000]
        puts "\aToast is ready!"
    }
    method clean {} {
        puts "Cleaning toaster..."
        after 2000
        puts "Toaster is clean"
    }
}

puts "Starting test program"
Toaster machine
machine clean
machine setToastTime 5
puts "Toast time set to [machine getToastTime]"
machine toast
delete object machine
```

Alphabetical Summary of Commands

---

className

className objName [*arg...*]

Create an object of class *className* with name *objName*. Any arguments
are passed to the constructor. The string #auto inside an *objName* is
replaced with a unique automatically generated name.

---

objName

objName method [*arg...*]

Invoke method *method* on object *objName*. Any arguments are passed as
the argument list of the method. The method can be *constructor*, *destructor*, a
method appearing in the class definition, or one of the built-in methods listed
below.

objName cget -varName

Return the current value of public variable *varName*.

objName configure [-*varname*] [*value*]...

Provide access to public variables. With no arguments, return a list describing
all public variables. Each element contains a variable name, its initial value,
and its current value. With a single -*varname* option, return the same information for one variable. With one or more -*varname*-*value* pairs, set public

variable *varname* to value *value*. Any *configbody* code associated with the variable is also executed.

objName isa className

Return `true` if *className* can be found in the object's heritage; otherwise, return `false`.

objName info option [args...]

Return information about *objName* or its class definition. Accepts any of the arguments for the Tcl *info* command, as well as the following:

objName info class

Return the name of the most specific class for object *objName*.

objName info inherit

Return the list of base classes as they were defined in the *inherit* command, or an empty string if this class has no base classes.

objName info heritage

Return the current class name and the entire list of base classes in the order that they are traversed for member lookup and object destruction.

objName info function [cmdName] [-protection] [-type] [-name] [-args] [-body]

With no arguments, return a list of all class methods and procedures. If *cmd-Name* is specified, return information for a specific method or procedure. If no flags are specified, return a list with the following elements: the protection level, the type (method/proc), the qualified name, the argument list, and the body. Flags can be used to request specific elements from this list.

objName info variable [varName] [-protection] [-type] [-name] [-init] [-value] [-config]

With no arguments, return a list of all object-specific variables and common data members. If *varName* is specified, return information for a specific data member. If no flags are specified, return a list with the following elements: the protection level, the type (variable/common), the qualified name, the initial value, and the current value. If *varName* is a public variable, the *configbody* code is included in this list. Flags can be used to request specific elements from this list.

---

body

body className::function args body

Define or redefine a class method or procedure that was declared in a *class* command. The name of the method or procedure is specified by *className::function*; the arguments are specified using the list *args*, followed by the Tcl command script *body*.

---

class

class className *definition*

Define a new class named *className*. The properties of the class are described by *definition*, a list containing any of the following Tcl statements:

inherit [baseClass...]

Cause class to inherit characteristics from one or more existing base classes.

constructor args [init] body

Define the argument list and body for the constructor method called when an object is created. Can optionally specify *init* statement to pass parameters to base class constructors. Constructor always returns the class name.

destructor body

Define the code body for the destructor method called when an object is deleted.

method name [args] [body]

Declare a method named *name*. Can define the argument list *args* and code body *body*. The *body* command can define or redefine the method body outside of the class definition.

proc name [args] [body]

Declare a procedure named *name*. Can define the argument list *args* and code body *body*. The *body* command can define or redefine the body outside of the class definition.

variable varName [init] [config]

Define an object-specific variable named *varName*. Optional string *init* supplies an initial value for the variable when the object is created. Optional script *config* specifies code to be executed whenever a public variable is modified using the *configure* command.

common varName [init]

Declare a common variable (shared by all class objects) named *varName*. Optional string *init* supplies a value for the variable to be initialized with whenever a new object is created.

public command [arg...]

Declares that the element defined by *command* is to be publicly accessible (i.e., accessible from any namespace). The parameter *command* can be any of the subcommands *method, proc, variable, common*, or a script containing several member definitions.

protected command [*arg...*]

Declares that the element defined by *command* is to have protected access (i.e., accessible from the same class namespace and any namespaces nested within it).

private command [*arg...*]

Declares that the element defined by *command* is to have private access (i.e., accessible only from the same class namespace).

set varName [*value*]

Set the initial value of a *variable* or *common* variable.

array option [*arg...*]

A standard Tcl *array* command can be used within a class definition, typically to initialize variables.

code

code [*-namespace name*] *command* [*arg...*]

Create a scoped value for a command and its associated arguments. The scoped value is a list with three elements: the @scope keyword, a namespace context, and a value string.

configbody

configbody className::varName body

Allows you to change the configuration code associated with a public variable. The name *className::varName* identifies the public variable being updated. The configuration code is automatically executed when a variable is modified using an object's *configure* command.

delete

delete option [*arg...*]

Used to delete various things in the interpreter. Accepts the following options:

delete class name...

Delete one or more classes, as well as objects in the class and derived classes.

delete object name...

Delete one or more objects. Destructors in the class hierarchy are called, and the object is removed as a command from the interpreter.

delete namespace name...

Delete one or more namespaces, including commands, variables, and child namespaces.

ensemble

ensemble `name command args...`

Create or modify an ensemble command (i.e., a command such as *info*, which is a composite of many different functions). If an ensemble command *name* already exists, then it is updated; otherwise, a new command is created.

The command accepts zero or more **command** arguments that take one of two forms. The `part` command defines a new part for the ensemble, adding it as a new option to the command. The argument list and body are defined as for the *proc* command. The **command** parameter can also be `ensemble`, allowing another subensemble to be nested.

Example

```
ensemble wait {
    part variable {name} {
      uplevel vwait $name
    }
    part visibility {name} {
      tkwait visibility $name
    }
    part window {name} {
      tkwait window $name
    }
}
```

find

find `option` [*arg...*]

Return information about classes or objects. The command takes one of two forms:

find classes [`pattern`]

Return a list of classes available in the current namespace context matching glob pattern `pattern`, or all classes if `pattern` is omitted.

find objects [`pattern`] [*-class className*] [*-isa className*]

Return a list of objects available in the current namespace context matching glob pattern `pattern`, or all objects if `pattern` is omitted. Can use the *-class* option to restrict list to objects whose most specific class is `class-Name`. Can also restrict list to objects having the given class name anywhere in their heritage, using the *-isa* option.

itcl_class

Obsolete; see the *class* command.

itcl_info

Obsolete; see the *find* command.

local

local className objName [arg...]

Create an object that is local to the current stack frame. Object is automatically deleted when stack frame goes away.

scope

scope string

Create a scoped value for a string. The scoped value is a list with three elements: the @scope keyword, a namespace context, and a value string.

CHAPTER 8

[incr Tk]

[incr Tk] is not part of the core Tcl/Tk package, but can be obtained for free at *http://www.tcltk.com/itk*. This chapter covers Version 3.0. *

[incr Tk] provides an object-oriented framework for creating new graphical widgets, known as *mega-widgets*. Mega-widgets are made up of standard Tk widgets, and one mega-widget can contain nested mega-widgets. The widgets and mega-widgets that go into a mega-widget are called *components*.

Using the basic widgets provided by the Tk toolkit and the object-oriented programming capabilities of [incr Tcl], [incr Tk] allows the user to write new widgets in Tcl that look and act just like the ordinary Tk widgets.

The [incr Tk] distribution also comes with more than 30 predefined mega-widgets.

Basic Structure of a Mega-widget

The following code fragment shows the general structure of a mega-widget.

```
class className {
    inherit itk::Widget        # or itk::Toplevel

    constructor {args} {
        itk_option define optName {...}
        itk_component add compName {...}
        pack $itk_component(compName) ...
        eval itk_initialize $args
    }
    public method methodName ...
    protected method methodName ...
    private variable varName ...
```

* This chapter is based on the quick reference in Michael McLennan's Chapter 3 of *Tcl/Tk Tools* (O'Reilly & Associates).

```
    }

usual className {
    ...
}
```

Special Variable

itcl::library
> Name of directory containing library of [incr Tk] scripts; can be set using ITK_LIBRARY environment variable.

Methods and Variables

New mega-widgets built using [incr Tk] should be derived from either `itk::Widget` or `itk::Toplevel`. Both classes are subclasses of `itk::Archetype`.

Public Methods

The following methods are built into all mega-widgets. For a mega-widget having the Tk name *pathName*, the following methods are supported:

pathname cget *-option*
> Return the current value of option *option*.

pathname component
> Return a list of the well-known components.

pathname component name command [arg...]
> Invoke the given command *command* as a method on the component called *name*, optionally with additional arguments.

pathname configure
> Return a list describing all of the available options.

pathname configure *-option*
> Return the current value of option *option*.

pathname configure *-option* value...
> Set the value of option *option* to *value*. Multiple option-value pairs can be supplied.

The *cget* and *configure* commands work just like the corresponding Tk widget commands.

Protected Methods

These methods are used in the implementation of a mega-widget:

```
itk_component add
[-protected] [-private] [--]
```

```
symbolicName {
    widget pathName [arg...]
} [ {
    ignore -option...
    keep  -option...
    rename -option -newName resourceClass resourceClass
    usual [tag]
} ]
```

Commands in this format create a widget and register it as a mega-widget component. The optional block containing *ignore*, *keep*, *rename*, and *usual* commands
controls how the configuration options for this component are merged into the
master option list for the mega-widget.

Ignore removes one or more configuration options from the composite list (the
default behavior). Keep integrates one or more configuration options into the
composite list, keeping them the same. Rename integrates the configuration
option into the composite list with a different name. Usual finds the usual option
handling commands for the specified tag name and executes them.

itk_option add optName...
> Add an option that was previously ignored back into the master option
> list.

itk_option remove name...
> Remove an option that was previously merged into the master option list.

itk_option define -option resourceName resourceClass init
[configBody]
> Define a new configuration option for a mega-widget class.

itk_initialize [-option value ...]
> Called when a mega-widget is constructed to initialize the master option
> list.

Protected Variables

The following variables can be accessed within a mega-widget class:

itk_option(*symbolicName*)
> An array element containing the Tk window pathname for the compo-
> nent named *symbolicName*.

itk_interior
> Contains the name of the top-level widget or frame within a mega-widget
> that acts as a container for new components.

itk_option(*-option*)
> An array element containing the current value of the configuration option
> named *option*.

Alphabetical Summary of Commands

usual

usual tag [*commands*]

Query or set "usual" option-handling commands for a widget in class *tag*.

CHAPTER 9

Tix

Tix, written by Ioi Lam, is not part of the core Tcl/Tk package, but can be obtained for free at *http://www.neosoft.com/tcl/*. This chapter covers Version 4.1.0.*

Tix Overview

Tix, which stands for the Tk interface extension, adds an object-oriented framework for defining new widget types from existing widget types. Instances of these new widget types are called *mega-widgets*. Tix includes over 40 predefined mega-widget classes and several commands for designing new ones. Figure 9-1 shows some examples of the mega-widgets added by Tix.

Tix also adds a few new standard widgets, commands for communicating with the Motif window manager, a form-based geometry manager, and two new image types: `compound` and `pixmap`.

Tix scripts are usually run using the supplied *tixwish* command interpreter. The command-line arguments for *tixwish* are the same as for Tk's *wish*. Tix can also be dynamically loaded into a running Tcl interpreter using the command:

```
package require Tix
```

if the system is properly configured for dynamic loading.

Special Variables

The following global variables are defined by Tix:

`tix_library`	Directory containing the Tix script library
`tix_patchLevel`	Current patch level of Tix extension

---

* At the time of writing, the Tix web site at *http://www.xpi.com/tix* was down due to lack of funding.

205

Figure 9–1: Examples of some of the Tix mega-widgets

| `tix_release` | Release level of the Tix extension |
| `tix_version` | Current version of Tix extension |

Group Listing of Tix Commands

This section briefly lists all Tix commands, grouped logically by function.

Mega-widgets

tixBalloon	Create a tixBalloon mega-widget.
tixButtonBox	Create a tixButtonBox mega-widget.
tixCheckList	Create a tixCheckList mega-widget.
tixComboBox	Create a tixComboBox mega-widget.
tixControl	Create a tixControl mega-widget.
tixDialogShell	Create a tixDialogShell mega-widget.
tixDirList	Create a tixDirList mega-widget.
tixDirSelectBox	Create a tixDirSelectBox mega-widget.
tixDirSelectDialog	Create a tixDirSelectDialog mega-widget.
tixDirTree	Create a tixDirTree mega-widget.
tixExFileSelectBox	Create a tixExFileSelectBox mega-widget.
tixExFileSelectDialog	Create a tixExFileSelectDialog mega-widget.
tixFileComboBox	Create a tixFileComboBox mega-widget.
tixFileEntry	Create a tixFileEntry mega-widget.
tixFileSelectBox	Create a tixFileSelectBox mega-widget.
tixFileSelectDialog	Create a tixFileSelectDialog mega-widget.
tixLabelEntry	Create a tixLabelEntry mega-widget.
tixLabelFrame	Create a tixLabelFrame mega-widget.
tixLabelWidget	Create a tixLabelWidget mega-widget.
tixListNoteBook	Create a tixListNoteBook mega-widget.
tixMeter	Create a tixMeter mega-widget.
tixNoteBook	Create a tixNoteBook mega-widget.

tixOptionMenu	Create a tixOptionMenu mega-widget.
tixPanedWindow	Create a tixPanedWindow mega-widget.
tixPopupMenu	Create a tixPopupMenu mega-widget.
tixPrimitive	Create a tixPrimitive mega-widget.
tixScrolledGrid	Create a tixScrolledGrid mega-widget.
tixScrolledHList	Create a tixScrolledHList mega-widget.
tixScrolledListBox	Create a tixScrolledListBox mega-widget.
tixScrolledTList	Create a tixScrolledTList mega-widget.
tixScrolledText	Create a tixScrolledText mega-widget.
tixScrolledWidget	Create a tixScrolledWidget mega-widget.
tixScrolledWindow	Create a tixScrolledWindow mega-widget.
tixSelect	Create a tixSelect mega-widget.
tixShell	Create a tixShell mega-widget.
tixStackWindow	Create a tixStackWindow mega-widget.
tixStdButtonBox	Create a tixStdButtonBox mega-widget.
tixStdDialogShell	Create a tixStdDialogShell mega-widget.
tixTree	Create a tixTree mega-widget.
tixVStack	Create a tixVStack mega-widget.
tixVTree	Create a tixVTree mega-widget.

Standard Widgets

tixGrid	Create a tixGrid widget.
tixHList	Create a tixHList widget.
tixInputOnly	Create a tixInputOnly widget.
tixNBFrame	Create a tixNBFrame widget.
tixTList	Create a tixTList widget.

Core Commands

tix	Access the Tix application context.
tixCallMethod	Call method of derived class.
tixChainMethod	Call method of superclass.
tixClass	Declare a new Tix class.
tixDescendants	Get descendants of a widget.
tixDestroy	Destroy a Tix class object.
tixDisableAll	Disable a widget and its descendants.
tixDisplayStyle	Create a style for display items.
tixEnableAll	Enable a widget and its descendants.
tixForm	Communicate with the tixForm geometry manager.
tixGetBoolean	Get the boolean value of a string.
tixGetInt	Get the integer value of a string.
tixMwm	Communicate with the Motif window manager.
tixPushGrab	Set a grab on a window and push it on the grab stack.
tixPopGrab	Release a grab on a window and pop it off the grab stack.
tixWidgetClass	Declare a new Tix widget class.

Tix Mega-widget Overview

Tix mega-widgets are created and manipulated in the same manner as standard Tk widgets. Options can be set both at creation or with the widget's *configure* method. All mega-widgets let you specify option values using the Tk options database and query option values with the *cget* method.

The widgets that are used to compose a mega-widget can be standard widgets or other mega-widgets. Each of these subwidgets is identified by a unique name defined in the mega-widget's API. All mega-widgets support the *subwidget* method to directly access their subwidgets. This method has the form:

```
pathName subwidget subwidget [method [args ...]]
```

where *subwidget* is the unique name given to the subwidget by the mega-widget. When the *method* argument is omitted, the widget pathname of the subwidget is returned. Otherwise, the method *method* of the subwidget is called with any optional arguments and the results returned. For example, to change the background color of the entry widget contained in the tixControl mega-widget .c, one would use this code:

```
.c subwidget entry configure -bg white
```

The subwidget root is present in all mega-widgets and is the equivalent to the name of the created mega-widget (i.e., the *pathName* argument to the mega-widget creation command). It is the base container upon which each mega-widget is built and is almost always either a frame or top-level widget.

The object-oriented framework for defining a mega-widget class supports inheritance from another mega-widget class. The class being inherited from is called the *superclass* of the class being defined. The mega-widget class tixPrimitive is at the top of the mega-widget class hierarchy for the classes supplied with Tix. All other classes are descendants of tixPrimitive. A mega-widget inherits all the commands, options, and subwidgets of its superclass.

Tix Mega-widgets

This section describes the predefined mega-widget classes that are present in the Tix extension. For options that are equivalent to the standard Tk widget options, only the names are listed. Refer to the "Standard Widget Options" section of Chapter 3, *Tk Core Commands*, for the full definition of these options. Since almost all mega-widget classes are derived from another mega-widget class, it is important to refer to the description of the superclass to see the full API of a mega-widget class. Inherited commands, options, and subwidgets are sometimes listed for a mega-widget class when they are overridden or are an integral part of the mega-widget's function.

Balloon

tixBalloon pathName `[option value...]`

The *tixBalloon* command creates a new tixBalloon mega-widget named *pathName*. The `tixBalloon` class is derived from the `tixShell` class. A tixBalloon widget can be bound to one or more widgets so that when the mouse cursor is inside the target widget, a window pops up with a descriptive message. In addition, a message can be displayed in a connected status bar.

Widget-Specific Options

-initwait `milliseconds`   `(initWait, InitWait)`

How long the balloon should wait after the mouse cursor enters an associated widget before popping up the balloon message. If the mouse cursor leaves the widget before this time has elapsed, no message is popped up.

-state `state`   `(state, State)`

Which help messages should be displayed. Valid values for *state* are `both` (balloon and status bar), `balloon` (balloon only), `status` (status bar only), and `none` (display no message).

-statusbar `pathName`   `(statusBar, StatusBar)`

Which widget to use as the status bar of the balloon. Any widget that supports a *-text* configuration option can be a status bar.

Subwidgets

`label`

The label widget containing the arrow bitmap in the pop-up window.

`message`

The message widget that shows the descriptive message in the pop-up window.

Methods

pathName `bind` *window* `[option value...]`

Arrange for the tixBalloon widget to be invoked when the mouse pointer enters the widget *window*. The available options are as follows:

-balloonmsg `string`

String to show in the pop-up window.

-statusmsg `string`

String to show on the status bar.

-msg `string`

String to show in both the pop-up window and status bar. This option has the lowest precedence.

pathName `unbind` *window*

Cancel the tixBalloon widget's binding to *window*.

Example

```
label .status -relief sunken -bd 1 -width 40
button .btn1 -text Exit -command exit
tixBalloon .balloon1 -statusbar .status
.balloon1 bind .btn1 -balloonmsg "Exit Application" \
    -statusmsg {Press this button to exit the applications}
pack .btn1 .status
```

ButtonBox

tixButtonBox `pathName` [`option value...`]

The *tixButtonBox* command creates a new tixButtonBox mega-widget named `pathName`. The `tixButtonBox` class is derived from the `tixPrimitive` class. It serves as a container widget for button widgets, most commonly in dialogs.

Widget-Specific Options

-orientation `orientation`   (`orientation`, `Orientation`)
> Orientation of the button subwidgets, either `horizontal` (the default) or `vertical`.

-padx `size`   (`padX`, `Pad`)
> Horizontal padding between two neighboring button subwidgets.

-pady `size`   (`padY`, `Pad`)
> Vertical padding between two neighboring button subwidgets.

-state `state`   (`state`, `State`)
> State of all the button subwidgets, either `normal` or `disabled`.

Methods

`pathName` *add* `buttonName` [`option value...`]
> Add a new button subwidget with name `buttonName` into the box. Options are those valid for a normal button widget.

`pathName` *invoke* `buttonName`
> Invoke the button subwidget `buttonName`.

CheckList

tixCheckList `pathName` [`option value...`]

The *tixCheckList* command creates a new tixCheckList mega-widget named `pathName`. The `tixCheckList` class is derived from the `tixTree` class. It displays a hierarchical list of items that can be selected by the user. The status of an item can be one of four possible values: on (indicated by a check bitmap), off (indicated by a cross bitmap), default (indicated by a gray box bitmap), or none (no bitmap). Items with on, off, and default status may be selected. The default status for an item is none.

Widget-Specific Options

-browsecmd tclCommand   (browseCmd, BrowseCmd)
>   Command to call whenever the user browses an entry (usually by a single click). The pathname of the entry is appended as an argument.

-command tclCommand   (command, Command)
>   Command to call whenever the user invokes an entry (usually by a double click). The pathname of the entry is appended as an argument.

-radio boolean   (radio, Radio)
>   Whether only one item at a time can be selected.

Subwidgets

hlist
>   The tixHList mega-widget that displays the tixCheckList. Entries to the tix-CheckList are added directly to the hlist subwidget. Entries must be display items of type imagetext. Once an entry is added, the *tixCheckList setstatus* command should be called to set the entry's status:

```
tixCheckList .c
.c subwidget hlist add choice1 -itemtype imagetext
    -text "Choice 1"
.c setstatus choice1 on
```

hsb
>   The horizontal scrollbar widget.

vsb
>   The vertical scrollbar widget.

Methods

pathName getselection [status]
>   Return a list of items whose status is *status* (default is on).

pathName getstatus entryPath
>   Return the current status of *entryPath*.

pathName setstatus entryPath status
>   Set the status of *entryPath* to be *status*.

Example

```
tixCheckList .clist -scrollbar auto
set hlist [.clist subwidget hlist]
foreach attr {Bold Italic Underline} {
    $hlist add $attr -itemtype imagetext -text $attr
    .clist setstatus $attr off
}
.clist setstatus Bold on
pack .clist
```

ComboBox

tixComboBox pathName [*option value...*]

The *tixComboBox* command creates a new tixComboBox mega-widget named `pathName`. The `tixComboBox` class is derived from the `tixLabelWidget` class. It provides an entry widget whose value is connected to the selected item of a listbox widget.

The tixComboBox supports two selection modes with the *-selectmode* option. When the mode is `immediate`, the current value is changed immediately when the user enters a keystroke in the entry subwidgets or clicks (or drags over) an item in the listbox. When the mode is `browse`, the current value is not changed until the user presses the Return key or double-clicks an item in the listbox. The selected item in the listbox or what the user has typed so far is made the temporary value (see the *-selection* option). If the user presses the Escape key, the string displayed in the entry is changed back to the current value.

Widget-Specific Options

-anchor anchorPos (anchor, Anchor)
How the string in the entry subwidget should be aligned.

-arrowbitmap bitmap (arrowBitmap, ArrowBitmap)
Bitmap to use for arrow button beside the entry subwidget.

-browsecmd tclCommand (browseCmd, BrowseCmd)
Command to be called when the selection mode is `browse` and the temporary value has changed.

-command tclCommand (command, Command)
Command to be called when *tixComboBox* is invoked or when its current value is changed.

-crossbitmap bitmap (crossBitmap, CrossBitmap)
Bitmap to use in cross button to the left of the entry subwidget.

-disablecallback boolean (disableCallback, DisableCallback)
Whether callbacks (specified by the *-command* option) are disabled.

-dropdown boolean (dropDown, DropDown)
Whether the listbox should be in a drop-down window.

-editable boolean (editable, Editable)
Whether user is allowed to type into the entry subwidget.

-fancy boolean (fancy, Fancy)
Whether cross and tick button subwidgets should be shown.

-grab grabPolicy (grab, Grab)
Grab policy for listbox when in a drop-down window. Valid values are `global` (default), `local`, or `none`.

-historylimit integer   (historyLimit, HistoryLimit)
How many previous user inputs are remembered in history list.

-history boolean   (history, History)
Whether to store previous user inputs in a history list.

-label string   (label, Label)
String to use as label for the tixComboBox.

-labelside position   (labelSide, LabelSide)
Where to position the tixComboBox label. Valid values are top, left, right, bottom, none, or acrosstop.

-listcmd tclCommand   (listCmd, ListCmd)
Command to call whenever the listbox is dropped down.

-listwidth tclCommand   (listWidth, ListWidth)
Width for listbox subwidget.

-prunehistory boolean   (pruneHistory, PruneHistory)
Whether previous duplicate user inputs should be pruned from history list.

-selection tclCommand   (selection, Selection)
The temporary value of the tixComboBox when the selection mode is browse.

-selectmode mode   (selectMode, SelectMode)
The selection mode of the tixComboBox. Valid values are browse and immediate.

-state state   (state, State)
Current state of the tixComboBox. Valid values are normal and disabled.

-tickbitmap bitmap   (tickBitmap, TickBitmap)
Bitmap to display in tick button to the left of the entry subwidget.

-validatecmd tclCommand   (validateCmd, ValidateCmd)
Command to call when the current value of the tixComboBox is about to change. The candidate new value is appended as an argument. The command should return the value it deems valid.

-value string   (value, Value)
The current value of the tixComboBox.

-variable varName   (variable, Variable)
Global variable that should be set to track the value of the tixComboBox. Direct changes to the variable will also change the value of the tixComboBox.

Subwidgets

arrow

The down arrow button widget.

cross

The cross button widget (when *-fancy* is set).

entry

The entry widget that shows the current value.

label

The label widget.

listbox

The listbox widget that holds the list of possible values.

slistbox

The tixScrolledListBox widget.

tick

The tick button widget (when *-fancy* is set).

Methods

pathName addhistory `string`

Add `string` to the beginning of the listbox.

pathName appendhistory

Append `string` to the end of the listbox.

pathName flash

Flash the tixComboBox by alternating between active and normal colors.

pathName insert `index string`

Insert `string` into the listbox at specified index.

pathName pick `index`

Change the current value to that of the item at `index` in the listbox.

Example

```
tixComboBox .cb -label Encoding: -dropdown true -editable false \
    -options { listbox.height 4 label.width 10 label.anchor w }
foreach type { Latin1 Latin2 Latin3 Latin4 Cyrillic Arabic Greek } {
    .cb insert end $type
}
tixSetSilent .cb Latin1
pack .cb
```

Control

tixControl `pathName` [`option value...`]

The *tixControl* command creates a new tixControl mega-widget named `pathName`. The `tixControl` class is derived from the `tixPrimitive` class. The tixControl widget, also known as a spinbox, is generally used to control a denumerable value. The user can adjust the value by pressing the two arrow buttons or by entering the value directly into the entry.

The tixControl supports two selection modes with the *-selectmode* option. When the mode is `immediate`, the current value is changed immediately when the user enters a keystroke. When the mode is `normal`, the current value is not changed until the user presses the Return key. If the user presses the Escape key, the string displayed in the entry is changed back to the current value.

Widget-Specific Options

-allowempty boolean   (allowEmpty, AllowEmpty)
   Whether an empty string is a valid input value.

-autorepeat boolean   (autoRepeat, AutoRepeat)
   Whether increment and decrement buttons should autorepeat when held down.

-command tclCommand   (command, Command)
   Command to call when the current value is changed. The value is appended as an argument.

-decrcmd tclCommand   (decrCmd, DecrCmd)
   Command to call when the user presses the decrement button. The current value is appended as an argument. The return value is made the new current value.

-disablecallback boolean   (disableCallback, DisableCallback)
   Whether callbacks (specified by the *-command* option) are disabled.

-disabledforeground color   (disabledForeground,
                                           DisabledForeground)
   Color to use for the foreground of the entry subwidget when the tixControl widget is disabled.

-incrcmd tclCommand   (incrCmd, IncrCmd)
   Command to call when the user presses the increment button. The current value is appended as an argument. The return value is made the new current value.

-initwait milliseconds   (initWait, InitWait)
   How long to wait before entering autorepeat mode.

-integer boolean   (integer, Integer)
   Whether only integer values are allowed.

-label string   (label, Label)
   String to display as the label of the tixControl widget.

-labelside position   (labelSide, LabelSide)
   Where to position the tixControl label. Valid values are top, left, right, bottom, none, or acrosstop.

-max value   (max, Max)
> Upper-limit value of the tixControl. If set to the empty string, there is no limit.

-min value   (min, Min)
> Lower-limit value of the tixControl. If set to the empty string, there is no limit.

-repeatrate milliseconds   (repeatRate, RepeatRate)
> Time between increments or decrements when in autorepeat mode.

-selectmode mode   (selectMode, SelectMode)
> The selection mode of the tixControl. Valid values are normal and immediate.

-state state   (state, State)
> Current state of the tixControl. Valid values are normal and disabled.

-step value   (step, Step)
> How much the value should be incremented or decremented when the user presses the increment or decrement buttons.

-validatecmd tclCommand   (validateCmd, ValidateCmd)
> Command to call when the current value of the tixControl is about to change. The candidate new value is appended as an argument. The command should return the value it deems valid.

-value value   (value, Value)
> The current value of the tixControl.

-variable varName   (variable, Variable)
> Global variable that should be set to track the value of the tixControl. Direct changes to the variable will also change the value of the tix-Control.

Subwidgets

decr
> The decrement button widget.

entry
> The entry widget that shows the current value.

incr
> The increment button widget.

label
> The label widget.

Methods

pathName decr
> Decrement the current value of the tixControl.

pathName incr
> Increment the current value of the tixControl.

pathName invoke
> Flash the tixControl by alternating between active and normal colors.

pathName update
> Update the current value to whatever the user has typed in the entry sub-widget.

Example

```
tixControl .ctl -label "Point Size:" -integer true \
    -variable fontsize -min 1 -max 30
pack .ctl
```

DialogShell

tixDialogShell pathName [*option value...*]

The *tixDialogShell* command creates a new tixDialogShell mega-widget named *pathName*. The `tixDialogShell` class is derived from the `tixShell` class. It is used as a superclass for more functional dialog mega-widgets.

Widget-Specific Options

-minheight tclCommand   (minHeight, MinHeight)
> The minimum height of the dialog for resizing.

-minwidth tclCommand   (minWidth, MinWidth)
> The minimum width of the dialog for resizing.

-transient tclCommand   (transient, Transient)
> Whether dialog window should be a transient window.

Methods

pathName center [*window*]
> Arrange for the dialog's position on the screen to be centered over *window* (defaults to dialog's parent). The position is adjusted to make sure the dialog is fully visible.

pathName popdown
> Withdraw the dialog from the screen.

pathName popup [*window*]
> Pop up the dialog on the screen, centered on *window* (defaults to dialog's parent).

DirList

tixDirList pathName [option value...]

The *tixDirList* command creates a new tixDirList mega-widget named *path-Name*. The tixDirList class is derived from the tixScrolledHList class. It displays a list of the subdirectories and parent directory of a target directory. The user can choose one of the directories or change to another directory.

Widget-Specific Options

-browsecmd tclCommand   (browseCmd, BrowseCmd)
> Command to call whenever the user browses on a directory (usually by a single click). The directory is appended as an argument.

-command tclCommand   (command, Command)
> Command to call whenever the user activates a directory (usually by a double click). The directory is appended as an argument.

-dircmd tclCommand   (dirCmd, DirCmd)
> Command to call when a directory listing is needed. Two arguments are appended: the name of the directory to be listed and a boolean that signifies whether hidden subdirectories should be listed. The return values should be the list of subdirectories in the given directory. If this option is not specified, the default is to read the directory as a Unix directory.

-disablecallback boolean   (disableCallback, DisableCallback)
> Whether callbacks (*-command*) are disabled.

-showhidden boolean   (showHidden, ShowHidden)
> Whether hidden directories should be shown.

-root directory   (root, Root)
> Name of the root directory.

-rootname string   (rootName, RootName)
> Text string to display as the root directory. Default is same as *-root* option.

-value directory   (value, Value)
> Name of the current directory displayed.

Subwidgets

hlist
> The tixHList mega-widget that displays the directory list.

hsb
> The horizontal scrollbar widget.

vsb
> The vertical scrollbar widget.

Methods

pathName *chdir* *directory*
> Change the current directory to *directory*.

DirSelectBox

tixDirSelectBox *pathName* [*option value...*]

The *tixDirSelectBox* command creates a new tixDirSelectBox mega-widget named *pathName*. The `tixDirSelectBox` class is derived from the `tix-Primitive` class. It combines a tixFileComboBox with a tixDirList to provide a method for a user to select a directory by both keyboard entry and listbox selection.

Widget-Specific Options

-command *tclCommand*   (command, Command)
> Command to call when the current directory value is changed. The value is appended as an argument.

-disablecallback *boolean*   (disableCallback, DisableCallback)
> Whether callbacks (*-command*) are disabled.

-value *directory*   (value, Value)
> Name of the current directory displayed.

Subwidgets

`dircbx`
> The tixFileComboBox mega-widget.

`dirlist`
> The tixDirList mega-widget.

DirSelectDialog

tixDirSelectDialog *pathName* [*option value...*]

The *tixDirSelectDialog* command creates a new tixDirSelectDialog mega-widget named *pathName*. The `tixDirSelectDialog` class is derived from the `tixDialogShell` class. It presents a tixDirSelectBox in a pop-up dialog window.

Widget-Specific Options

-command *tclCommand*   (command, Command)
> Command to call when the user chooses a directory in the dialog box. The complete pathname of the directory is appended as an argument.

Subwidgets

`dirbox`
> The tixDirSelectBox mega-widget.

cancel

> The Cancel button widget. Invoking this button pops down the dialog with no choice being made.

ok

> The OK button widget. Invoking this button pops down the dialog and makes the current selected directory the user's choice.

DirTree

tixDirTree pathName [*option value...*]

The *tixDirTree* command creates a new tixDirTree mega-widget named *pathName*. The tixDirTree class is derived from the tixVTree class. It displays a tree-style list of directories and their subdirectories for the user to choose from.

Widget-Specific Options

-browsecmd tclCommand   (browseCmd, BrowseCmd)
> Command to call whenever the user browses on a directory (usually by a single click). The directory is appended as an argument.

-command tclCommand   (command, Command)
> Command to call whenever the user activates a directory (usually by a double click). The directory is appended as an argument.

-dircmd tclCommand   (dirCmd, DirCmd)
> Command to call when a directory listing is needed. Two arguments are appended: the name of the directory to be listed and a boolean that signifies whether hidden subdirectories should be listed. The return values should be the list of subdirectories in the given directory. If this option is not specified, the default is to read the directory as a Unix directory.

-disablecallback boolean   (disableCallback, DisableCallback)
> Whether callbacks (*-command*) are disabled.

-showhidden boolean   (showHidden, ShowHidden)
> Whether hidden directories should be shown.

-value directory   (value, Value)
> Name of the current directory displayed.

Subwidgets

hlist
> The tixHList mega-widget that displays the directory list.

hsb
> The horizontal scrollbar widget.

vsb
> The vertical scrollbar widget.

Methods

pathName *chdir* `directory`
> Change the current directory to `directory`.

ExFileSelectBox

tixExFileSelectBox `pathName` [`option value...`]

The *tixExFileSelectBox* command creates a new tixExFileSelectBox mega-widget named `pathName`. The `tixExFileSelectBox` class is derived from the `tixPrimitive` class. It provides a method for a user to select a file similar to the style used in Microsoft Windows.

Widget-Specific Options

-browsecmd `tclCommand`   (browseCmd, BrowseCmd)
> Command to call whenever the user browses on a file (usually by a single click). The filename is appended as an argument.

-command `tclCommand`   (command, Command)
> Command to call whenever the user activates a file (usually by a double click). The filename is appended as an argument.

-dialog `dialog`   (dialog, Dialog)
> Dialog box that contains this tixExFileSelectBox widget (internal use only).

-dircmd `tclCommand`   (dirCmd, DirCmd)
> Command to call when a file listing is needed. Three arguments are appended: the name of the directory to be listed, a list of file patterns, and a boolean that signifies whether hidden files should be listed. The return value should be a list of files in the given directory. If this option is not specified, the default is to read the directory as a Unix directory.

-directory `directory`   (directory, Directory)
> The current directory whose files and subdirectories are displayed.

-disablecallback `boolean`   (disableCallback, DisableCallback)
> Whether callbacks (*-command*) are disabled.

-filetypes `fileTypes`   (fileTypes, FileTypes)
> List of file types that can be selected from the "List Files of Type" tix-ComboBox subwidget. Each item is a list of two items: a list of file patterns and a description (e.g., `{{*.c *.h} {C source files}}`).

-showhidden `boolean`   (showHidden, ShowHidden)
> Whether hidden files and subdirectories should be shown.

-pattern `pattern`   (pattern, Pattern)
> List of file patterns to match with the files in the current directory.

-value `fileName`   (value, Value)
> Name of the currently selected file.

Subwidgets

cancel
> The Cancel button widget.

dir
> The tixComboBox mega-widget for the current directory.

dirlist
> The tixDirList mega-widget for listing directories.

file
> The tixComboBox mega-widget for the current file.

filelist
> The tixScrolledListBox mega-widget for listing files.

hidden
> The checkbutton widget for toggling display of hidden files.

ok
> The OK button widget.

types
> The tixComboBox mega-widget for selecting file filter types.

Methods

pathName filter
> Force refiltering of listed filenames according to the *-pattern* option.

pathName invoke
> Force the widget to perform actions as if the user had pressed the OK button.

ExFileSelectDialog

tixExFileSelectDialog pathName [*option value...*]

The *tixExFileSelectDialog* command creates a new tixExFileSelectDialog mega-widget named *pathName*. The tixExFileSelectDialog class is derived from the tixDialogShell class. It simply presents a tixExFileSelectBox mega-widget in a dialog.

Widget-Specific Options

-command tclCommand   (command, Command)
> Command to call when the user chooses a file (clicks the OK button). The name of the chosen file is appended as an argument.

Subwidgets

fsbox
> The tixExFileSelectBox mega-widget.

FileComboBox

tixFileComboBox pathName [option value...]

The *tixFileComboBox* command creates a new tixFileComboBox mega-widget named *pathName*. The tixFileComboBox class is derived from the tix-Primitive class. It provides a combo box for entering file and directory names.

Widget-Specific Options

-command tclCommand   (command, Command)
 Command to be called when *tixFileComboBox* is invoked or when its current value is changed. A list describing the file is appended as an argument. The first element of the list is the absolute pathname to the file, the second element is the directory part file's pathname, and the third element is the base filename.

-defaultfile fileName   (defaultFile, DefaultFile)
 If the value entered into the tixFileComboBox is a directory, *fileName* is appended to the value before calling the associated command.

-directory directory   (directory, Directory)
 Set the current working directory for the tixFileComboBox to *directory*.

-text fileName   (text, Text)
 Change the value of the tixFileComboBox to *fileName*. The associated command is not invoked.

Subwidgets

combo
 The tixComboBox mega-widget.

Methods

pathName invoke
 Invoke the tixFileComboBox.

FileEntry

tixFileEntry pathName [option value...]

The *tixFileEntry* command creates a new tixFileEntry mega-widget named *pathName*. The tixFileEntry class is derived from the tixLabel-Widget class. It provides an entry box for a user to enter a filename, along with a button that will pop up a file selection dialog.

The *tixFileEntry* supports two selection modes with the *-selectmode* option. When the mode is immediate, the current value is changed immediately when the user enters a keystroke. When the mode is normal, the current value is not changed until the user presses the Return key.

Widget-Specific Options

-activatecmd tclCommand   (activateCmd, ActivateCmd)
　　Command to call when user activates the button subwidget. This com-
　　mand is called before the file dialog is popped up.

-command tclCommand   (command, Command)
　　Command to call when the current value of the tixFileEntry is changed.
　　The filename is appended as an argument.

-dialogtype dialogClass   (dialogType, DialogType)
　　The type of file selection dialog that should be popped up when the user
　　invokes the button subwidget. Valid values are tixFileSelectDialog
　　and tixExFileSelectDialog.

-disablecallback boolean   (disableCallback, DisableCallback)
　　Whether callbacks (*-command*) are disabled.

-disabledforeground color   (disabledForeground,
　　　　　　　　　　　　　　　　　　　　　　　　　DisabledForeground)
　　Foreground color for entry subwidget when the tixFileEntry is disabled.

-filebitmap bitmap   (fileBitmap, FileBitmap)
　　Bitmap to display in the button subwidget.

-label string   (label, Label)
　　String to display as the label of the tixFileEntry.

-labelside position   (labelSide, LabelSide)
　　Where to position the tixFileEntry label. Valid values are top, left,
　　right, bottom, none, or acrosstop.

-selectmode mode   (selectMode, SelectMode)
　　The selection mode of the tixFileEntry. Valid values are normal and
　　immediate.

-state state   (state, State)
　　Current state of the tixFileEntry. Valid values are normal and dis-
　　abled.

-validatecmd tclCommand   (validateCmd, ValidateCmd)
　　Command to call when the current value of the tixFileEntry is about to
　　change. The candidate new value is appended as an argument. The
　　command should return the value it deems valid.

-value value
　　The current value of the tixFileEntry.

-variable varName
　　Global variable that should be set to track the value of the tixFileEntry.
　　Direct changes to the variable will also change the value of the tixFile-
　　Entry.

Subwidgets

button
> The button widget for popping up a file selection dialog.

entry
> The entry widget for entering a filename.

Methods

pathName invoke
> Force the tixFileEntry to act as if the user has pressed the Return key inside the entry subwidget.

pathName filedialog [*method* [*args*]]
> If no additional arguments are given, the pathname of the file selection dialog associated with the tixFileEntry is returned. When additional arguments are given, they translate to a method call on the file selection dialog.

pathName update
> Update the current value of the tixFileEntry to the current contents of the entry subwidget. Useful only in normal selection mode.

FileSelectBox

tixFileSelectBox pathName [*option value...*]

The *tixFileSelectBox* command creates a new tixFileSelectBox mega-widget named *pathName*. The tixFileSelectBox class is derived from the tix-Primitive class. It provides a method for a user to select a file similar to the style used in Motif.

Widget-Specific Options

-browsecmd tclCommand   (browseCmd, BrowseCmd)
> Command to call whenever the user browses a file (usually by a single click). The filename is appended as an argument.

-command tclCommand   (command, Command)
> Command to call whenever the user activates a file (usually by a double-click). The absolute path of the filename is appended as an argument.

-directory directory   (directory, Directory)
> The current directory whose files and subdirectories are displayed.

-disablecallback boolean   (disableCallback, DisableCallback)
> Whether callbacks (*-command*) are disabled.

-pattern pattern   (pattern, Pattern)
> List of file patterns to match with the files in the current directory.

-value fileName   (value, Value)
> Name of the currently selected file.

`dirlist`
> The tixScrolledListBox mega-widget for listing directories.

`filelist`
> The tixScrolledListBox mega-widget for listing files.

`filter`
> The tixComboBox mega-widget for the filter string.

`selection`
> The tixComboBox mega-widget for the selected file.

Methods

pathName filter
> Force refiltering of listed filenames according to the *-pattern* option.

pathName invoke
> Call the command given by *-command* with the current filename.

FileSelectDialog

tixFileSelectDialog `pathName` [`option value...`]

The *tixFileSelectDialog* command creates a new tixFileSelectDialog mega-widget named `pathName`. The `tixFileSelectDialog` class is derived from the `tixStdDialogShell` class. It simply presents a tixFileSelectBox mega-widget in a dialog.

Widget-Specific Options

-command `tclCommand`   (command, Command)
> Command to call when the user chooses a file (clicks the OK button). The name of the chosen file is appended as an argument.

Subwidgets

`btns`
> The tixStdButtonBox mega-widget containing the OK, Filter, Cancel, and Help button widgets.

`fsbox`
> The tixFileSelectBox mega-widget.

LabelEntry

tixLabelEntry `pathName` [`option value...`]

The *tixLabelEntry* command creates a new tixLabelEntry mega-widget named `pathName`. The `tixLabelEntry` class is derived from the `tixLabel-Widget` class. It provides an entry box with an attached label.

Widget-Specific Options

-disabledforeground color   (disabledForeground,
                                                 DisabledForeground)
> Color to use for the foreground of the entry subwidget when the tix-
> LabelEntry widget is disabled.

-label string   (label, Label)
> String to display as the label of the tixLabelEntry widget.

-labelside position   (labelSide, LabelSide)
> Where to position the tixLabelEntry label. Valid values are top, left,
> right, bottom, none, or acrosstop.

-state state   (state, State)
> Current state of the tixLabelEntry. Valid values are normal and dis-
> abled.

Subwidgets

entry
> The entry subwidget.

label
> The label subwidget.

LabelFrame

tixLabelFrame pathName [option value...]

The *tixLabelFrame* command creates a new tixLabelFrame mega-widget
named *pathName*. The tixLabelFrame class is derived from the tix-
LabelWidget class. It provides a labeled frame for containing other widgets,
which should be children of the frame subwidget.

Widget-Specific Options

-label string   (label, Label)
> String to display as the label of the tixLabelFrame widget.

-labelside position   (labelSide, LabelSide)
> Where to position the tixLabelFrame label. Valid values are top, left,
> right, bottom, none, or acrosstop.

-padx amount   (padX, PadX)
> Amount of horizontal padding around the frame subwidget.

-pady amount   (padY, PadY)
> Amount of vertical padding around the frame subwidget.

Subwidgets

frame
> The frame subwidget, which should be the parent of any widget to be
> contained.

label
> The label subwidget.

Methods

pathName frame [*method* [*args*]]
> Shortcut to subwidget `frame`.

LabelWidget

tixLabelWidget *pathName* [*option value...*]

The *tixLabelWidget* command creates a new tixLabelWidget mega-widget named *pathName*. The `tixLabelWidget` class is derived from the `tix-Primitive` class. Its main purpose is to provide a base class for labeled mega-widgets.

Widget-Specific Options

-label `string`   (label, Label)
> String to display as the label of the tixLabelWidget widget.

-labelside `position`   (labelSide, LabelSide)
> Where to position the tixLabelWidget label. Valid values are `top`, `left`, `right`, `bottom`, `none`, or `acrosstop`.

-padx `amount`   (padX, PadX)
> Amount of horizontal padding around the frame subwidget.

-pady `amount`   (padY, PadY)
> Amount of vertical padding around the frame subwidget.

Subwidgets

`frame`
> The frame subwidget upon which derived mega-widget classes should build.

`label`
> The label subwidget.

ListNoteBook

tixListNoteBook *pathName* [*option value...*]

The *tixListNoteBook* command creates a new tixListNoteBook mega-widget named *pathName*. The `tixListNoteBook` class is derived from the `tixVStack` class. Similar to the tixNoteBook, it allows the user to select one of several *pages* (windows) to be displayed at one time. The user chooses the page to display by selecting its name from an `hlist` subwidget.

Widget-Specific Options

-dynamicgeometry `boolean`   (`dynamicGeometry,`
                                                                  `DynamicGeometry`)

>   Whether the tixListNoteBook should dynamically resize to match the size
>   of the current page. The default is `false`, in which case the size of the
>   tixListNoteBook will match the size of the largest page.

-ipadx `amount`   (`ipadX, Pad`)

>   Amount of internal horizontal padding around the sides of the page sub-
>   widgets.

-ipady `amount`   (`ipady, Pad`)

>   Amount of internal vertical padding around the sides of page subwidgets.

Subwidgets

`hlist`

>   The tixHList mega-widget that displays the names of the pages.

pageName

>   The frame widget of a notebook page as returned by the *add* method.

Methods

pathName add pageName [`option value...`]

>   Add a new page to the tixListNoteBook. The *pageName* option must be
>   the name of an existing entry in the `hlist` subwidget. The pathname of
>   the page's master frame widget is returned. Available options are:

>   *-createcmd* `tclCommand`
>   >   Command to be called the first time a page is to be displayed.

>   *-raisecmd* `tclCommand`
>   >   Command to be called whenever the page is raised by the user.

pathName delete pageName

>   Delete the given page from the tixListNoteBook.

pathName pagecget pageName `option`

>   Similar to the *cget* method, but operates on the page *pageName*.
>   `Option` may have any of the values accepted by the *add* method.

pathName pageconfigure pageName [`option value...`]

>   Similar to the *configure* method, but operates on the page *pageName*.
>   `Option` may have any of the values accepted by the *add* method.

pathName pages

>   Return a list of the names of all the pages.

pathName raise pageName

>   Raise the page *pageName*.

pathName raised

>   Return the name of the currently raised page.

Meter

tixMeter *pathName* [*option value...*]

The *tixMeter* command creates a new tixMeter mega-widget named *path-Name*. The `tixMeter` class is derived from the `tixPrimitive` class. It provides a way to show the progress of a time-consuming background job.

Widget-Specific Options

-fillcolor color   (fillColor, FillColor)
   Color of the progress bar.

-text string   (text, Text)
   Text to place inside the progress bar. Defaults to percentage value specified by the *-value* option.

-value value   (value, Value)
   A real value between 0.0 and 1.0 that specifies the amount of progress.

NoteBook

tixNoteBook *pathName* [*option value...*]

The *tixNoteBook* command creates a new tixNoteBook mega-widget named *pathName*. The `tixNoteBook` class is derived from the `tixVStack` class. It allows the user to select one of several pages (windows) to be displayed at one time. The user chooses the page to display by selecting a tab at the top of the tixNoteBook widget.

Widget-Specific Options

-dynamicgeometry boolean   (dynamicGeometry,
                                                     DynamicGeometry)
   Whether the tixNoteBook should dynamically resize to match the size of the current page. The default is `false`, in which case the size of the tixNoteBook will match the size of the largest page.

-ipadx amount   (ipadX, Pad)
   Amount of internal horizontal padding around the sides of the page subwidgets.

-ipady amount   (ipadY, Pad)
   Amount of internal vertical padding around the sides of the page subwidgets.

Subwidgets

nbframe
   The tixNoteBookFrame that displays the tabs of the notebook. Most of the display options of the page tabs are controlled by this subwidget.

pageName
> The frame widget of a notebook page as returned by the *add* method.

Methods

`pathName` *add* `pageName` [`option value...`]
> Add a new page to the tixNoteBook. The `pageName` option must be the name of an existing entry in the `hlist` subwidget. The pathname of the page's master frame widget is returned. Available options are as follows:

-anchor `anchorPos`
> Specifies how the information in a page's tab (e.g., text or bitmap) should be anchored. Must be one of `n`, `nw`, `w`, `sw`, `s`, `se`, `e`, `ne`, or `center`.

-bitmap `bitmap`
> Bitmap to display in tab.

-createcmd `tclCommand`
> Command to be called the first time a page is to be displayed.

-image `imageName`
> Name of image to display in tab.

-justify `position`
> How multiple lines of text in a tab should be justified. Must be one of `left`, `right`, or `center`.

-label `string`
> Text to display in the tab. Overrides *-image* and *-bitmap*.

-raisecmd `tclCommand`
> Command to be called whenever the page is raised by the user.

-state `state`
> Whether page can be raised by the user. Must be either `normal` or `disabled`.

-underline `index`
> Integer index (starting from 0) of character in text label to underline in the tab. Used by default bindings to set up keyboard traversal of tabs.

-wraplength `chars`
> Maximum line length of text in the tab. If value is 0 or less, no wrapping is done.

`pathName` *delete* `pageName`
> Delete the given page from the tixNoteBook.

`pathName` *pagecget* `pageName` `option`
> Similar to the *cget* method, but operates on the page `pageName`. `Option` may have any of the values accepted by the *add* method.

pathName pageconfigure pageName [option value...]
> Similar to the *configure* method, but operates on the page *pageName*. *Option* may have any of the values accepted by the *add* method.

pathName pages
> Return a list of the names of all the pages.

pathName raise pageName
> Raise the page *pageName*.

pathName raised
> Return the name of the currently raised page.

Example

```
tixNoteBook .nb -ipadx 6 -ipady 6 -options
    { nbframe.backpagecolor gray }
.nb add fonts -label "Fonts" -underline 0
set f1 [frame [.nb subwidget fonts].f]
pack [listbox $f1.lb]
$f1.lb insert end Courier Helvetica Utopia
.nb add colors -label "Colors" -underline 0
set f2 [frame [.nb subwidget colors].f]
pack [listbox $f2.lb]
$f2.lb insert end Red Green Blue
pack .nb $f1 $f2 -expand true -fill both
```

OptionMenu

tixOptionMenu pathName [option value...]

The *tixOptionMenu* command creates a new tixOptionMenu mega-widget named *pathName*. The tixOptionMenu class is derived from the tix-LabelWidget class. It provides a method for the user to select an option from a pop-up menu.

Widget-Specific Options

-command tclCommand   (command, Command)
> Command to call when the current value of the tixOptionMenu is changed. The filename is appended as an argument.

-disablecallback boolean   (disableCallback, DisableCallback)
> Whether callbacks (*-command*) are disabled.

-dynamicgeometry boolean   (dynamicGeometry, DynamicGeometry)
> Whether the size of the menubutton subwidget should change dynamically to match the width of the currently selected menu entry. If false, its width is wide enough to contain the largest entry.

-label string   (label, Label)
> String to display as the label of the tixOptionMenu.

-labelside position   (labelSide, LabelSide)

Where to position the tixOptionMenu label. Valid values are `top`, `left`, `right`, `bottom`, `none`, or `acrosstop`.

-state state   (state, State)

Current state of the tixOptionMenu. Valid values are `normal` and `disabled`.

-value value   (value, Value)

The current value of the tixOptionMenu, which is the name of the menu entry currently displayed in the menubutton subwidget.

-variable varName   (variable, Variable)

Global variable that should be set to track the value of the tixOption-Menu. Direct changes to the variable will also change the value of the tixOptionMenu.

Subwidgets

menu

The menu widget that is popped up when the user presses the menubutton widget.

menubutton

The menubutton widget that displays the current selection.

Methods

pathName add type entryName [*option value...*]

Add a new entry to the tixOptionMenu named *entryName*. *Type* must be either `command` or `separator`. The options are any of the valid options for a menu entry of the given type, except *-command*.

pathName delete entryName

Delete the entry *entryName* from the tixOptionMenu.

pathName disable entryName

Disable the entry *entryName*.

pathName enable entryName

Enable the entry *entryName*.

pathName entrycget entryName option

Similar to the *cget* method, but operates on the entry *entryName*. *Option* may have any of the values accepted by the *add* method.

pathName entryconfigure entryName [*option value...*]

Similar to the *configure* method, but operates on the entry *entryName*. *Option* may have any of the values accepted by the *add* method.

pathName entries

Return a list of the names of all entries in the tixOptionMenu.

PanedWindow

tixPanedWindow pathName [option value...]

The *tixPanedWindow* command creates a new tixPanedWindow mega-widget named `pathName`. The `tixPanedWindow` class is derived from the `tix-Primitive` class.

Widget-Specific Options

-command `tclCommand`   (command, Command)
> Command to call when the panes change their sizes. A list of the new sizes in the order of each pane's creation is appended as an argument.

-dynamicgeometry `boolean`   (dynamicGeometry, DynamicGeometry)
> Whether the size of the tixPanedWindow will dynamically change if the size of any of its panes is changed. If `false`, the size of the tixPaned-Window will increase but not decrease.

-handleactivebg `color`   (handleActiveBg, HandleActiveBg)
> Active background color for the resize handles.

-handlebg `color`   (handleBg, HandleBg)
> Background color for the resize handles.

-height `amount`   (height, Height)
> Desired height for the tixPanedWindow.

-orientation `orientation`   (orientation, Orientation)
> Orientation of the panes. Must be either `vertical` or `horizontal`.

-paneborderwidth `amount`   (paneBorderWidth, PaneBorderWidth)
> Border width of the panes.

-panerelief `relief`   (paneRelief, PaneRelief)
> Border relief of the panes.

-separatoractivebg `color`   (separatorActiveBg, SeparatorActiveBg)
> Active background color of the separators.

-separatorbg `color`   (separatorBg, SeparatorBg)
> Background color of the separators.

-width `amount`   (width, Width)
> Desired width of the tixPanedWindow.

Subwidgets

`paneName`
> The frame widget of pane `paneName` as returned by the *add* method.

Methods

pathName *add* *paneName* [option value...]
> Add a new pane named *paneName*. The frame widget to serve as the master container for the pane is returned. Available options are:

> *-after paneName*
>> Place the pane after the pane named *paneName*.

> *-before paneName*
>> Place the pane before the pane named *paneName*.

> *-expand* factor
>> The weighting factor by which the pane should grow or shrink when the tixPanedWindow is resized. The default is 0.0. If all panes have a 0.0 factor, only the last visible pane is resized.

> *-max* amount
>> The maximum size, in pixels, for the pane.

> *-min* amount
>> The minimum size, in pixels, for the pane.

> *-size* amount
>> Desired size of the pane along the tixPanedWindow's orientation. If not given, the pane's natural default size is used.

pathName *delete* *paneName*
> Remove the pane *paneName* and delete its contents.

pathName *forget* *paneName*
> Remove the pane *paneName* but do not delete its contents, so that it may be added back using the *manage* method.

pathName *manage* *paneName* [option value...]
> Add the pane *paneName* back to those currently managed by the tix-PanedWindow. Available options are the same as for the *add* method.

pathName *panecget* *paneName* option
> Similar to the *cget* method, but operates on the pane *paneName*. *Option* may have any of the values accepted by the *add* method.

pathName *paneconfigure* *paneName* [option value...]
> Similar to the *configure* method, but operates on the pane *paneName*. *Option* may have any of the values accepted by the *add* method.

pathName *panes*
> Return a list of the names of all panes in the tixPanedWindow.

pathName *setsize* *paneName* newSize [direction]
> Set the size of pane *paneName* to *newSize*. *Direction* may be next (the default) or prev and directs the pane to grow or shrink by moving the boundary between itself and the pane to its right or bottom (next) or by moving the pane to its left or top (prev).

PopupMenu

tixPopupMenu pathName [*option value...*]

The *tixPopupMenu* command creates a new tixPopupMenu mega-widget named *pathName*. The tixPopupMenu class is derived from the tixShell class. It provides a replacement for the *tk_popup* command with easier configuration and a menu title.

Widget-Specific Options

-buttons buttonList   (buttons, Buttons)
> A list that specifies the mouse buttons and key modifiers that pop up the menu. Each item is a list with two elements: the button number and a list of key modifiers. For example, {{1 {Control Meta}} {3 {Any}}}. The default is {3 {Any}}.

-postcmd tclCommand   (postCmd, PostCmd)
> Command to call just before the menu is popped up. The x- and y-coordinates of the button event are appended as the final two arguments. The command must return a boolean value to indicate whether the menu should be posted.

-spring boolean   (spring, Spring)
> Whether the menu should automatically pop down when the user releases the mouse button outside the menu without invoking any menu commands. The default is true. If false, the user must press the Escape key to cancel the menu.

-state state   (state, State)
> Current state of the tixPopupMenu. Valid values are normal and disabled. When disabled, the menu will not pop up.

-title string   (title, Title)
> Text for the title of the tixPopupMenu.

Subwidgets

menu
> The menu widget that pops up.

menubutton
> The menubutton widget used for the title.

Methods

pathName bind window [*window...*]
> Arrange for the tixPopupMenu to be bound to the configured button events over the given windows.

pathName post window x y
> Post the tixPopupMenu inside *window* at the coordinates *x, y*.

pathName unbindwindow[*window...*]

Cancel the tixPopupMenu's binding to the given windows.

Primitive

tixPrimitive pathName [*option value...*]

The *tixPrimitive* command creates a new tixPrimitive mega-widget named *pathName*. The tixPrimitive is a virtual base class that provides a root widget that derived mega-widgets use as a base container upon which to build. In fact, *pathName* is used as the pathname of the base widget. Unless overridden by a derived class, this base widget is a frame widget. The only class in the Tix core mega-widgets that overrides this is the tixShell class, which uses a top-level widget for its root.

Widget-Specific Options

The tixPrimitive mega-widget supports the following options, which are simply passed to the underlying root widget. See the *frame* widget command in Chapter 3.

-background	-borderwidth	-cursor
-height	-highlightbackground	-highlightcolor
-highlightthickness	-relief	-takefocus
-width		

The tixPrimitive mega-widget supports the following special option to make it easy for descendant classes to pass options to subwidgets:

-options optionList   (options, Options)

List of resource options and values to apply to mega-widget. Each odd element is the resource specification relative to the mega-widget. Each following even element is its value. This option is mainly used to configure a mega-widget's subwidgets at creation time. For example:

```
tixComboBox .cb -label Color: -dropdown true \
    -options { listbox.height 4 label.width 10 label.anchor e }
```

Subwidgets

root

The base frame widget in which derived mega-widgets should be built. This will equal the *pathName* argument of the mega-widget creation command (e.g., tixPrimitive) and therefore is almost never needed.

ScrolledGrid

tixScrolledGrid pathName [*option value...*]

The *tixScrolledGrid* command creates a new tixScrolledGrid mega-widget named *pathName*. The tixScrolledGrid class is derived from the tixScrolledWidget class. It provides a scrollable tixGrid widget.

Subwidgets

`grid`

> The tixGrid widget that will be scrolled.

`hsb`

> The horizontal scrollbar widget.

`vsb`

> The vertical scrollbar widget.

ScrolledHList

tixScrolledHList pathName [*option value...*]

The *tixScrolledHList* command creates a new tixScrolledHList mega-widget named `pathName`. The `tixScrolledHList` class is derived from the `tixScrolledWidget` class. It provides a scrollable tixHList mega-widget.

Subwidgets

`hlist`

> The tixHList mega-widget that will be scrolled.

`hsb`

> The horizontal scrollbar widget.

`vsb`

> The vertical scrollbar widget.

ScrolledListBox

tixScrolledListBox pathName [*option value...*]

The *tixScrolledListBox* command creates a new tixScrolledListBox mega-widget named `pathName`. The `tixScrolledListBox` class is derived from the `tixScrolledWidget` class. It provides a scrollable listbox widget.

Widget-Specific Options

-browsecmd tclCommand   (browseCmd, BrowseCmd)

> Command to call whenever the user browses an entry (usually by a single click).

-command tclCommand   (command, Command)

> Command to call whenever the user activates an entry (usually by a double click).

-state state   (state, State)

> Current state of the listbox subwidget. Valid values are `normal` and `disabled`.

Subwidgets

listbox
> The listbox widget that will be scrolled.

hsb
> The horizontal scrollbar widget.

vsb
> The vertical scrollbar widget.

ScrolledText

tixScrolledText pathName [option value...]

The *tixScrolledText* command creates a new tixScrolledText mega-widget named *pathName*. The tixScrolledText class is derived from the tixScrolledWidget class. It provides a scrollable text widget.

Subwidgets

text
> The text widget that will be scrolled.

hsb
> The horizontal scrollbar widget.

vsb
> The vertical scrollbar widget.

ScrolledTList

tixScrolledTList pathName [option value...]

The *tixScrolledTList* command creates a new tixScrolledTList mega-widget named *pathName*. The tixScrolledTList class is derived from the tixScrolledWidget class. It provides a scrollable tixTList mega-widget.

Subwidgets

tlist
> The tixTList mega-widget that will be scrolled.

hsb
> The horizontal scrollbar widget.

vsb
> The vertical scrollbar widget.

ScrolledWidget

tixScrolledWidget pathName [option value...]

The *tixScrolledWidget* command creates a new tixScrolledWidget mega-widget named *pathName*. The tixScrolledWidget class provides a virtual base class for deriving mega-widgets that wrap scrollbars around a contained widget.

Widget-Specific Options

-scrollbar policy   (scrollbar, Scrollbar)
　　The display policy for the scrollbars. Valid values for policy are:

　　auto [xPolicy] [yPolicy]
　　　　Scrollbars are shown when needed. XPolicy may be +x or -x, which state that the tixScrolledWidget should always or never show the horizontal scrollbar, respectively. Similarly, yPolicy may be +y or -y for the vertical scrollbar.

　　both
　　　　Always show both scrollbars.

　　none
　　　　Never show either scrollbar.

　　x　　At all times, show only the horizontal scrollbar.

　　y　　At all times, show only the vertical scrollbar.

Subwidgets

hsb
　　The horizontal scrollbar widget.

vsb
　　The vertical scrollbar widget.

ScrolledWindow

tixScrolledWindow pathName [option value...]

The *tixScrolledWindow* command creates a new tixScrolledWindow mega-widget named pathName. The tixScrolledWindow class is derived from the tixScrolledWidget class. It provides a scrollable frame widget in which any arbitrary windows may be placed.

Widget-Specific Options

-expandmode mode   (expandMode, ExpandMode)
　　If mode is expand (the default), the size of the scrolled window will be expanded to fill its containing frame. The size of the scrolled window will not be expanded if mode is the empty string.

-shrink mode   (shrink, Shrink)
　　If mode is x, the width of the scrolled window will be reduced to fit its containing frame. The width of the scrolled window will not be reduced if mode is the empty string (the default).

Subwidgets

window

> The frame widget that will be scrolled and that will serve as the container for other widgets.

hsb

> The horizontal scrollbar widget.

vsb

> The vertical scrollbar widget.

Select

tixSelect pathName [*option value*...]

The *tixSelect* command creates a new tixSelect mega-widget named *path-Name*. The tixSelect class is derived from the tixLabelWidget class. It provides a set of button subwidgets that provide a radiobox or checkbox style of selection options for the user.

Widget-Specific Options

-allowzero boolean   (allowZero, AllowZero)

> Whether the selection can be empty. When **false**, at least one button subwidget must be selected at any time. At creation time, the selection is alway empty no matter what the value of *-allowzero*.

-buttontype type   (buttonType, ButtonType)

> Type of buttons to be used as subwidgets inside the tixSelect mega-widget. The default is the standard Tk button widget.

-command tclCommand   (command, Command)

> Command to call when the current value of the tixSelect mega-widget is changed. Two arguments will be appended: the name of the button sub-widget toggled and a boolean value indicating whether that button is selected.

-disablecallback boolean   (disableCallback, DisableCallback)

> Whether callbacks (*-command*) are disabled.

-label string   (label, Label)

> String to display as the label of the tixSelect mega-widget.

-labelside position   (labelside, Labelside)

> Where to position the label. Valid values are top, left, right, bottom, none, or acrosstop.

-orientation orientation   (orientation, Orientation)

> Orientation of the button subwidgets. Must be either horizontal or vertical. This option can only be set at creation.

-padx amount   (padX, Pad)

> Horizontal padding to add between button subwidgets.

-pady amount   (padY, Pad)
> Vertical padding to add between button subwidgets.

-radio boolean   (radio, Radio)
> Whether only one button subwidget can be selected at any time. This option can only be set at creation.

-selectedbg color   (selectedBg, SelectedBg)
> Background color for all the selected button subwidgets.

-state state   (state, State)
> Current state of the tixSelect mega-widget. Valid values are normal and disabled.

-validatecmd tclCommand   (validateCmd, ValidateCmd)
> Command to call when the current value of the tixSelect mega-widget is about to change. The candidate new value is appended as an argument. The command should return the value it deems valid.

-value value   (value, Value)
> The current value of the tixSelect mega-widget, which is a list of names of the selected button subwidgets.

-variable varName   (variable, Variable)
> Global variable that should be set to track the value of the tixSelect mega-widget. Changes directly to the variable will also change the value of the tixSelect mega-widget.

Subwidgets

label
> The label widget.

buttonName
> The button widget identified by the name *buttonName* as created by the *add* method.

Methods

pathName add buttonName [*option value*...]
> Add a new button subwidget named *buttonName*. Available options are those valid for the type of button selected by *-buttontype*, with the exclusion of *-command* and *-takefocus*.

pathName invoke buttonName
> Invoke the button subwidget named *buttonName*.

Shell

tixShell pathName [*option value*...]

The *tixShell* command creates a new tixShell mega-widget named *pathName*. The tixShell class is derived from the tixPrimitive class. It provides a base class for mega-widgets that need a top-level root window.

Widget-Specific Options

The tixShell mega-widget supports the following options of the top-level widget. See the *toplevel* command in Chapter 3.

-background	*-borderwidth*	*-colormap*
-container	*-cursor*	*-height*
-highlightbackground	*-highlightcolor*	*-highlightthickness*
-relief	*-takefocus*	*-use*
-screen	*-visual*	*-width*

The tixShell mega-widget also supports the following option:

-title `string`   (`title, Title`)
> Text to display in the titlebar (if any) of the top-level window.

Subwidgets

`root`
> The top-level widget.

StackWindow

tixStackWindow pathName [`option value...`]

The *tixStackWindow* command creates a new tixStackWindow mega-widget named `pathName`. The `tixStackWindow` class is derived from the `tix-VStack` class. Similar to the tixNoteBook, it allows the user to select one of several pages (windows) to be displayed at one time. The user chooses the page to display by selecting its name from a tixSelect mega-widget.

Widget-Specific Options

-dynamicgeometry `boolean`   (`dynamicGeometry,`
                                                 `DynamicGeometry`)
> Whether the tixStackWindow should dynamically resize to match the size of the current page. The default is `false`, in which case the size of the tixStackWindow will match the size of the largest page.

-ipadx `amount`   (`ipadX, Pad`)
> Amount of internal horizontal padding around the sides of the page subwidgets.

-ipady `amount`   (`ipadY, Pad`)
> Amount of internal vertical padding around the sides of the page subwidgets.

Subwidgets

`tabs`
> The Stack mega-widget that displays a button for each page.

`pageName`
> The frame widget of a page as returned by the *add* method.

Methods

pathName *add* **pageName** [*option value...*]

Add a new page to the tixStackWindow and a button to select it in the Select subwidget. The **pageName** option will be the name of the page and the button in the Select subwidget. The pathname of the page's master frame widget is returned. Available options are as follows:

-createcmd **tclCommand**

Command to be called the first time a page is to be displayed.

-label **tclCommand**

Text label for the button in the Select subwidget.

-raisecmd **tclCommand**

Command to be called whenever the page is raised by the user.

pathName *delete* **pageName**

Delete the given page from the tixStackWindow.

pathName *pagecget* **pageName** *option*

Similar to the *cget* method, but operates on the page **pageName**. *Option* may have any of the values accepted by the *add* method.

pathName *pageconfigure* **pageName** [*option value...*]

Similar to the *configure* method, but operates on the page **pageName**. *Option* may have any of the values accepted by the *add* method.

pathName *pages*

Return a list of the names of all the pages.

pathName *raise* **pageName**

Raise the page **pageName**.

pathName *raised*

Return the name of the currently raised page.

StdButtonBox

tixStdButtonBox **pathName** [*option value...*]

The *tixStdButtonBox* command creates a new tixStdButtonBox mega-widget named **pathName**. The tixStdButtonBox class is derived from the tixButtonBox class. It adds four predefined buttons (OK, Apply, Cancel, Help) for Motif-like dialog boxes.

Widget-Specific Options

-applycmd **tclCommand**   (applyCmd, ApplyCmd)

Command to call when the Apply button is pressed.

-cancelcmd **tclCommand**   (cancelCmd, CancelCmd)

Command to call when the Cancel button is pressed.

-helpcmd tclCommand   (helpCmd, HelpCmd)
> Command to call when the Help button is pressed.

-okcmd tclCommand   (okCmd, OkCmd)
> Command to call when the OK button is pressed.

Subwidgets

apply
> The Apply button widget.

cancel
> The Cancel button widget.

help
> The Help button widget.

ok
> The OK button widget.

StdDialogShell

tixStdDialogShell pathName [*option value*...]

The *tixStdDialogShell* command creates a new tixStdDialogShell mega-widget named *pathName*. The `tixStdDialogShell` class is derived from the `tixDialogShell` class. It provides a base class for dialog mega-widgets that need a tixStdButtonBox.

Subwidgets

btns
> The tixStdButtonBox mega-widget.

Tree

tixTree pathName [*option value*...]

The *tixTree* command creates a new tixTree mega-widget named *pathName*. The `tixTree` class is derived from the `tixVTree` class. It provides a display of hierarchical data in a tree form. The user can adjust the view of the tree by opening (expanding) or closing (collapsing) parts of the tree.

Widget-Specific Options

-browsecmd tclCommand   (browseCmd, BrowseCmd)
> Command to call whenever the user browses an entry (usually by a single click). The pathname of the entry is appended as an argument.

-closecmd tclCommand   (closeCmd, CloseCmd)
> Command to call whenever an expanded entry needs to be closed. The pathname of the entry is appended as an argument. The default action is to hide all child entries of the specified entry.

-command tclCommand   (command, Command)
  Command to call whenever the user activates an entry (usually by a double click). The pathname of the entry is appended as an argument.

-ignoreinvoke boolean   (ignoreInvoke, IgnoreInvoke)
  If `true`, an entry is not expanded or collapsed when the entry is activated. The default is `false`.

-opencmd tclCommand   (openCmd, OpenCmd)
  Command to call whenever an expanded entry needs to be opened. The pathname of the entry is appended as an argument. The default action is to show all child entries of the specified entry.

Subwidgets

`hlist`
  The tixHList mega-widget that displays the tree. Entries to the tree are added directly to the `hlist` subwidget using its *add* method.

`hsb`
  The horizontal scrollbar widget.

`vsb`
  The vertical scrollbar widget.

Methods

pathName autosetmode
  Call the *setmode* method for all entries. If an entry has no children, its mode is set to none. If an entry has any hidden children, its mode is set to open. Otherwise, the entry's mode is set to `close`.

pathName close entryPath
  Close the entry given by *entryPath* if its mode is `close`.

pathName getmode entryPath
  Return the current mode of the entry given by *entryPath*.

pathName open entryPath
  Open the entry given by *entryPath* if its mode is `open`.

pathName setmode entryPath mode
  Set the mode of the entry given by *entryPath* to *mode*. If *mode* is open, a (+) indicator is drawn next to the entry. If *mode* is close, a (-) indicator is drawn next to the entry. If *mode* is none (the default), no indicator is drawn.

Example

```
tixTree .tree -options { separator "/" }
set hlist [.tree subwidget hlist]
foreach d { Adobe Adobe/Courier Adobe/Helvetica Adobe/Times \
    Bitstream Bitstream/Charter Bitstream/Courier } {
  $hlist add $d -itemtype imagetext -text [file tail $d] \
      -image [tix getimage folder]
}
.tree autosetmode
pack .tree
```

tixVStack pathName [option value...]

The *tixVStack* command creates a new tixVStack mega-widget named *path-Name*. The `tixVStack` class is derived from the `tixPrimitive` class. It serves as a virtual base class for tixNoteBook-style mega-widgets.

Widget-Specific Options

-dynamicgeometry boolean   (dynamicGeometry,
                                              DynamicGeometry)
> Whether the tixVStack should dynamically resize to match the size of the current page. The default is `false`, in which case the size of the tix-VStack will match the size of the largest page.

-ipadx amount   (ipadX, Pad)
> Amount of internal horizontal padding around the sides of the page sub-widgets.

-ipady amount   (ipadY, Pad)
> Amount of internal vertical padding around the sides of the page subwid-gets.

Subwidgets

pageName
> The frame widget of a notebook page as returned by the *add* method.

Methods

pathName add pageName [option value...]
> Add a new page to the tixVStack named *pageName*. The pathname of the page's master frame widget is returned. Available options are:
>
> *-createcmd tclCommand*
> > Command to be called the first time a page is to be displayed.
>
> *-raisecmd tclCommand*
> > Command to be called whenever the page is raised by the user.

pathName delete pageName
> Delete the given page from the tixVStack.

pathName pagecget pageName option
> Similar to the *cget* method, but operates on the page *pageName*. *Option* may have any of the values accepted by the *add* method.

pathName pageconfigure pageName [option value...]
> Similar to the *configure* method, but operates on the page *pageName*. *Option* may have any of the values accepted by the *add* method.

pathName pages
> Return a list of the names of all the pages.

pathName raise pageName
> Raise the page *pageName*.

pathName raised
> Return the name of the currently raised page.

VTree

tixVTree pathName [*option value...*]

The *tixVTree* command creates a new tixVTree mega-widget named *path-Name*. The tixVTree class is derived from the tixScrolledHList class. It serves as a virtual base class for tree-style mega-widgets.

Widget-Specific Options

-ignoreinvoke boolean   (ignoreInvoke, IgnoreInvoke)
> If true, an entry is not expanded or collapsed when the entry is activated. The default is false.

Subwidgets

hlist
> The tixHList mega-widget that displays the tree.

hsb
> The horizontal scrollbar widget.

vsb
> The vertical scrollbar widget.

Tix Standard Widgets Overview

Tix adds five new standard widgets to Tk: tixGrid, tixHList, tixInputOnly, tixNote-BookFrame, and tixTList. These widgets add new features to Tk that could not be constructed from the standard Tk widgets.

Display Items

Three of the standard widgets added to Tk by Tix are designed to arrange and display items in a list or grid without regard to how each item is actually drawn. They simply treat the items as rectangular boxes and leave the drawing part to the item itself. To this end, all three widgets, called *host widgets*, support a set of items with a common interface, called *display items*.

Tix currently has four types of display items: image, text, imagetext, and window. A C API exists for the programmer to add more item types. The appearance of each item is controlled by option-value pairs specified at creation in a manner similar to how items of the canvas widget are configured. Each host widget also supports an *entryconfigure* method for changing options for existing items.

Since several or all items in a host widget will share common display attributes, Tix supports the concept of *display styles*. Each display item supports the *-style* option, which accepts as a value a display style as returned by the *tixDisplayStyle* command. The *tixDisplayStyle* command is described in detail in the "Tix Core Commands" section, later in this chapter. In short, it defines a style by defining values for a subset of the style options a display item type supports. Display items are configured to use the style using the *-style* option. Changes to the style at a later time will be reflected in all display items connected to the style.

Image Items

Display items of the type `image` are used to display Tk images. Image items support the following options:

> *-image imageName*   (image, Image)
>   Image to display in the item.
>
> *-style displayStyle*   (imageStyle, ImageStyle)
>   Display style to which to connect the item.

Image items support the following standard widget options as style options:

-activebackground	-activeforeground	-anchor
-background	-disabledbackground	-disabledforeground
-foreground	-padx	-pady
-selectbackground	-selectforeground	

Imagetext Items

Display items of the type `imagetext` are used to display an image and a text string together. Imagetext items support the following options:

> *-bitmap bitmap*   (bitmap, Bitmap)
>   Bitmap to display in the item.
>
> *-image imageName*   (image, Image)
>   Image to display in the item. Overrides the *-bitmap* option.
>
> *-style displayStyle*   (imageTextStyle, ImageTextStyle)
>   Display style to which to connect the item.
>
> *-showimage boolean*   (showImage, ShowImage)
>   Whether image/bitmap should be displayed.
>
> *-showtext boolean*   (showText, ShowText)
>   Whether text string should be displayed.
>
> *-text string*   (text, Text)
>   Text string to display in the item.
>
> *-underline string*   (underline, Underline)
>   Text string to display in the item.

Imagetext items support the following standard widget options as style options:

-activebackground	-activeforeground	-anchor
-background	-disabledbackground	-disabledforeground
-font	-foreground	-justify
-padx	-pady	-selectbackground
-selectforeground	-wraplength	

Imagetext items support the following special style option:

-*gap* amount   (gap, Gap)
        Distance in pixels between the bitmap/image and the text string.

Text Items

Display items of the type text are used to display a simple text string. Text items support the following options:

-*style* displayStyle   (textStyle, TextStyle)
        Display style to which to connect the item.

-*text* string   (text, Text)
        Text string to display in the item.

-*underline* string   (underline, Underline)
        Text string to display in the item.

Text items support the following standard widget options as style options:

-activebackground	-activeforeground	-anchor
-background	-disabledbackground	-disabledforeground
-font	-foreground	-justify
-padx	-pady	-selectbackground
-selectforeground	-wraplength	

Window Items

Display items of the type window are used to display a subwindow in a host widget. Window items support the following options:

-*style* displayStyle   (windowStyle, WindowStyle)
        Display style to which to connect the item.

-*window* pathName   (window, Window)
        Pathname of widget to display as a subwindow in the item.

Window items support the following standard widget options as style options:

-anchor   -padx   -pady

Tix Standard Widgets

Grid

tixGrid `pathName` [`option value...`]

The *tixGrid* command creates a new tixGrid widget named `pathName`. A tix-Grid widget presents a 2D grid of cells. Each cell may contain one Tix display item and can be formatted with a wide range of attributes.

Standard Options

-background	*-borderwidth*	*-cursor*
-font	*-foreground*	*-highlightbackground*
-highlightcolor	*-highlightthickness*	*-padx*
-pady	*-relief*	*-selectbackground*
-selectborderwidth	*-selectforeground*	*-takefocus*
-xscrollcommand	*-yscrollcommand*	

Widget-Specific Options

-editdonecmd `tclCommand`   (`editDoneCmd, EditDoneCmd`)
  Command to call when the user has edited a grid cell. The column and row numbers of the cell are appended as arguments.

-editnotifycmd `tclCommand`   (`editNotifyCmd, EditNotifyCmd`)
  Command to call when the user tries to edit a grid cell. The column and row numbers of the cell are appended as arguments. The command should return a boolean value to indicate whether the cell is editable.

-formatcmd `tclCommand`   (`formatCmd, FormatCmd`)
  Command to call when the grid cells need to be formatted on the screen. Five arguments are appended: `Type x1 y1 x2 y2`. `type` is the logical type of the region. It may be one of `x-region` (the horizontal margin), `y-region` (the vertical margin), `s-region` (area where margins are joined), or `main` (any other region). The last four arguments give the column and row numbers of the top left cell and bottom right cell of the affected region.

-height `integer`   (`height, Height`)
  Number of rows in the grid. The default is 10.

-itemtype `tclCommand`   (`itemType, ItemType`)
  The default item type for a cell when set with the *set* method. The default is `text`.

-leftmargin `integer`   (`leftMargin, LeftMargin`)
  Number of cell columns, starting at column 0, that make up the vertical margin. The default is 1. Left margin columns are not scrolled.

-selectmode `mode`   (`selectMode, SelectMode`)
  Specifies one of several styles understood by the default bindings for manipulation of the selection. Supported styles are `single`, `browse`,

multiple, and extended. Any arbitrary string is allowed, but the programmer must extend the bindings to support it.

-selectunit `tclCommand`   (selectUnit, SelectUnit)
The unit of selection. Valid values are `cell`, `column`, or `row`.

-sizecmd `tclCommand`   (sizeCmd, SizeCmd)
Command to call whenever the grid is resized or the size of a row or column is changed with the *size* method.

-state `tclCommand`   (state, State)
Current state of the grid. Valid values are `normal` and `disabled`.

-topmargin `tclCommand`   (topMargin, TopMargin)
Number of cell rows, starting from row 0, that make up the horizontal margin. The default is 1. Rows in the top margin are not scrolled.

-width `integer`   (width, Width)
Number of columns in the grid. The default is 4.

Methods

pathName anchor `operation` [`args`...]
Manipulate the anchor cell of the grid. Available operations are:

`clear`
Make no cell the anchor cell.

`get`
Return the column and row of the anchor cell as a two-item list. A result of {-1 -1} indicates there is no anchor cell.

`set` *x y*
Set the anchor cell to the cell at column *x* and row *y*.

pathName delete `what` `from` [`to`]
Delete specified rows or columns. *What* may be `row` or `column`. If *to* is omitted, only the row (or column) at *from* is deleted. Otherwise, all rows (or columns) from position *from* through *to*, inclusive, are deleted.

pathName edit apply
Un-highlight any cell currently being edited and apply the changes.

pathName edit set `x y`
Highlight the cell at column *x*, row *y* for editing.

pathName entrycget `x y` `option`
Similar to the *cget* method, but operates on the cell at *x y*. *Option* may have any of the values accepted by the *set* method used for that cell.

pathName entryconfigure `x y` [`option value`...]
Similar to the *configure* method, but operates on the cell at *x y*. *Option* may have any of the values accepted by the *set* method for that cell.

pathName format *borderType x1 y1 x2 y2* [option value...]

Format the grid cells contained in the rectangular region with its top left cell at *x1,y1* and bottom right cell at *x2,y2*. This command can only be called from the format command handler set with the *-formatcmd* option. The *borderType* argument may be either border or grid. The following options are supported by both border types:

-background color   (background, Background)

Background color for 3D borders when border type is border. When *-filled* is true, the background of the cell is also drawn in this color for both types. Otherwise, the tixGrid widget's background color is used.

-borderwidth amount   (borderWidth, BorderWidth)

Width of the border.

-filled boolean   (filled, Filled)

Whether the *-background* and *-selectbackground* options should override the tixGrid widget's options. The default is false.

-selectbackground color   (selectBackground, Foreground)

The background color of the cell when it is selected. Used only when *-filled* is true.

-xon xon   (xon, Xon)

Using the *-xon*, *-xoff*, *-yon*, and *-yoff* options, borders can be drawn around groups of cells. The given region is divided into subregions, starting from the top left cell, that are *xon+xoff* cells wide by *yon+yoff* cells high. Within this subregion, the border is drawn only around the rectangular regions in the top left corner that are *xon* cells wide and *yon* cells high. The default values are 1 for *-xon* and *-yon* and 0 for *-xoff* and *-yoff*, which results in borders being drawn around each individual cell.

-xoff xoff   (xoff, Xoff)

See *-xon*.

-yon yon   (yon, Yon)

See *-xon*.

-yoff yoff   (yoff, Yoff)

See *-xon*.

When *borderType* is border, cell borders are standard Tk 3D borders. Available options are as follows:

-relief relief   (relief, Relief)

3D effect for border.

When *borderType* is grid, cell borders are plain grid lines. Available options are as follows:

-anchor anchorPos   (anchor, Anchor)

For grid lines, only one or two of the border's sides are actually drawn. *AnchorPos* identifies on which sides of the rectangular region the grid lines are drawn. For example, ne states that grid lines are drawn on the top and right sides, whereas e states that a grid line is drawn only on the right side.

-bordercolor color   (borderColor, BorderColor)

Color of the grid lines.

pathName info exists x y

Return a 1 if the cell at row *x*, column *y* contains a display item. Otherwise, return 0.

pathName move what from to offset

Move the specified rows or columns. *What* may be row or column. Move rows (or columns) from position *from* through *to*, inclusive, by the distance *offset*.

pathName nearest x y

Return the row and column of the cell nearest to coordinates *x y* inside the grid.

pathName set x y [*-itemtype type*] [*option value*...]

Create a new display item at row *x*, column *y*. If given, *type* specifies the type of the display item. Valid options are those allowed for the selected display item type. If a display item already exists in the cell, it will be deleted automatically.

pathName size what index [*option value*...]

Query or set the size of the row or column. *What* may be row or column. *Index* may be the integer position of the row (or column) or the string default, which sets the default size for all rows (or columns). Available options are as follows:

-pad0 pixels

Padding to the left of a column or the top of a row.

-pad1 pixels

Padding to the right of a column or the bottom of a row.

-size amount

Width of a column or height of a row. *Amount* may be a real number in screen units or one of the following:

auto

Autosize to largest cell in column or row.

default

Use the default size (10 times the average character widths for columns and 1.2 times the average character height for rows).

nchar

> Set the size to *n* times the average character width for columns and *n* times the average character height for rows.

pathName *unset* x y

> Remove the display item from the cell at row *x*, column *y*.

pathName *xview*

> Return a two-element list describing the currently visible horizontal region of the widget. The elements are real numbers representing the fractional distance that the view's left and right edges extend into the horizontal span of the widget. Columns in the left margin are not part of the scrollable region.

pathName *xview moveto* fraction

> Adjust the visible region of the widget so that the point indicated by fraction along the widget's horizontal span appears at the region's left edge.

pathName *xview scroll* number what

> Horizontally scroll the visible columns outside the left margin by **number**. If **what** is units, then **number** is in units of columns. If **what** is pages, then **number** is in units of the visible region's width.

pathName *yview*

> Return a two-element list describing the currently visible vertical region of the widget. The elements are real numbers representing the fractional distance that the view's top and bottom edges extend into the vertical span of the widget. Rows in the top margin are not part of the scrollable region.

pathName *yview moveto* fraction

> Adjust the visible region of the widget so that the point indicated by fraction along the widget's vertical span appears at the region's top edge.

pathName *yview scroll* number what

> Vertically scroll the visible rows outside the top margin by **number**. If **what** is units, then **number** is in units of rows. If **what** is pages, then **number** is in units of the visible region's height.

Example

```
proc SimpleFormat {w area x1 y1 x2 y2} {
   array set bg {s-margin gray65 x-margin gray65 \
      y-margin gray65 main gray20 }
   case $area {
     main { $w format grid $x1 $y1 $x2 $y2 -anchor se -fill 0 \
                 -relief raised -bd 1 -bordercolor $bg($area)
     }
     {x-margin y-margin s-margin} {
           $w format border $x1 $y1 $x2 $y2 \
               -fill 1 -relief raised -bd 1 -bg $bg($area)
        }
      }
   }
```

```
set grid [[tixScrolledGrid .sg -bd 0] subwidget grid]
$grid configure -formatcmd "SimpleFormat $grid"
for {set x 0} {$x < 10} {incr x} {
    $grid size col $x -size auto
    for {set y 0} {$y < 10} {incr y} {
        $grid set $x $y -itemtype text -text ($x,$y)
    }
}
$grid size col 0 -size 10char
pack .sg -expand true -fill both
```

HList

tixHList pathName [*option value...*]

The *tixHList* command creates a new tixHList widget named *pathName*. A tixHList is used to display any data that has a hierarchical structure (e.g., filesystem directory trees).

Standard Options

-background	*-borderwidth*	*-cursor*
-font	*-foreground*	*-highlightbackground*
-highlightcolor	*-highlightthickness*	*-padx*
-pady	*-relief*	*-selectbackground*
-selectborderwidth	*-selectforeground*	*-takefocus*
-xscrollcommand	*-yscrollcommand*	

Widget-Specific Options

-browsecmd tclCommand   (browseCmd, BrowseCmd)
    Command to call whenever the user browses an entry (usually by a single click). The pathname of the entry is appended as an argument.

-columns integer   (columns, Columns)
    Number of columns in the tixHList. Can be set at creation only. Column numbering begins at 0. List entries alway appear in column 0. Arbitrary display items can be placed in the columns to the right of an entry (e.g., file sizes and owner's name).

-command tclCommand   (command, Command)
    Command to call whenever the user browses an entry (usually by a single click). The pathname of the entry is appended as an argument.

-drawbranch boolean   (drawBranch, DrawBranch)
    Whether branch lines should be drawn to connect list entries to their parents.

-header boolean   (header, Header)
    Whether headers should be displayed at the top of each column.

-height amount   (height, Height)
    Height for the window in lines of characters.

-indent amount   (indent, Indent)
> Horizontal indentation between a list entry and its children.

-indicator boolean   (indicator, Indicator)
> Whether indicators should be displayed.

-indicatorcmd tclCommand   (indicatorCmd, IndicatorCmd)
> Command to call when an entry's indicator is activated. The *entryPath*
> of the entry is appended as an argument.

-itemtype type   (itemType, ItemType)
> The default item type for a new entry. The default is text.

-selectmode mode   (selectMode, SelectMode)
> Specifies one of several styles understood by the default bindings for
> manipulation of the selection. Supported styles are single, browse,
> multiple, and extended. Any arbitrary string is allowed, but the pro-
> grammer must extend the bindings to support it.

-separator char   (separator, Separator)
> Character that serves as path separator for entry pathnames. The default
> is the "." character.

-sizecmd tclCommand   (sizeCmd, SizeCmd)
> Command to call whenever the tixHList changes its size.

-wideselection boolean   (wideSelection, WideSelection)
> Whether selection highlight extends the entire width of the tixHList or
> just fits the selected entry. Default is true.

-width amount   (width, Width)
> Width of the tixHList in characters.

Methods

pathName add entryPath [option value...]
> Add a new top-level list entry with pathname *entryPath*. This path-
> name is also the method's return value. Available options are those
> appropriate to the selected display item type, with these additions:

-at index
> Insert the new entry at position *index*, an integer starting from 0.

-after afterWhich
> Insert the new entry after the entry *afterWhich*.

-before beforeWhich
> Insert the new entry before the entry *beforeWhich*.

-data string
> String to associate with the new entry that will be returned by the
> *info* method.

-itemtype type
> Display item type for the new entry. Otherwise, the type is taken
> from the tixHList's *-itemtype* option.

-state `state`

>Whether entry can be selected and invoked. *State* must be either `normal` or `disabled`.

pathName addchild `parentPath`

>Add a new child entry underneath entry *parentPath*. If *parentPath* is the empty string, a top-level entry is created. The pathname of the new entry is returned. Available options are the same as for the *add* method.

pathName anchor set `entryPath`

>Set the selection anchor to the entry *entryPath*.

pathName anchor clear

>Make it so no entry is the selection anchor.

pathName column width `col` [[*-char*] `width`]

>Set the width of column *col* to `width`, which is in screen units. If *-char* is specified, the width is in characters. If `width` is the empty string, the column is autosized to the widest element. If the only argument given is *col*, the current width of column *col* is returned in pixels.

pathName delete `what` [*entryPath*]

>Delete one or more entries. *What* may be one of the following:

`all`

>Delete all of the entries in the tixHList.

`entry`

>Delete the entry *entryPath* and all of its children.

`offsprings`

>Delete all the children of entry *entryPath*.

`siblings`

>Delete all entries that share the same parent as the entry *entry-Path* (which is not deleted).

pathName entrycget `entryPath option`

>Similar to the *cget* method, but operates on the entry *entryPath*. *Option* may have any of the values accepted by the entry's display item type.

pathName entryconfigure `entryPath` [*option value...*]

>Similar to the *configure* method, but operates on the entry *entryPath*. *Option* may have any of the values accepted by the entry's display item type.

pathName header cget `col option`

>Similar to the *cget* method, but operates on the header for column *col*. *Option* may have any of the values accepted by the *header create* method.

pathName header configure `col` [*option value...*]

>Similar to the *configure* method, but operates on the header for column *col*. *Option* may have any of the values accepted by the *header create* method.

pathName **header create** co1 [*-itemtype type*] [*option value*...]
> Create a new display item to serve as the header for column *col*. If *type* is not given, the default is that of the tixHList's *-itemtype* option. Available options are those appropriate to the selected display item type, with the following additions:

> *-borderwidth amount*   (borderWidth, BorderWidth)
>> Border width for header item.

> *-headerbackground color*   (headerBackground, Background)
>> Background color for header item.

> *-relief relief*   (relief, Relief)
>> Relief for header item.

pathName **header delete** co1
> Delete the header item for column *col*.

pathName **header exists** co1
> Return 1 if a header item exists for column *col*, 0 otherwise.

pathName **header size** co1
> Return the size of the header in column *col* as a two-item list of its width and height, or an empty list if no header item exists.

pathName **hide entry** *entryPath*
> Hide the list entry *entryPath*.

pathName **indicator cget** *entryPath* option
> Similar to the *cget* method, but operates on the indicator for entry *entryPath*. *Option* may have any of the values valid for the display item type of the indicator.

pathName **indicator configure** *entryPath* [*option value*...]
> Similar to the *configure* method, but operates on the indicator for entry *entryPath*. *Option* may have any of the values valid for the display item type of the indicator.

pathName **indicator create** *entryPath* [*-itemtype type*] [*option value*...]
> Create a new display item to be the indicator for the entry *entryPath*. If *type* is not given, the default is that of the tixHList's *-itemtype* option. Available options are those appropriate to the selected display item type.

pathName **indicator delete** *entryPath*
> Delete the indicator display item for the entry *entryPath*.

pathName **indicator exists** *entryPath*
> Return 1 if entry *entryPath* has an indicator, 0 otherwise.

pathName **indicator size** *entryPath*
> Return the size of the indicator for the entry *entryPath* as a two-item list of its width and height (or an empty list if no indicator exists).

pathName info anchor
> Return the pathname of the entry that is the current anchor.

pathName info bbox entryPath
> Return a coordinate list of the form {*x1 y1 x2 y2*} giving an approximate bounding box for the currently visible area of entry *entryPath*.

pathName info children [*entryPath*]
> If *entryPath* is given, return a list of that entry's children. Otherwise, return a list of the top-level entries.

pathName info data entryPath
> Return the associated data string for entry *entryPath*.

pathName info exists entryPath
> Return 1 if an entry with pathname *entryPath* exists, 0 otherwise.

pathName info hidden entryPath
> Return 1 if the entry *entryPath* is hidden, 0 otherwise.

pathName info next entryPath
> Return the pathname of the entry immediately below entry *entryPath* in the list. An empty string is returned if *entryPath* is the last entry.

pathName info parent entryPath
> Return the pathname of the entry that is the parent of entry *entryPath*. An empty string is returned if *entryPath* is a top-level entry.

pathName info pref entryPath
> Return the pathname of the entry immediately above entry *entryPath* in the list. An empty string is returned if *entryPath* is the first entry.

pathName info selection
> Return a list of the selected entries in the tixHList.

pathName item cget entryPath option
> Similar to the *cget* method, but operates on the display item in column *col* on the same line as entry *entryPath*. *Option* may have any of the values valid for the display item's type.

pathName item configure entryPath col [*option value...*]
> Similar to the *configure* method, but operates on the display item in column *col* on the same line as entry *entryPath*. *Option* may have any of the values valid for the display item's type.

pathName item create entryPath col [*-itemtype type*] [*option value...*]
> Create a new display item in column *col* on the same line as entry *entryPath*. If *type* is not given, the default is that of the tixHList's *-itemtype* option. Available options are those appropriate to the selected display item type. If *col* is 0, the display item of entry *entryPath* is replaced with the new item.

pathName *item delete* `entryPath` `col`
> Delete the display item in column `col` that is on the same line as entry `entryPath`. `Col` must be greater than 0. Use the *delete entry* method to delete the entry.

pathName *item exists* `entryPath` `col`
> Return 1 if a display item in column `col` exists on the same line as entry `entryPath`, 0 otherwise.

pathName *nearest* `y`
> Return the pathname of the entry nearest to the y-coordinate `y`.

pathName *see* `entryPath`
> Adjust the view in the tixHList so the entry `entryPath` is visible.

pathName *selection clear* [`from` [`to`]]
> With no arguments, all entries are deselected. If only `from` is given, just the entry with pathname `from` is deselected. If `to` is also given, all entries from the entry `from` up to and including the entry `to` are deselected.

pathName *selection get*
> Return a list of the selected entries in the tixHList.

pathName *selection includes* `entryPath`
> Return 1 if entry `entryPath` is selected, 0 otherwise.

pathName *selection set* `from` [`to`]
> If only `from` is given, just the entry with pathname `from` is selected. If `to` is also given, all entries from the entry `from` up to and including the entry `to` are selected.

pathName *show entry* `entryPath`
> If entry `entryPath` is hidden, unhide it.

pathName *xview*
> Return a two-element list describing the currently visible horizontal region of the widget. The elements are real numbers representing the fractional distance that the view's left and right edges extend into the horizontal span of the widget. Columns in the left margin are not part of the scrollable region.

pathName *xview* `entryPath`
> Adjust the view so that the entry `entryPath` is aligned at the left edge of the window.

pathName *xview moveto* `fraction`
> Adjust the visible region of the widget so that the point indicated by `fraction` along the widget's horizontal span appears at the region's left edge.

pathName *xview scroll* `number` `what`
> Scroll the view horizontally in the window by `number`. If `what` is units, then `number` is in units of characters. If `what` is pages, then `number` is in units of the visible region's width.

pathName **yview**

> Return a two-element list describing the currently visible vertical region of the widget. The elements are real numbers representing the fractional distance that the view's top and bottom edges extend into the vertical span of the widget. Rows in the top margin are not part of the scrollable region.

pathName **yview** `entryPath`

> Adjust the view so that the entry `entryPath` is aligned at the top edge of the window.

pathName **yview** *moveto* `fraction`

> Adjust the visible region of the widget so that the point indicated by `fraction` along the widget's vertical span appears at the region's top edge.

pathName **yview** scroll *number* what

> Scroll the view vertically in the window by *number*. If *what* is units, then *number* is in units of characters. If *what* is pages, then *number* is in units of the visible region's height.

InputOnly

tixInputOnly `pathName` [`option value...`]

The *tixInputOnly* command creates a new tixInputOnly widget named *path-Name*. TixInputOnly widgets are not visible to the user. The only purpose of a tixInputOnly widget is to accept input from the user. It is useful for intercepting events to other widgets when mapped invisibly on top of them.

Standard Options

-cursor   *-width*   *-height*

NoteBookFrame

tixNoteBookFrame `pathName` [`option value...`]

The *tixNoteBookFrame* command creates a new tixNoteBookFrame widget named `pathName`. It provides page tabs for use in tixNoteBook-style mega-widgets and serves as the container for any page frames to be controlled. It is up to the programmer to set up event bindings to properly connect page tabs and frames.

Standard Options

-background	*-borderwidth*	*-cursor*
-disabledforeground	*-font*	*-foreground*
-height	*-relief*	*-takefocus*
-width		

Widget-Specific Options

-backpagecolor *color*   (backPageColor, BackPageColor)
> Color for the background behind the page tabs.

-focuscolor *color*   (focusColor, FocusColor)
> Color for the tab focus highlight.

-inactivebackground *color*   (inactiveBackground, Background)
> Background color for inactive tabs. The active tab always has the same
> background color as the tixNoteBookFrame.

-slave *boolean*   (slave, Slave)
> Whether the tixNoteBookFrame is a slave and therefore should not make
> its own geometry requests.

-tabpadx *amount*   (tabPadX, Pad)
> Horizontal padding around the text labels on the page tabs.

-tabpady *amount*   (tabPadY, Pad)
> Vertical padding around the text labels on the page tabs.

Methods

pathName *activate* **tabName**
> Make the page tab *tabName* the active tab and also give it the tab focus.
> Note that this does not raise the page frame associated with the tab. If
> *tabName* is the empty string, no tab will be active or have the tab focus.

pathName *add* **tabName** [*option value...*]
> Add a new page tab named *tabName* to the tixNoteBookFrame. It is up
> to the programmer to create a new frame widget to associate with the
> page tab. The frame must be a descendant of the tixNoteBookFrame.
> Available options are as follows:

> **-anchor** *anchorPos*
>> Specifies how the information in a page's tab (e.g., text or bitmap)
>> should be anchored. Must be one of n, nw, w, sw, s, se, e, ne, or
>> center.

> **-bitmap** *bitmap*
>> Bitmap to display in tab.

> **-image** *imageName*
>> Name of image to display in tab.

> **-justify** *position*
>> How multiple lines of text in the tab should be justified. Must be
>> left, right, or center.

> **-label** *string*
>> Text to display in the tab. Overrides *-image* and *-bitmap*.

> **-state** *state*
>> Whether page tab can be made active. Must be either normal or
>> disabled.

-underline index

Integer index (starting from 0) of character in text label to underline in the tab. Used by default bindings to set up keyboard traversal of tabs.

-wraplength chars

Maximum line length of text in the tab. If value is 0 or less, no wrapping is done.

pathName delete tabName

Delete the page tab *tabName*.

pathName focus tabName

Give the page tab *tabName* the tab focus. If *tabName* is the empty string, no tab will have the focus.

pathName geometryinfo

Return a two-item list of the form {*width height*} describing the size of the area containing the page tabs.

pathName identify x y

Return the name of the page tab that contains the coordinates *x y*. Returns an empty string if the coordinates are outside the tab area.

pathName info what

Return information about *what* in the tixNoteBookFrame. Valid values for *what* are as follows:

pages

Return a list of the page tab names in the tixNoteBookFrame.

active

Return the name of the currently active page tab.

focus

Return the name of the page tab that currently has the focus.

focusnext

Return the name of the page tab that lies in the focus ring after the current page tab with the focus.

focusprev

Return the name of the page tab that lies in the focus ring before the current page tab with the focus.

pathName pagecget tabName option

Similar to the *cget* method, but operates on the page tab *tabName*. *Option* may have any of the values accepted by the *add* method.

pathName pageconfigure tabName [option value...]

Similar to the *configure* method, but operates on the page tab *tabName*. *Option* may have any of the values accepted by the *add* method.

TList

tixTList pathName [*option value...*]

The *tixTList* command creates a new tixTList widget named *pathName*.

Standard Options

-background	*-borderwidth*	*-cursor*
-font	*-foreground*	*-highlightcolor*
-highlightthickness	*-padx*	*-pady*
-relief	*-selectbackground*	*-selectborderwidth*
-selectforeground	*-takefocus*	*-xscrollcommand*
-yscrollcommand		

Widget-Specific Options

-browsecmd tclCommand   (browseCmd, BrowseCmd)
> Command to call whenever the user browses an entry (usually by a single click). The pathname of the entry is appended as an argument.

-command tclCommand   (command, Command)
> Command to call whenever the user browses an entry (usually by a double click). The pathname of the entry is appended as an argument.

-height amount   (height, Height)
> Height for the window in lines of characters.

-itemtype type   (itemType, ItemType)
> The default item type for a new entry. The default is text.

-orient orient   (orient, Orient)
> Order for tabularizing the list entries. *Orient* may be vertical (entries are arranged from top to bottom in columns) or horizontal (entries are arranged from left to right in rows).

-selectmode mode   (selectMode, SelectMode)
> Specifies one of several styles understood by the default bindings for manipulation of the selection. Supported styles are single, browse, multiple, and extended. Any arbitrary string is allowed, but the programmer must extend the bindings to support it.

-sizecmd tclCommand   (sizeCmd, SizeCmd)
> Command to call whenever the tixTList changes its size.

-state state   (state, State)
> Whether tixTList entries can be selected or activated. *State* must be either normal or disabled.

-width amount   (width, Width)
> Width of the tixTList in characters.

Methods

pathName anchor set `index`

Set the selection anchor to the entry at `index`.

pathName anchor clear

Make it so no entry is the selection anchor.

pathName delete `from` [`to`]

Delete all list entries between the indices `from` and `to`, inclusive. If `to` is omitted, only the entry at `from` is deleted.

pathName entrycget `index` `option`

Similar to the *cget* method, but operates on the entry at `index`. `Option` may have any of the values accepted by the *insert* method used to create the entry.

pathName entryconfigure `index` [`option` `value`...]

Similar to the *configure* method, but operates on the entry at `index`. `Option` may have any of the values accepted by the *insert* method used to create the entry.

pathName insert `index` [*-itemtype* `type`] [`option` `value`...]

Create a new entry at position `index`. If `type` is not given, the default is that of the tixTList's *-itemtype* option. Available options are those appropriate to the selected display item type, with the following addition:

-state `state`

State of the individual entry. Must be either `normal` or `disabled`.

pathName info anchor

Return the pathname of the entry that is the current anchor.

pathName info selection

Return a list of the selected entries in the tixTList.

pathName nearest `x` `y`

Return the index of the entry nearest to the coordinates `x` `y`.

pathName see `index`

Adjust the view in the tixTList so the entry at `index` is visible.

pathName selection clear [`from` [`to`]]

With no arguments, all entries are deselected. If only `from` is given, just the entry at index `from` is deselected. If `to` is also given, all entries from the entry at `from` up to and including the entry at `to` are deselected.

pathName selection includes `index`

Return 1 if the entry at `index` is selected, 0 otherwise.

pathName selection set `from` [`to`]

If only `from` is given, just the entry at index `from` is selected. If `to` is also given, all entries from the entry at `from` up to and including the entry at `to` are selected.

pathName **xview**

Return a two-element list describing the currently visible horizontal region of the widget. The elements are real numbers representing the fractional distance that the view's left and right edges extend into the horizontal span of the widget. Columns in the left margin are not part of the scrollable region.

pathName **xview** *index*

Adjust the view so that the entry at *index* is aligned at the left edge of the window.

pathName **xview moveto** *fraction*

Adjust the visible region of the widget so that the point indicated by *fraction* along the widget's horizontal span appears at the region's left edge.

pathName **xview scroll** *number* **what**

Scroll the view horizontally in the window by *number*. If *what* is units, then *number* is in units of characters. If *what* is pages, then *number* is in units of the visible region's width.

pathName **yview**

Return a two-element list describing the currently visible vertical region of the widget. The elements are real numbers representing the fractional distance that the view's top and bottom edges extend into the vertical span of the widget. Rows in the top margin are not part of the scrollable region.

pathName **yview** *index*

Adjust the view so that the entry at *index* is aligned at the top edge of the window.

pathName **yview moveto** *fraction*

Adjust the visible region of the widget so that the point indicated by *fraction* along the widget's vertical span appears at the region's top edge.

pathName **yview scroll** *number* **what**

Scroll the view vertically in the window by *number*. If *what* is units, then *number* is in units of characters. If *what* is pages, then *number* is in units of the visible region's height.

Tix Core Commands

This section describes the commands added by the Tix extension that do not create widgets or mega-widgets. These commands cover new mega-widget class definition, method writing, and configuration of the Tix internal state.

tix operation [*arg arg...*]

Access aspects of Tix's internal state and the Tix application context.

Application-Context Options

Several of Tix's internal settings are manipulated using the *cget* and *configure* operations, which operate in the same manner as the identically named widget methods. The settings that can be set this way are as follows:

-debug boolean
> Whether Tix widget should run in debug mode.

-fontset fontSet
> The font set to use as defaults for Tix widgets. Valid values are TK (standard Tk fonts), 12Point, and 14Point (the default).

-scheme scheme
> Color scheme to use for the Tix widgets. Valid values are TK (standard Tk colors), Gray, Blue, Bisque, SGIGray, and TixGray (the default).

-schemepriority priority
> Priority level of the options set by the Tix schemes. See the Tk *option* command for a discussion of priority levels. The default is 79.

Operations

tix addbitmapdir directory
> Add *directory* to the list of directories searched by the *getimage* and *getbitmap* operations for bitmap and image files.

tix filedialog [*class*]
> Returns the pathname of a file selection mega-widget that can be shared among different modules of the application. The mega-widget will be created when this operation is first called. The *class* argument may be used to specify the mega-widget class of the file selection dialog, either tixFileSelectDialog (the default) or tixExFileSelectDialog.

tix getbitmap name
> Search the bitmap directories for a file with the name *name.xbm* or *name*. If found, return the full pathname to the file, prefixed with an @ character to make the result suitable for *-bitmap* options.

tix getimage name
> Search the bitmap directories for a file with the name *name.xpm*, *name.gif*, *name.ppm*, *name.xbm*, or *name*. If found, the name of a newly created Tk image is returned, suitable for use with *-image* options.

tix option get option
> Return the setting of a Tix scheme option. Available options are:

-active_bg	*-active_fg*	*-bg*
-bold_font	*-dark1_bg*	*-dark1_fg*

-dark2_bg	-dark2_fg	-disabled_fg
-fg	-fixed_font	-font
-inactive_bg	-inactive_fg	-input1_bg
-input2_bg	-italic_font	-light1_bg
-light1_fg	-light2_bg	-light2_fg
-menu_font	-output1_bg	-output2_bg
-select_bg	-select_fg	-selector

tix resetoptions `newScheme newFontSet [newSchemePriority]`

Reset the scheme and font set of the Tix application context to `newScheme` and `newFontSet`. `NewSchemePriority` can be specified to change the priority level of the scheme options in the Tk options database. This command is preferred to using *tix configure* for the *-scheme*, *-fontset*, and *-schemepriority* settings.

CallMethod

tixCallMethod `pathName method [arg arg...]`

Invoke method `method` of the mega-widget `pathName` with the given arguments. Most commonly used by a base class to call a method that a derived class may have overridden.

ChainMethod

tixChainMethod `pathName method [arg arg...]`

Invoke the method `method` with the given arguments in the context of the superclass of mega-widget `pathName`. Most commonly used by a derived class to call a method of its superclass that it has overridden.

Class

tixClass `className { ... }`

Define a new class in the Tix Intrinsics named `className`. *TixClass* is almost identical to the *tixWidgetClass* command, except that it is not associated with a widget. The new command that is created, named `className`, therefore lacks widget-related methods, such as *subwidget*. Also, there are no methods such as *initWidgetRec* that must be defined for the class.

There is one syntactical difference compared with the *tixWidgetClass* command. Each item in the *-configspec* list for *tixClass* is only a two- or three-element list: the option, the default value, and an optional verification command. One example of a nonwidget Tix class is the *tix* command, which is defined at runtime using the *tixClass* command.

Descendants

tixDescendants `window`

Return a list of all the descendants of the widget `window`.

Destroy

tixDestroy objectName

Destroy the Tix object *objectName*, which must be an instance of class defined with *tixClass* or *tixWidgetClass*. The *Destructor* method of the object is called first, if defined.

DisableAll

tixDisableAll window

Set the *-state* option of *window* and all its descendants that have a *-state* option to disabled.

DisplayStyle

tixDisplayStyle itemType [*-stylename styleName*] [*-refwindow refWindow*][option value...]

Create a new display item style of type *itemType*. The name of the new style will be *styleName*, if specified. Otherwise, a unique name is generated and returned. Valid *options* are those defined for the chosen display item type.

If *refWindow* is specified, the default values for the style will be taken from the matching options of the window *refWindow*. Note that *refWindow* need not exist; however, any options specified for it in the Tk resource database will be used. If *refWindow* is omitted, the main window is used.

A new Tix object is created with the same name as the style (i.e., *style-Name*). This object has the following methods:

styleName cget option
Return the current value of the configuration option *option* for the display style.

styleName configure [*option* [*value* [*option value*...]]]
Query or modify the configuration options of the display style in the same manner as the standard widget *configure* method.

styleName delete
Destroy the display style object.

EnableAll

tixEnableAll window

Set the *-state* option of *window* and all its descendants that have a *-state* option to normal.

Form

tixForm operation [*arg arg...*]

Communicate with the Tix Form geometry manager that arranges widgets inside their master according to various attachment rules. The *tixForm* command can take the following forms:

tixForm slave [*slave...*] [*options*]
> Same as *tixForm configure*.

tixForm check master
> Return 1 if there is a circular dependency in the attachments for *master*s slaves, 0 otherwise.

tixForm configure slave [*slave...*] [*options*]
> Configure how the slave window *slave* should be managed by its Form geometry master. Supported options are as follows:

> *-bottom attachment*
>> Attachment for bottom edge of the slave. (Abbreviation: *-b*)

> *-bottomspring weight*
>> Weight of the spring at the bottom edge of the slave. (Abbreviation: *-bs*)

> *-fill fill*
>> Direction slave should fill. *Fill* may be x, y, both, or none.

> *-in master*
>> Insert the slave in master window *master*, which must either be the slave's parent (the default) or a descendant of the slave's parent.

> *-left attachment*
>> Attachment for left edge of the slave. (Abbreviation: *-l*)

> *-leftspring weight*
>> Weight of the spring at the left edge of the slave. (Abbreviation: *-ls*)

> *-padbottom amount*
>> How much external padding to add to the bottom side of the slave. (Abbreviation: *-bp*)

> *-padleft amount*
>> How much external padding to add to the left side of the slave. (Abbreviation: *-lp*)

> *-padright amount*
>> How much external padding to add to the right side of the slave. (Abbreviation: *-rp*)

> *-padtop amount*
>> How much external padding to add to the top side of the slave. (Abbreviation: *-tp*)

-padx amount
> How much external padding to add to both the right and left sides of the slave.

-pady amount
> How much external padding to add to both the top and bottom sides of the slave.

-right attachment
> Attachment for right edge of the slave. (Abbreviation: *-r*)

-rightspring weight
> Weight of the spring at the right edge of the slave. (Abbreviation: *-rs*)

-top attachment
> Attachment for top edge of the slave. (Abbreviation: *-t*)

-topspring weight
> Weight of the spring at the top edge of the slave. (Abbreviation: *-ts*)

tixForm forget slave [slave...]
> Remove each given slave from the list of slaves managed by its master and unmap its window. The grid configuration options for each *slave* are forgotten.

tixForm grid master [xSize ySize]
> Set the number of horizontal and vertical grid cells in the master window *master* to *xSize* and *ySize*, respectively. If the grid sizes are omitted, the current setting is returned as a list of the form *{xSize ySize}*.

tixForm info slave
> Return the current configuration state of the slave *slave* in the same option-value form given to *tixForm configure*. The first two elements will be *-in master*.

tixForm slaves master
> Return a list of all the slaves managed by the master window *master*.

Attachments

The *attachment* argument to the *-right, -left, -top,* and *-bottom* configuration options takes the general form *{anchorPoint offset}*. The second element, *offset*, is given in screen units. If positive, it indicates a shift in position to the right of or down from the anchor point. If negative, it indicates a shift in position to the left of or up from the anchor point.

The first element, *anchorPoint*, specifies where the slave will be positioned on the master. It may have the following forms:

%gridline
> The slave's side is attached to an imaginary grid line. By default, the master window is divided into 100×100 grid cells. An anchor point of *%0* specifies the first grid line (the left or top edge of the master), and an anchor point of *%100* specifies the last grid line (the right or bottom edge

of the master). The number of grid cells can be changed with the *tix-Form grid* method.

pathName
> The slave's side is aligned to the opposite side of the window `path-Name`, which must also be a slave. For example, a configuration `option-value` of *-top {.a 0}* will align the top side of the slave at the same vertical position as the bottom side of the slave `.a`.

&pathName
> The slave's side is aligned with the same side of the window `pathName`, which must also be a slave. For example, a configuration `option-value` of *-top {.a 0}* will align the top side of the slave at the same vertical position as the top side of the slave `.a`.

none
> The slave's side is attached to nothing. When none is the anchor point, the offset must be 0. The side is unconstrained and its position determined from the attachments for the other sides and the slave's natural size.

The value `attachment` can be abbreviated as a single element. If the value can be interpreted as an anchor point, the offset defaults to 0. If it can be interpreted as an offset, the anchor point defaults to %0 for positive offsets and to %100 (or whatever the maximum grid line is) for negative offsets.

GetBoolean

tixGetBoolean [*-nocomplain*] `string`

Return 0 if the string is a valid Tcl boolean value for `false`. Return 1 if the string is a valid Tcl boolean value for `true`. Otherwise, an error is generated unless *-nocomplain* is specified, in which case a 0 is returned.

GetInt

tixGetInt [*-nocomplain*] [*-trunc*] `string`

Convert string into an integer if it is a valid Tcl numerical value. Otherwise, an error is generated unless *-nocomplain* is specified, in which case a 0 is returned. By default, the value is rounded to the nearest integer. If *-trunc* is specified, the value is truncated instead.

Mwm

tixMwm `operation` [`arg arg`...]

Communicate with *mwm*, the Motif window manager. The *tixMwm* command can take the following forms:

tixMwm decoration `pathName` [`option` [`value` [`option value`...]]]
Query or modify the Motif window decoration options for the top-level window `pathName` in the same manner as the standard widget *configure* method. Valid options are *-border*, *-menu*, *-maximize*, *-minimize*, *-resizeb*, and *-title*.

tixMwm ismwmrunning `pathName`
Return 1 if *mwm* is running on `pathName`'s screen, 0 otherwise.

tixMwm protocol `pathName`
Return a list of all protocols associated with the top-level window *path-Name*.

tixMwm protocol `pathName` *activate* `protocol`
Activate the given *mwm* protocol in *mwm*'s menu.

tixMwm protocol `pathName` *add* `protocol` `menuMsg`
Add a new *mwm* protocol named `protocol` and add an item in *mwm*'s menu according to *menuMsg* that will invoke the protocol. *MenuMsg* is a valid X resource for a *mwm* menu item. The protocol invocation can be caught using the Tk *wm protocol* command.

tixMwm protocol `pathName` *deactivate* `protocol`
Deactivate the given protocol in *mwm*'s menu.

tixMwm protocol `pathName` *delete* `protocol`
Delete the given protocol from *mwm*'s menu.

PopGrab

tixPopGrab

Release the last grab set with the *tixPushGrab* command and pop it off the Tix grab stack.

PushGrab

tixPushGrab [*-global*] `window`

Identical to the standard Tk *grab set* command, with the added feature that the grab is placed on Tix's internal grab stack. The *tixPopGrab* command must be used to release the grab.

WidgetClass

tixWidgetClass `className` { `option value` ... }

Define a new mega-widget class named `className`. A Tcl command named `className` is also defined, which will create new instances of the class. Available options are as follows:

-alias aliasList
> Aliases for the options defined by *-flag*. Each element of *aliasList* is a two-item list consisting of the alias followed by the full option to which it maps.

-classname classResName
> Resource class name for the mega-widget for use by Tk resource database. By convention, *classResName* is the same as the *class-Name* argument with the first letter capitalized.

-configspec configList
> Configuration of each option that the new mega-widget supports (see *-flag*). Each element of *configList* is a four- or five-item list. The required four elements are the option name (including the hyphen), resource name, resource class, and default value. The optional fifth element is a Tcl command used to validate a value for the option. This command is called once the option is initialized at creation and whenever its value is set with the *configure* method. The candidate value is appended to the call as an argument. The command should return the value to actually be used or generate an error.

-default resList
> List of Tk resource specifications to be applied for each instance of the mega-widget. These resources are most often used to set up configuration defaults for subwidgets of the mega-widget. Each element of *resList* is a two-item list giving the *pattern* and *value*, as for an *option add* command.

-flag optionList
> List of options (also known as public variables) that the mega-widget class supports.

-forcecall optionList
> List of options that should have their private configuration methods called during initialization of a mega-widget instance. Normally, an option's configuration method is called only when the option is set with the *configure* method.

-method methodList
> List of public methods that the mega-widget class supports.

-readonly optionList
> List of options that cannot be set or changed by the user.

-static optionList
> List of options that can be set only at mega-widget creation (i.e., cannot be changed with the *configure* method).

-superclass superClass
> Superclass of the class being defined. All the options and methods of the superclass are inherited. Note that *superClass* is the command name of the superclass, not the resource class name from the *-classname* option.

-virtual `boolean`

> Whether the class is a virtual class. If `true`, then instances of the class cannot be created.

Example

Here is an example class definition for a scrolling banner mega-widget:

```
tixWidgetClass tixScrollingBanner {
    -classname   TixScrollingBanner
    -superclass tixPrimitive
    -method {
        start stop
    }
    -flag {
        -orientation -rate -text
    }
    -static {
        -orientation
    }
    -configspec {
        {-orientation orientation Orientation horizontal}
        {-rate rate Rate 2}
        {-text text Text {}}
    }
    -alias {
        {-orient -orientation}
    }
    -default {
        {*Label.anchor e}
        {*Label.relief sunken}
    }
}
```

Writing Methods

The methods for a class are defined using the Tcl *proc* command with three special requirements. First, the name of the procedure for a method must match the format `className::method`. For the example above, the programmer will need to define the Tcl procedures *tixScrollingBanner::start* and *tixScrollingBanner::stop*. Second, each procedure must accept at least one argument, which must be named w, which will be set to the name of the class instance (i.e., mega-widget) for which the method was invoked. Additional arguments can be defined if the method accepts any arguments.

The third requirement is that the first command executed in the procedure be:

```
upvar #0 $w data
```

which sets up access to the instance's subwidgets and public and private variables through the Tcl array `data`. Public variables are available using the name of the option (with the leading hyphen) as the element name. The programmer is free to create other elements in the `data` array as private variables, with the exception of the following reserved elements: `ClassName`, `className`, `context`, and `rootCmd`. By convention, the names of subwidgets should be assigned to array elements with names beginning with the prefix `w:` followed by the name of the subwidget known to the user. Using this format will give the user access to the subwidget using the mega-widget *subwidget* method inherited from `tixPrimitive`. Private subwidgets should use the prefix `pw:`. For example, the *stop* method for our `tixScrolling-Banner` example may be defined as follows:

```
proc tixScrollingBanner::stop {w {ms 0}} {
    upvar #0 $w data
    after cancel $data(afterid)
    if {$t > 0} {
        set data(afterid) [after $ms
                                tixScrollingBanner::advance $w]
    } else {
        $data(w:label) configure -text {}
    }
}
```

This method stops the scrolling of the banner by canceling the timeout set for the next banner advance. If an optional argument is given, it specifies that the scrolling will be paused only for the given number of milliseconds (if non-zero). Otherwise, the banner is cleared. Note the call to the procedure *tixScrollingBanner::advance*. This is a private method of the class, since **advance** is not in the list given to the *-method* option of the class definition.

Initialization Methods

When a new instance of a mega-widget is created, the private methods *InitWidgetRec*, *ConstructWidget*, and *SetBindings* are called, in that order. The purpose of the *InitWidgetRec* method is to initialize the private variables of the mega-widget instance. The *ConstructWidget* method is used to create and initialize its subwidgets, and the *SetBindings* method is used to create its initial event bindings.

The procedures to define the methods must follow the three rules outlined previously. When defined, the methods override the respective methods of their superclass. Therefore, the programmer should normally use the *tix-ChainMethod* command to call the superclass's version of the method as a first step. For example, the *ConstructWidget* method for the scrolling banner example might be defined as follows:

```
proc tixScrollingBanner::ContructWidget {w} {
    upvar #0 $w data
    tixChainMethod $w ConstructWidget
    set data(w:label) [label $w.label]
    pack $w.label -expand yes -fill x
}
```

Public Variables

When the configure mega-widget method is used to set the value of a public variable, Tix will attempt to call a method with the name *config-option* with the name of the mega-widget and the value as arguments. The programmer should define this method when he or she needs to know immediately when the value of a public variable changes. For example, the **text** option for the scrolling banner example could be handled as follows:

```
proc tixScrollingBanner::config-text {w value} {
    upvar #0 $w data
```

```
$data(w:label) configure -text $value
}
```

An option's configuration method is called after any validation command specified in the *-configspec* entry for the option. During the call to the method, the element for the option in the data array will still be set to the old value in case it is needed. One may override the value passed by explicitly setting the public variable's element in the data array to the desired value and also returning the value from the method. A public variable's configuration method is not called when a mega-widget is created unless the option is listed in the *-forcecall* option of the class definition.

Tix Extensions to Tk image Command

Tix extends the standard Tk *image* command by adding support for two additional image types: compound and pixmap.

image

image create compound imageName [*option value...*]

The compound image type allows a single image to be composed of multiple lines, each of which contains one or more text items, bitmaps, or other images. Available options are as follows:

-background color
Background color for the image and for bitmap items in the image.

-borderwidth amount
Width of 3D border drawn around the image.

-font font
Default font for text items in the image.

-foreground color
Foreground color for the bitmap and text items in the image.

-padx amount
Extra space to request for padding on the left and right side of the image.

-pady amount
Extra space to request for padding on the top and bottom side of the image.

-relief relief
3D effect for the border around the image.

-showbackground boolean
Whether the background and 3D border should be drawn or the image should have a transparent background. The default is false.

-window pathName
> Window in which the compound image is to be drawn. When the window is destroyed, the image is also destroyed. This option must be specified when a compound image is created and cannot be changed.

When a compound image is created, a Tcl command with the same name as the image is created. This command supports the following operations:

imageName add line [*-anchor anchorPos*] [*-padx amount*]
> Create a new line for items at the bottom of the image. If *anchorPos* is specified, it specifies how the line should be aligned horizontally. If *amount* is specified, it specifies the amount of padding to add to the left and right of the line in the image.

imageName add itemType [*option value...*]
> Add a new item of the specified type to the end of the last line of the compound image. *ItemType* may be bitmap, image, space, or text. All item types support the following options:

> *-anchor anchorPos*
>> How the item should be aligned on its line along the vertical axis.

> *-padx amount*
>> Amount of padding to add to the left and right side of the item.

> *-pady amount*
>> Amount of padding to add to the top and bottom side of the item.

Bitmap items support the following options:

> *-background color*
>> Background color for the bitmap.

> *-bitmap bitmap*
>> Bitmap to add to the compound image.

> *-foreground color*
>> Foreground color for the bitmap.

Image items support the following option:

> *-image imageName*
>> Name of an image to add to the compound image.

Space items reserve empty space in the image. Space items support the following options:

> *-height amount*
>> Height of space to add to the compound image.

> *-width amount*
>> Width of space to add to the compound image.

Text items support the following options:

-background `color`
> Background color for the text.

-font `font`
> Font to be used for the text.

-foreground `color`
> Foreground color for the text.

-justify `justify`
> How to justify multiple lines of text. `Justify` may be `left`, `right`, or `center`.

-text `string`
> Text string to be added to the compound image.

-underline `integer`
> Integer index of a character in the text that should be underlined.

-wraplength `chars`
> Maximum line length in characters. If `chars` is less than or equal to 0, no wrapping is done.

imageName cget *option*
> Return the current value of the configuration option *option* for the compound image.

imageName configure [*option* [*value* [*option* *value*...]]
> Query or modify the configuration options of the compound image in the same manner as the standard widget *configure* method.

---

image

> *image create pixmap* `imageName` [*option* *value*...]

Create a Tk image using XPM format. Supported options are as follows:

-data `string`
> Source for the XPM image is specified in `string`. Takes precedence over the *-file* option.

-file `fileName`
> Source for the XPM image is to be read from the file `fileName`.

When a pixmap image is created, a Tcl command with the same name as the image is created. This command supports the *cget* and *configure* operations for querying and changing the image options.

CHAPTER 10

TclX

TclX, also known as Extended Tcl, was developed by Karl Lehenbauer and Mark Diekhans. TclX is not part of the core Tcl/Tk package, but can be obtained for free at *http://www.neosoft.com/TclX*. This chapter covers TclX Version 8.0.2.

TclX enhances the Tcl language with a number of features designed to make it more suited to general-purpose programming. The TclX software includes a number of new Tcl commands, a new Tcl shell, a standalone help facility, and a library of handy Tcl procedures. Some features of TclX have proven so useful that, over time, they have been integrated into the core Tcl distribution.

This chapter describes only the commands in TclX that are not in standard Tcl. As noted in the text, some commands are not supported or have reduced functionality when running on the Windows 95, Windows 98, and Windows NT platforms. TclX does not support the Macintosh platform.

Special Variables

The following global variables have special meaning to the Extended Tcl interpreter (the programs *tcl* and *wishx*):

argc
> Number of command-line arguments, not including the name of the script file

argv
> List containing command-line arguments

argv0
> Filename being interpreted, or name by which script was invoked

auto_path
Path to search to locate autoload libraries

tcl_interactive
1 if running interactively, 0 otherwise

tcl_prompt1
Primary prompt

tcl_prompt2
Secondary prompt for incomplete commands

tclx_library
Location of Extended Tcl libraries

tkx_library
Location of Extended Tcl Tk libraries

TCLXENV
Array containing information about Tcl procedures

Group Listing of Commands

This section briefly lists all Extended Tcl commands, grouped logically by function.

General Commands

commandloop	Create an interactive command loop.
dirs	List directories in directory stack.
echo	Write strings to standard output.
for_array_keys	Loop over each key in an array.
for_recursive_glob	Loop recursively over files matching a pattern.
host_info	Return information about a network host.
infox	Return information about Extended Tcl.
loop	Loop over a range of values.
mainloop	Call event loop handler.
popd	Pop top entry from the directory stack.
pushd	Push entry onto directory stack.
recursive_glob	Return list of files recursively matching pattern.
tclx_errorHandler	User-defined procedure to handle errors.
try_eval	Evaluate code and trap errors.

Debugging and Development Commands

cmdtrace	Trace command execution.
edprocs	Edit source code for procedures.
profile	Collect performance data.
profrep	Generate report from performance data.
saveprocs	Save procedure definitions to file.
showproc	List definitions of procedures.

Unix Access Commands

alarm	Send alarm signal.
chroot	Change root directory.
execl	Start a new program.
fork	Create a child process.
id	Set, get, or convert user, group, and process identifiers.
kill	Send signal to a process.
link	Create a hard or symbolic link.
nice	Set or get process priority.
readdir	Return list of directory entries.
signal	Handle Unix signals.
sleep	Delay process execution.
sync	Flush pending buffered output.
system	Execute shell command.
times	Return process and child execution times.
umask	Set or get file creation permission mask.
wait	Wait for command to terminate.

File Commands

bsearch	Search lines of file for a string.
chgrp	Set group ID of files.
chmod	Set file permissions.
chown	Set owner of files.
dup	Duplicate an open file identifier.
fcntl	Set or get attributes of file identifier.
flock	Apply lock on an open file.
for_file	Loop over contents of a file.
fstat	Return status information about an open file identifier.
ftruncate	Truncate a file to a specified length.
funlock	Remove lock from an open file.
lgets	Read Tcl list from a file.
pipe	Create a pipe.
read_file	Read file contents into a string.
select	Check file identifiers for change in status.
write_file	Write strings to a file.

File Scanning Commands

scancontext	Create, delete, or modify file scan contexts.
scanfile	Perform file context scanning.
scanmatch	Specify commands for file context scanning.

Math Commands

These commands operate in the same fashion as their counterparts that are built into the *expr* command. They accept as arguments any expression accepted by the *expr* command. The trigonometric functions use values expressed in radians.

abs	Absolute value.
acos	Arc cosine.
asin	Arc sine.
atan	Arc tangent.
atan2	Arc tangent (accepts two parameters).
ceil	Round up to the nearest integer.
cos	Cosine.
cosh	Hyperbolic cosine.
double	Convert numeric value to double-precision floating-point value.
exp	*e* raised to the power of the argument.
floor	Round down to the nearest integer.
fmod	Floating-point remainder (accepts two arguments).
hypot	Hypotenuse function (accepts two arguments).
int	Convert to integer by truncating.
log	Natural logarithm.
log10	Base 10 logarithm.
max	Maximum value (accepts one or more arguments).
min	Minimum value (accepts one or more arguments).
pow	Exponentiation (accepts two parameters).
random	Return random floating-point number.
round	Convert to integer by rounding.
sin	Sine.
sinh	Hyperbolic sine.
sqrt	Square root.
tan	Tangent.
tanh	Hyperbolic tangent.

List Manipulation Commands

intersect	Return list of elements common to two lists.
intersect3	Accept two lists, returning items common to, and unique to, each list.
lassign	Assign list elements to variables.
lcontain	Return 1 if element is contained in a list.
lempty	Return 1 if a list is empty.
lmatch	Search list for elements matching a pattern.
lrmdups	Remove duplicate list elements.
lvarcat	Concatenate lists onto a variable.
lvarpop	Delete or replace list element contained in a variable.
lvarpush	Insert element into list contained in a variable.
union	Return logical union of two lists.

Keyed List Commands

keyldel	Delete entry from keyed list.
keylget	Return value from keyed list.
keylkeys	Return list of keys from keyed list.
keylset	Set value in keyed list.

String and Character Manipulation Commands

ccollate	Return collation ordering of two strings.
cconcat	Concatenate strings.
cequal	Compare strings for equality.
cindex	Return one character from a string.
clength	Return length of a string.
crange	Return range of characters from a string.
csubstr	Return substring of a string.
ctoken	Parse a token out of a string.
ctype	Return type of characters in a string.
replicate	Replicate a string several times.
translit	Transliterate characters in a string.

XPG/3 Message Catalog Commands

catclose	Close a message catalog.
catgets	Retrieve message from a catalog.
catopen	Open a message catalog.

Help Commands

apropos	Locate help information based on a pattern.
help	Online help system for Extended Tcl.
helpcd	Change current location in tree of help subjects.
helppwd	List current help subject location.

Library and Package Commands

auto_commands	List names of loadable commands.
auto_load_file	Source a file using autoload path.
auto_packages	Return names of defined packages.
buildpackageindex	Build index files for package libraries.
convert_lib	Convert Tcl index and source files into a package.
loadlibindex	Load a package library index.
searchpath	Search a path of directories for a file.

Alphabetical Summary of Commands

This section describes all Extended Tcl commands, listed in alphabetical order.

---

abs

> *abs* `arg`
>
> Return the absolute value of expression `arg`. The argument may be in either integer or floating-point format and the result is returned in the same form.

acos

acos `arg`

Return the arc cosine of expression `arg`.

alarm

alarm `seconds`

Instruct the system to send an alarm signal (SIGALRM) to the command interpreter *seconds* seconds in the future. The time is specified as a floating-point value. A value of 0 cancels any previous alarm request. This command is not supported under Windows.

apropos

apropos `pattern`

Search the online help system for entries that contain the regular expression `pattern` in their summaries.

asin

asin `arg`

Return the arc sine of expression `arg`.

atan

atan `arg`

Return the arc tangent of expression `arg`.

atan2

atan2 `x,y`

Return the arc tangent of expression `x` divided by expression `y`, using the signs of the arguments to determine the quadrant of the result.

auto_commands

auto_commands [*-loaders*]

List the names of all known loadable procedures. If the *-loaders* option is specified, the output also lists the commands that will be executed to load each command.

auto_load_file

auto_load_file `file`

Load a file, as with the Tcl *source* command, but use the search path defined by *auto_path* to locate the file.

auto_packages

auto_packages [*-location*]

Return a list of all defined package names. With the *-location* option, return a list of pairs of package name and the *.tlib* pathname, offset, and length of the package within the library.

bsearch

bsearch `fileId key` [*retvar*] [`compare_proc`]

Search file opened with `fileId` for lines of text matching the string `key`. Return the line that was found, or an empty string if no match exists. If the variable name is specified with `retvar`, the matching line is stored in the variable and the command returns 1 if the key matched or 0 if there was no match. Can optionally specify a procedure *compare_proc* that will compare the key and each line, returning a value indicating the collation order (see *ccollate*).

buildpackageindex

buildpackageindex `libfilelist`

Build index files for package libraries. Argument `libfilelist` is a list of package libraries. Each name must end with the suffix *.tlib*. A corresponding *.tndx* file will be built.

catclose

catclose [*-fail* \ *-nofail* `cathandle`

Close a previously opened message catalog.

Options

-fail
> Return an error if the catalog cannot be closed.

-nofail
> Ignore any errors when closing (default).

catgets

> *catgets* `catHandle setnum msgnum defaultstr`

Retrieve a message from a message catalog. The message catalog handle returned by *catopen* should be contained in `catHandle`. The message set number and message number are specified using `setnum` and `msgnum`. If the message catalog was not opened or the message set or message number cannot be found, then the default string, `defaultstr`, is returned.

catopen

> *catopen* [*-fail*| *-nofail*] `catname`

Open a message catalog using `catname`, which can be an absolute or relative pathname. Return a handle that can be used for subsequent *catgets* and *catclose* commands.

Options

-fail

> Return an error if the catalog cannot be opened.

-nofail

> Ignore any errors when opening (default).

ccollate

> *ccollate* [*-local*] `string1 string2`

Compare two strings and return their collation ordering. Return −1 if `string1` is less than `string2`, 0 if they are equal, and 1 if `string1` is greater than `string2`. With the option *-local*, compares according to current locale.

cconcat

> *cconcat* [`string...`]

Concatenate the strings passed as arguments and return the resulting string.

ceil

> *ceil* `arg`

Return the value of expression `arg`, rounded up to the nearest integer.

cequal

> *cequal* `string1 string2`

Compare two strings, returning 1 if they are identical, 0 if not.

chgrp

chgrp [-fileId] group filelist

Set the group ID of files in the list `filelist` to `group`, which can be either a group name or a group ID number.

With option *-fileId*, the file list consists of open file identifiers rather than filenames. This command is not supported under Windows.

chmod

chmod [-fileId] mode filelist

Set permissions on the files specified in list `filelist` to `mode`, which can be a numeric mode or symbolic permissions as accepted by the Unix *chmod* command.

With option *-fileId*, the file list consists of open file identifiers rather than filenames. This command is not supported under Windows.

chown

chown [-fileId] owner filelist
chown [-fileId] {owner group} filelist

Set the ownership of each file in list `filelist` to `owner`, which can be a username or numeric user ID. In the second form, a list consisting of the owner and group names can be specified.

With option *-fileId*, the file list consists of open file identifiers rather than filenames. This command is not supported under Windows.

chroot

chroot dirname

Set the process root directory to `dirname`. Can be run only by the superuser.

cindex

cindex string indexExpr

Return the character with index `indexExpr` in string `string`. Indices start at 0; the words end and len can be used at the beginning of the expression to indicate the index of the last character and length of the string, respectively.

clength

clength string

Return the length of `string` in characters.

cmdtrace

cmdtrace `level` [*noeval*] [*notruncate*] [*procs*] [`fileId`] [*command* `cmd`]

Print a trace statement when commands are executed at depth `level` (1 being the top level) or at all levels if the level is specified as on.

Options

noeval
>   Cause arguments to be printed before being evaluated.

notruncate
>   Turn off truncation of output, which normally occurs when a command line is longer than 60 characters.

procs
>   Enable tracing of procedure calls only.

fileId
>   Cause output to be written to an open file identifier.

command
>   Rather than producing normal output, the given command is executed during tracing.

cmdtrace off

Turn off all tracing.

cmdtrace depth

Return the current trace depth level, or 0 if tracing is not enabled.

commandloop

commandloop [*-async*] [*-interactive* on|off|tty] [*-prompt1* *cmd*] [*-prompt2* *cmd*] [*-endcommand* *cmd*]

Enter a command loop, reading from standard input and writing to standard output.

Options

-async
>   Interpret commands on standard input.

-interactive
>   Controls interactive command mode (prompting of commands and display of results). If the argument is on, interactive mode is enabled; if off, it is disabled; if tty, it is enabled if standard input is associated with a terminal.

-prompt1
> The argument supplies a command that is executed and the result used as the primary command prompt.

-prompt2
> The argument supplies a command that is executed and the result used as the secondary command prompt.

-endcommand
> The argument supplies a command that is executed when the command loop terminates.

convert_lib

convert_lib `tclIndex packagelib` [`ignore`]

Convert a Tcl index file `tclIndex` and its associated source files into an Extended Tcl package library `packagelib`. The list `ignore` can specify files that should not be included in the library.

cos

cos `arg`

Return the cosine of expression `arg`.

cosh

cosh `arg`

Return the hyperbolic cosine of expression `arg`.

crange

crange `string firstExpr lastExpr`

Return a range of characters from string `string`, from index `firstExpr` through `lastExpr`.

Indices start at 0, and the words end and len can be used at the beginning of an expression to indicate the index of the last character and length of the string, respectively.

csubstr

csubstr `string firstExpr lengthExpr`

Return a range of characters from string `string` from index `firstExpr` for a range of `lengthExpr` characters.

Indices start at 0, and the words end and len can be used at the beginning of an expression to indicate the index of the last character and length of the string, respectively.

ctoken

ctoken `strvar separators`

Parse the next token from the string contained in variable `strvar`. Tokens are separated by the characters specified in the string `separators`. Returns the next token and removes it from the string.

ctype

ctype [*-failindex* *var*] `class string`

Examine the characters in `string` and determine if they conform to the specified `class`. Return 1 if they conform, 0 if they do not or the string is empty. The `class` option takes one of the following forms:

`alnum`
> All characters are alphabetic or numeric.

`alpha`
> All characters are alphabetic.

`ascii`
> All characters are ASCII characters.

`char`
> Converts the string, which must be a number from 0 through 255, to an ASCII character.

`cntrl`
> All characters are control characters

`digit`
> All characters are decimal digits.

`graph`
> All characters are printable and nonspace.

`lower`
> All characters are lowercase.

`ord`
> Converts the first character in the string to its decimal numeric value.

`space`
> All characters are whitespace.

`print`
> All characters are printable (including space).

`punct`
> All characters are punctuation.

upper
> All characters are uppercase.

xdigit
> All characters are valid hexadecimal digits.

With the option *-failindex*, the index of the first character in the string that did not conform to the class is placed in the variable named *var*.

dirs

> *dirs*

List the directories in the directory stack.

double

> *double* **arg**

Evaluate the expression **arg**, convert the result to floating-point, and return the converted value.

dup

> *dup* **fileId** [**targetFileId**]

Create a new file identifier that refers to the same device as the open file identifier **fileId**. The new file identifier is returned.

Can optionally specify the name of an existing file identifier **targetFileId** (normally **stdin**, **stdout**, or **stderr**). In this case the **targetFileId** device is closed if necessary, and then becomes a duplicate that refers to the same device as **fileId**.

On Windows, only **stdin**, **stdout**, **stderr**, or a nonsocket file handle number may be specified for **targetFileId**.

echo

> *echo* [**string**...]

Write zero or more strings to standard output, followed by newline character.

edprocs

> *edprocs* [**proc**...]

Write the definitions for the named procedures (by default, all currently defined procedures) to a temporary file, invoke an editor, then reload the definitions if they were changed. Uses the editor specified by the EDITOR environment variable, or *vi* if none is specified.

execl

execl [-argv0 argv0] prog [arglist]

Perform an *execl* system call, replacing the current process with program *prog* and the arguments specified in the list `arglist`. The command does not return unless the system call fails.

The *-argv0* option specifies the value to be passed as `argv[0]` of the new program.

Under Windows, the *execl* command starts a new process and returns the process ID.

exp

exp arg

Return the value of the constant *e* raised to the power of the expression *arg*.

fcntl

fcntl fileId attribute [value]

Modifiy or return the current value of a file option associated with an open file identifier. If only `attribute` is specified, its current value is returned. If a boolean `value` is specified, the attribute is set. Some values are read only. The following attributes may be specified:

RDONLY
> File is opened for reading (read only).

WRONLY
> File is opened for writing (read only).

RDWR
> File is opened for reading and writing (read only).

READ
> File is readable (read only).

WRITE
> File is writable (read only).

APPEND
> File is opened for appending.

NONBLOCK
> File uses nonblocking I/O.

CLOEXEC
> Close the file upon execution of a new process.

NOBUF

File is not buffered.

LINEBUF

File is line buffered.

KEEPALIVE

Keep-alive option is enabled for a socket.

The **APPEND** and **CLOEXEC** attributes are not available on Windows.

Tc/X

flock

flock options fileId [start] [length] [origin]

Place a lock on all or part of the file open with identifier *fileId*. The file data is locked from the beginning of byte offset *start* for a length of *length* bytes. The default start position is the start of file, and the default length is to the end of file. If the file is currently locked, the command waits until it is unlocked before returning.

The value of *origin* indicates the offset for the data locked and is one of the strings **start** (relative to start of file, the default), **current** (relative to current access position), or **end** (relative to end of file, extending backward).

This command is not supported on Windows 95/98. Also see *funlock.*

Options

-read

Place a read lock on the file.

-write

Place a write lock on the file.

-nowait

Do not block if lock cannot be obtained. Return 1 if the file could be locked, or 0 if it could not.

floor

floor arg

Return the value of expression *arg* rounded down to the nearest integer.

fmod

fmod x y

Return the remainder after dividing expression *x* by expression *y.*

for_array_keys

for_array_keys var array_name code

Perform a *foreach*-style loop for each key in the array `array_name`.

Example

```
for_array_keys key tcl_platform {
    echo $key => $tcl_platform($key)
}
```

for_file

for_file var filename code

Loop over the file `filename`, setting `var` to the line and executing `code` for each line in the file.

Example

```
for_file line /etc/passwd {
    echo $line
}
```

for_recursive_glob

for_recursive_glob var dirlist globlist code

Perform a *foreach*-style loop over files that match patterns. All directories in the list `dirlist` are recursively searched for files that match the glob patterns in list `globlist`. For each matching file the variable `var` is set to the file path and code `code` is evaluated.

Example

```
for_recursive_glob file {~ /tmp} {*.tcl *.c *.h} {
    echo $file
}
```

fork

fork

Call the *fork* system call to duplicate the current process. Returns 0 to the child process, and the process number of the child to the parent process. This command is not supported under Windows.

fstat

fstat fileId [item] | [*stat* arrayvar]

Return status information about the file opened with identifier `fileId`. If one of the keys listed below is specified, the data for that item is returned. If *stat* `arrayvar` is specified, the information is written into array `arrayvar` using the listed keys. If only a file identifier is specified, the data is returned as a keyed list.

The following keys are used:

`atime`
> Time of last access.

`ctime`
> Time of last file status change.

`dev`
> Device containing a directory for the file.

`gid`
> Group ID of the file's group.

`ino`
> Inode number.

`mode`
> Mode of the file.

`mtime`
> Time of last file modification.

`nlink`
> Number of links to the file.

`size`
> Size of file in bytes.

`tty`
> 1 if the file is associated with a terminal, otherwise 0.

`type`
> Type of the file, which can be `file`, `directory`, `character-Special`, `blockSpecial`, `fifo`, `link`, or `socket`.

`uid`
> User ID of the file's owner.

The following additional keys may be specified, but are not returned with the array or keyed list forms:

`remotehost`
> If *fileId* is a TCP/IP socket connection, a list is returned, with the first element being the remote host IP address. If the remote hostname can be found, it is returned as the second element of the list. The third element is the remote host IP port number.

`localhost`
> If *fileId* is a TCP/IP socket connection, a list is returned, with the first element being the local host IP address. If the local hostname can be found, it is returned as the second element of the list. The third element is the local host IP port number.

ftruncate

ftruncate [-fileId] file newsize

Truncate a file to a length of at most *newsize* bytes. With the *-fileId* option, the *file* argument is an open file identifier rather than a filename. The *-fileId* option is not available on Windows.

funlock

funlock fileId [start] [length] [origin]

Remove a file lock that was previously set using an *flock* command on the file open with identifier *fileId*. The portion of the file data that is locked is from the beginning of byte offset *start* for a length of *length* bytes. The default start position is the start of file, and the default length is to the end of file.

The value of *origin* indicates the offset for the locked data and is one of the strings start (relative to start of file, the default), current (relative to the current access position), or end (relative to end of file).

This command is not supported on Windows 95/98. Also see *flock*.

help

help [options]

Invoke the online Tcl help facility to provide information on all Tcl and Extended Tcl commands. Information is structured as a hierarchical tree of subjects with help pages at the leaf nodes. Without arguments, the command lists all of the help subjects and pages under the current help subject.

help subject
Display all help pages and lower-level subjects (if any) under the subject *subject*.

help subject/helppage
Display the specified help page.

help help|?
Display help on using the help facility itself. Valid at any directory level.

helpcd

helpcd [subject]

Change the current subject in the hierarchical tree of help information. Without a *subject*, goes to the top level of the help tree.

helppwd

helppwd

Display the current subject in the hierarchical documentation tree of online help information.

host_info

host_info `option host`

Return information about a network host. The command takes one of the following three forms:

host_info addresses `host`
Return a list of the IP addresses for `host`.

host_info official_name `host`
Return the official name for `host`.

host_info aliases `host`
Return a list of aliases for `host`.

hypot

hypot **x y**

Return the hypotenuse function, equivalent to *sqrt*($x^*x + y^*y$). The arguments are expressions.

id

id `options`

Provides various functions related to getting, setting, and converting user, group, and process identifiers. Some functions can be performed only by the superuser. Under Windows only the *host* and *process* options are implemented.

id user [name]

Without a *name* option, return the current username. With an option, sets the real and effective user to *name*.

id userid [`uid`]

Without a `uid` option, return the current numeric user ID. With an option, set the real and effective user to `uid`.

id convert userid `uid`

Return the username corresponding to numeric user ID `uid`.

id convert user `name`

Return the numeric user ID corresponding to user `name`.

id group [name]

Without a *name* option, return the current group ID name. With an option, set the real and effective group ID to *name*.

id groupid [gid]

Without a *gid* option, return the current numeric group ID. With an option, set the real and effective group ID to *gid*.

id groups

Return a list of group names for the current process.

id groupids

Return a list of numeric group IDs for the current process.

id convert groupid gid

Return the group name corresponding to numeric group ID *gid*.

id convert group name

Return the numeric group ID corresponding to group *name*.

id effective user

Return the effective username.

id effective userid

Return the effective user ID number.

id effective group

Return the effective group name.

id effective groupid

Return the effective group ID number.

id host

Return the hostname of the system on which the program is running.

id process

Return the process ID of the current process.

id process parent

Return the process ID of the parent of the current process.

id process group

Return the process group ID of the current process.

id process group set

Set the process group ID of the current process to its process ID.

infox

infox *option*

Return information about the Extended Tcl interpreter or current application. The command can take the following forms:

infox *version*

Return the Extended Tcl version number.

infox *patchlevel*

Return the Extended Tcl patch level.

infox *have_fchown*

Return 1 if the *fchown* system call is available otherwise. If available, the *-fileId* option on the *chown* and *chgrp* commands is supported.

infox *have_fchmod*

Return 1 if the *fchmod* system call is available otherwise. If available, the *-fileId* option on the *chmod* command is supported.

infox *have_flock*

Return 1 if the *flock* command is defined, 0 if it is not available.

infox *have_fsync*

Return 1 if the *fsync* system call is available and the *sync* command will sync individual files, 0 if *fsync* is not available and the *sync* command will always sync all file buffers.

infox *have_ftruncate*

Return 1 if the *ftruncate* or *chsize* system call is available. If it is, the *ftruncate* command *-fileId* option may be used.

infox *have_msgcats*

Return 1 if XPG message catalogs are available, 0 if they are not. The *catgets* command is designed to continue to function without message catalogs, always returning the default string.

infox *have_posix_signals*

Return 1 if POSIX signals (*block* and *unblock* options for the *signal* command) are available.

infox *have_truncate*

Return 1 if the *truncate* system call is available. If it is, the *ftruncate* command may truncate by file path.

infox *have_waitpid*

Return 1 if the *waitpid* system call is available and the *wait* command has full functionality, 0 if the *wait* command has limited functionality.

infox appname

Return the symbolic name of the current application linked with the Extended Tcl library. The C variable `tclAppName` must be set by the application to return an application-specific value for this variable.

infox applongname

Return a natural language name for the current application. The C variable `tclLongAppName` must be set by the application to return an application-specific value for this variable.

infox appversion

Return the version number for the current application. The C variable `tcl-AppVersion` must be set by the application to return an application-specific value for this variable.

infox apppatchlevel

Return the patch level for the current application. The C variable `tclApp-Patchlevel` must be set by the application to return an application-specific value for this variable.

---

int

int arg

Evaluate the expression *arg*, convert the result to an integer, and return the converted value.

---

intersect

intersect list1 list2

Return the logical intersection of two lists, i.e., a list of all elements contained in both *list1* and *list2*. The returned list is sorted alphabetically.

---

intersect3

intersect3 list1 list2

Return a list containing three lists. The first consists of all elements of *list1* that are not in *list2*. The second contains the intersection of the two lists. The third contains all elements of *list2* that are not in *list1*. The returned lists are sorted alphabetically.

---

keyldel

keyldel listvar key

Delete the field specified by *key* from the keyed list in variable *listvar*. Removes both the key and the value from the keyed list.

---

keylget

keylget `listvar` [*key*] [*retvar* | {}]

Return the value associated with *key* from the keyed list in variable *list-var*. If *retvar* is not specified, the value will be returned as the result of the command. In this case, if *key* is not found in the list, an error will result.

If *retvar* is specified and *key* is in the list, the value is returned in the variable *retvar* and the command returns 1 if the key was present within the list. If *key* is not in the list, the command will return 0, and *retvar* will be left unchanged. If {} is specified for *retvar*, the value is not returned, allowing the programmer to determine if a key is present in a keyed list without setting a variable as a side effect.

If *key* is omitted, a list of all the keys in the keyed list is returned.

keylkeys

keylkeys `listvar` [*key*]

Return a list of the keys in the keyed list contained in variable `listvar`. If *key* is specified, it is used as the name of a key field whose subfield keys are to be retrieved.

keylset

keylset `listvar key value`...

Set the value associated with *key* to `value` in the keyed list contained in variable `listvar`. If `listvar` does not exist, it is created. If *key* is not currently in the list, it is added. If it already exists, `value` replaces the existing value. Multiple keywords and values may be specified if desired.

kill

kill [*-pgroup*] [`signal`] `idlist`

Send a signal to each process in the list `idlist`, if permitted. Parameter `signal`, if present, is the signal number or symbolic name of the signal. The default is 15 (SIGTERM).

If *-pgroup* is specified, the numbers in `idlist` are taken as process group IDs and the signal is sent to all of the processes in that process group. A process group ID of 0 specifies the current process group. This command is not supported under Windows.

lassign

lassign `list var`...

Assign successive elements of a list to specified variables. If there are more variable names than fields, the remaining variables are set to the empty string.

If there are more elements than variables, a list of the unassigned elements is returned.

lcontain

lcontain `list element`

Return 1 if `element` is an element of list `list`; otherwise, return 0.

lempty

lempty `list`

Return 1 if `list` is an empty list; otherwise, return 0.

lgets

lgets `fileId` [`varName`]

Read a Tcl list from the file given by file identifier `fileId`, discarding the terminating newline. If `varName` is specified, the command writes the list to the variable and returns the number of characters read; otherwise, it returns the list.

link

link [*-sym*] `srcpath destpath`

Create a link from existing pathname `srcpath` to `destpath`. With option *-sym*, creates a symbolic rather than hard link. This command is not supported under Windows.

lmatch

lmatch [*mode*] `list pattern`

Return a new list, consisting of the elements of `list` that match `pattern`. The type of pattern matching is determined by the `mode` parameter:

-exact
> Exact match

-glob
> Glob-style matching (default)

-regexp
> Regular expression matching

loadlibindex

loadlibindex `libfile.tlib`

Load the package library index of the library file `libfile.tlib`.

log

log arg

Return the natural logarithm of expression *arg*.

log10

log10 arg

Return the base 10 logarithm of expression *arg*.

loop

loop var first limit [increment] body

Loop construct in which the beginning and ending loop index variables and increment are fixed. The loop index is variable *var*, which is initialized to *first*. In each iteration of the loop, if the index is not equal to *limit*, the command *body* is evaluated and the index is increased by the value *increment*.

Example

```
# count from ten down to one
loop i 10 0 -1 {
    echo $i
}
```

lrmdups

lrmdups list

Remove duplicate elements from *list*; return the result, sorted alphabetically.

lvarcat

lvarcat var string...

Concatenate one or more string arguments to the end of the list contained in variable *var*, storing the result in *var* and returning the resulting list. String arguments that are lists are deconstructed into individual elements before being concatenated into the result list.

lvarpop

lvarpop var [indexExpr] [string]

Remove the element of the list contained in *var* having index *indexExpr* (default 0). If *string* is given, the deleted element is replaced with the string. Returns the replaced or deleted item.

Indices start at 0, and the words end and len can be used at the beginning of the expression to indicate the index of the last element and length of the list, respectively.

lvarpush

lvarpush var string [indexExpr]

Insert **string** as an element of the list stored in **var** before position **index-Expr** (default 0).

Indices start at 0, and the words end and len can be used at the beginning of the expression to indicate the index of the last element and length of the list, respectively.

mainloop

mainloop

Start a top-level event handler. Process events until there are no more active event sources, then exit.

max

max number...

Return the argument having the highest numeric value. The arguments can be any mixture of integer or floating-point values.

min

min number...

Return the argument having the lowest numeric value. The arguments can be any mixture of integer or floating-point values.

nice

nice [priorityIncr]

Without arguments, return the current process priority. With a numeric argument, add **priorityIncr** to the current process priority. A negative value increases the process priority (this will work only for the superuser). This command is not supported under Windows.

pipe

pipe [fileId_var_r fileId_var_w]

Create a pipe. Without options, return a list containing the file identifiers for the read and write ends of the pipe. If passed two variable names, they are set to the file identifiers for the opened pipe.

popd

popd

Remove the top entry from the directory stack; make it the current directory.

pow

pow x y

Return the value of expression *x* raised to the power of expression *y*.

TclX

profile

profile [*-commands*] [*-eval*] *on*

Start collection of data for performance profiling of procedures. With the *-commands* option, also profiles commands within a procedure. With the *-eval* option, uses the procedure call stack rather than the procedure scope stack when reporting usage.

profile off arrayVar

Turn off profiling and store the results in variable `arrayVar` for later analysis by the *profrep* command.

profrep

profrep profDataVar sortKey [*outFile*] [*userTitle*]

Generate a report using profile data generated by the *profile* command. Data must have been previously stored in variable `profDataVar`. The parameter `sortKey` has one of the values `calls`, `cpu`, or `real`, indicating how to sort the output. The output can optionally be written to file `outFile` (default is standard out) using an optional title `userTitle`.

pushd

pushd [*dir*]

Push the current directory onto the directory stack and change to directory `dir`. If no directory is specified, the current directory is pushed but remains unchanged.

random

random limit

Return a pseudorandom integer greater than or equal to 0 and less than `limit`.

random seed [`seedval`]

Reset the random number generator using the number **`seedval`**, or if omitted, a seed based on the current date and time.

read_file

read_file [*-nonewline*] `fileName` [`numBytes`]

Read the entire contents of file **`fileName`** and return it as a string. The *-nonewline* option discards any final newline character in the file. The **`numBytes`** option specifies the number of bytes to read.

readdir

readdir [*-hidden*] `dirPath`

Return a list of the files contained in directory **`dirPath`**. The option *-hidden* causes hidden files to be included in the list (Windows platforms only).

recursive_glob

recursive_glob `dirlist globlist`

Recursively search the directories in list **`dirlist`** for files that match any of the patterns in **`globlist`**. Returns a list of matching files.

replicate

replicate `string countExpr`

Return **`string`** replicated the number of times indicated by integer expression **`countExpr`**.

round

round `arg`

Evaluate the expression **`arg`**, convert the result to an integer by rounding, and return the converted value.

saveprocs

saveprocs `fileName` [`proc`...]

Save the definitions of the listed Tcl procedures (by default, all procedures) to file **`fileName`**.

scancontext

scancontext [`option`]

Create, delete, or modify file scan contexts.

scancontext create

Create a new scan context.

scancontext delete `contexthandle`

Delete the scan context identified by `contexthandle`.

scancontext copyfile `contexthandle`

Return the file handle to which unmatched lines are copied.

scancontext copyfile `contexthandle` [`filehandle`]

Set the file handle to which unmatched lines are copied. A file handle of { } removes any file copy specification.

scanfile

scanfile [*-copyfile* `copyFileId`] `contexthandle fileId`

Scan the file specified by `fileId` starting from the current file position. Check all patterns in the scan context specified by `contexthandle`, executing the match commands corresponding to patterns matched.

If the optional *-copyfile* argument is specified, the next argument is a file ID to which all lines not matched by any pattern (excluding the default pattern) are to be written. If the copy file is specified with this flag, instead of using the *scancontext copyfile* command, the file is disassociated from the scan context at the end of the scan.

scanmatch

scanmatch [*-nocase*] `contexthandle` [`regexp`] `commands`

Specify Tcl commands to be evaluated when `regexp` is matched by a *scanfile* command. The match is added to the scan context specified by `contexthandle`. Any number of match statements may be specified for a given context. With option *-nocase*, the pattern matching is case insensitive.

searchpath

searchpath `pathList file`

Search the directories in list `pathList` for file `file`. Return the full path if found; otherwise, return an empty string.

select

select `readfileIds` [`writefileIds`] [`exceptfileIds`] [`timeout`]

Wait for a change of status in file identifiers. Up to three lists, containing file identifiers for files to be polled for read, write, or exceptions, can be specified. An optional parameter `timeout` indicates the maximum time, in seconds, to wait (it can be 0 for polling). The command returns three lists, corresponding to the file descriptors in each of the three categories that have a change in status.

On Windows, only sockets can be used with the *select* command.

showproc

showproc [`procname`...]

List the definitions of the named Tcl procedures (by default, all procedures).

signal

signal `action siglist [command]`

Set the action to take when a Unix signal is received. The `siglist` parameter lists one or more signal names or numbers. Parameter `action` indicates the action to take, as described in the following:

default
Take system default action.

ignore
Ignore the signal.

error
Generate a catchable Tcl error.

trap
Execute command indicated by `command` parameter.

get
Return current settings for the specified signals as a keyed list.

set
Set signals from a keyed list in the format returned by *get*.

block
Block signals from being received.

unblock
Allow the specified signal to be received.

sin

sin `arg`

Return the sine of expression `arg`.

sinh

sinh `arg`

Return the hyperbolic sine of expression `arg`.

sleep

sleep `seconds`

Delay execution of the current process for `seconds` seconds, which must be an integer value.

sqrt

sqrt `arg`

Return the square root of expression `arg`.

sync

sync `[fileId]`

With no options, issue a *sync* system call to write pending data to disk. With a file identifier `fileId` corresponding to a file open for writing, schedule output for that file to disk. On platforms that do not support the *fsync* system call, the `fileId` parameter is ignored.

system

system `cmdstring`...

Concatenate one or more command strings with space characters and execute the command using the system command interpreter (*/bin/sh* on Unix and *command.com* on Windows). Returns the numeric return code of the command.

tan

tan `arg`

Return the tangent of expression `arg`.

tanh

tanh `arg`

Return the hyperbolic tangent of expression `arg`.

tclx_errorHandler

tclx_errorHandler `message`

A user-written procedure to handle errors. Called before returning to the top-level command interpreter after an unhandled error.

times

times

Return a list containing four process CPU usage time values, in the form *utime stime cutime cstime*.

translit

translit inrange outrange string

Transliterate characters in *string*, replacing the characters occurring in *inrange* to the corresponding characters in *outrange*. The ranges may be lists of characters or a range in the form *lower-upper*.

Example

```
translit a-z A-Z "A string"
```

try_eval

try_eval code catch [finally]

Evaluate the command string *code*. If an error occurs, evaluate *code* and return the result. Last, execute the command string *finally*.

Example

```
try_eval {
    # code
    puts -nonewline stderr "Enter a number: "
    set ans [gets stdin]
    # could fail, e.g. due to divide by zero
    set res [expr 1.0 / $ans]
    puts stderr "1 / $ans = $res"
} {
    # catch
    set msg [lindex $errorCode end]
    puts stderr "Error: $msg"
} {
    # finally
    puts stderr "End of example"
}
```

umask

umask [octalmask]

Set the file creation mode mask to *octalmask*, which must be an octal (base 8) number. With no parameters, return the current mask.

union

union list1 list2

Return the logical union of two lists, i.e., a list of all elements contained in either *list1* or *list2*. The returned list is sorted alphabetically and has no duplicate elements.

wait

wait [*-nohang*] [*-untraced*] [*-pgroup*] [*pid*]

Wait for a child process with process ID *pid* to terminate (or any process if *pid* is omitted).

Options

-nohang
   Don't block waiting on the process to terminate.

-untraced
   Return status of other child processes.

-pgroup
   Wait on any processes in process group.

The command returns a list with three elements: the process ID of the process that terminated, the reason code (*EXIT, SIG, SIGSTP,* or *STOP*), and the numeric exit code.

write_file

write_file *fileName string...*

Write one or more strings to the file named *fileName*. Each string is terminated with a newline character.

CHAPTER 11

BLT

BLT, written by George A. Howlett, is not part of the core Tcl/Tk package, but can be obtained for free at *http://www.tcltk.com/blt*. At the time of this writing, the final 2.4 version of BLT had not been released. However, because of the addition of the tabset and hierbox widgets, it is bound to quickly become a popular version. Therefore, this chapter documents prerelease 2.4f, which should be extremely close to the final version. Footnotes in the description denote where changes may be expected.

BLT is an extension to Tcl/Tk designed to simplify a number of tasks that would normally require considerable coding. It provides commands for producing graphs and managing numerical data, a table-based geometry manager, a drag-and-drop facility, and several other graphical and utility commands. Several of BLT's commands have been partially incorporated into the standard Tcl/Tk distribution. It works with Unix under the X Window System and with Windows.

BLT can be loaded from existing Tcl applications or one can use the supplied *bltwish* command interpreter. In the former case, BLT can be loaded using the command:

```
package require BLT
```

on a properly configured system. The BLT commands will be defined in the `blt::` namespace. To make the BLT commands globally accessible, issue the command:

```
namespace import blt::*
```

Figure 11-1 shows some examples of BLT widgets.

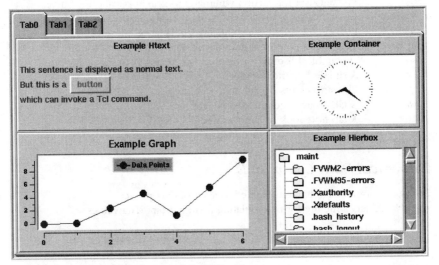

Figure 11-1: Examples of some of the BLT widgets

Environment Variable

The following environment variable is used by the BLT toolkit:

BLT_LIBRARY
    Directory containing Tcl scripts and other files needed by BLT at runtime

Special Variables

The following global variables have special meaning to the BLT toolkit:

`blt_library`
    Directory containing Tcl scripts and other files related to BLT. Uses the BLT_LIBRARY environment variable if set; otherwise uses a compiled-in library.

`blt_version`
    The current version of BLT in the form *major-number.minor-number*.

Group Listing of Commands

This section briefly lists all BLT commands, grouped logically by function.

Graphical Commands

barchart   Plot two-dimensional bar chart of data in a window.
bitmap   Read and write bitmaps using inline Tcl code.

busy	Prevent user interaction when a graphical application is busy.
container	Container for a window from another application.
drag&drop	Provide a drag-and-drop facility for Tk applications.
graph	Plot two-dimensional graphics of data in a window.
hierbox	Hierarchical listbox for displaying ordered trees.
htext	A simple hypertext widget.
stripchart	Plot strip charts of data in a window.
table	A table-based geometry manager.
tabset	A tab notebook or simple tabset.
winop	Raise, lower, map, or unmap a window.

Numerical Data Commands

spline	Compute a spline curve fitted to a set of data points.
vector	A data structure for manipulating floating-point data values.

Tile Widget Commands

tilebutton	Version of Tk *button* supporting background tiles.
tilecheckbutton	Version of Tk *checkbutton* supporting background tiles.
tileframe	Version of Tk *frame* supporting background tiles.
tilelabel	Version of Tk *label* supporting background tiles.
tileradiobutton	Version of Tk *radiobutton* supporting background tiles.
tilescrollbar	Version of Tk *scrollbar* supporting background tiles.
tiletoplevel	Version of Tk *toplevel* supporting background tiles.

Utility Commands

beep	Ring the keyboard bell.
bgexec	Similar to the Tcl *exec* command, but allows Tk to handle events while a process is executing.
bltdebug	Simple Tcl command tracing facility.
cutbuffer	Manipulate the eight X Window System cut buffers.
watch	Call user-defined procedures before or after execution of Tcl commands.

Alphabetical Summary of Commands

This section describes all BLT commands, listed in alphabetical order.

barchart

> *barchart* pathName [option value...]

See the *graph* command.

beep

beep `percent`

Ring the keyboard bell. `Percent` is relative to the base volume of the bell and can range from −100 to 100 inclusive, such that the actual volume will be between 0 and 100. The default `percent` is 50.

bgexec

bgexec `varName` [`options`...] `command` [`arg arg`...]

Run an external program, like the Tcl *exec* command, but allow Tk to process events while the program is running.

Parameter `varName` is a global variable that will be set to the program's exit status when the command is completed. Setting the variable will cause the program to be terminated with a signal.

Parameters `command` and `args` specify an external command with optional arguments in the same form as accepted by the Tcl *exec* command.

Normally, *bgexec* returns the results of the program. However, if the last argument is the ampersand (&), *bgexec* immediately returns a list of the spawned process IDs. The variable `varName` can be used with the *tkwait* command to wait for the program to finish.

Options

-error `varName`
> Cause `varName` to be set to the contents of standard error when the command has completed.

-update `varName`
> Cause `varName` to be set whenever data is written to standard output by the command.

-keepnewline `boolean`
> Enable or disable truncation of newline from last line of output.

-killsignal `signal`
> Specify (by name or number) the signal to be sent to the command when terminating. The default signal is SIGKILL.

-lasterror `varName`
> Same as the *-error* option, except `varName` is updated as soon as new data is available.

-lastoutput `varName`
> Same as the *-output* option, except `varName` is updated as soon as new data is available.

-onerror cmdPrefix
> When new data from standard error is available, evaluate the command *cmdPrefix* with the new data appended as an argument.

-onoutput cmdPrefix
> When new data from standard output is available, evaluate the command *cmdPrefix* with the new data appended as an argument.

-output varName
> Cause *varName* to be set to the contents of standard output when the command has completed.

-update varName
> Deprecated. Same as the *-lastoutput* option.

- -

> Mark the end of options (useful for commands that may start with a dash).

Example

```
global myStatus myOutput
set dir /tmp
bgexec myStatus -output myOutput du -s $dir
puts "Disk usage for $dir is $myOutput"
```

---

bitmap

bitmap operation bitmapName [arg arg...]

Create or return information about a bitmap created using inline Tcl code. The following operations are defined:

bitmap compose bitmapName text [option value...]
> Create a new bitmap from a text string and associate it with the name *bitmapName*. The bitmap is defined by the text in the parameter *text*. The following options are available:

> *-font fontName*
>> Specify the font to use when drawing text in the bitmap.

> *-rotate theta*
>> Rotate the bitmap by *theta* degrees.

> *-scale value*
>> Scale the bitmap by the factor of floating-point number *value*.

bitmap data bitmapName
> Return a list of the bitmap data. The first element is a list of the height and width, the second is a list of the source data.

bitmap define bitmapName data [option value...]
> Create a new bitmap and associate it with the name *bitmapName*. The bitmap is defined by parameter *data*, which is a list containing two elements. The first element is a list defining the height and width. The second element is a list of the source data.

The following options are available:

-rotate `theta`
> Rotate the bitmap by `theta` degrees.

-scale `value`
> Scale the bitmap by the factor of floating-point number `value`.

bitmap exists `bitmapName`
> Return 1 if a bitmap named `bitmapName` exists; otherwise, return 0.

bitmap height `bitmapName`
> Return the height of a bitmap in pixels.

bitmap source `bitmapName`
> Return the source data for a bitmap as a list of hexadecimal values.

bitmap width `bitmapName`
> Return the width of a bitmap in pixels.

Example

```
bitmap define crosshatch {{8 8} {0xaa 0x55 0xaa 0x55 0xaa 0x55 0xaa
    0x55}}
toplevel .t
tk_dialog .t title "<- Sample Bitmap" crosshatch 0 Continue

bitmap compose text "Some\nText" -rotate 90 -scale 2
toplevel .t
tk_dialog .t title "<- Sample Bitmap" text 0 Continue
```

bltdebug

bltdebug [`level`]

Trace Tcl commands by printing each command before it is executed. The command is shown both before and after substitutions. The integer value `level` indicates the number of stack levels to trace. A level of 0 disables all tracing. If `level` is omitted, the current level is returned.

busy

busy operation [`arg arg...`]

Make Tk widgets busy, temporarily blocking user interaction. In many cases, the *busy* command provides a more flexible alternative to the Tk *grab* command. The following operations are defined:

busy hold `window` [*-cursor* `cursor`]
> Make the widget `window` and all of its descendants busy. The *-cursor* option specifies the cursor to be displayed when busy. It accepts any of the standard Tk cursors; the default is `watch`. It can also be defined in the Tk resource database using resource and class names `busyCursor` and `BusyCursor`, respectively.

busy configure window [*option* [*value* [*option value*...]]]

   Query or modify the configuration parameters for a window previously
   made busy in the same manner as the general widget *configure* method.
   Available options are the same as for the *hold* operation.

busy forget window...

   Restore user interaction to the given *windows*. The input-only window
   used by *busy* is destroyed.

busy isbusy [*pattern*]

   Return the pathnames of all windows that are currently busy. With an
   optional pattern, return the names of busy widgets matching the pattern.

busy release window...

   Restore user interaction to the given *windows*. The input-only window
   used by *busy* is not destroyed.

busy status window

   Return the status of a window previously made busy. Return 1 if the window is busy, 0 otherwise.

busy windows [*pattern*]

   Return the pathnames of all windows that have previously been made
   busy or are currently busy. With an optional pattern, return the names of
   busy windows matching the pattern.

Example

```
frame .f
button .f.b -text "BUTTON"
pack .f.b
pack .f
busy hold .f.b
update
after 5000
busy release .f.b
```

---

container

container pathName [*option value*...]

The *container* command creates a new container widget named *pathName*.
A container widget is similar to a frame widget but is intended to contain a
window belonging to another application. Although the frame widget can do
this between other Tk applications, *container* works with non-Tk applications. This command is not supported under Windows.

Standard Options

-background	*-borderwidth*	*-cursor*
-highlightbackground	*-highlightcolor*	*-highlightthickness*
-relief	*-takefocus*	

Widget-Specific Options

-height `amount`   (`height`, `Height`)
> Desired height, in screen units, for the window.

-width `amount`   (`width`, `Width`)
> Desired width, in screen units, for the window.

-window `windowID`   (`window`, `Window`)
> The hexadecimal, platform-specific identifier for a window to be contained in the widget.

Example

```
container .c -window 0x3c00009
pack .c
```

cutbuffer

> *cutbuffer* `operation` [`arg`...]

Read or modify the eight X Window System cut buffer properties. This command is not supported under Windows. The following operations are defined:

cutbuffer get [`number`]
> Return the contents of cut buffer `number`, a number between 0 (the default) and 7. Any NULL bytes are converted to the @ character.

cutbuffer rotate [`count`]
> Rotate the cut buffers by `count`, a number between −7 and 7. The default is 1.

cutbuffer set `value` [`number`]
> Set the contents of cut buffer `number` to `value`. The default is 1.

drag&drop

> *drag&drop* `operation` [`arg arg`...]

Provide a drag-and-drop facility for Tk applications. Widgets registered as a drag-and-drop source can export data to other widgets registered as targets. The following operations are defined:

drag&drop active
> Return 1 if a drag-and-drop operation is in progress, 0 otherwise. A drag-and-drop operation officially starts after the package command has been executed successfully, and ends after the send handler has been executed (successfully or otherwise).

drag&drop drag `window x y`
> Handle dragging of the token window for source `window` during a drag-and-drop operation. If the token window is unmapped, the *-packagecmd* for the source window is executed. If this command is successful and returns a non-null string, the token window is mapped. On subsequent calls, the token window is moved to the given `x y` location.

drag&drop drop `window` *x* *y*

Handle the end of a drag-and-drop operation. If the location *x* *y* is over a compatible target window, the appropriate source handler for the first compatible data type is invoked. If the data transfer is successful, the token window is unmapped. Otherwise, a rejection symbol is drawn on the token window, and the window is unmapped after a small delay.

drag&drop errors [`proc`]

Specify that the Tcl procedure `proc` be used to handle errors that occur during drag-and-drop operations. If `proc` is not specified, the current error handler is returned. By default, all errors are sent to the usual *tkerror* command and therefore appear in a dialog box to the user.

drag&drop location [*x* *y*]

Set the pointer location during a drag-and-drop operation to location *x* *y*. If the coordinates are not given, then the last reported location is returned as a two-element list.

drag&drop source

Return a list of the pathnames of widgets registered as drag-and-drop sources.

drag&drop source `window` [`option` [`value` [`option` `value`...]]]

Register `window` as a drag-and-drop source with the given options, or modify the options for an existing source. The available options are as follows:

-button n   (`buttonBinding`, `ButtonBinding`)

Specify the mouse button (1–5) for invoking the drag-and-drop operation. The default is button 3. `ButtonPress` and `Motion` events for this button will be bound to the *drag* operation, and `Button-Release` events will be bound to the *drop* operation. If *n* is 0, then no binding is made.

-packagecmd command   (`packageCommand`, `PackageCommand`)

Specify a Tcl command used to establish the appearance of the token window at the start of each drag-and-drop operation.

The following substitutions are made in the command string before it is executed: `%t` is replaced with the window pathname for the token that represents the data being dragged; `%W` is replaced with the window pathname for the drag-and-drop source.

The return value of the command is remembered by the drag-and-drop manager and made available to the appropriate source handler command through the `%v` substitution. If no source handler command is defined, the value is used for the `%v` substitution for the target handler.

-rejectbg color   (`rejectBackground`, `Background`)

Specify the color used to draw the background of the rejection symbol on the token window. This appears whenever communication fails.

-rejectfg `color`   (`rejectForeground, Foreground`)
Specify the color used to draw the foreground of the rejection symbol on the token window.

-rejectstipple `pattern`   (`rejectStipple, Stipple`)
Specify the stipple pattern used to draw the rejection symbol on the token window.

-selftarget `boolean`   (`selfTarget, SelfTarget`)
Whether a widget defined as a drag-and-drop source and target will be permitted to transmit to itself. The default is `false`.

-send `list`   (`send, Send`)
Specify a list of the data types enabled for communication. Only data types defined with the *source window handler* operation are allowed. The order of data types in the list defines their priority for targets that handle multiple types. The default is `all`, which enables all data types in the order they were defined.

-sitecmd `command`   (`siteCommand, Command`)
Specify a Tcl command used to update the appearance of the token window while being dragged.

The following substitutions are made in the command string before it is executed: `%s` is replaced with 1 if the token window is over a compatible target, and 0 otherwise; `%t` is replaced with the window pathname for the token that represents the data being dragged.

-tokenactivebackground `color`   (`tokenActiveBackground, ActiveBackground`)
Specify the color used to draw the background of the token window when it is active.

-tokenanchor `anchor`   (`tokenAnchor, Anchor`)
Specify how the token window is positioned relative to the mouse pointer coordinates passed to the *drag&drop drag* operation. The default is `center`.

-tokenbg `color`   (`tokenBackground, Background`)
Specify the color used to draw the background of the token window.

-tokenborderwidth `size`   (`tokenBorderWidth, BorderWidth`)
Specify the width, in pixels, of the border around the token window. The default is 3.

-tokencursor `cursor`   (`tokenCursor, Cursor`)
Specify the cursor used when a token window is active. The default is `center_ptr`.

-tokenoutline `color`   (`tokenOutline, Outline`)
Specify the color for the outline drawn around the token window.

BLT

drag&drop source `window handler` [`dataType` [`command arg arg`...]]

Define `dataType` as a data type for which `window` is a drag-and-drop source. If `command` is given, it is concatenated with any `args` and evaluated whenever a target requests data of type `dataType` from the source `window`. If only `dataType` is given, it is defined if necessary and any command associated with it is returned.

The following substitutions are made in the command string before it is executed: `%i` is replaced with the name of the interpreter for the target application; `%v` is replaced with the value returned from the *-packagecmd* command, and `%w` is replaced with the window pathname for the target window. The return value of the command is made available to the target handler's command through its `%v` substitution.

drag&drop target

Return a list of pathnames for widgets registered as drag-and-drop targets.

drag&drop target `window handler` [`dataType command arg`...]

Register `window` as a drag-and-drop target capable of handling source data of type `dataType`. `Command` is concatenated with any `args` and evaluated whenever data of type `dataType` is dropped on the target.

The following substitutions are made in the command string before it is executed: `%v` is replaced with the value returned from the source's handler command (or the source's *-packagecmd* command if there is no handler); `%W` is replaced with the window pathname for the target window.

drag&drop target `window handle dataType`

Search for data type `dataType` among the handlers registered for the target `window` and invoke the appropriate command. An error is generated if no handler is found.

drag&drop token `window` [`option value`...]]]

With no options, return the pathname of the token window associated with drag-and-drop source `window`. The token window is used to represent data as it is being dragged from the source to a target. When a source is first established, its token window must be filled with widgets to display the source data.

If options are specified, they specify configuration options for the token. Available options are as follows:

-activebackground color   (activeBackground,
                                              ActiveBackground)

Specify the color used to draw the background of the token window when it is active.

-activeborderwidth size   (activeBorderWidth,
                                              ActiveBorderWidth)

Specify the width, in pixels, of the border around the token window when it is active.

-activerelief relief   (activeBackground, ActiveBackground)
    3D effect for border of the token window when it is active.

-anchor anchor   (anchor, Anchor)
    Specify how the token window is positioned relative to the mouse
    pointer coordinates passed to the *drag&drop drag* operation. The
    default is center.

-background color   (background, Background)
    Specify the color used to draw the background of the token win-
    dow.

-borderwidth size   (borderWidth, BorderWidth)
    Specify the width, in pixels, of the border around the token window.
    The default is 3.

-cursor cursor   (cursor, Cursor)
    Specify the cursor used when a token window is active. The default
    is center_ptr.

-outline color   (outline, Outline)
    Specify the color for the outline drawn around the token window.

-rejectbg color   (rejectBackground, Background)
    Specify the color used to draw the background of the rejection sym-
    bol on the token window. This appears whenever communication
    fails.

-rejectfg color   (rejectForeground, Foreground)
    Specify the color used to draw the foreground of the rejection sym-
    bol on the token window.

-rejectstipple pattern   (rejectStipple, Stipple)
    Specify the stipple pattern used to draw the rejection symbol on the
    token window.

-relief relief   (relief, Relief)
    3D effect for border of the token window.

Example

For a complete example of using this command, see the demo programs
included with the BLT distribution.

---

graph

graph pathName [option value...]

stripchart pathName [option value...]

barchart pathName [option value...]

BLT supports three types of charts with the *graph*, *stripchart*, and *barchart*
commands. The methods and options for each of these widgets are nearly
identical; therefore, all three are described here with the differences noted as
appropriate.

The *graph* command creates a new graph widget named *pathName* for plotting two-dimensional data (x- and y-coordinates) using symbols and/or connecting lines. A graph widget is composed of several components: coordinate axes, data elements, a legend, a grid, crosshairs, pens, a PostScript generator, and annotation markers. Methods exist for creating (if necessary) and manipulating each of these components.

The *stripchart* command creates a new strip chart widget named *pathName*. A strip chart widget is almost exactly the same as a graph widget except that the x-axis typically refers to time points and has better support for maintaining a view of recent data. The primary difference is support for the *-autorange* and *-shiftby* axis options.

The *barchart* command creates a new bar chart widget named *pathName*. A bar chart widget is essentially the same as a graph widget except that vertical bars are used to represent the data rather than symbols and lines. Therefore the bar chart has very different element and pen configuration options. It also supports the additions to the axis configuration used by the strip chart to handle dynamic data.

Any number of independent coordinate axes can be created and used to map data points. Axes consist of the axis line, title, major and minor ticks, and tick labels. Only four axes can be displayed at one time. They are drawn along the four borders of the plotting area. Four axes are automatically created for each graph. These are named x, x2, y, and y2, which are associated with the bottom, top, left, and right boundaries, respectively. Only x and y are shown by default.

Grid lines can be drawn to extend the major and minor ticks from axes. Crosshairs can be displayed to track the position of the mouse on the plotting area.

A set of data values plotted on the chart is called an *element*. Each element can be drawn with connecting lines, symbols, or both. Pens can be defined for controlling the display attributes of both lines and symbols. Each element may use multiple pens. A legend can be displayed anywhere on the chart to identify the plotted elements.

Six types of annotations, called *markers*, are supported: text, line, image, bitmap, polygon, and window. A marker is created and manipulated with the *marker* methods and can be placed at an arbitrary position on the chart. Markers are similar in operation to canvas items.

Standard Options

-background	*-borderwidth*	*-cursor*
-font	*-foreground*	*-relief*
-takefocus		

Widget-Specific Options

-aspect ratio   (aspect, Aspect)

> The height or width of the plotting area will be shrunk to maintain a ratio of width to height of *ratio*.

-barmode mode   (barMode, BarMode)

[bar chart only] How bars with the same x-coordinate should be displayed. Valid values for *mode* are as follows:

normal
> No effort is made to keep bars from obscuring each other.

aligned
> Bars are reduced in width and drawn side by side in display order so they do not overlap.

overlap
> Bars are slightly offset and reduced in width so all bars are visible but overlap each other in display order.

stacked
> Bars are stacked on top of each other in display order.

-barwidth amount   (barWidth, BarWidth)

[bar chart only] Width of bars in chart x-coordinates. The default is 1.0.

-baseline y   (baseline, Baseline)

[bar chart only] Baseline along y-axis for bars. Bars for values greater than *y* are drawn upward, and bars for values less than *y* are drawn downward. The default is 0.0. For a log scale y-axis, the baseline is always 1.0.

-bottommargin amount   (bottomMargin, Margin)

Size, in screen units, of the margin from x-coordinate axis to the bottom of the window. If *amount* is 0, the margin is autosized.

-bottomvariable varName   (bottomVariable, BottomVariable)

Variable that will be automatically updated with the current size of the bottom margin.

-bufferelements boolean   (bufferElements, BufferElements)

Whether to use a pixmap to cache the display elements. Useful if data points are frequently redrawn. The default is true.

-halo amount   (halo, Halo)

Threshold distance when searching for the closest data point.

-height amount   (height, Height)

Desired height, in screen units, for the window.

-invertxy boolean   (invertXY, InvertXY)

Whether placement of the x- and y-axis should be inverted.

-justify justify   (justify, Justify)

How the title should be aligned on the chart. Parameter *justify* may be left, right, or center (the default).

-leftmargin amount   (leftMargin, Margin)

Size, in screen units, of the margin from the left edge of the window to the y-coordinate axis. If *amount* is 0, the margin is autosized.

-leftvariable varName   (leftVariable, LeftVariable)
Variable that will be automatically updated with the current size of the left margin.

-plotbackground color   (plotBackground, Background)
Background color for the plotting area.

-plotborderwidth amount   (plotBorderWidth, BorderWidth)
Window of 3D border drawn around the plotting area.

-plotpadx amount   (plotPadX, PlotPad)
Amount of padding, in screen units, to add to the left and right sides of the plotting area. Parameter *amount* may be a list of two screen distances to set the left and right padding separately.

-plotpady amount   (plotPadY, PlotPad)
Amount of padding, in screen units, to add to the top and bottom sides of the plotting area. Parameter *amount* may be a list of two screen distances to set the top and bottom padding separately.

-plotrelief relief   (plotRelief, Relief)
3D relief for border drawn around the plotting area.

-rightmargin amount   (rightMargin, Margin)
Size, in screen units, of the margin from the plotting area to the right edge of the window.

-rightvariable varName   (rightVariable, RightVariable)
Variable that will be automatically updated with the current size of the right margin.

-shadow color   (shadow, Shadow)
Color for the shadow drawn beneath the title text. The default is the empty string (i.e., transparent).

-tile image   (tile, Tile)
Image to use for a tiled background for the chart. If *image* is the empty string (the default), no tiling is done.

-title string   (title, Title)
Title for the chart. If *string* is the empty string (the default), no title is displayed.

-topmargin amount   (topMargin, Margin)
Size, in screen units, of the margin from the top edge of the window to the plotting area.

-topvariable varName   (topVariable, TopVariable)
Variable that will be automatically updated with the current size of the top margin.

-width amount   (width, Width)
Desired width, in screen units, for the window.

Methods

pathName *axis cget* `axisName option`

Return the current value of the option `option` for the axis `axisName` in the same manner as the general widget *cget* method. Supported options are those available to the *axis create* method used to create the axis.

pathName *axis configure* `axisName` [`axisName...`] [`option value...`]

Query or modify the configuration options for the axes `axisName`s in the same manner as the general widget *configure* method. Supported options are those available for the *axis create* method.

pathName *axis create* `axisName` [`option value...`]

Create a new axis in the chart named `axisName` configured with the given options. Supported options are as follows:

-autorange range　　　　　　　　　　(autoRange, AutoRange)

[bar chart and strip chart only] Set the allowed range (difference between the maximum and minimum limit values) for the axis to `range`. If `range` is 0.0 (the default), the range is determined from the limits of the data. The option is overridden by the *-min* and *-max* options.

-color color　　　　　　　　　　　　(color, Color)

Foreground color for the axis and its labels.

-command tclCommand　　　　　　　　(command, Command)

Command to call when formatting the axis labels. The pathname of the chart and the numeric value of the axis label are appended as arguments. The return value of the command is used as the final label.

-descending boolean　　　　　　　(descending, Descending)

Whether coordinate values should decrease along the axis. The default is `false`.

-hide boolean　　　　　　　　　　　(hide, Hide)

Whether axis should be hidden (not drawn).

-justify justify　　　　　　　　　(justify, Justify)

How multiple lines in the axis title should be aligned. justify must be `left`, `right`, or `center` (the default).

-limitcolor color　　　　　　　　(limitColor, Color)

Color used to draw axis limits.

-limitfont font　　　　　　　　　(limitFont, Font)

Font used to draw axis limits.

-limits formatStr　　　　　　　　(limits, Limits)

A *printf*-like format string to format the minimum and maximum limits. If `formatStr` is a list with two elements, the two elements are the format strings for the minimum and maximum limits. If `formatStr` is the empty string (the default), the limits are not displayed.

-limitshadow color   (limitShadow, Shadow)
    Color to use to draw the shadow for axis limits.

-linewidth amount   (lineWidth, LineWidth)
    Line width for the axis and its ticks. The default is 1.

-logscale boolean   (logScale, LogScale)
    Whether the scale of the axis should be logarithmic. The default is
    false.

-loose boolean   (loose, Loose)
    Whether the axis range, when autoscaling, should fit loosely around
    the data points at the outer tick intervals. The default is false.

-majorticks majorList   (majorTicks, MajorTicks)
    Where to display major axis ticks. Parameter *majorList* is a list of
    axis coordinates designating the location of major ticks. No minor
    ticks are drawn. If the list is empty, major ticks are automatically
    computed.

-max value   (max, Max)
    The maximum limit of the axis. Data points above this limit are
    clipped. If *value* is the empty string, the maximum value of the
    axis is autoscaled.

-min value   (min, Min)
    The minimum limit of the axis. Data points below this limit are
    clipped. If *value* is the empty string, the minimum value of the
    axis is autoscaled.

-minorticks minorList   (minorTicks, MinorTicks)
    Where to display minor axis ticks. Parameter *minorList* is a list of
    real values between 0.0 and 1.0 designating the location of minor
    ticks between each pair of major ticks. If the list is empty, minor
    ticks are automatically computed.

-rotate theta   (rotate, Rotate)
    Angle, in degrees, to rotate the axis labels. The default is 0.0.

-shiftby value   (shiftBy, ShiftBy)
    [bar chart and strip chart only] How much to automatically shift the
    range of the axis when new data exceeds the current axis maximum
    limit. The limit is increased in increments of *value*. If *value* is 0.0
    (the default), no automatic shifting is done.

-showticks boolean   (showTicks, ShowTicks)
    Whether axis ticks should be drawn. The default is true.

-stepsize value   (stepSize, StepSize)
    The step size between major axis ticks. If the value is not greater
    than zero or is greater than the full range of the axis, the step size is
    automatically calculated.

-subdivisions number   (subdivisions, Subdivisions)
> Number of minor axis tick intervals between major ticks. The default is 2, corresponding to one minor tick being drawn.

-tickfont fontName   (tickFont, Font)
> Font to use for drawing the axis tick labels.

-ticklength amount   (tickLength, TickLength)
> Length of the major ticks. Minor ticks are set to half this length. If *amount* is negative, tick will point away from the plotting area.

-tickshadow color   (tickShadow, Shadow)
> Color to use for drawing the shadow for the axis tick labels.

-title string   (title, Title)
> Title for the axis.

-titlecolor color   (titleColor, Color)
> Foreground color to use for drawing the axis title.

-titlefont fontName   (titleFont, Font)
> Font to use for drawing the axis title.

-titleshadow color   (titleShadow, Shadow)
> Foreground color to use for drawing the axis title.

pathName axis delete axisName...
> Delete the given axes. An axis is not really deleted until all elements and markers mapped to it are deleted.

pathName axis invtransform axisName coord
> Perform an inverse coordinate transformation, mapping the screen coordinate *coord* to its corresponding chart coordinate on the axis *axisName*. The calculated chart coordinate is returned.

pathName axis limits axisName
> Return a list of two coordinates representing the minimum and maximum limits of the axis.

pathName axis names [pattern...]
> Return a list of axes with names that match any of the given patterns. If no pattern is specified, the names of all axes are returned.

pathName axis transform axisName coord
> Transform the chart coordinate *coord* on the axis *axisName* to its corresponding screen coordinate. The calculated screen coordinate is returned.

pathName bar operation arg...
> The *bar* method is identical to the *element* method in bar chart widgets. In a future version of BLT, the *bar* method will be supported by graph widgets in order to mix line- and bar-type elements.

pathName crosshairs cget *option*

> Return the current value of the option *option* for the crosshairs in the same manner as the general widget *cget* method. Supported options are those available to the *crosshairs configure* method.

pathName crosshairs configure [option value...]

> Query or modify the configuration options for the chart's crosshairs in the same manner as the general widget *configure* method. Supported options are as follows:

> *-color color*   (color, Color)
> > Color for the crosshair lines.

> *-dashes dashStyle*   (dashes, Dashes)
> > Dash style for the crosshair lines. Parameter *dashStyle* is a list of up to 11 numbers that alternately represent the lengths of the dashes and gaps. Each number must be between 1 and 255, inclusive. If *dashStyle* is the empty string (the default), a solid line is drawn.

> *-hide boolean*   (hide, Hide)
> > Whether crosshairs should be hidden (not drawn). The default is true.

> *-linewidth amount*   (lineWidth, LineWidth)
> > Line width for the crosshairs.

> *-position @x,y*   (position, Position)
> > The chart *x*- and *y*- coordinates of the crosshairs.

pathName crosshairs *off*

> Turn off the drawing of the crosshairs.

pathName crosshairs *on*

> Turn on the drawing of the crosshairs.

pathName crosshairs *toggle*

> Toggle drawing of the crosshairs.

pathName element activate *elemName* [index...]

> Make the data points in element *elemName* at the given indices active. If no indices are specified, all data points in the element are made active.

pathName element bind *tagName* [sequence [command]]

> Bind *command* to all elements with tag *tagName* so it is invoked when the given event *sequence* occurs for the element. The syntax for this method is the same as for the standard Tk *bind* command except that it operates on graph elements. *TagName* may be the name of a single element, the special tag all (bind to all elements), or an arbitrary string. Only keyboard and mouse events can be bound.

pathName element cget *elemName option*

> Return the current value of the option *option* for the element *elemName* in the same manner as the general widget *cget* method. Supported options are those available to the *element create* method used to create the axis.

pathName *element* *closest* *winX* *winY* *varName* [*option* *value*...] [*elemName*...]

Find the data point closest to window coordinates *winX* and *winY*. If found, a 1 is returned and the variable *varName* is set equal to a list containing the name of the closest element, the index of the closest point, and the chart xy-coordinates of the point. If no data point is found within the threshold distance given by the *-halo* option, a 0 is returned. The optional *elemName* arguments restrict the search to the given elements. The following options can be specified to further modify the search:

-halo *amount*

Threshold distance outside of which points are ignored in search. Overrides the chart *-halo* option.

-interpolate *boolean*

Whether interpolated points should also be considered in the search. Useful for graph widgets only.

pathName *element* *configure* *elemName* [*elemName*...] [*option* *value*...]

Query or modify the configuration options for the elements *elemNames* in the same manner as the general widget *configure* method. Supported options are those available for the *element create* method.

pathName *element* *create* *elemName* [*option* *value*...]

Create a new element in the chart named *elemName* configured with the given options. Options supported by all three chart widgets are:

-activepen *penName*   (activePen, ActivePen)

Name of pen to use to draw element when it is active.

-bindtags *tagList*   (bindTags, BindTags)

The binding tag list for the element, which determines the order of evaluation of the commands for matching event bindings. Implicitly, the name of the element itself is always the first tag in the list. The default value is all.

-data *coordList*   (data, Data)

Chart coordinates for the data points to be plotted. Parameter *coordList* is a list of real numbers representing x- and y-coordinate pairs.

-hide *boolean*   (hide, Hide)

Whether element is hidden (not drawn).

-label *string*   (label, Label)

Label for the element in the legend.

-labelrelief *relief*   (labelRelief, LabelRelief)

3D effect of border around label for the element in the legend.

-mapx *xaxis*   (mapX, MapX)

Name of x-axis onto which to map element's data. The default is x.

-mapy yaxis   (mapY, MapY)
  Name of y-axis onto which to map element's data. The default is y.

-pen penName   (pen, Pen)
  Name of pen to use to draw element when it is not active. The pen's
  options override those explicitly set with *element configure.*

-styles styleList   (styles, Styles)
  Styles used to draw the data point symbols or bars. Each element of
  styleList is a list consisting of a pen name and, optionally, two
  numbers defining a minimum and maximum range. Data points
  whose weights fall inside this range are drawn with this pen. If no
  range is specified, the default range is a single value equal to the
  index of the pen in the list.

-weights wVec   (weights, Weights)
  Weights of the individual data points. Parameter *wVec* is a BLT vector or list.

-xdata xvec   (xData, XData)
  The x-coordinates of the data points for the element. Overrides *-data*
  option. Parameter *xvec* is a BLT vector or list.

-ydata yvec   (yData, YData)
  The y-coordinates of the data points for the element. Overrides *-data*
  option. Parameter *yvec* is a BLT vector or list.

Options supported by only the graph and strip chart widgets are as follows:

-color color   (color, Color)
  Color for traces connecting the data points.

-dashes dashStyle   (dashes, Dashes)
  Dash style for lines. Parameter *dashStyle* is a list of up to 11 numbers that alternately represent the lengths of the dashes and gaps.
  Each number must be between 1 and 255, inclusive. If *dashStyle*
  is the empty string (the default), a solid line is drawn.

-fill color   (fill, Fill)
  Interior color for the data point symbols. If *color* is the empty
  string, the color is transparent. If *color* is defcolor (the default),
  the color is the same as the value for the *-color* option.

-linewidth amount   (lineWidth, LineWidth)
  Width of connecting lines between data points.

-offdash color   (offDash, OffDash)
  Color for stripes when traces are dashed. If *color* is the empty
  string, the color is transparent. If *color* is defcolor (the default),
  the color is the same as the value for the *-color* option.

-outline color   (outline, Outline)

Color for outline drawn around each symbol. If `color` is the empty string, the color is transparent. If `color` is defcolor (the default), the color is the same as the value for the *-color* option.

-outlinewidth amount   (outlineWidth, OutlineWidth)

Width of the outline drawn around each symbol. The default is 1.0.

-pixels amount   (pixels, Pixels)

Size of the symbols. If *amount* is zero, no symbol is drawn. The default is 0.125i.

-scalesymbols boolean   (scaleSymbols, ScaleSymbols)

Whether the size of the symbols should change to scale with future changes to the scale of the axes.

-smooth type   (smooth, Smooth)

How connecting lines are drawn between the data points. If *type* is linear, a single line segment is drawn. If *type* is step, first a horizontal line is drawn to the next x-coordinate and then a vertical line to the next y-coordinate. If *type* is natural or quadratic, multiple segments are drawn between the data points using a cubic or quadratic spline, respectively. The default is linear.

-symbol symbol   (symbol, Symbol)

Type of symbol to use for data points. Parameter *symbol* may be square, circle, diamond, plus, cross, splus, scross, triangle, or a bitmap. Bitmaps are represented as a list specifying the bitmap and an optional mask. If *symbol* is the empty string, no symbol is drawn. The default is circle.

-trace type   (trace, Trace)

[graph only] How to draw lines between data. If *type* is increasing, lines are drawn only between monotonically increasing points. If *type* is decreasing, lines are drawn only between monotonically decreasing points. If *type* is both, lines between points are always drawn. The default is both.

Options supported by only the bar chart widget are as follows:

-background color   (background, Background)

Color of border around each bar.

-barwidth amount   (barWidth, BarWidth)

Width of the bar in x-coordinate values. Overrides the widget's *-barwidth* option.

-borderwidth amount   (borderWidth, BorderWidth)

Width of 3D border drawn around each bar.

-foreground color   (foreground, Foreground)

Color of the interior of each bar.

-relief relief   (relief, Relief)
>   3D relief for border drawn around each bar.

-stipple bitmap   (stipple, Stipple)
>   Stipple pattern used to draw each bar. If *bitmap* is the empty string
>   (the default), the bar is drawn in solid color.

pathName element deactivate pattern...
>   Deactivate all elements whose names match any of the given patterns.

pathName element delete elemName...
>   Delete all the given elements from the chart.

pathName element exists elemName
>   Return 1 if an element named *elemName* exists, 0 otherwise.

pathName element names [*pattern...*]
>   Return a list of the names of all the elements that match the given pat-
>   terns. If no patterns are specified, the names of all elements in the chart
>   are returned.

pathName element show [*nameList*]
>   If *nameList* is specified, it is a list of elements that should be displayed
>   on the chart and in what order. Otherwise, the current display list is
>   returned. Elements not in the list are not drawn.

pathName element type elemName
>   Return the type of element *elemName*, either `bar` for bar charts or `line`
>   for graphs and strip charts.

pathName extents Item
>   Return the size of an item in the chart. *Item* must be `leftmargin`,
>   `rightmargin`, `topmargin`, `bottommargin`, `plotwidth`, or
>   `plotheight`.

pathName grid cget option
>   Return the current value of the option *option* for the grid in the same
>   manner as the general widget *cget* method. Supported options are those
>   available to the *grid configure* method.

pathName grid configure [*option value...*]
>   Query or modify the configuration options for the chart's grid in the same
>   manner as the general widget *configure* method. By default, the grid is
>   hidden for the graph and strip chart widgets, and only horizontal grid
>   lines are shown for the bar chart widget. Supported options are as fol-
>   lows:

-color color   (color, Color)
>   Color for the grid lines.

-dashes dashStyle   (dashes, Dashes)
>   Dash style for grid lines. Parameter *dashStyle* is a list of up to 11
>   numbers that alternately represent the lengths of the dashes and
>   gaps. Each number must be between 1 and 255, inclusive. If *dash-
>   Style* is the empty string (the default), a solid line is drawn.

-hide boolean   (hide, Hide)
> Whether the grid lines should be hidden (not drawn). The default is
> true.

-linewidth amount   (lineWidth, LineWidth)
> Line width for the grid lines.

-mapx xaxis   (mapX, MapX)
> Name of x-axis onto which to map vertical grid lines. If *xaxis* is
> the empty string, no vertical grid lines are drawn. The default is the
> empty string for bar charts and x for graphs and strip charts.

-mapy yaxis   (mapY, MapY)
> Name of y-axis onto which to map horizontal grid lines. If *yaxis* is
> the empty string, no horizontal grid lines are drawn. The default is y.

-minor boolean   (minor, Minor)
> Whether grid lines should be drawn for minor ticks. The default is
> true.

pathName grid off
> Turn off the drawing of the grid lines.

pathName grid on
> Turn on the drawing of the grid lines.

pathName grid toggle
> Toggle drawing of the grid lines.

pathName invtransform winX winY
> Perform an inverse coordinate transformation, mapping the given win-
> dow coordinates to chart coordinates. The calculated x- and y- chart
> coordinates are returned.

pathName inside x y
> Return 1 if the given screen coordinates *x y* are inside the plotting area,
> 0 otherwise.

pathName legend activate pattern...
> Activate all legend entries whose names match the given patterns.

pathName legend bind elemName [sequence [command]]
> Bind *command* to the legend entry associated with element *elemName*
> so it is invoked when the given event *sequence* occurs for the entry.
> The syntax for this method is the same as for the standard Tk *bind* com-
> mand except that it operates on legend entries. If *elemName* is all, the
> binding applies to all entries. Only keyboard and mouse events can be
> bound.

pathName legend cget option
> Return the current value of the option *option* for the legend in the
> same manner as the general widget *cget* method. Supported options are
> those available to the *legend configure* method.

BLT

pathName legend configure [option value...]

Query or modify the configuration options for the chart's legend in the same manner as the general widget *configure* method. Supported options are as follows:

-activebackground color   (activeBackground, ActiveBackground)

Background color for active legend entries.

-activeborderwidth amount   (activeBorderWidth, ActiveBorderWidth)

Width of 3D border around active legend entries.

-activeforeground color   (activeForeground, ActiveForeground)

Foreground color for active legend entries.

-activerelief relief   (activeRelief, ActiveRelief)

Relief of border around active legend entries.

-anchor anchorPos   (anchor, Anchor)

How legend should be positioned relative to its positioning point. The default is center. How *anchorPos* is interpreted depends on the value of the positioning point (see the *-position* option).

-background color   (background, Background)

Background color for the legend. The default is an empty string (transparent).

-borderwidth amount   (borderWidth, BorderWidth)

Width of the 3D border around the legend.

-font fontName   (font, Font)

Font to use for the labels of legend entries.

-foreground color   (foreground, Foreground)

Foreground color for the legend.

-hide boolean   (hide, Hide)

Whether the legend should be hidden (not drawn).

-ipadx amount   (iPadX, Pad)

Internal horizontal padding between the legend border and entries. If *amount* has two elements, it specifies the padding for the left and right sides, in that order.

-ipady amount   (iPadY, Pad)

Internal vertical padding between the legend border and entries. If *amount* has two elements, it specifies the padding for the top and bottom, in that order.

-padx amount   (padX, Pad)

Extra padding on the left and right side of the legend. If *amount* has two elements, it specifies the padding for the left and right sides, in that order.

-pady `amount`   (`padY, Pad`)
> Extra padding on the top and bottom side of the legend. If `amount` has two elements, it specifies the padding for the top and bottom, in that order.

-position `position`   (`position, Position`)
> Positioning point for the legend in window coordinates. Valid values for `position` (the default is `right`) are as follows:

> `@x,y`
>> Legend is placed so its anchor point is at the given window coordinates.

> `left` or `right`
>> Legend is drawn in left or right margin. The anchor point affects only the vertical position.

> `top` or `bottom`
>> Legend is drawn in the top or bottom margin. The anchor point affects only the horizontal position.

> `plotarea`
>> Legend is placed inside the plotting area. The anchor point of the legend is placed at the same cardinal point of the plotting area. For example, if the anchor is `ne`, the legend will occupy the upper-right corner of the plotting area.

-raised `boolean`   (`raised, Raised`)
> Whether legend should be drawn above data elements when in the plotting area. The default is `false`.

-relief `relief`   (`relief, Relief`)
> Relief of the border around the legend.

-shadow `color`   (`shadow, Shadow`)
> Color for the shadow drawn beneath the entry labels. The default is the empty string (i.e., transparent).

`pathName` *legend deactivate* `pattern...`
> Deactivate the legend entries whose names match the given patterns.

`pathName` *legend get* `@x,y`
> Return the name of the element with a legend entry at window coordinates *x,y* in the legend.

`pathName` *line operation* `arg...`
> The *line* method is identical to the *element* method in graph and strip chart widgets. In a future version of BLT, the *line* method will be supported by bar chart widgets in order to mix line- and bar-type elements.

`pathName` *marker after* `markerId` [`markerId`]
> Reorder the marker display list, placing the first specified marker after the second. If the second `markerId` is omitted, the marker is placed at the end of the list. Markers are drawn in order from this list.

pathName **marker before** `markerId` [`markerId`]

Reorder the marker display list, placing the first specified marker before the second. If the second `markerId` is omitted, the marker is placed at the beginning of the list. Markers are drawn in order from this list.

pathName **marker bind** `tagName` [`sequence` [`command`]]

Bind `command` to all markers with tag `tagName` so it is invoked when the given event `sequence` occurs for the marker. The syntax for this method is the same as for the standard Tk *bind* command except that it operates on graph markers. *TagName* may be the name of a single marker, a capitalized marker type (e.g., `Line`, for all line markers), the special tag `all` (bind to all markers), or an arbitrary string. Only keyboard and mouse events can be bound.

pathName **marker cget** `markerId` `option`

Return the current value of the option `option` for the marker `markerId` in the same manner as the general widget *cget* method. Supported options are those available to the *marker create* method used to create the marker.

pathName **marker configure** `markerId` [`option value`...]

Query or modify the configuration options for the marker `markerId` in the same manner as the general widget *configure* method. Supported options are those available to the *marker create* method used to create the marker.

pathName **marker create** `type` [`option value`...]

Create a new marker in the chart of the selected type configured with the given options. *Type* may be `text`, `bitmap`, `image`, `line`, `polygon`, or `window`. A unique marker identifier for the newly created marker is returned (see the *-name* option). Options that are specific to each marker type are described in the following sections. Options that are supported by all marker types are as follows:

-bindtags `tagList`   (bindtags, bindTags)

The binding tag list for the marker, which determines the order of evaluation of the commands for matching event bindings. Implicitly, the name of the marker itself is always the the first tag in the list. The default value is `all`.

-coords `coordList`   (coords, Coords)

A list of real numbers that represent the appropriate x- and y-coordinate pairs for the marker. For text and window markers, only two coordinates are needed, which give the position point of the marker. Bitmap and image markers can take two or four coordinates. Line markers require at least four coordinates (two pairs), and polygon markers require at least six (three pairs).

-element `elemName`   (element, Element)

Indicates that the marker should be drawn only if element `elemName` is currently displayed.

-hide boolean   (hide, Hide)
> Whether markers should be hidden (not drawn).

-mapx xaxis   (mapX, MapX)
> The x-axis onto which to map the marker's x-coordinates. Parameter *xaxis* must be the name of an axis. The default is x.

-mapy xaxis   (mapY, MapY)
> The y-axis onto which to map the marker's y-coordinates. Parameter *xaxis* must be the name of an axis. The default is y.

-name markerId
> ID to use to identify the marker. Parameter *markerId* must not be used by another marker. If this option is not specified at creation, a unique ID is generated.

-under boolean   (under, Under)
> Whether marker is drawn below the data elements so as not to obscure them.

-xoffset amount   (xOffset, XOffset)
> Screen distance by which to offset the marker horizontally.

-yoffset amount   (yOffset, YOffset)
> Screen distance by which to offset the marker vertically.

pathName marker delete markerId...
> Delete all markers from the chart with the given IDs.

pathName marker exists markerId
> Return 1 if a marker with ID *markerId* exists, 0 otherwise.

pathName marker names [pattern]
> Return a list of marker IDs defined in the chart. If pattern is given, only those IDs that match it are returned.

pathName marker type markerId
> Return the type of the marker *markerId*.

pathName pen cget penName option
> Return the current value of the option option for the pen *penName* in the same manner as the general widget *cget* method. Supported options are those available to the *pen create* method used to create the axis.

pathName pen configure penName [penName...] [option value...]
> Query or modify the configuration options for the pens *penNames* in the same manner as the general widget *configure* method. Supported options are those available for the *pen create* method.

pathName pen create penName [-type type] [option value...]
> Create a new pen of the specified type in the chart named *penName* configured with the given options. *Type* may be line or bar. If type is not given, it defaults to line for graph and strip chart widgets and to bar for bar chart widgets.

Supported options for pens of type `line` are as follows:

-color color   (color, Color)
Color of the traces connecting the data points.

-dashes dashStyle   (dashes, Dashes)
Dash style for lines. Parameter *dashStyle* is a list of up to 11 numbers that alternately represent the lengths of the dashes and gaps. Each number must be between 1 and 255, inclusive. If *dashStyle* is the empty string (the default), a solid line is drawn.

-fill color   (fill, Fill)
Interior color for the data point symbols. If *color* is the empty string, the color is transparent. If *color* is defcolor (the default), the color is the same as the value for the *-color* option.

-linewidth amount   (lineWidth, LineWidth)
Width of connecting lines between data points. The default is 0.

-offdash color   (offDash, OffDash)
Color for stripes when traces are dashed. If *color* is the empty string, the color is transparent. If *color* is defcolor (the default), the color is the same as the value for the *-color* option.

-outline color   (outline, Outline)
Color for outline drawn around each symbol. If *color* is the empty string, the color is transparent. If *color* is defcolor (the default), the color is the same as the value for the *-color* option.

-outlinewidth amount   (outlineWidth, OutlineWidth)
Width of the outline drawn around each symbol. The default is 1.0.

-pixels amount   (pixels, Pixels)
Size of the symbols. If *amount* is 0, no symbol is drawn. The default is 0.125i.

-symbol symbol   (symbol, Symbol)
Type of symbol to use for data points. Parameter *symbol* may be square, circle, diamond, plus, cross, splus, scross, triangle, or a bitmap. Bitmaps are represented as a list specifying the bitmap and an optional mask. If *symbol* is the empty string, no symbol is drawn. The default is circle.

Supported options for pens of type `bar` are as follows:

-background color   (background, Background)
Color of border around each bar.

-borderwidth amount   (borderWidth, BorderWidth)
Width of 3D border drawn around each bar.

-foreground color   (foreground, Foreground)
Color of the interior of each bar.

-relief `relief`   `(relief, Relief)`
3D relief for border drawn around each bar.

-stipple `bitmap`   `(stipple, Stipple)`
Stipple pattern used to draw each bar. If `bitmap` is the empty string
(the default), the bar is drawn in solid color.

`pathName` *pen delete* `penName`...
Delete the given pens. A pen is not really deleted until all elements using
it are deleted.

`pathName` *pen names* [`pattern`...]
Return a list of the names of all pens that match the given patterns. If no
patterns are specified, the names of all pens in the chart are returned.

`pathName` *postscript cget* `option`
Return the current value of the PostScript option `option` in the same
manner as the general widget *cget* method. Supported options are those
available to the *postscript configure* method used to create the axis.

`pathName` *postscript configure* [`option value`...]
Query or modify the configuration options for PostScript generation in
the same manner as the general widget *configure* method. Supported
options are as follows:

-center `boolean`   `(psCenter, PsCenter)`
Whether plot should be centered on the PostScript page. The default
is `true`.

-colormap `varName`   `(psColorMap, PsColorMap)`
A global array variable that specifies the color mapping from the X
color to PostScript code to set that color. If no element of the array is
found for a color, default code is generated using RGB intensities.

-colormode `mode`   `(psColorMode, PsColorMode)`
How to output color information. Parameter `mode` may be `color`,
`gray`, or `mono`. The default is `color`.

-decorations `boolean`   `(psDecorations, PsDecorations)`
Whether PostScript commands generate color backgrounds and 3D
borders in the output. The default is `true`.

-fontmap `varName`   `(psFontMap, PsFontMap)`
A global array variable that specifies the font mapping from X font
name to a two-element list specifying a PostScript font and point
size. If no mapping exits, BLT makes a best guess for Adobe X fonts
and uses Helvetica Bold for others.

-height `amount`   `(psHeight, PsHeight)`
Height of the plot. If `amount` is 0, then the height is the same as the
widget height.

-landscape boolean   (psLandscape, PsLandscape)
>   Whether the printed area is to be rotated 90 degrees.

-maxpect boolean   (psMaxpect, PsMaxpect)
>   Scale the plot so it fills the PostScript page. The aspect ratio is retained. The default is `false`.

-padx amount   (psPadX, PsPadX)
>   Padding on the left and right page borders. If *amount* has two elements, it specifies the padding for the left and right sides, in that order. The default is 1i.

-pady amount   (psPadY, PsPadY)
>   Padding on the top and bottom page borders. If *amount* has two elements, it specifies the padding for the top and bottom, in that order. The default is 1i.

-paperheight amount   (psPaperHeight, PsPaperHeight)
>   Set the height of the PostScript page. The default is 11.0i.

-paperwidth amount   (psPaperWidth, PsPaperWidth)
>   Set the width of the PostScript page. The default is 8.5i.

-preview boolean   (psPreview, PsPreview)
>   Whether an EPSI thumbnail preview image should be inserted into the generated PostScript.

-width amount   (psWidth, PsWidth)
>   Width of the plot. If *amount* is 0, the the width is the same as the widget width.

pathName postscript output [`filename`] [`option value`...]
>   Output the chart as encapsulated PostScript. The output is written to the file `filename`, if specified. Otherwise, the output is returned as the method's results.

pathName print
>   Prompt for a printer and print the image to the printer selected. This is supported on Windows only.*

pathName snap photoName
>   Take a snapshot of the chart and store it in the contents of Tk photo image *photoName* (which must already exist).

pathName transform x y
>   Transform the chart coordinates *x* and *y* into window coordinates. The x and y window coordinates are returned. Results for chart coordinates outside the axes' region are not guaranteed to be accurate.

pathName xaxis cget option
>   Same as the *axis cget* method for whichever axis is used along the bottom boundary.

---

* The format of this command may change for the final Version 2.4 to require a specific printer ID.

---

pathName xaxis configure [option value...]
> Same as the *axis configure* method for whichever axis is used along the bottom boundary.

pathName xaxis invtransform coord
> Same as the *axis invtransform* method for whichever axis is used along the bottom boundary.

pathName xaxis limits
> Same as the *axis limits* method for whichever axis is used along the bottom boundary.

pathName xaxis transform coord
> Same as the *axis transform* method for whichever axis is used along the bottom boundary.

pathName xaxis use [axisName]
> Designate that axis axisName is to be used as the bottom boundary axis. Parameter axisName cannot be already in use at another location. If axisName is omitted, the name of the axis currently used for the bottom axis is returned.

pathName x2axis cget option
> Same as the *axis cget* method for whichever axis is used along the top boundary.

pathName x2axis configure [option value...]
> Same as the *axis configure* method for whichever axis is used along the top boundary.

pathName x2axis invtransform coord
> Same as the *axis invtransform* method for whichever axis is used along the top boundary.

pathName x2axis limits
> Same as the *axis limits* method for whichever axis is used along the top boundary.

pathName x2axis transform coord
> Same as the *axis transform* method for whichever axis is used along the top boundary.

pathName x2axis use [axisName]
> Designate that axis axisName is to be used as the top boundary axis. Parameter axisName cannot be already in use at another location. If axisName is omitted, the name of the axis currently used for the top axis is returned.

pathName yaxis cget option
> Same as the *axis cget* method for whichever axis is used along the left boundary.

pathName yaxis configure [`option value`...]
Same as the *axis configure* method for whichever axis is used along the left boundary.

pathName yaxis invtransform `coord`
Same as the *axis invtransform* method for whichever axis is used along the left boundary.

pathName yaxis limits
Same as the *axis limits* method for whichever axis is used along the left boundary.

pathName yaxis transform `coord`
Same as the *axis transform* method for whichever axis is used along the left boundary.

pathName yaxis use [`axisName`]
Designate that axis `axisName` is to be used as the left boundary axis. Parameter `axisName` cannot be already in use at another location. If `axisName` is omitted, the name of the axis currently used for the left axis is returned.

pathName y2axis cget `option`
Same as the *axis cget* method for whichever axis is used along the right boundary.

pathName y2axis configure [`option value`...]
Same as the *axis configure* method for whichever axis is used along the right boundary.

pathName y2axis invtransform `coord`
Same as the *axis invtransform* method for whichever axis is used along the right boundary.

pathName y2axis limits
Same as the *axis limits* method for whichever axis is used along the right boundary.

pathName y2axis transform `coord`
Same as the *axis transform* method for whichever axis is used along the right boundary.

pathName y2axis use [`axisName`]
Designate that axis `axisName` is to be used as the right boundary axis. Parameter `axisName` cannot be already in use at another location. If `axisName` is omitted, the name of the axis currently used for the right axis is returned.

Bitmap Markers

A bitmap marker displays a bitmap image. If two coordinates are specified for the -coords option, they specify the position of the top-left corner of the bitmap and the bitmap retains its normal width and height. If four coordinates are specified, the last pair of coordinates represents the bottom-right corner for the bitmap. The bitmap will be stretched or reduced as necessary to fit into the bounding rectangle. Options specific to bitmap markers are:

-anchor anchorPos   (anchor, Anchor)
> How to position the bitmap relative to the position point for the bitmap. The default is `center`.

-background color   (background, Background)
> Same as the *-fill* option.

-bitmap bitmap   (bitmap, Bitmap)
> The bitmap to display.

-fill color   (fill, Fill)
> Background color for the bitmap. The default is the empty string (i.e., transparent).

-foreground color   (foreground, Foreground)
> Same as the *-outline* option.

-outline color   (outline, Outline)
> Foreground color for the bitmap. The default is `black`.

-rotate theta   (rotate, Rotate)
> Angle in degrees to rotate the bitmap.

Image Markers

An image marker displays a Tk named image. Options specific to image markers are as follows:

-anchor anchorPos   (anchor, Anchor)
> How to position the image relative to the position point for the image. The default is `center`.

-image imageName   (image, Image)
> Name of the Tk image to display.

Line Markers

A line marker displays one or more connected line segments on the chart. Options specific to line markers are as follows:

-cap style   (cap, Cap)
> How caps are drawn at endpoints of lines. *Style* may be `butt` (the default), `projecting`, or `round`.

-dashes dashStyle   (dashes, Dashes)
> Dash style for lines. Parameter *dashStyle* is a list of up to 11 numbers that alternately represent the lengths of the dashes and gaps. Each number must be between 1 and 255, inclusive. If *dashStyle* is the empty string (the default), a solid line is drawn.

-fill color   (fill, Fill)
>   Background color for the line when dashed or stippled. The default is the
>   empty string (i.e., transparent).

-join style   (join, Join)
>   How line joints are drawn. *Style* may be bevel, miter (the default),
>   or round.

-linewidth amount   (lineWidth, LineWidth)
>   Width of the line. The default is 0.

-outline color   (outline, Outline)
>   Foreground color for the line. The default is black.

-stipple bitmap   (stipple, Stipple)
>   Stipple pattern used to draw the line.

-xor boolean   (xor, Xor)
>   Whether outline and fill color should be determined from a logical XOR
>   of the colors on the plot underneath the marker. Overrides the *-fill* and
>   *-outline* options.

Polygon Markers

A polygon marker displays a closed region of two or more connected line
segments on the chart. Options specific to polygon markers are as follows:

-cap style   (cap, Cap)
>   How caps are drawn at endpoints of lines. *Style* may be butt (the
>   default), projecting, or round.

-dashes dashStyle   (dashes, Dashes)
>   Dash style for lines. Parameter *dashStyle* is a list of up to 11 numbers
>   that alternately represent the lengths of the dashes and gaps. Each num-
>   ber must be between 1 and 255, inclusive. If *dashStyle* is the empty
>   string (the default), a solid line is drawn.

-fill color   (fill, Fill)
>   Fill color for the polygon. If *color* is the empty string, the interior of the
>   polygon is transparent.

-join style   (join, Join)
>   How line joints are drawn. *Style* may be bevel, miter (the default),
>   or round.

-linewidth amount   (lineWidth, LineWidth)
>   Width of the outline. The default is 0.

-outline color   (outline, Outline)
>   Color for the outline of the polygon.

-stipple bitmap   (stipple, Stipple)
>   Bitmap to use as a stipple pattern for drawing the fill color.

-xor boolean   `(xor, Xor)`

> Whether outline and fill color should be determined from a logical XOR of the colors on the plot underneath the marker. Overrides the *-fill* and *-outline* options.

Text Markers

A text marker displays a string of characters at an arbitrary position inside the chart. Embedded newlines cause line breaks. Options specific to text markers are as follows:

-anchor anchorPos   `(anchor, Anchor)`

> How to position the text relative to the position point for the marker. The default is `center`.

-background color   `(background, Background)`

> Same as the *-fill* option.

-fill color   `(fill, Fill)`

> Background color for the text. The default is the empty string (i.e., transparent).

-font font   `(font, Font)`

> Font to use for the text.

-foreground color   `(foreground, Foreground)`

> Same as the *-outline* option.

-justify justify   `(justify, Justify)`

> How multiple lines of text should be justified. Parameter *justify* may be `left`, `right`, or `center` (the default).

-outline color   `(outline, Outline)`

> Foreground color for the text. The default is `black`.

-padx amount   `(padX, PadX)`

> Amount of padding to add to the left and right sides of the text. Parameter *amount* may be a list of two screen distances to set the left and right padding separately.

-pady amount   `(padY, PadY)`

> Amount of padding to add to the top and bottom sides of the text. Parameter *amount* may be a list of two screen distances to set the top and bottom padding separately.

-rotate theta   `(rotate, Rotate)`

> Angle, in degrees, to rotate the text.

-shadow color   `(shadow, Shadow)`

> Color for the shadow drawn beneath the text. The default is the empty string (i.e., transparent).

-text string   `(text, Text)`

> The text string to display.

Window Markers

A window marker displays the window of a Tk widget at an arbitrary position inside the chart. Options specific to window markers are as follows:

-anchor anchorPos   (anchor, Anchor)
> How to position the window relative to the position point for the marker. The default is `center`.

-height amount   (height, Height)
> Height to assign to the window. If not specified, the height will be whatever the window requests.

-width amount   (width, Width)
> Width to assign to the window. If not specified, the width will be whatever the window requests.

-window pathName   (window, Window)
> Pathname of window to use for the marker. The window must be a descendant of the chart widget.

Example

```
set x {0.0 1.0 2.0 3.0 4.0 5.0 6.0}
set y {0.0 0.1 2.3 4.5 1.2 5.4 9.6}
graph .g -title "Example Graph"
.g element create x -label "Data Points" -xdata $x -ydata $y
pack .g
```

---

hierbox

hierbox pathName [*option value...*]

The *hierbox* command creates a new hierbox widget named *pathName*. A hierbox widget displays a hierarchy tree of entries for navigation and selection. Each entry consists of an icon image, a text label, and an optional text or image data field. Also, an entry can contain a list of subentries, which in turn can have their own subentries. Entries with subentries can be expanded or collapsed using an optional open/close button drawn to the entry's left side.

Standard Options

-activebackground	*-activeforeground*	*-background*
-borderwidth	*-cursor*	*-exportselection*
-font	*-foreground*	*-highlightbackground*
-highlightcolor	*-highlightthickness*	*-relief*
-selectbackground	*-selectborderwidth*	*-selectforeground*
-takefocus	*-xscrollcommand*	*-yscrollcommand*

Widget-Specific Options

-activerelief relief   (activeRelief, Relief)
> 3D effect for the active entry.

-allowduplicates boolean   (allowDuplicates, AllowDuplicates)
> Whether entries with identical names are allowed. The default is true.

-autocreate boolean   (autoCreate, AutoCreate)
> Whether an entry's ancestors should automatically be created and inserted if they do not exist when the entry is inserted. The default is false.

-closecommand command   (closeCommand, CloseCommand)
> Tcl command to evaluate when an entry is closed. The following percent sign substitutions are done on *command*:

> %%   Replaced with a single percent sign
> %n   Entry ID number of affected entry
> %P   Full pathname of affected entry
> %p   Tail part of the pathname of affected entry
> %W   Pathname of hierbox widget

-closerelief relief   (closeRelief, Relief)
> 3D effect for buttons of closed entries.

-dashes number   (dashes, Dashes)
> Dash style for lines connecting entries. Parameter *dashStyle* is a list of up to 11 numbers that alternately represent the lengths of the dashes and gaps. Each number must be between 1 and 255, inclusive. If *dashStyle* is the empty string (the default), a solid line is drawn.

-height amount   (height, Height)
> Requested height of the hierbox widget window.

-hideroot boolean   (hideRoot, HideRoot)
> Whether root entry should be hidden. The default is false.

-linecolor color   (lineColor, LineColor)
> Color of the lines connecting entries.

-linespacing pixels   (lineSpacing, LineSpacing)
> Set the vertical spacing between entries. The default is 0.

-linewidth pixels   (lineWidth, LineWidth)
> Width of the lines connecting entries. The default is 1.

-opencommand command   (openCommand, OpenCommand)
> Tcl command to be evaluated when an entry is opened. The same percent sign substitutions are made as for the widget *-closecommand*.

-openrelief relief   (openRelief, Relief)
> 3D effect for buttons of open entries.

-scrollmode mode   (scrollMode, ScrollMode)
> Whether scrolling should follow the model of the Tk listbox widget or the Tk canvas widget. *Mode* must be either listbox (the default) or canvas.

BLT

-scrolltile boolean   (scrollTile, ScrollTile)
> Whether tile should appear to scroll when the widget is scrolled.

-selectmode mode   (selectMode, SelectMode)
> Specifies one of several styles understood by the default hierbox bindings for manipulation of the entry selection. Supported styles are single, active, and multiple. Any arbitrary string is allowed, but the programmer must extend the bindings to support it. Default is multiple.

-separator string   (separator, Separator)
> Path separator string of components of entries. The default is the empty string, which implies no sublevels.

-tile imageName   (tile, Tile)
> Image to use as a tiled background for the widget.

-trimleft string   (trimLeft, Trim)
> Leading characters to trim from entry pathnames.

-width amount   (width, Width)
> Requested width of the hierbox widget window.

-xscrollincrement amount   (xScrollIncrement, ScrollIncrement)
> Increment, in pixels, for horizontal scrolling by units (see *view* method).

-yscrollincrement amount   (yScrollIncrement, ScrollIncrement)
> Increment, in pixels, for vertical scrolling by units (see *view* method).

Entry Indices

The following special indices can be used to identify entries in the hierbox:

number
> Integer ID number of the entry. This number does not indicate the location of the entry in the hierbox. However, the root entry will always be number 0.

current
> Entry that is currently active, usually the one under the mouse pointer.

anchor
> Entry that is the anchor point for selection.

focus
> Entry that currently has the focus.

root
> The root entry of the hierarchy.

end
> Last entry currently displayed (i.e., not hidden by closing) in the hierbox.

up
> Entry immediately above the one that currently has the focus.

down

    Entry immediately below the one that currently has the focus.

prev

    Entry above the one that currently has the focus. Unlike **up**, wraps around to last entry.

next

    Entry below the one that currently has the focus. Unlike **down**, wraps around to top entry.

parent

    Entry that is the parent of the one that currently has the focus.

nextsibling

    Next sibling of the entry that currently has the focus.

prevsibling

    Previous sibling of the entry that currently has the focus.

view.top

    First partially visible entry in the hierbox.

view.bottom

    Last partially visible entry in the hierbox.

path

    Absolute pathname of the entry.

@x,y

    The entry that covers the pixel with window coordinates *x* and *y*.

Methods

pathName **bind** *tagName* [*sequence* [*command*]]

    Bind *command* to all entries with tag *tagName* so it is invoked when the given event *sequence* occurs for the entry. The syntax for this method is the same as for the standard Tk *bind* command except that it operates on entries. *TagName* may be the pathname of an entry, the special tag **all** (bind to all entries), or an arbitrary string. Only keyboard and mouse events can be bound.

pathName **bbox** [*-screen*] *entryIndex* [*entryIndex*...]

    Return a coordinate list of the form {*x1 y1 x2 y2*} giving an approximate bounding box enclosing all the given entries. If the *-screen* switch is given, the coordinates are for the screen rather than the widget.

pathName **button activate** *entryIndex*

    If entry *entryIndex* has a button, make it the active button. Only one button in the hierbox may be active at a given time.

pathName **button bind** *tagName* [*sequence* [*command*]]

    Bind *command* to all buttons with tag *tagName* so it is invoked when the given event *sequence* occurs for the button. The syntax for this method is the same as for the standard Tk *bind* command except that it operates on hierbox buttons. *tagName* may be the name of a button's entry, the special tag all (bind to all buttons), or an arbitrary string. Only keyboard and mouse events can be bound.

pathName button cget option

Return the current value of the hierbox button option *option* in the same manner as the general widget *cget* method. Supported options are those available to the *button configure* method.

pathName button configure [option [value [option value...]]]

Query or modify the configuration options for the hierbox's buttons in the same manner as the general widget *configure* method. Supported options are as follows:

-activebackground color   (activeBackground, Background)
Background color for non-image buttons when active.

-activeforeground color   (activeForeground, Foreground)
Foreground color for non-image buttons when active.

-background color   (background, Background)
Background color for buttons.

-borderwidth amount   (borderWidth, BorderWidth)
Width of 3D border drawn around buttons.

-foreground color   (foreground, Foreground)
Foreground color for buttons.

-images imageList   (images, Images)
The images to use for closed and open buttons. If *imageList* contains two images, the first is used as the button for closed entries and the second for open entries. If *imageList* contains one image, it is used for both. If *imageList* is empty (the default), the default (+/-) symbols are used.

pathName close [-recurse] entryIndex [entryIndex...]

Close (do not display the subentries) each specified entry. If the *-recurse* option is given, then each subentry is recursively closed.

pathName curselection

Return a list containing the entry IDs of all entries in the hierbox currently selected.

pathName delete entryIndex [first [last]]

Delete the entry at *entryIndex* and all its subentries. If *first* and *last* are specified, they designate a range of subentries to delete by position within their parent. If *last* is the string end, it signifies the last subentry. If *last* is omitted, only the subentry at *first* is deleted. The root entry cannot be deleted.

pathName entry activate entryIndex

Make the entry at *entryIndex* the active entry.

pathName entry cget entryIndex option

> Return the current value of the hierbox entry option *option* in the same manner as the general widget *cget* method. Supported options are those available to the *insert* method.

pathName entry children entryIndex [first last]

> Return the entry IDs of the subentries belonging to the entry at *entryIndex* within the given range of positions, inclusive. The positions *first* and *last* are either integers or the string end. An integer position is the index of the subentry among its siblings. For example, the range 0 end would identify all the subentries, which is the default if a range is not specified.

pathName entry configure entryIndex [option [value [option value...]]]

> Query or modify the configuration options for the hierbox's buttons in the same manner as the general widget *configure* method. Supported options are those available to the *insert* method.

pathName entry hidden entryIndex

> Return 1 if the entry at *entryIndex* is not currently displayed, either by being explicitly hidden or in a closed hierarchy. Return 0 otherwise.

pathName entry open entryIndex

> Return 1 if the entry at *entryIndex* has subentries and is currently open, 0 otherwise.

pathName entry size [-recurse] entryIndex

> Return the number of subentries belonging to the entry at *entryIndex*. If the *-recurse* switch is given, the count will include the number of subentries at all levels below the entry.

pathName find [switches] [firstIndex [lastIndex]]

> Return as a list the entry IDs of entries matching the search specification provided. The entries searched are restricted to those between the entries *firstIndex* and *lastIndex*, inclusive. If *lastIndex* is omitted, it defaults to the last entry in the hierbox. Also, any use of the special index end specifies the last entry in the hierbox rather than the last displayed one. If *firstIndex* is also not given, it defaults to the root entry.

The search specification is defined using the following switches:

option pattern

> *option* must be a valid entry configuration option (see the *insert* method). The value of the option for each searched entry is matched against *pattern*.

-count max

> Specifies maximum matches before search is finished. If *max* is 0 (the default), there is no limit.

BLT

-exact

The search patterns must be matched exactly (i.e., no special inter-pretation of characters in the pattern). This is the default.

-exec command

The Tcl command *command* is evaluated for each matching entry. The same percent sign substitutions as for the *-closecommand* wid-get are done.

-full pattern

The full pathname of each entry is matched against *pattern*.

-glob

Patterns are treated as glob patterns, as for the Tcl *glob* command.

-name pattern

The tail part of the full pathname is matched against *pattern*.

-nonmatching

Invert search so that the indices for those entries that do not match the given patterns are returned.

-regexp

Patterns are treated as regular expressions, as for the Tcl *regexp* command.

- -

Marks the end of switches.

pathName focus entryIndex

Make the entry at *entryIndex* the entry with the keyboard focus.

pathName get [-full] entryIndex [entryIndex...]

If *-full* is given, a list of the full pathnames for the given entries is returned. Otherwise, the list contains only the tail part of the pathnames.

pathName hide [switches] entryIndex [entryIndex...]

Hide the given entries. The entries to hide are specified using *switches* to define a search specification, by explicit entry index, or both. Valid switches for the search specification are as follows:

option value

option must be a valid entry configuration option (see the *insert* method). The value of the option for each searched entry is matched against *pattern*.

-exact

The search patterns must be matched exactly (i.e., no special inter-pretation of characters in the pattern). This is the default.

-full pattern

The full pathname of each entry is matched against *pattern*.

-glob

Patterns are treated as glob patterns, as for the Tcl *glob* command.

-name pattern
> The tail part of the full pathname is matched against *pattern*.

-nonmatching
> Invert search so it applies to those entries that do not match the given patterns.

-regexp
> Patterns are treated as regular expressions, as for the Tcl *regexp* command.

- -
> Marks the end of switches.

pathName index [*-at focusIndex*] *entryIndex*
> Return the ID number of the entry specified by the non-numerical index *entryIndex*. If *focusIndex* is given, it identifies the entry to be considered the focus entry in the evaluation. Note that, if *entryIndex* is an integer, it is treated as an entry name rather than an ID. All other methods will treat an integer for *entryIndex* as an entry ID number.

pathName insert [*-at parentIndex*] *position name* [*name*...] [*option value*...]
> Insert one or more new entries with the given names into the hierbox just before the subentry at *position* belonging to *parentIndex*. The *position* argument may be an integer position (e.g., 0 is the first subentry) or the string end (position after the last subentry).* If *parentIndex* is not given, it defaults to root. The following entry configuration options are available:

-bindtags tagList   (bindTags, BindTags)
> The binding tag list for the entry, which determines the order of evaluation of the commands for matching event bindings. Implicitly, the name of the entry itself is always the first tag in the list. The default value is all.

-closecommand command   (entryCloseCommand,
                                            EntryCloseCommand)
> Tcl command to evaluate when the entry is closed. Overrides default widget *-closecommand* option.

-data string   (data, Data)
> Arbitrary data string to associate with the entry.

-button mode   (button, Button)
> Whether an open/close button should be displayed for the entry. *Mode* may be a boolean value or auto (the default), which will display a button for an entry automatically if it has subentries.

---

* The format of this command may change in the final Version 2.4 to use normal entry indices for positioning.

-icons imageList (icons, Icons)

The images to use for the entry's icons. If *imageList* contains two images, the first is used as the icon when the entry does not have the focus and the second when it does. If *imageList* contains one image, it is used for both. If *imageList* is empty (the default), a simple miniature folder icon is used for both.

-images imageList (images, Images)

ImageList is a list of zero or more images to be drawn in the data field for the entry. If not empty, this overrides the *-text* option.

-label string (label, Label)

Text string for the entry's label. The default is the tail of the full pathname of the entry.

-labelcolor color (labelColor, LabelColor)

Foreground color for drawing the entry's label.

-labelfont font (labelFont, LabelFont)

Font for drawing the entry's label.

-labelshadow color (labelShadow, LabelShadow)

Color of shadow for entry's label. The default is the empty string (i.e., transparent).

-opencommand command (entryOpenCommand, EntryOpenCommand)

Tcl command to evaluate when the entry is opened. Overrides default widget *-opencommand* option.

-text text (text, Text)

Text string to be drawn in the entry's data field.

-textcolor color (textColor, TextColor)

Foreground color for text string in data field.

-textfont font (textFont, TextFont)

Font for text string in data field.

-textshadow color (textShadow, Shadow)

Shadow color for text string in data field. The default is the empty string (i.e., transparent).

pathName move fromIndex where toIndex

Move the entry at *fromIndex* to a position relative to *toIndex* according to *where*. *Where* can be after, before, or into (append to end of *toIndex*'s children). It is an error if *fromIndex* is an ancestor of *toIndex*.

pathName nearest x y

Return the entry ID of the entry nearest to screen coordinates *x y*.

pathName open [*-recurse*] *entryIndex* [*entryIndex*...]

Open (display the subentries) of each specified entry. If the *-recurse* option is given, each subentry is recursively opened.

pathName range [*-open*] *firstIndex* [*lastIndex*]

Return a list of the entry IDs of the entries between entry indices *firstIndex* and *lastIndex*, inclusive. If the switch *-open* is specified, only the indices of entries currently displayed (i.e., not closed) are returned.

pathName scan dragto x y

Scroll the widget's view horizontally and vertically. The distance scrolled is equal to 10 times the difference between this command's *x* and *y* arguments and the *x* and *y* arguments to the last *scan mark* command for the widget.

pathName scan mark x y

Record the screen coordinates *x y* as anchors for a following *scan dragto* method call.

pathName see [*-anchor anchorPos*] *entryIndex*

Adjust the current view in the hierbox, if necessary, so that entry *entryIndex* is visible. If *anchorPos* is given, it specifies a cardinal point of the entry that should be made visible at the same cardinal point of the view. For example, if *anchorPos* is nw, then the top left corner of the entry will be visible at the top left corner of the view.

pathName selection anchor entryIndex

Set the anchor for selection dragging to the element at *entryIndex*.

pathName selection cancel

Cancel temporary selection operation started with a previous call to the *selection dragto* method without changing the real selections.

pathName selection clear firstIndex [*lastIndex*]

Deselect any selected entries between *firstIndex* and *lastIndex*, inclusive.

pathName selection dragto entryIndex action

Perform a temporary selection action on the entries between the selection anchor and *entryIndex*, inclusive. *Action* can be clear, set, or toggle, corresponding to the identically named *selection* methods. The selection changes are temporary in that the hierbox is redrawn to make it look as if the selection has changed on the affected entries. However, the internal selection flags of the entries are not changed. This temporary state is canceled by making a call to any other selection method except *selection includes*.

pathName selection includes entryIndex

Return 1 if the entry at *entryIndex* is selected, 0 otherwise.

pathName *selection set* `firstIndex` [`lastIndex`]
> Select all entries between `firstIndex` and `lastIndex`, inclusive.

pathName *selection toggle* `firstIndex` [`lastIndex`]
> Toggle the selection state of all entries between `firstIndex` and `lastIndex`, inclusive.

pathName *show* [`switches`] `entryIndex` [`entryIndex`...]
> Show the given entries if they are hidden. The entries to show are specified using `switches` to define a search specification, by explicit entry index, or both. Valid switches for the search specification are the same as for the *hide* method.

pathName *sort* [`-recurse`] [`-command command`] `entryIndex` [`entryIndex`...]
> Sort the subentries of the given entries. If the *-recurse* switch is specified, then the sort routine will recursively sort subentries of subentries, and so on. The sort will be in ascending order unless a sorting command is passed with *-command*. `Command` is a Tcl command, which must take three arguments: the pathname of the hierbox widget and the tail of the pathnames of two entries. It should return a integer less than, equal to, or greater than zero to signify the order of the entries.

pathName *toggle* `entryIndex`
> Open the entry at `entryIndex` if it is closed, or close it if it is open.

pathName *xview*
> Return a two-element list describing the currently visible horizontal region of the hierbox. The elements are real numbers representing the fractional distance that the view's left and right edges extend into the horizontal span of the widget.

pathName *xview moveto* `fraction`
> Adjust the visible region of the hierbox so that the point indicated by `fraction` along the widget's horizontal span appears at the region's left edge.

pathName *xview scroll* `number` `what`
> Shift the visible region of the hierbox horizontally by `number`. If `what` is `units`, then `number` is in units of the *-xscrollincrement* option. If `what` is `pages`, then `number` is in units of nine-tenths the visible region's width.

pathName *yview*
> Return a two-element list describing the currently visible vertical region of the hierbox. The elements are real numbers representing the fractional distance that the view's top and bottom edges extend into the vertical span of the widget.

pathName *yview moveto* `fraction`
> Adjust the visible region of the hierbox so that the point indicated by `fraction` along the widget's vertical span appears at the region's top edge.

pathName yview scroll *number* what
> Shift the visible region of the hierbox vertically by *number*. If *what* is units, then *number* is in units of the *-yscrollincrement* option. If *what* is pages, then *number* is in units of nine-tenths the visible region's height.

Example

```
hierbox .h -separator "/" -trimleft "."
.h entry configure root -label [file tail [pwd]]
catch { exec find . } files
eval .h insert end [lsort [split $files \n]]
.h find -glob -name *.gif -exec {
    %W entry configure %n -labelcolor red
}
pack .h
```

htext

htext *pathName* [option value...]

Create a hypertext widget window named *pathName*. Options may be specified on the command line or in the option database.

The contents of the hypertext widget are defined by a text string or file. Any text surrounded by two special characters (by default, %%) is interpreted as Tcl commands.

Standard Options

-background	*-cursor*	*-exportselection*
-font	*-foreground*	*-selectbackground*
-selectborderwidth	*-selectforeground*	*-takefocus*
-xscrollcommand	*-yscrollcommand*	

Widget-Specific Options

-file `fileName`   (file, File)
> Specify the file containing the htext text to be displayed. See "Text Format," later in this section.

-height `amount`   (height, Height)
> Requested height of the htext widget window.

-linespacing `pixels`   (lineSpacing, LineSpacing)
> Set the spacing between each line of text. The default is 1 pixel.

-maxheight `pixels`   (maxHeight, MaxHeight)
> Maximum height allowed for the htext widget window.

-maxwidth `amount`   (maxWidth, MaxWidth)
> Maximum width allowed for the htext widget window.

-specialchar `number`   (specialChar, SpecialChar)
> Specify the ASCII code of the character used to delimit embedded Tcl commands in htext's text. The default is 0×25 (percent sign).

-text text   (text, Text)
> Specify the text to be displayed in the htext widget. See the "Text Format" section later in this chapter.

-tile imageName   (tile, Tile)
> Image to use as a tiled background for the widget.

-tileoffset boolean   (tileOffset, TileOffset)
> Whether the background tile should scroll with the widget. The default is true.

-width amount   (width, Width)
> Requested width of the htext widget window.

-xscrollunits pixels   (xScrollUnits, ScrollUnits)
> Specify the horizontal scrolling distance. The default is 10 pixels.

-yscrollunits pixels   (yScrollUnits, ScrollUnits)
> Specify the vertical scrolling distance. The default is 10 pixels.

Text Indices

Several widget operations accept as arguments indices that define a location of a character (or embedded window) in the text. These can take the following forms:

number
> Raw position of character in the text, starting at zero.

line.char
> Character position *char* of line *line*. Both are numbers starting at zero. The character position can be omitted to indicate the first position.

@x,y
> The character that covers the pixel with window coordinates *x* and *y*.

end
> The end of the text.

anchor
> The anchor point for the selection.

sel.first
> The first character of the selection.

sel.last
> The character immediately after the last one of the selection.

Text Format

The text to be displayed in the htext is set either using the value of the *-text* option or the contents of the file specified by the *-file* option. Whichever of the two options is set last takes precedence and resets the other to an empty string. If both are set at the same time, *-file* takes precedence.

The basic format for the text of the htext widget is plain ASCII. However, any text enclosed by double percent signs (or by another character chosen by the

-specialchar option) is interpreted and evaluated as Tcl commands. Typically, these commands create and configure a widget that is finally embedded in the htext at the current location using the *append* method of the htext. The commands are evaluated in the global scope.

The following global variables are set when parsing an htext file for use by the embedded Tcl commands:

`htext(widget)`
> The pathname of the htext widget.

`htext(file)`
> The name of the htext file currently being parsed (empty if the *-text* option is used).

`htext(line)`
> The current line number in the text.

Methods

`pathName append window [options...]`
> Embed child widget `window` in the htext widget `pathName` at the current text location. The following options configure the appearance of the child window:
>
> *-anchor* `anchorPos`
>> Specify how the child window will be positioned if there is extra space in the cavity surrounding the window. The default is `center`.
>
> *-fill* `style`
>> Specify how the child window should be stretched to occupy the extra space in the cavity surrounding it. One of `x`, `y`, `both`, or `none` (the default).
>
> *-cavityheight* `amount`
>> Requested height for the cavity surrounding the window. Overrides the *-relcavityheight* option. If the value of both this option and *-relcavityheight* is 0, the height of the cavity will be set to the height of the window plus the border width and any padding.
>
> *-cavitywidth* `amount`
>> Requested width for the cavity surrounding the window. Overrides the *-relcavitywidth* option. If the value of both this option and *-relcavitywidth* is 0, the width of the cavity will be set to the width of the window plus the border width and any padding.
>
> *-height* `pixels`
>> Requested height for the window. The default is 0, which will use the window's own requested height. Overrides the *-relheight* option.
>
> *-justify* `justify`
>> Specify how to justify the window with respect to the line it is on. `Justify` must be one of `top`, `bottom`, or `center` (the default).

-padx `pad`

Specify the padding on the left and right sides of the window. Can be a list of two numbers, specifying the padding for the left and right sides, or one number, specifying the padding to use for both sides. The default is 0.

-pady `pad`

Specify the padding on the top and bottom of the window. Can be a list of two numbers, specifying the padding for the top and bottom, or one number, specifying the padding to use for both. The default is 0.

-relcavityheight `fraction`

Specify the height of the cavity containing the child window as a fraction of the height of the htext widget. If the value of both this option and *-cavityheight* is 0, then the height of the cavity will be set to the height of the window plus the border width and any padding.

-relcavitywidth `fraction`

Specify the width of the cavity containing the child window as a fraction of the width of the htext widget. If the value of both this option and *-cavitywidth* is 0, then the width of the cavity will be set to the width of the window plus the border width and any padding.

-relheight `fraction`

Specify the height of the window containing the child window as a fraction of the height of the htext widget. If the value of both this option and *-height* is 0, then the height of the window will be set to the requested height of the window.

-relwidth `fraction`

Specify the width of the window containing the child window as a fraction of the width of the htext widget. If the value of both this option and *-width* is 0, then the width of the window will be set to the requested width of the window.

-width `pixels`

Requested width for the window. The default is 0, which will use the window's own requested width. Overrides the *-relwidth* option.

pathName configure `window` [`option value`...]

Query or modify the configuration options for the embedded child window `window` in the same manner as the standard widget *configure* method. Available options are those defined for the *append* method.

Note that when `window` is omitted, this method is the standard widget *configure* method for the htext itself.

pathName gotoline [`index`]

Set the top line of the text to `index`. With no `index` parameter, returns the current line number.

pathName index `index`

    Returns the raw character position of the character or window at `index`.

pathName linepos `index`

    Return the position of the character or window at `index` in the form `line.char`.

pathName range [`first` [`last`]]

    Return the text of the htext widget covering the range of characters from `first` to `last`, inclusive. If `first` or `last` are omitted, they default to `sel.first` and `sel.last`, respectively. If there is no selection, they default to the beginning and end of the text.

pathName scan dragto `@x,y`

    Scroll the widget's view horizontally and vertically. The distance scrolled is equal to 10 times the difference between this command's x and y arguments and the given x and y arguments to the last *scan mark* command for the widget.*

pathName scan mark `@x,y`

    Record the screen coordinates x y as anchors for a following *scan dragto* method call.

pathName search `pattern` [`from` [`to`]]

    Return the number of the next line matching `pattern`. Parameter `pattern` is a string that obeys the matching rules of the Tcl *string match* command. Parameters `from` and `to` are text indices (inclusive) that bound the search. If no match for pattern can be found, –1 is returned.

pathName selection adjust `index`

    Locate the end of the selection nearest to `index`, adjust that end to be at `index`, and make the other end of the selection the anchor point. If the selection isn't currently owned by the htext, this method behaves the same as the *select to* widget method.

pathName selection clear

    Clear the selection if it is owned by the htext.

pathName selection from `index`

    Set the selection anchor point to be just before the character given by `index`.

pathName selection line `index`

    Select the line containing the character at `index`.

pathName selection present

    Return 1 if the htext currently owns the selection, 0 otherwise.

---

* The format of the *scan* commands may change to match the newer syntax, in which x and y are specified as separate arguments.

pathName **selection range** `first` `last`

Shortcut for doing a *selection from* `first` followed by a *selection to* `last`.

pathName **selection to** `index`

Set the selection to consist of those characters between the anchor point and `index`. If no anchor point has been set, it defaults to `index`. The new selection will always include the character given by `index`; it will include the character given by the anchor point only if it exists and is less than or equal to `index`.

pathName **selection word** `index`

Select the word containing the character at `index`.

pathName *windows* [`pattern`]

Return a list of the pathnames of all windows embedded in the htext. If `pattern` is specified, only names matching the pattern are returned.

pathName *xview*

Return a two-element list describing the currently visible horizontal region of the htext. The elements are real numbers representing the fractional distance that the view's left and right edges extend into the horizontal span of the widget.

pathName *xview moveto* `fraction`

Adjust the visible region of the htext so that the point indicated by `fraction` along the widget's horizontal span appears at the region's left edge.

pathName *xview scroll* `number` `what`

Shift the visible region of the htext horizontally by `number`. If `what` is `units`, then `number` is in units of the *-xscrollunits* option. If `what` is `pages`, then `number` is in units of nine-tenths the visible region's width.

pathName *yview*

Return a two-element list describing the currently visible vertical region of the htext. The elements are real numbers representing the fractional distance that the view's top and bottom edges extend into the vertical span of the widget.

pathName *yview moveto* `fraction`

Adjust the visible region of the htext so that the point indicated by `fraction` along the widget's vertical span appears at the region's top edge.

pathName *yview scroll* `number` `what`

Shift the visible region of the htext vertically by `number`. If `what` is `units`, then `number` is in units of the *-yscrollunits* option. If `what` is `pages`, then `number` is in units of nine-tenths the visible region's height.

Example

```
set text {
This will be displayed as normal text.
But this will become a %%
```

```
button .demo.button -text "button" -fg red
.demo append .demo.button %%
which can invoke a Tcl command.
}
htext .demo -text $text -foreground blue -background green
pack .demo
```

spline

spline type *x y sx sy*

Compute a spline fitted to a set of data points. The `type` argument is either `natural` or `quadratic`.

Parameters *x* and *y* are vectors representing points of data to be fitted to the spline. Values of *x* must be monotonically increasing.

Parameter *sx* is a vector containing the x-coordinates of the new points to be interpolated by the spline function. These must also be monotonically increasing and lie between the first and last values of *x*.

The *spline* command creates a new vector *sy*, which contains the y-coordinates corresponding to the x-coordinate values stored in *sx* calculated using the spline function.

Example

```
vector x y sx sy
x set {0.1 1.5 3.4 5.6}
y set {0.2 4.5 1.3 9.8}
x populate sx 10
spline natural x y sx sy
graph .graph
.graph element create original -x x -y y -color blue
.graph element create spline -x sx -y sy -color red
table . .graph
```

stripchart

stripchart pathName [*option value*...]

See the *graph* command.

table

table operation [*arg arg*...]

Arrange widgets in a table. The alignment of widgets is determined by their row and column positions and the number of rows or columns that they span. The following operations are defined:

table master [*slave index option value* ...]

Add the widget *slave* to the table at *index*. Parameter *index* is a position in the table in the form *row,column*, where *row* and *column* are the respective row and column numbers and 0,0 is the upper leftmost position. If a table doesn't exist for *master*, one is created. Parameter *slave* is the pathname of the window, which must already exist, to be arranged inside of *master*. Parameters *option* and *value* are described later in the "Slave Options" section.

table arrange master
> Force the table to compute its layout immediately rather than waiting until the next idle point.

table cget master [*item*] *option*
> Return the current value of the configuration option specific to *item* given by *option*, where *item* is either a row or column index or the pathname of a slave window. Parameter *item* can be in any form described for the *configure* method. If no *item* argument is provided, the configuration option is for the table itself. Parameter *option* may be any of the options described in the appropriate options section for the item.

table configure master [*item*...] [*option* [*value* [*option value*...]]]
> Query or modify the configuration options specific to *item* in the same manner as the standard widget *configure* method. If the argument *item* is omitted, the specified configuration options are for the table itself, as specified in the "Table Options" section. If options are being modified, multiple *item* arguments of the same form are allowed. The *item* arguments must take one of the following forms:

> C*i*   Specifies the column of the master to be configured, where *i* is the index of the column. Valid options are specified in the "Column Options" section.

> R*i*   Specifies the row of the master to be configured, where *i* is the index of the row. Valid options are specified in the "Row Options" section.

> *slave*
>> Specifies a slave window of the master to be queried, where *slave* is the pathname of a slave window packed in *master*. Valid options are specified in the "Slave Options" section.

table extents master index
> Query the location and dimensions of rows and columns in the table. Parameter *index* can be either a row or column index or a table index in the form described for the configure method. Returns a list of the xy-coordinates (upper-left corner) and dimensions (width and height) of the cell, row, or column.

table forget slave [*slave*...]
> Request that *slave* no longer have its geometry managed. Parameter *slave* is the pathname of the window currently managed by some table. The window will be unmapped so that it no longer appears on the screen. If *slave* is not currently managed by any table, an error message is returned; otherwise, the empty string is returned.

table info master [*item* [*item*...]]

Return a list of the current configuration options for the given items. The list returned is in exactly the form that might be specified for the *table* command. It can be used to save and reset table configurations. The *item* parameters must be one of the following:

C*i*   Specifies the column of *master* to be queried, where *i* is the index of the column.

R*i*   Specifies the row of *master* to be queried, where *i* is the index of the row.

slave

Specifies a slave window of the master to be queried, where *slave* is the pathname of a slave window packed in *master*.

No argument

Specifies that the table itself is to be queried.

table locate master x y

Return the table index (row,column) of the cell containing the given screen coordinates. The *x* and *y* arguments specify the coordinates of the sample point to be tested.

table masters [*options*]

Return a list of all master windows matching the criteria specified using the options. If no options are given, the names of all master windows (only those using the *table* command) are returned. The following are valid options (only one may be specified):

-pattern pattern

Return a list of pathnames of all master windows matching *pattern*.

-slave window

Return the name of the master window of the table managing *window*. The *window* parameter must be the pathname of a slave window. If *window* is not managed by any table, the empty string is returned.

table search master [*options*...]

Return the names of all the slave windows in *master* matching the criteria given by *options*. The *master* parameter is the name of the master window associated with the table to be searched. The name of the slave window is returned if any one option criterion matches. If no option arguments are given, the names of all slave windows managed by *master* are returned. The following options are available:

-pattern pattern

Return the names of the slave windows matching *pattern*.

-span index

Return the names of slave windows that span *index*. A slave window does not need to start at *index* to be included. Parameter *index* must be in the form *row,column*.

-start index
> Return the names of slave windows that start at *index*. Parameter *index* must be in the form *row,column*.

Table Options

table configure master [option value...]

To configure the table itself, omit the *item* argument when invoking the *configure* operation. The following options are available for the table:

-columns number
> Set the number of columns in the table. By default, the table creates new columns whenever they are needed. If the number of columns is less than currently in the master, any slave windows located in those columns are removed from the table.

-padx pad
> Set how much padding to add to the left and right exteriors of the table. Parameter *pad* can be a list of one or two numbers. If it has two elements, the left side of the table is padded by the first value and the right side by the second value. If it has just one value, both the left and right sides are padded evenly by the value. The default is 0.

-pady pad
> Set how much padding to add to the top and bottom exteriors of the table. Parameter *pad* can be a list of one or two numbers. If it has two elements, the area above the table is padded by the first value and the area below by the second value. If it is just one number, both the top and bottom areas are padded by the value. The default is 0.

-propagate boolean
> Indicate if the table should override the requested width and height of the master window. If *boolean* is false, the master will not be resized, and will be its requested size. The default is true.

-rows number
> Set the number of rows in the table. By default, the table creates new rows whenever they are needed. If the number of rows is less than currently in the master, any slave windows located in those rows will be unmapped.

Slave Options

table configure master slave [option value...]

Slave windows are configured by specifying the name of the slave when invoking the *configure* operation. Parameter *slave* must be the pathname of a window already packed in the table associated with *master*. The following options are available for slave windows:

-anchor anchor
> Anchor slave to a particular edge of the cells in which it resides. This option takes effect only if the space of the spans surrounding the slave is

larger than the slave. Parameter *anchor* specifies how the slave will be positioned in the space. The default is center.

-columnspan *number*
Set the number of columns the slave will span. The default is 1.

-columnweight *weight*
Specify how much weight the width slave should have when the table computes the sizes of the columns it spans. Weight is one of normal (the default), none, or full.

-fill *fill*
If the space in the span surrounding the slave is larger than the slave, *fill* indicates if slave should be stretched to occupy the extra space. Fill is one of none (the default), x, y, or both.

-ipadx *pixels*
Set how much horizontal padding to add internally on the left and right sides of the slave. Parameter *pixels* must be a valid screen distance, such as 2 or 0.3i. The default is 0.

-ipady *pixels*
Set how much vertical padding to add internally on the top and bottom of the slave. Parameter *pixels* must be a valid screen distance, such as 2 or 0.3i. The default is 0.

-padx *pad*
Set how much padding to add to the left and right exteriors of the slave. Parameter *pad* can be a list of one or two numbers. If it has two elements, the left side of the slave is padded by the first value and the right side by the second value. If it has just one value, both the left and right sides are padded evenly by the value. The default is 0.

-pady *pad*
Set how much padding to add to the top and bottom exteriors of the slave. Parameter *pad* can be a list of one or two numbers. If it has two elements, the area above the slave is padded by the first value and the area below by the second value. If it is just one number, both the top and bottom areas are padded by the value. The default is 0.

-reqheight *height*
Specify the limits of the requested height for the slave. Parameter *height* is a list of bounding values. See the "Bounding Sizes" section for a description of this list. By default, the height of the slave is its requested height with its internal padding (see the *-ipady* option). The bounds specified by *height* either override the height completely or bound the height between two sizes. The default is " ".

-reqwidth *width*
Specify the limits of the requested width for the slave. Parameter *width* is a list of bounding values. See the "Bounding Sizes" section for a description of this list. By default, the width of the slave is its requested width with its internal padding (see the *-ipadx* option). The bounds spec-

ified by *width* either override the width completely or bound the height between two sizes. The default is " ".

-rowspan *number*
> Set the number of rows the slave will span. The default is 1.

-rowweight *weight*
> Specify how much weight the height slave should have when the table computes the sizes of the rows it spans. Weight is one of `normal` (the default), `none`, or `full`.

Column Options

table configure **master** `Ci` [*option value...*]

To configure a column in the table, specify the column index as `Ci`, where *i* is the index of the column to be configured. If the index is specified as `C*`, all columns of the table will be configured. The following options are available:

-padx *pad*
> Set the padding to the left and right of the column. Parameter *pad* can be a list of one or two numbers. If *pad* has two elements, the left side of the column is padded by the first value and the right side by the second value. If *pad* has just one value, both the left and right sides are padded evenly by the value. The default is 0.

-resize *mode*
> Indicate that the column can expand or shrink from its normal width when the table is resized. Parameter *mode* must be one of the following: `none`, `expand`, `shrink`, or `both`. If *mode* is `expand`, the width of the column is expanded if there is extra space in the master window. If *mode* is `shrink`, its width may be reduced beyond its normal width if there is not enough space in the master. The default is `none`.

-width *width*
> Specify the limits within which the width of the column may expand or shrink. Parameter *width* is a list of bounding values. See the section "Bounding Sizes" for a description of this list. By default, there are no constraints.

Row Options

table configure **master** `Ri` [*option value...*]

To configure a row in the table, specify the row index as `Ri`, where *i* is the index of the row to be configured. If the index is specified as `R*`, then all rows of the table will be configured. The following options are available for table rows:

-height *height*
> Specifies the limits of the height to which the row may expand or shrink. Parameter *height* is a list of bounding values. See the section "Bounding Sizes" for a description of this list. By default, there are no constraints.

-pady pad

Sets the padding above and below the row. Parameter *pad* can be a list of one or two numbers. If *pad* has two elements, the area above the row is padded by the first value and the area below by the second value. If *pad* is just one number, both the top and bottom areas are padded by the value. The default is 0.

-resize mode

Indicates that the row can expand or shrink from its normal height when the table is resized. Parameter *mode* must be one of the following: none, expand, shrink, or both. If *mode* is expand, the height of the row is expanded if there is extra space in the master window. If *mode* is shrink, its height may be reduced if there is not enough space in the master. The default is none.

Bounding Sizes

You can bound the sizes of the master window, a slave window, a row, or a column. The *-width*, *-height*, *-reqwidth*, and *-reqheight* options take a list of one, two, or three values:

{}

With an empty list, no bounds are set. The default sizing is performed.

{ x }

Fixes the size at *x*. The window or partition cannot grow or shrink.

{ min max }

Set minimum and maximum limits for the size of the window or partition. The window or partition cannot be reduced less than *min* nor can it be stretched beyond *max*.

{ min max nom }

Specify minimum and maximum size limits, but also specify a nominal size *nom*. This overrides the calculated size of the window or partition.

Example

```
label .title -text "Example Table"
button .ok -text "Ok"
button .cancel -text "Cancel"
table . .title 0,0 -cspan 2 .ok 1,0 .cancel 1,1
```

---

tabset

tabset pathName [option value...]

The *tabset* command creates a new tabset widget named *pathName*. A tabset widget displays a a series of overlapping widget layout folders. Only the contents of one folder, selected by using its tab, is displayed at one time. The tabset widget is similar to the notebook mega-widget in the Tix extension.

BLT

Standard Options

-activebackground	*-activeforeground*	*-background*
-borderwidth	*-cursor*	*-font*
-foreground	*-highlightbackground*	*-highlightcolor*
-highlightthickness	*-relief*	*-selectbackground*
-selectborderwidth	*-selectforeground*	*-takefocus*

Widget-Specific Options

-dashes `dashStyle`   (dashes, Dashes)
  Dash style for focus outline around selected tab's label. Parameter
  `dashStyle` is a list of up to 11 numbers that alternately represent the
  lengths of the dashes and gaps. Each number must be between 1 and
  255, inclusive. If `dashStyle` is the empty string, a solid line is drawn.
  The default is {5 2}.

-gap `size`   (gap, Gap)
  Gap, in pixels, between tabs. The default is 2.

-height `height`   (height, Height)
  Desired height, in screen units, for the window. If `height` is 0 (the
  default), the height is autosized.

-pageheight `height`   (pageHeight, PageHeight)
  Desired height, in screen units, for the area under the tabs for displaying
  the page contents. If `height` is 0 (the default), the height is autosized.

-pagewidth `width`   (pageWidth, PageWidth)
  Desired width, in screen units, for the area under the tabs for displaying
  the page contents. If `width` is 0 (the default), the width is autosized.

-rotate `theta`   (rotate, Rotate)
  Rotate the text in tab labels by `theta` degrees.

-samewidth `boolean`   (sameWidth, SameWidth)
  Whether each tab should be the same width. If `true`, each tab will be as
  wide as the widest tab. The default is `false`.

-scrollcommand `cmdPrefix`   (scrollCommand, ScrollCommand)
  Prefix for a command used to communicate with an associated scrollbar
  used to scroll through available tabs. Typically `scrollbar set`, where
  `scrollbar` is the pathname of a scrollbar widget.

-scrollincrement `amount`   (scrollIncrement, ScrollIncrement)
  Increment, in pixels, for scrolling by units (see *view* method).

-selectcommand `command`   (selectCommand, SelectCommand)
  Default command to be evaluated when a tab is invoked. See the *invoke*
  method.

-selectpad `amount`   (selectPad, SelectPad)
  Padding to be added around the selected tab. The default is 5.

-shadowcolor color   (shadowColor, ShadowColor)
> Color of shadow around pages.

-side side   (side, Side)
> The side of the tabset on which the tabs should be displayed. *Side* must be left, right, top (the default), or bottom.

-tabbackground color   (tabBackground, Background)
> Default background color for tabs.

-tabborderwidth amount   (tabBorderWidth, BorderWidth)
> Width of 3D border drawn around tabs.

-tabforeground color   (tabForeground, Foreground)
> Default foreground color for tabs.

-tabrelief relief   (tabRelief, TabRelief)
> 3D effect desired for the border around tabs.

-textside side   (textSide, TextSide)
> Specify on which side of a tab its text label is placed if both images and text are displayed in a tab. *Side* must be left, right, top (the default), or bottom.

-tiers number   (tiers, Tiers)
> Maximum number of tiers to use for displaying tabs. Default is 1.

-tile imageName   (tile, Tile)
> Image to use as a tile for the background of the tabset.

-width amount   (width, Width)
> Desired width, in screen units, for the window. If *amount* is 0 (the default), the width is autosized.

Tab Indices

Several tabset widget methods support a *tabIndex* argument that identifies a specific tab in the tabset. This index can take one of the following forms:

number
> The *number*th tab in the tabset.

tabName
> The tab named *tabName*.

@x,y
> The tab that covers the pixel whose coordinates within the tabset window are *x* and *y*.

tabSelect
> Tab whose page is currently selected and displayed.

tabActive
> Tab that is currently active. Typically, the tab with the mouse pointer over it.

`tabFocus`

Tab that currently has the widget's focus.

`tabDown`

Tab immediately below the tab that currently has the focus, if there is one.

`tabLeft`

Tab immediately left of the tab that currently has the focus, if there is one.

`tabRight`

Tab immediately right of the tab that currently has the focus, if there is one.

`tabUp`

Tab immediately above the tab that currently has the focus, if there is one.

`tabEnd`

Last tab in the tabset.

Methods

pathName activate tabIndex

Make the tab `tabIndex` the active tab. If `tabIndex` is the empty string, no tab will be active.

pathName bind tagName [*sequence* [*command*]]

Bind *command* to all tabs with tag *tagName* so it is invoked when the given event *sequence* occurs for the tab. The syntax for this method is the same as for the standard Tk *bind* command except that it operates on tabs. *TagName* may be the name of a tab, the special tag *all* (bind to all tabs), or an arbitrary string. Only keyboard and mouse events can be bound.

pathName delete first [*last*]

Delete the range of tabs from *first* to *last*, inclusive. If *last* is omitted, then only the tab *first* is deleted.

pathName focus tabIndex

Make tab `tabIndex` the current focus tab.

pathName get tabIndex

Return the numeric index of the tab identified by `tabIndex`.

pathName insert position tabName [*option value*...] [*tabName* [*option value*...]]...

Create one or more new tabs with names specified by the *tabName* arguments and configured with the following options. The tabs are inserted just before the tab *position*. If *position* is the special tag *end*, the tab is added to the end of the tab list. *TabName* should be chosen not to conflict with any of the special index strings. The following tab configuration options are available:

-activebackground color   (activeBackground,
                                             ActiveBackground)

 Background color for tab when it is active.

-activeforeground color   (activeForeground,
                                             ActiveForeground)

 Foreground color for tab when it is active.

-anchor anchorPos   (anchor, Anchor)
 Anchor point for placing the tab's embedded widget inside the tab's
 page. The default is center.

-background color   (background, Background)
 Background color for the tab. Overrides the *-tabbackground* option
 of the widget.

-bindtags tagList   (bindTags, BindTags)
 The binding tag list for the tab, which determines the order of evaluation of the commands for matching event bindings. Implicitly, the
 name of the tab itself is always the first tag in the list. The default
 value is all.

-command command   (command, Command)
 Command to be evaluated when the tab is invoked. Overrides the
 widget's *-selectcommand* option.

-data string   (data, Data)
 Arbitrary data string to associate with the tab.

-fill fill   (fill, Fill)
 How the tab's embedded widget should be stretched when its
 requested size is smaller than the size of tab's page. *Fill* must be
 one of x, y, both, or none (the default).

-font font   (font, Font)
 Font to use for the tab's text label.

-foreground color   (foreground, Foreground)
 Foreground color for the tab. Overrides the widget's *-tabforeground*
 option.

-image imageName   (image, Image)
 Image to be drawn in the tab's label.

-ipadx amount   (iPadX, PadX)
 Horizontal padding to the left and right of the tab's label. If *amount*
 has two elements, the first specifies the padding for the left side and
 the second for the right.

-ipady amount   (iPadY, PadY)
 Vertical padding to the top and bottom of the tab's label. If *amount*
 has two elements, the first specifies the padding for the left side and
 the second for the right.

-padx amount   (padX, PadX)
> Horizontal padding to the left and right of the tab's embedded widget. If *amount* has two elements, the first specifies the padding for the left side and the second for the right.

-pady amount   (padY, PadY)
> Vertical padding to the top and bottom of the tab's embedded widget. If *amount* has two elements, the first specifies the padding for the left side and the second for the right.

-selectbackground color   (selectBackground, Background)
> Background color for tab when it is selected. Overrides the widget's *-selectbackground* option.

-shadow color   (shadow, Shadow)
> Color for the shadow under the tab's text label. The default is the empty string (i.e., transparent).

-state state   (state, State)
> State for the tab. *State* must be normal or disabled.

-stipple bitmap   (stipple, Stipple)
> Stipple pattern to use for the background of the page window when tab's embedded window is torn off. The default is BLT.

-text string   (text, Text)
> Text for the tab's text label.

-window pathName   (window, Window)
> Name of widget to be embedded into tab's page. It must be a child of the tabset. The tabset will "pack" and manage the size and placement of the widget.

-windowheight height   (windowHeight, WindowHeight)
> Desired height, in screen units, for the tab's page. If *height* is 0 (the default), the height is set to the maximum height of all embedded tab widgets.

-windowwidth width   (windowWidth, WindowWidth)
> Desired width, in screen units, for the tab's page. If *width* is 0 (the default), the width is set to the maximum width of all embedded tab widgets.

pathName invoke tabIndex
> Select the tab *tabIndex*, map the tab's embedded widget, and execute any associated command. The return value will be the return value of the command if there is one, an empty string otherwise. This command does nothing if the tab's state is disabled. The following substitutions are made to the command before it is evaluated:

> %%   An actual percent sign
> %W   Pathname of tabset widget
> %i   Numeric index of invoked tab
> %n   Name of invoked tab

pathName move `tabIndex` *where* `position`
> Move the tab `tabIndex` to a position immediately before or after the tab `position`. *Where* must be either `before` or `after`.

pathName nearest `x y`
> Return the name of the tab nearest to screen coordinates `x y`.

pathName scan dragto `x y`
> Scroll the widget's view horizontally and vertically. The distance scrolled is equal to 10 times the difference between this command's `x` and `y` arguments and the `x` and `y` arguments to the last *scan mark* command for the widget.

pathName scan mark `x y`
> Record the screen coordinates `x y` as anchors for a following *scan dragto* method call.

pathName see `tabIndex`
> Scroll the tabset so that tab `tabIndex` is visible.

pathName size
> Return the number of tabs in the tabset.

pathName tab cget `tabIndex option`
> Return the current value of configuration option `option` for tab `tabIndex`.

pathName tab configure `tabIndex` [`tabIndex`...] [`option value`...]
> Query or modify the configuration options for the tabs identified by the `tabIndex` arguments in the same manner as the general widget *configure* method. Supported options are those available for the *insert* method.

pathName tab names [`pattern`]
> Return the names of all tabs in the tabset. If `pattern` is given, only tab names matching the pattern are returned.

pathName tab tearoff `tabIndex` [`newName`]
> Reparent the embedded widget belonging to tab `tabIndex` inside of `newName`. If `newName` is the pathname of the tabset widget itself, the embedded widget is put back into its page. Otherwise, the widget *newName* must not already exist. If no *newName* argument is given, the current parent of the embedded widget is returned. An empty string is returned if there is no embedded widget for tab `tabIndex`.

pathName view
> Return a two-element list describing the currently visible region of the tabset. The elements are the fractional distances of the view's left and right (or bottom and top) edges into the span of the widget's width (or height).

pathName view moveto `fraction`
> Adjust the visible region of the tabset so that the point indicated by `fraction` along the widget's span appears at the region's left (or top) edge.

pathName view scroll *number* what
> Shift the visible region of the tabset by *number*. If *what* is units, then *number* is in units of the *-scrollincrement* option. If *what* is pages, then *number* is in number of tabs.

Example

```
image create photo stopImg -file images/stopsign.gif
image create photo rainImg -file images/rain.gif
tabset .t
.t insert end t0 -text Stop -window [label .t.10 -image stopImg]
.t insert end t1 -text Rain -window [label .t.11 -image rainImg]
pack .t
```

tile

tilebutton pathName [*option value...*]

tilecheckbutton pathName [*option value...*]

tileframe pathName [*option value...*]

tilelabel pathName [*option value...*]

tileradiobutton pathName [*option value...*]

tilescrollbar pathName [*option value...*]

tiletoplevel pathName [*option value...*]

These commands are identical to their Tk counterparts without the "tile" prefix, with the addition of support for textured backgrounds using the following options:

-activetile imageName   (activeTile, Tile)
> Image to use as background tile for widget when the widget is active (i.e., it would normally be drawn with its *-activebackground* color).

-tile imageName   (tile, Tile)
> Image to use as background tile for widget.

The *tilescrollbar* command is not supported under Windows.

Example

```
image create photo paper -file tan_paper.gif
tileframe .frame -tile paper
```

vector

vector operation [*arg arg...*]

Create and manipulate vectors, that is, ordered sets of real numbers. BLT's vectors are more efficient than standard Tcl lists and arrays for accessing and manipulating large sets of real numbers. The following operations are defined:

vector vecSpec [*vecSpec*...] [*option value*...]
>   Same as *vector create*.

vector create [*vecSpec*...] [*option value*...]
>   Create one or more new vectors according to **vecSpec** and the follow-
>   ing options. The name of the last vector created is returned. The **vec-**
>   **Spec** argument specifies the vector's name and size according to these
>   valid forms:
>
>   **vecName**
>   >   A vector named **vecName** with no components.
>
>   **vecName(size)**
>   >   A vector named **vecName** with **size** components, all initialized to
>   >   0.0 and with the index starting from 0.
>
>   **vecName(first:last)**
>   >   A vector named **vecName** with components indexed from **first** to
>   >   **last**, inclusive, all initialized to 0.0.

The following options are available to the *create* operation:

>   *-variable varName*
>   >   Name of a Tcl array to be associated with the vector. By default, the
>   >   variable is the same as the vector name (this may change in a future
>   >   release of BLT). Any existing array by this name is deleted. If **var-**
>   >   **Name** is an empty string, then no variable will be mapped. See the
>   >   "Accessing Vectors as Arrays" section for how this array variable can
>   >   be used.
>
>   *-command cmdName*
>   >   Name of a Tcl command to be mapped to the vector. A Tcl com-
>   >   mand by that name cannot already exist. If the command name is
>   >   the empty string, then no command will be mapped and you will
>   >   lose access to the vector's Tcl command interface. See the "Instance
>   >   Operations" section for the syntax of the created command.
>
>   *-watchunset boolean*
>   >   Whether vector should automatically destroy itself if the variable
>   >   associated with it is unset. The default is **false**. This should most
>   >   likely be set to **true** for temporary vectors used in procedures.

vector destroy vecName [*vecName*...]
>   Destroy the vectors named by the **vecName** arguments. Any associated
>   variable is unset and its instance command undefined.

vector expr expression
>   Return the result of evaluating **expression** for each component of the
>   included vectors in the expression. Usually this is a list of the results of
>   the expression for each component. However, if the expression includes
>   specific statistical functions, the result may be a single value. If more than
>   one vector appears in the expression, they must be of equal length or
>   have only one component (i.e., a scalar value).

The syntax of *expression* is the same as for the general Tcl *expr* command. However, the operators and functions supported are slightly different. For results of boolean operations, the value 1.0 or 0.0 is returned. Supported operators in order of precedence are as follows:

– !
Unary minus and logical NOT.

^
Exponentiation.

* / %
Multiply, divide, remainder.

+ –
Add, subtract.

<< >>
Circularly shift vector values left and right (not implemented yet).

< > <= >=
Boolean comparison for less than, greater than, less than or equal, greater than or equal.

== !=
Boolean test for equality, inequality.

&& Logical AND.

|| Logical OR.

x?y:z
If-then-else (not implemented yet).

The following functions are supported, which are identical to the Tcl *expr* functions of the same name:

abs	*acos*	*asin*	*atan*
ceil	*cos*	*cosh*	*exp*
floor	*hypot*	*log*	*log10*
random	*round*	*sin*	*sinh*
sqrt	*tan*	*tanh*	

The following statistical functions are supported, which take a vector (or vector result) as their sole argument. All functions except *norm* and *sort* return a single value:

adev	Average deviation
kertosis	Degree of peakedness (fourth moment)
length	Number of components
max	Vector's maximum value
mean	Vector's mean value
median	Vector's median value
min	Vector's minimum value
norm	Scale vector to lie in range [0.0..1.0]
q1	First quartile
q3	Third quartile

prod	Product of the components
sdev	Standard deviation
skew	Skewness (third moment)
sort	Sorted components in ascending order
sum	Sum of the components
var	Variance

vector names [`pattern`]

   Return a list of defined vector names. If `pattern` is specified, return only those vectors whose names match the pattern.

Accessing Vectors as Arrays

A Tcl array is normally associated with each vector, having the same name as the vector unless overridden with the *-variable* option to the *create* operation. The data in the array can be accessed or set using indices that take the following forms:

vecName(`index`)

   The `index`th component of *vecName*.

vecName(`expression`)

   Same as the previous index, except that `expression` is a simple math expression that evaluates to an integer index.

vecName(`first:last`)

   The whole range of components from the `first` to `last`, inclusive. You can omit `first` or `last`, in which case they default to the first and last elements, respectively.

The following special indices can be used:

`min`

   The component with the minimum value.

`max`

   The component with the maximum value.

`end`

   The last component.

`++end`

   Extends the vector by 1. Component access for setting value only.

Instance Operations

After a vector is created, a new Tcl command is defined having the same name unless overridden with the *-command* option to the *create* operation. This command supports the following operations:

vecName append `item`...

   Append one or more items to a vector. Each item can be another vector or a list of numeric values.

vecName clear
> Clear the index and value strings from the Tcl array associated with the vector. The components of the vector itself are not affected, and the array elements will be automatically recreated if accessed.

vecName delete index...
> Remove from the vector one or more elements having the specified index values.

vecName dup destName
> Create a duplicate vector *destName* that is a copy of the original vector. The new vector is created if necessary.

vecName expr expression
> Reset the values of the vector to the results of evaluating *expression*. See the *vector expr* operation for details on vector expressions.

vecName length [newSize]
> Change the size of a vector to be *newSize* elements, which can be larger or smaller than the original size. If *newSize* is omitted, the current size is returned.

vecName merge srcName...
> Return a list consisting of the merged components of *vecName* and one or more *srcName* vectors.

vecName normalize [destName]
> Normalize the values of the vector to lie between 0.0 and 1.0. If a *dest-Name* argument is provided, the resulting vector after normalizing is stored in the vector named *destName*. This command is deprecated in favor of using the *norm* function in the *expr* operation.

vecName notify when
> Control how clients of the vector are notified of changes. The *when* parameter is one of always, never, whenidle, now, cancel, or pending.

vecName offset [value]
> Shift the indices of the vector by integer number *value*. With no *value* parameter, the current offset is returned.

vecName populate destName density
> Create a new vector *destName* that contains all of the elements of the original vector as well as *density* new values, evenly distributed between each of the original values. Useful for generating abscissas to be interpolated along a spline.

vecName range firstIndex lastIndex
> Return a list of the values of the vector from index *firstIndex* through *lastIndex*.

vecName search value [value]
> With one *value* argument, return a list of the element indices that have the given value. With two arguments, return a list of elements whose values range between the two values.

---

vecName set *item*
> Set the vector to the elements specified by *item*, which can be either a list of numeric expressions or another vector.

vecName seq *start* *finish* [*step*]
> Set the vector to the values generated by stepping from value *start* to *finish*, inclusive, with interval *step*. The default step is 1.0.

vecName sort [*-reverse*] [*argName*...]
> Sort the elements of the vector. The *-reverse* option changes the sort order to decreasing. Optional *argName* arguments can specify the names of vectors to be rearranged in the same order when sorting. This is useful for sorting x- and y-coordinates stored as pairs of vectors.

vecName variable *varName*
> Associate the Tcl variable *varName* with the vector, creating another means for accessing the vector. The variable cannot already exist. This overrides any previous variable mapping the vector may have had.

Example

```
vector create q(10)
q set {2 3 5 7 11 13 17 19 23}
set q(++end) 29
q dup x
x expr {2.0 * sqrt(q) + 3.0}
puts $x(:)
```

watch

watch *operation* [*arg arg*...]

Execute Tcl procedures before and after the execution of each Tcl command. The following operations are defined:

watch *activate* *watchName*
> Activate a previously created watch.

watch *create* *watchName* [*option value*...]
> Create a new watch. Options are the same as those for the *configure* operation.

watch *configure* *watchName* [*option value*...]
> Query or modify the configuration options for the watch *watchName* in the same manner as the standard widget *configure* method. The available options are as follows:

-active *boolean*
> Specify if the watch should be made active. By default, watches are active when created.

-postcmd *string*
> Specify the Tcl procedure and additional arguments to be called after executing each Tcl command. When the procedure is invoked, it is passed the specified arguments with the following appended: (1) the current level, (2) the current command line, (3) a list containing the

command after substitutions and split into words, (4) the return code of the command, and (5) the results of the command.

-precmd `string`

Specify the Tcl procedure and additional arguments to be called before executing each Tcl command. When the procedure is invoked, it is passed the specified arguments with the following appended: (1) the current level, (2) the current command line, and (3) a list containing the command after substitutions and split into words.

-maxlevel `number`

The maximum evaluation depth to watch Tcl commands. The default is 10000.

watch deactivate `watchName`

Deactivate a watch, causing its pre- and postcommand procedures to no longer be invoked. It can be reactivated.

watch delete `watchName`

Delete a watch. Its pre- and postcommand procedures will no longer be invoked.

watch info `watchName`

Return configuration information about a previously created watch.

watch names `[state]`

Return a list of watches defined for a given state, where `state` can be one of `active`, `idle`, or `ignore`. If `state` is omitted, all watches are listed.

Example

```
proc preCmd { level command argv } {
    set name [lindex $argv 0]
    puts stderr "$level $name => $command"
}
proc postCmd { level command argv retcode results } {
    set name [lindex $argv 0]
    puts stderr "$level $name => $argv ($retcode) $results"
}
watch create trace -postcmd postCmd -precmd preCmd
```

winop

winop `operation` `[[window]` `[arg arg...]]`

Perform assorted window operations on Tk windows using Xlib functions. Also, some miscellaneous image operations are defined in preparation for a new image type in a later BLT release. The following operations are defined:

winop convolve `srcPhoto` `destPhoto` `filter`

Set the photo image `destPhoto` to the result of the convolution of photo image `srcPhoto` with the given filter. `Filter` is a list of N×N real numbers representing the square matrix for the mean filter.

winop lower [`window...`]
> Lower given `window`s to the bottom of window stack.

winop map [`window...`]
> Map given `window`s to screen (ignored if already mapped).

winop move `window x y`
> Move the window to the screen coordinates specified by `x` and `y`.

winop raise [`window...`]
> Raise given `window`s to top of window stack.

winop readjpeg `filename photoName`
> Read the JPEG image data from the file `filename` into the photo image `photoName`, which must already exist. Only available if BLT was compiled with JPEG image support.

winop resample `srcPhoto destPhoto` [`horzFilter` [`vertFilter`]]
> Set the photo image `destPhoto` to the result of resampling the photo image `srcPhoto` with the given filters. Valid values for `horzFilter` and `vertFilter` are `bell`, `box`, `bessel`, `bspline`, `catrom`, `default`, `dummy`, `gaussian`, `lanczos3`, `mitchell`, `none`, `sinc`, and `triangle`.

winop snap `window photoName` [`width height`]
> Take a snapshot of the window and store the contents in photo image `photoName`. The window must be totally visible and `photoName` must already exist. If `width` and `height` are specified, they constrain the size of the snapshot.

winop subsample `srcPhoto destPhoto x y width height` [`horzFilter` [`vertFilter`]]
> Set the photo image `destPhoto` to the result of subsampling the photo image `srcPhoto` with the given filters. The region of the source image to subsample is given by `x y width height`. Valid values for `horzFilter` and `vertFilter` are the same as for the *resample* operation.

winop unmap [`window...`]
> Unmap given `window`s from the screen.

winop warpto [`window`]
> Move the mouse pointer to `window`. Window can also be specified in the form `@x,y` to indicate `@x,y` to indicate specific coordinates. If `window` is omitted, returns the current x- and y-coordinates of the mouse pointer as a two-element list.

Example

```
set img [image create photo]
winop snap .h $img
winop warpto @100,100
```

CHAPTER 12

Oratcl

The Oratcl extension is not part of the core Tcl/Tk package, but can be obtained for free at *http://www.nyx.net/~tpoindex*. This chapter discusses Oratcl Version 2.5.

Oratcl provides access to Oracle, a commercial relational database from Oracle Corporation. Oratcl makes connecting to databases and manipulating relational data easy and convenient using the Tcl language.

Oratcl comes with sample applications and works with standard Tcl, Tk, and common extensions, including Extended Tcl.

Overview

You connect to a database using the *oralogon* command, which returns a logon handle. To perform queries and retrieve database rows you use the *oraopen* command, which returns a cursor. Multiple cursors can be open over a single login connection.

The *orasql* command sends an SQL query to the database server for execution. To retrieve data rows, the *orafetch* command is used.

When finished, use *oraclose* to close each cursor handle, and *oralogoff* to close a logon handle.

The global array variable **oramsg** stores information related to the current database operations.

These are the most basic commands used for Oratcl operations. Other commands support more advanced functions.

Example

```
tclsh> oralogon scott/tiger
oratcl0
tclsh> oraopen oratcl0
oratcl0.0
tclsh> orasql oratcl0.0 "select empno, ename from emp"
0
tclsh> orafetch oratcl0.0
7379 Smith
tclsh> orafetch oratcl0.0
7499 Allen
tclsh> oralogoff oratcl0
```

Environment Variables

Oratcl optionally uses two environment variables to determine the default Oracle server name and directory:

ORACLE_HOME
> Base directory for Oracle files

ORACLE_SID
> Default Oracle server system ID

Special Variables

Oratcl stores information related to its operation in the global variable oramsg. The variable is an array and contains the keys described in the following list:

collengths
> A list of the column lengths returned by *oracols*.

colprecs
> A list of the precision of the numeric columns returned by *oracols*.

colscales
> A list of the scales of the numeric columns returned by *oracols*.

coltypes
> A list of the types of the columns returned by *oracols*.

errortxt
> The error message text associated with the last SQL command.

handle
> The handle of the last Oratcl command.

maxlong
> Set to limit the amount of data returned by an *orafetch* or *orareadlong* command; default is 32,768 bytes.

nullvalue

String value to return for null results. The default value `default` will return 0 for numeric types and a null string for others.

ocifunc

The numeric Oracle Call Interface (OCI) status code of the last OCI function performed.

ociinfo

List of features present in Oracle library when Oratcl was compiled.

peo

Parse error offset; index into SQL string that failed due to error.

rc

Numeric Oracle error number associated with the last SQL command (see the following list).

rowid

Row ID of the row affected by SQL insert, update, or delete command.

rows

The number of rows affected by an SQL insert, update, or delete command or number of rows fetched by *orafetch*.

sqlfunc

The numeric OCI status code of the last SQL function performed.

version

Version of Oratcl.

The following are typical error status values returned in the `$oramsg(rc)` variable. Refer to the Oracle documentation for an exhaustive set of codes and messages.

0

Normal command completion; no error.

900–999

Invalid SQL statements, keywords, column names, etc.

1000–1099

Program interface error.

1400–1499

Execution errors or feedback.

1403

End of data reached on *orafetch* command.

1406

Column fetched by *orafetch* command was truncated.

3123

Asynchronous execution is pending completion (not an error).

One or more of the following features can be returned in the `$oramsg(oci-info)` variable:

`version_6`
>   Compiled under Oracle version 6

`version_7`
>   Compiled under Oracle version 7

`non_blocking`
>   Supports nonblocking SQL execution

`cursor_variables`
>   Supports PL/SQL cursor variables

Group Listing of Commands

Database Server Setup Commands

oralogon	Log on to Oracle server.
oraopen	Open an SQL cursor to a server.
oraclose	Close an SQL cursor to a server.
oralogoff	Log off from Oracle server.

Data Manipulation Commands

oraautocom	Enable/disable autocommit of SQL statements.
orabindexec	Execute a previously parsed SQL statement, optionally binding to variables.
orabreak	Interrupt an executing SQL statement.
oracancel	Cancel pending SQL commands.
oracols	Return column names from last *orasql* or *oraplexec* command.
oracommit	Commit pending transactions.
orafetch	Return next row from last SQL statement executed.
oraplexec	Execute an anonymous PL/SQL block.
orapoll	Poll for data during asynchronous execution.
oraroll	Roll back pending transactions.
orasql	Send SQL statements to server.
orareadlong	Return LONG or LONG RAW column data and write to file.
orawritelong	Write file contents to a LONG or LONG RAW column.

Alphabetical Summary of Commands

In the following command descriptions, arguments that are logon and cursor handles are shown as `logon` and `cursor`, respectively. Commands will raise a Tcl error if the arguments do not refer to valid handles.

oraautocom

oraautocom logon on|off

Turn on or off automatic commit of SQL commands sent to the server opened using *logon*. By default autocommit is turned off. Affects all cursors opened with the logon handle.

orabindexec

orabindexec cursor [*-async*] [*:varname value*...]

Execute a statement previously parsed using *orasql -parseonly*.

Option *-async* specifies that the command should run asynchronously, i.e., return immediately without waiting for the statement to complete.

Optional name-value pairs allow substitution on SQL bind variables before execution. Variable names must begin with a colon.

Returns a numeric return code, which is 0 for successful execution, 3123 when *-async* is specified, and non-zero for errors. Updates the `oramsg` array variable element `rowid`.

orabreak

orabreak cursor

Cause the currently executing SQL statement to be interrupted.

oracancel

oracancel cursor

Cancel any pending results from a prior *orasql* command sent using *cursor*.

oraclose

oraclose cursor

Close the SQL cursor associated with *cursor*.

oracols

oracols cursor

Return the names of the columns from the last *orasql*, *orafetch*, or *oraplexec* command as a list.

Updates the `oramsg` array variable elements `collengths`, `coltypes`, `colprecs`, and `colscales`.

oracommit

oracommit logon

Commit pending transactions from prior *orasql* commands sent using *logon*. Affects all cursors opened with the logon handle.

orafetch

orafetch cursor [commands] [substitution-character] [tclvarname colnum...]

Return the next row of data from the SQL statements executed by the last *orasql* command. Returns a list with all columns converted to strings.

The optional *commands* parameter can specify a command string to repeatedly execute for each row until no more data is available. Command substitution is performed, where the strings @1, @2, @3, etc., are replaced with the results from the appropriate columns. The string @0 is replaced with the entire row, as a list.

An optional parameter *substitution-character* can specify a different substitution character to be used instead of @. A null string may be specified, in which case column substitutions are not performed.

Tcl variables may also be set for each row that is processed. One or more matching pairs of variable names and column numbers can be specified.

The command updates many of the elements of the oramsg array variable.

oralogoff

oralogoff logon

Log off from the Oracle server connection associated with *logon*.

oralogon

oralogon connect-str

Connect to an Oracle server. The connect string *connect-str* should be in one of the following forms:

```
name
name/password
name@dbname
name/password@dbname
name/password@(SQL*Net V2 string)
```

Returns a logon handle that can be used in subsequent Oratcl commands. Raises an error if the connection cannot be made. The environment variable ORACLE_SID is used as the server if the connect string does not specify a database.

oraopen

oraopen logon

Open an SQL cursor to the server and return a cursor handle that can be used for subsequent Oratcl commands. Multiple cursors can be opened against the same logon handle.

oraplexec

oraplexec cursor pl-block [:varname value...]

Execute an anonymous PL block. Parameter *pl-block* can be a complete PL/SQL procedure or a call to a stored procedure coded as an anonymous PL/SQL block.

Optional name-value pairs may be specified that match the substitution bind names in the procedure. Variable names must begin with a colon.

The command returns the contents of each variable name, after execution, as a list.

orapoll

orapoll cursor [-all]

Return a list of cursor handles that have results available, or a null string if no results are available. The *cursor* parameter must be a valid open cursor handle.

The optional parameter *-all* indicates to return a list of all cursor handles that have asynchronous requests pending.

orareadlong

orareadlong cursor rowid table column filename

Read the contents of a LONG or LONG RAW column and write the results to a file. The row ID, table name, column name, and file to be written to must be specified. Returns the number of bytes written as a decimal number.

Raises an error if *rowid*, *table*, or *column* are invalid or the row does not exist.

oraroll

oraroll logon

Roll back any pending transactions from prior *orasql* commands sent using *logon*. Affects all cursors opened with the logon handle.

orasql

orasql `cursor sql-statement` [*-parseonly*] [*-async*]

Send an SQL statement to the server using cursor handle `cursor`. Returns a numeric return code, which is 0 for successful execution, 3123 when *-async* is specified, and non-zero for errors. Updates the `oramsg` array variable elements `rc`, `rows`, and `rowid`.

Options

-parseonly
> Parse, but do not execute, SQL statement (used with *orabindexec*).

-async
> Execute asynchronously, i.e., without waiting for command to complete.

Raises an error if there is a syntax error in the SQL statement.

orawritelong

orawritelong `cursor rowid table column filename`

Write the contents of a file to a LONG or LONG RAW column. The row ID, table name, column name, and file containing the data must be specified. Returns the number of bytes written as a decimal number.

Raises an error if `rowid`, `table`, or `column` are invalid or the row does not exist.

CHAPTER 13

Sybtcl

Sybtcl, a Tcl extension developed by Tom Poindexter, is not part of the core Tcl/Tk package, but can be obtained for free at *http://www.nyx.net/~tpoindex*. This chapter covers Version 2.5.

Sybtcl provides access to Sybase, a commercial relational database from Sybase, Inc. Sybtcl makes connecting to databases and manipulating relational data easy and convenient, using the Tcl language. The Sybtcl extension comes with sample applications and works with standard Tcl, Tk, and common extensions, including Extended Tcl.

Overview

You connect to a Sybase server using the *sybconnect* command, which returns a connection handle. To select which database on the server to access, you use the *sybuse* command.

The *sybsql* command sends an SQL query to the database server for execution. To retrieve data rows, the *sybnext* command is used.

When finished, use *sybclose* to close the connection handle to the database server.

The global array variable **sybmsg** stores information related to the current database operations.

These are the most basic commands used for Sybtcl operations. Other commands support more advanced functions.

Example

```
tclsh> sybconnect mysybaseuserid mypassword MYSERVER
sybtcl0
tclsh> sybuse sybtcl0 pubs2
tclsh> sybsql sybtcl0 "select au_fname, au_lname from authors"
REG_ROW
tclsh> sybnext sybtcl0
Abraham Bennet
tclsh> sybnext sybtcl0
Reginald Blotchet-Halls
tclsh> sybclose sybtcl0
```

Environment Variables

Sybtcl optionally uses two environment variables to control the default Sybase server name and directory:

DSQUERY
> Default Sybase server name

SYBASE
> Base directory for Sybase files

Special Variables

The global variable `sybmsg` is used by Sybtcl to store information related to its operation. The variable is an array and contains the keys described in the following list:

collengths
> A list of the column lengths of the columns returned by *sybcols*.

coltypes
> A list of the types of the columns returned by *sybcols*.

dateformat
> Controls formatting of dates. Can be set to a string containing substitution strings, described at the end of this section.

dberr
> Error number generated by the last DB-Library routine.

dberrstr
> Error text associated with dberr.

fixedchar
> Normally, trailing spaces are trimmed from character data. If set to yes, trailing spaces are retained.

floatprec
> Number of decimal places to use for floating-point values. Default is 17.

handle

The handle of the last Sybtcl command.

line

Line number of the SQL command or stored procedure that generated the last message.

maxtext

Sets maximum amount of data returned by *sybnext* and *sybreadtext* commands. Default is 32,768 bytes.

msgno

Message number from the last Sybase server message.

msgtext

Message text associated with msgno.

nextrow

Indicates result of last SQL command. Possible values are described in the next list.

nullvalue

String value to return for null results. The default value default will return 0 for numeric types and a null string for others.

oserr

Operating system error number associated with the last DB-Library error.

oserrstr

Error text associated with oserr.

procname

Name of stored procedure that generated the last message.

retstatus

Return code of the last stored procedure that was executed.

severity

Severity level of the last Sybase server message.

svrname

Name of the Sybase server that generated the last message.

The element $sybmsg(nextrow) can take the following values (which are also returned by the *sybsql* command):

FAIL

A server error has occurred.

NO_MORE_RESULTS

The final set of results has been processed.

NO_MORE_ROWS

All rows from the current result set have been processed, or the SQL command executed successfully but no rows are available.

PENDING
> Asynchronous execution of command is still in progress.

REG_ROW
> At least one row is available.

num
> The last row retrieved was a compute row having compute ID number *num*.

The `$sybmsg(dateformat)` variable, described earlier, can contain the following format strings:

YYYY	Four-digit year (e.g., 1900)
YY	Two-digit year (00–99)
MM	Two-digit month (1–12)
MONTH	Name of month (January–December)
MON	Abbreviated name of month (Jan–Dec)
DD	Two-digit day (1–31)
hh	Two-digit hour (0–23)
mm	Two-digit minute (0–59)
ss	Two-digit second (0–59)
ms	Three-digit millisecond (0–999)
dy	Three-digit day of year (0–365)
dw	One-digit day of week (1–7, for Monday–Sunday)

Group Listing of Commands

Database Server Setup Commands

sybconnect	Connect to a Sybase server.
sybuse	Set or get active database.
sybclose	Close connection to a server.

Data Manipulation Commands

sybsql	Execute SQL statements on server.
sybpoll	Poll for data during asynchronous execution.
sybnext	Retrieve data rows.
sybcols	Return column names.
sybcancel	Cancel pending SQL commands.
sybretval	Retrieve output variables from a stored procedure.
sybwritetext	Write file data to database.
sybreadtext	Store database data in file.

Alphabetical Summary of Commands

In the following command descriptions, an argument that refers to a database handle is shown as *handle*. Commands will raise a Tcl error if the argument does not refer to a valid handle.

sybcancel

sybcancel `handle`

Cancel pending results from last Sybtcl command. May be used before all results are obtained using *sybnext*.

sybclose

sybclose `handle`

Close a server connection.

sybcols

sybcols `handle`

Return a list of names of the columns associated with the last *sybnext* or *sybretval* command.

sybconnect

sybconnect `loginName password` [`server`] [`appName`] [`iFile`]

Connect to a Sybase server using `loginName` and `password`.

A `server` can be specified. If omitted, will use value of environment variable DSQUERY, and failing that, a server named SYBASE.

The command can optionally specify an application name `appName`.

A file `iFile` can be specified to resolve server addresses. Otherwise, the command uses the file *$SYBASE/interfaces*.

Returns a Sybase handle that can be used as a parameter to other Sybtcl commands to identify the database connection.

sybnext

sybnext `handle` [`commands`] [`substitutionCharacter`] [`tclvarname colnum...`]

Return the next row of data from the SQL statements executed by the last *sybsql* command. Returns a list with all columns converted to strings.

The optional `commands` parameter can specify a command string to repeatedly execute for each row until no more data is available. Command substitution is performed, where the strings @1, @2, @3, etc., are replaced with the results from the appropriate columns. The string @0 is replaced with the entire row, as a list.

An optional parameter `substitutionCharacter` can specify a different substitution character to be used instead of @. A null string may be specified, in which case column substitutions are not performed.

Tcl variables may also be set for each row that is processed. One or more matching pairs of variable names and column numbers can be specified.

sybpoll

sybpoll `handle` [`timeout`] [*-all*]

Return a list of handles that have results available, or a null string if no results are available. The `handle` parameter must be a valid Sybtcl handle.

An optional `timeout` parameter indicates how long to wait, in milliseconds, before returning. The timeout value can be 0 for polling (the default) or –1 to wait indefinitely until results are available.

The optional parameter *-all* indicates to check all Sybtcl handles that have asynchronous requests pending.

sybreadtext

sybreadtext `handle filename`

Read the contents of a text or image column and write the results to a file. The parameter `handle` must be an open Sybtcl handle and `filename` a writable file.

A single text or image column should have been previously selected using a *sybsql* command. Returns number of bytes read from the database column.

sybretval

sybretval `handle`

Return a list of the return values from a stored procedure.

sybsql

sybsql `handle sqlCommand` [*-async*]

Send one or more SQL statements to the Sybase server associated with handle `handle`.

Normally returns when a response is available. With the *-async* option, the command returns immediately. Returns one of the values described in the previous section under values for the variable `$sybmsg(nextrow)`.

sybuse

sybuse `handle` [*dbName*]

Return the name of the database currently in use. Attempts to use the database named *dbName*, if specified.

Raises an error if *dbName* is not a valid database name.

sybwritetext

sybwritetext `handle object columnNumber filename` [*-nolog*]

Write the contents of a file to a text or image column. The table and column name are specified using `object` in the format `table.column`. The relative position in the column is `columnNumber`. The name of the file containing text or image data is `filename`.

The option *-nolog* disables the logging of text and image writes that normally occurs.

CHAPTER 14

Tclodbc

The Tclodbc extension, created by Roy Nurmi, is not part of the core Tcl/Tk package, but can be obtained for free at *http://www.megalos.fi/~rnurmi*. This chapter covers Version 2.0.

Tclodbc is a Tcl interface to ODBC, the database protocol used by Microsoft Windows. It works with any database that has an ODBC driver. The distribution includes precompiled DLLs for Tcl versions 7.6, 8.0, and 8.1. Once installed using the supplied Tcl install program, the package can be loaded using the command *package require tclodbc*. The package adds one new command to the Tcl interpreter: *database*.

Overview

Tclodbc uses an object-based design. You first create a database connection with the *database connect* command. This returns a database object ID that is also a new Tcl command. SQL statements can then be passed to the database object ID command.

The database ID *statement* command creates a compiled SQL query, which can then be efficiently executed many times. The command returns a statement ID and creates a new Tcl command that accepts statement ID commands.

Multiple database IDs and statement IDs can be created and active at the same time.

Group Listing of Commands

Connection and Configuration Commands

database connect	Connect to an ODBC database.
database configure	Configure ODBC datasources.
database datasources	Return a list of ODBC datasources.
database drivers	Return a list of ODBC drivers.

Data Manipulation Commands

In the following commands, `database-id` is the database identifier for a database connection created using the *database connect* command:

`database-id` *SQL-clause*	Execute an SQL statement.
`database-id` *disconnect*	Disconnect from the database.
`database-id` *set*	Set connection-specific attributes.
`database-id` *get*	Get connection-specific attributes.
`database-id` *commit*	Commit current transaction.
`database-id` *rollback*	Cancel current transaction.
`database-id` *tables*	Return a list of database tables.
`database-id` *columns*	Return a list of database columns.
`database-id` *indexes*	Return a list of database indexes.
`database-id` *statement*	Create a statement object.

Statement Commands

In the following commands, `statement-id` is a statement identifier created using the `database-id` *statement* command:

`statement-id` *run*
> Execute the statement and return results.

`statement-id` *execute* [`args`]
> Execute the statement without returning results.

`statement-id` *fetch* [`arrayName`] [`columnNames`]
> With no parameters, read one row, returning the results or an empty string when there are no more results to be read. With an array name, read the results into an array. Column names can optionally be specified.

`statement-id` *columns*
> Return a list of statement column attributes.

`statement-id` *set*
> Set statement-specific attributes.

`statement-id` *get*
> Get statement-specific attributes.

`statement-id` *drop*
> Destroy the statement command.

Summary of Commands

This section describes the *database* command, followed by a list of commands that can be issued to a database (identified by *database-id*) and to a statement (identified by *statement-id*).

database

database `options`

This command is used to connect to a database and to query and change information related to database sources.

database [*connect*] `id datasource` [*userid*] [*password*]

Open a connection to a database, creating a database object named `id` (a new Tcl command) used to access the database. Accepts the datasource name (DSN) and optionally a user ID and password, returning the database ID. The *connect* keyword is optional.

Example

```
database db employeebase sysadm xxxxxx
```

database [*connect*] `id connectionstring`

An alternate form of the *connect* command that accepts a string of attribute-value pairs in the form `Attribute1=Value1 Attribute2=Value2`.

Example

```
database db "DRIVER=Microsoft Paradox Driver (*.db);DBQ=C:\\db"
```

database configure `operation driver attributes`

Configure an ODBC datasource. The `operation` parameter is one of the values in the following list. The `driver` parameter is the name of the ODBC driver to be used. The `attributes` argument is a driver-specific list of name and value pairs. Does not open a connection to the database.

Operations

add_dsn
    Add a datasource for the current user.

config_dsn
    Configure a datasource.

remove_dsn
    Remove the datasource.

add_sys_dsn
    Add a system datasource, visible to all users.

config_sys_dsn
>   Configure a system datasource.

remove_sys_dsn
>   Remove a system datasource.

database datasources

Return a list of configured ODBC datasources. Each element is a list consisting of the datasource name and the driver name.

database drivers

Return a list of configured ODBC drivers. Each element is a list consisting of the driver name and a list of driver attributes.

Example

```
set driver "Microsoft Access Driver (*.mdb)"
set attributes [list "DSN=mydsn" "DBQ=c:\mydb.mdb" "FIL=MS Access"]
database configure add_dsn $driver $attributes
```

database-id

database-id *options*

This command performs operations on the database associated with the *database-id* created using a previous *database connect* command.

database-id *SQL-clause* [*argtypedefs*] [*args*]

Execute the SQL statement *SQL-clause*, returning the result as a list. If the statement returns a single-column result set, the returned string is a simple list, or an empty string if nothing is found. If the command returns a multiple-column result set, a list is returned in which each element is a list representing a single row of the result. If the statement does not return a result set, the command returns OK.

SQL arguments may be given after *SQL-clause*, where the argument positions are marked with ? in the clause. This is usually used with precompiled statements; see the description in the *statement-id* command.

Example

```
db "select firstname, surname from employees, where id = $id"
```

database-id *disconnect*

Disconnect the database object from the datasource, removing the command from the interpreter.

database-id *set option value*

Set a connection-specific option to a value. The supported options and values are listed here:

autocommit `boolean`

> Turns autocommit on or off.

concurrency `mode`

> Set concurrency mode to one of `readonly`, `lock`, `values`, or `rowver`.

maxrows `number`

> Set the maximum number of rows.

timeout `number`

> Set timeout in seconds.

maxlength `number`

> Set the maximum length of data returned.

rowsetsize `number`

> Set the row set size.

cursortype `type`

> Set the cursor type to `type`, which must be one of `static`, `dynamic`, `forwardonly`, or `keysetdriven`.

Example

```
db set autocommit off
```

database-id `get option`

Return the value of a connection-specific option. The supported options are the same as those listed previously for the *get* command.

database-id *commit*

When autocommit mode is enabled, causes the current transaction to be committed.

database-id *rollback*

When autocommit mode is enabled, cancels the current transaction.

database-id *tables*

Return a list of all tables in the database. Each element is a list containing values for TABLE_QUALIFIER, TABLE_OWNER, TABLE_NAME, TABLE_TYPE, and REMARKS.

database-id *columns* [`tablename`]

Return a list of the columns in the database, or the columns in the specified table, if `tablename` is specified. Each element is a list containing values for TABLE_QUALIFIER, TABLE_OWNER, TABLE_NAME, COLUMN_NAME, DATA_TYPE, TYPE_NAME, PRECISION, LENGTH, SCALE, RADIX, NULLABLE, and REMARKS.

Tclodbc

database-id indexes tablename

Return a list of the indexes of table *tablename*. Each element is a list containing values for TABLE_QUALIFIER, TABLE_OWNER, TABLE_NAME, NON_UNIQUE, INDEX_QUALIFIER, INDEX_NAME, TYPE, SEQ_IN_INDEX, COLUMN_NAME, COLLATION, CARDINALITY, PAGES, and FILTER_CONDITION.

database-id statement id SQL-clause | tables | columns [argtypedefs]

Create a new *statement-id* object of one of the following types: SQL query, table query, or column query. The statement ID *id*, which is returned, becomes a new Tcl command which accepts any of the options described for a *statement-id*. The *SQL-clause* argument is an SQL statement which is compiled for later execution when the *statement-id* command is invoked.

Tclodbc tries to automatically determine the argument types for each argument. For drivers that do not support this function, the types can be explicitly defined using *argtypedefs*, which takes the form [*type*] [*scale*] [*precision*]. The supported types are the standard SQL types CHAR, NUMERIC, DECIMAL, INTEGER, SMALLINT, FLOAT, REAL, DOUBLE, VARCHAR, and the extended types DATE, TIME, TIMESTAMP, LONGVARCHAR, BINARY, VARBINARY, LONGVARBINARY, BIGINT, TINYINT, and BIT.

database-id eval proc SQL-clause [argtypedefs] [args]

First execute the given SQL clause and then evaluate the given Tcl procedure *proc* for each row in the result set. The argument count of the procedure must match the column count in the query. Only a single row is read into memory at one time, so very large tables can be accommodated.

database-id read arrayspec SQL-clause [argtypedefs] [args]

Read data from the database into one or more Tcl arrays. The first data column is used as the index for the array, and the remainder are stored into the array. The arrays may be specified as a list of names, which are used for the array names for each data column. Alternatively, one can specify only a single array name, which is used as a two-dimensional array. This command is not suitable for very large tables because the entire table is read into memory at one time.

Example

```
db statement s1 "select fullname from article where id=132"
db statement s2 "select fullname from article where id1=?" INTEGER
```

---

statement-id

statement-id options

This command performs operations on a precompiled SQL statement associated with the *statement-id* created using a previous *database-id statement* command.

statement-id [*run*] [*args*]

Execute the precompiled statement and return the result set immediately. If the command was defined with arguments, they should be specified using *args*, in the form of a list. The keyword [*run*] is optional.

Example

```
db statement s1 "select fullname from article where id=132"
s1
db statement s2 "select fullname from article where id1=?" INTEGER
s2 132
```

statement-id *execute*

Execute the precompiled statement but do not return the result set immediately. The results can be read one row at a time using the *fetch* command.

statement-id *fetch* [*arrayName*] [*columnNames*]

Return the next row of a result set from a statement previously executed using the *execute* command.

statement-id *columns* [*attribute*...]

Return a list of ODBC statement column attributes. The *attribute* parameter is a list specifying which attributes to return. The attributes are listed below. The default is `label`.

`label`
: Column label.

`name`
: Column name in the original table, if available.

`displaysize`
: The maximum string length of the column data.

`type`
: Standard numeric SQL type.

`typename`
: Database-specific type name string.

`precision`
: The precision of the column, if applicable.

`scale`
: The scale of the column, if applicable.

`nullable`
: 1 if the column is nullable.

`updatable`
: 1 if the column is updatable.

`tablename`

> Source table of the column, if available.

`qualifiername`

> Qualifier name of the table, if available.

`owner`

> Owner name of the table, if available.

statement-id set option value

Set a statement-specific option to a value. The supported options and values are listed here:

concurrency mode

> Set concurrency mode to one of `readonly`, `lock`, `values`, or `rowver`.

maxrows number

> Set the maximum number of rows.

timeout number

> Set timeout in seconds.

maxlength number

> Set the maximum length of data returned.

statement-id get option

Return the value of a statement-specific option. The supported options are the same as those listed previously for the *get* command.

statement-id drop

Clear the statement ID from memory and remove the command from the Tcl interpreter.

statement-id eval proc [args]

See the *database-id eval* command.

statement-id read arrayspec [args]

See the *database-id read* command.

CHAPTER 15

Hints and Tips for the Tcl Programmer

by Tom Poindexter

Tcl is simple compared with other computer languages. The Tcl(n) manual page, in just two pages, describes the syntax and semantics of the language with 11 concise rules. It's useful to review this document.

Programmers familiar with other languages, especially shell languages and C, usually feel comfortable with Tcl quickly. Browsing programs written in Tcl helps new programmers understand the language. What may not be obvious in reviewing Tcl programs is the best way to get your programming tasks accomplished within the bounds of those 11 rules.

This chapter is designed to help new Tcl programmers better understand the Tcl language, especially when written code does not perform as expected or produces errors. Much of the material in this chapter was selected from postings to the Usenet newsgroup *comp.lang.tcl*. Beginning programmers often seek help with coding problems, and suggested answers are given. These postings, along with the author's personal experiences, are presented here.

 Web addresses change over time. Use web search engines such as Yahoo!, AltaVista, Infoseek, and HotBot to help locate the Tcl FAQs if the links noted are out of date.

Hints and Tips

Other excellent sources of "how to" material available on the Web include these:

The Tcl Frequently Asked Questions (FAQ), by Larry Virden
  This is an up-to-date, comprehensive list of frequently asked questions and answers—well worth reading. See *http://www.teraform.com/~lvirden/tcl-faq/*.

Tcl Usage FAQ, by Joe Moss
> This covers specific Tcl language usage questions and answers. See *http://www.psg.com/~joem/tcl/faq.html*.

Tk Usage FAQ, by Jeffery Hobbs
> This document compiles questions and answers specific to the Tk toolkit. See *http://www.cs.uoregon.edu/research/tcl/faqs/tk/*.

Tcl Reference Pages, by Cameron Laird
> This is a collection of Tcl issues and explanations on a wide variety of topics. See *http://starbase.neosoft.com/~claird/comp.lang.tcl/tcl.html*.

Tcl Frequently Made Mistakes
> Cameron Laird has also compiled this list of frequent mistakes in Tcl. See *http://starbase.neosoft.com/~claird/comp.lang.tcl/fmm.html*.

Tcl WWW Information Pages, by Mike Hopkirk
> This is a comprehensive index to many Tcl resources, information, and source code. See *http://www.sco.com/Technology/tcl/Tcl.html*.

Scriptics Corporation Tcl Resource Center
> This is the home of Tcl's creator, John Ousterhout, and a focal point for Tcl development. Current and alpha/beta releases of new versions are available, as well as a comprehensive resource center. See *http://www.scriptics.com*.

The Tcl Consortium
> This is the home page of a nonprofit consortium to promote Tcl and contains links to many Tcl resources. See *http://www.tclconsortium.org*.

Neosoft, Inc. Archive
> This is a large archive of Tcl contributed software, including most extensions, applications, and utilities. See *http://www.neosoft.com/tcl*.

Usenet newsgroup *comp.lang.tcl*
> Usenet has ongoing discussion forums about Tcl issues, announcements, and online support. The *comp.lang.tcl* newsgroup is unmoderated and friendly; everyone is welcome to participate. Depending on your news feed and location, you may have access to other Tcl newsgroups.

Think Commands, Not Statements

Tcl is a syntactically simple language. The first word is the name of the command to be executed, and the remaining words are arguments to that command. *Words* of a command are sequences of characters separated by whitespace, but quoting can cause whitespace to be included in a word. Each of the lines in the following example are complete words:

```
abc
941.32
Long's\ Peak
$result
"the quick brown fox jumped over the lazy dog"
"checking if $somevar exists: [info exists $somevar]"
```

```
[llength $list]
{set area [expr {$pi * pow($r,2)}]; puts "area = $area"}
```

Problems occur when programmers do not pay enough attention to the differences between Tcl and other languages with which they may be familiar. It is sometimes a trap to try using idioms from other languages. Languages such as C have compilers that understand syntax and generate machine code that provides execution and instruction branching. Tcl has only commands and arguments; commands enable program flow control.

A good example of this difference is the *if* command. *If* is a command whose arguments are a conditional expression and blocks of Tcl code to be executed depending on the result of the expression. Tcl sees this *if* command as if it were a single list of three words:

```
{if} {$salary < 0} {puts "oops, salary is negative"}
```

It is quite common to write *if* commands as one would in C, breaking up the command over several lines, as in this example:

```
if {$salary < 0} {
    puts "oops, salary is negative"
}
```

Some programmers prefer a different formatting style, aligning the braces of the true condition block as follows:

```
if {$salary < 0}
    {
        puts "oops, salary is negative"
    }
```

When this code is run, Tcl reports an error with the *if* command, saying that no script follows the expression. The reason is that the *if* command was terminated by the newline character. The opening brace on the second line is treated as the start of a new command list.

The use of braces in Tcl to quote strings includes *all characters* up to the matching ending brace, *including* newline characters. The first *if* code fragment fully satisfies Tcl, since the opening brace to the true condition code block begins on the same line; the last one fails because the true condition code block begins on a new line, and newlines are used as command terminators in Tcl. The same operation applies to other commands typically written across multiple lines—*for*, *foreach*, *while*, *switch*, *proc*, and so forth. Don't forget that *if* commands with *else* clauses also need to be coded on the same logical line, as in this example:

```
set salary 60000.0
if {$salary < 0} {
    puts "oops, salary is negative"
} else {
    set monthlySalary [expr $salary / 12]
    puts "Monthly salary: $monthlySalary"
}
```

This code produces the following output:

```
Monthly salary: 5000.0
```

Whitespace is also required around the words of a command list. The code fragment in the following example fails because whitespace is missing between the expression and the true condition code block:

```
if {$salary < 0}{
    puts "oops, salary is negative"
}
```

Some readers will note that the earlier example can be fixed by quoting the newline character of the first line with a backslash, causing the logical command line to be continued on the second line:

```
if {$salary < 0} \
   {
       puts "oops, salary is negative"
   }
```

Although this is perfectly acceptable in Tcl, it adds noise characters to the code without much benefit. The best solution is to adopt the conventional Tcl coding style. In other cases, however, breaking up a long command with escaped newline characters (i.e., end of line quoted with "\") is useful to maintain readability in your code. This is especially true if you use a text editor that wraps lines instead of scrolling horizontally:

```
puts "At the sound of the tone, the time will be [clock format \
                [clock seconds] -format %H:%M]"
```

This code produces the following output:

```
At the sound of the tone, the time will be 12:43
```

Comments Are Treated as Commands

Comments in Tcl can be another source of frustration if the Tcl syntax rules are misinterpreted. Comments look like those in shell-type languages, a line that begins with a "#". However, Tcl fully parses lines before deciding that they should be executed (in the case of a command) or ignored (in the case of a comment). You should think of a comment as a "do nothing" command, rather than as a comment as in other languages. Comments may appear where Tcl expects a command to appear.

Two common problems arise when comments are included in the arguments of a command or are used to temporarily remove sections of code during testing or development. The *switch* command illustrates the first problem. *Switch* arguments include a test string followed by one of more pairs of patterns and Tcl code blocks. The problem in the following example occurs when comments are inserted among the pattern-code pairs:

```
switch $code {
    # decode red, green, blue color codes
    r {set color red}
```

```
        g {set color green}
        b {set color blue}
        default {puts "oops, unknown color code"}
    }
```

Since the *switch* command expects pairs of patterns and code blocks, the beginning "#" of the comment line is interpreted to be a pattern, followed by a code block (literally "decode"), another pattern ("red") with the code block "green," and so on. Tcl will announce "extra switch pattern with no body" if there is an odd number of words in the comment line, or perhaps yield an "invalid command name" if there is an even number of words in the comment line and a pattern was matched.

The solution is to either move comments out of the pattern-code pairs or include comments in the code blocks, where command lines are expected:

```
    # decode red, green, blue color codes
    switch $code {
        r {
            # the color is red
            set color red
        }
        g {set color green}
        b {set color blue}
        default {puts "oops, unknown color code"}
    }
```

Again, note that Tcl does not have much structure. Braces serve to quote a command's arguments, and nothing more. In the previous example, the comment for the pattern "r" is acceptable because the comment is actually part of code to be evaluated for the pattern and the comment character is found where a command is expected.

The second common problem with comments occurs when they are used to comment out parts of code. It is common during development to add extra code that is alternately commented and uncommented as development progresses. This example shows an extra *if* command that was used during testing but is now commented out:

```
    proc scaleByTen {x y} {
    #    if {$x > 9 && $y > 0} {
        if {$x > 9} {
            set x [expr $x * 10]
        }
        return $x
    }

    puts [scaleByTen 4  1]
    puts [scaleByTen 15 1]
```

Hints and Tips

The Tcl parser finds comments only after an entire command line is assembled. The ending open brace at the end of the comment line causes every character to be included until the matching close brace, consuming the entire body of the procedure. Running this code fragment as part of a program will cause a "missing close-brace" error. If you type this code into an interactive Tcl interpreter, Tcl will keep prompting you to finish the command with a closing brace.

The best way to avoid this problem is to ensure that comments look like full commands themselves, accounting for all braces that are contained in the comment.

Sometimes a small comment on the same line as your Tcl code is desirable. Tcl lets you add comments in this fashion; just terminate the preceding command with a semicolon and add a comment. Semicolons are another way to separate commands, in addition to newline characters:

```
set n {[0-9]} ;# regular expression to match a digit
```

Without the semicolon before the comment character, the *set* command will fail because it would receive too many arguments. Tcl treats "#" as an ordinary character if it is not at the beginning of a command.

A Symbolic Gesture

Much of Tcl's strength as a programming languages lies in the manipulation of strings and lists. Compare the following two methods for printing each element of a list:

```
set cpu_types [list pentium sparc powerpc m88000 alpha mips hppa]

# "C-like" method of iterative processing
for {set i 0} {$i < [llength $cpu_types]} {incr i} {
    puts [lindex $cpu_types $i]
}

# "The Tcl Way" - using string symbols
foreach cpu $cpu_types {
    puts $cpu
}
```

The loop coded with *for* is similar to how a C program might be coded, iterating over the list by the use of an integer index value. The second loop, coded with *foreach*, is more natural for Tcl. The loop coded with *foreach* contains over 50% less characters, contributing to greater readability and less code to maintain. In addition, the second loop executes much more quickly.

As a general rule, if you find that your code contains many *for* commands and integer indexing, check whether you may be able to reimplement your algorithms with lists and *foreach*.

Lists Are Strings, but Not All Strings Are Lists

Tcl's only data type is the string, and each command can interpret strings in special ways.* A list is a special interpretation of a string—a list of words separated by whitespace. Lists are a very powerful feature of Tcl: they are easy to visualize and

---

* Beginning with Tcl 8.0, data types also have an internal representation as string, integer, float, and list, but to the programmer all data types are still strings.

can be formed from simple strings. This example creates the variable name from a string and then causes the string to be interpreted as a list with *lindex*:

```
set names "bob carol ted alice"
puts [lindex $names 2]
```

This code produces the following output:

```
ted
```

Trouble begins when lists are assembled from arbitrary strings that may contain special Tcl characters. For example, suppose you are writing a program to count the number of words in each line of a file. You notice that Tcl has an *llength* command, which returns the number of words in a list, and decide to use it:

```
set fd [open $somefile]
gets $fd aLine
while {! [eof $fd]} {
    puts "line has [llength $aLine] words"
    gets $fd aLine
}
close $fd
```

You start running your program, and all is well until you read a file that contains:

```
Tcl has several quoting characters, which
include { to mark the beginning of a fully
quoted string, up to a matching }.
```

Your program then fails with "unmatched open brace in list." The opening brace in the second line is interpreted as the beginning of a quoted string, possibly a list itself.

The key is to not use list commands on arbitrary strings, and use only list commands to build lists. Tcl even includes a *list* command that builds properly quoted lists from various strings. The first example in this section can be built as follows:

```
set names [list bob carol ted alice]
```

The *list* command is also very useful for building Tcl commands to be executed at a later time, helping to ensure that a command contains the expected number of arguments (see "Common Tk Errors," later in this chapter, for an example).

To add to an existing list, use *lappend*. Like *list*, *lappend* ensures that strings are made into proper list elements as they are appended:

```
lappend names arnold beth
set newList [lreplace $names 2 3 george susan]
puts [lsort $newList]
```

This code produces the following output:

```
arnold beth bob carol george susan
```

Lists can be nested. Any list element that is itself a list is properly handled as one element during list processing on the outermost level. Extended Tcl (see Chapter 10, *TclX*) adds a data structure known as a *keyed list*, which mimics structures in C. A keyed list is a list made up of pairs of key identifiers followed by data. Ordinary Tcl list commands can pick apart keyed lists, but the keyed list commands in TclX make the job much easier and more efficient.

Strings are best manipulated with the Tcl commands *string, regexp, regsub, scan, format, append,* and *subst.* The *split* command can be used to make a string into a list while properly quoting any troublesome list elements.

Indirect References

A powerful programming construct is the use of common procedures that operate on a data structure of a particular type. In C, you might have a set of procedures to manipulate a `struct`; procedures are coded to accept pointers to the actual `struct`, so you pass a pointer to any number of structures to the procedures.

Tcl doesn't have a `struct` data type, but arrays indexed by elements are a close approximation. For example, you might have data on states of the United States and a procedure to calculate population density:

```
set mo(name) Missouri
set mo(pop) 5402058.0
set mo(area) 68945.0

set co(name) Colorado
set co(pop) 3892644.0
set co(area) 103598.0
```

How then to reference a specific state array based on the name of one of the arrays? The first instinct is to try to use two $ characters to deference the variable:

```
foreach aState [list mo co] {
    puts "State Name: $$aState(name)"
}
```

Tcl's parsing rules state that variable substitution is performed exactly once for each command, so the command fails, leaving an invalid variable name `$mo(name)`, rather than `mo(name)`.

The first way to deal with this situation is using a nested *set* command. *Set* without a third argument returns the current value of the variable. The variable `$aState` is first expanded by Tcl, leaving the correct variable name `mo(name)` for *set* to return its value:

```
set aState mo
puts "State Name: [set ${aState}(name)]"
```

This code produces the following output:

```
State Name: Missouri
```

Note that we must also use braces around `aState`; otherwise, the Tcl parser will think we are trying to reference an array element `aState(name)`, which doesn't exist.

Tcl's *upvar* command is another answer to coding indirect variable references. *Upvar* allows one to reference a variable or array by some other name. Using a first argument of 0 allows variables in the current scope to be accessed.

```
foreach state_array_name [list mo co] {
    upvar 0 $state_array_name aState
    set p [expr $aState(pop) / $aState(area)]
    puts "$aState(name) has a population density of $p"
}
```

This code produces the following output:

```
Missouri has a population density of 78.3531510624
Colorado has a population density of 37.5745091604
```

Upvar is also used when passing arrays to procedures, in which the default procedure scope frame (1) is used:

```
proc calc_pop_density {state_array_name} {
    upvar $state_array_name aState
    set p [expr $aState(pop) / $aState(area)]
    puts "$aState(name) has a population density of $p"
}
calc_pop_density mo
```

This code produces the following output:

```
Missouri has a population density of 78.3531510624
```

Sometimes the solution is to rethink your particular implementation. Lists can be used in many places where arrays can be used, and Extended Tcl's keyed list commands also provide struct-like data types. Multidimensional arrays can also be simulated in Tcl.

Executing Other Programs

A common complaint from beginners trying to execute other programs from Tcl is "It works in the shell but not in Tcl." Let's suppose you write a small Bourne shell script to strip the first word of each line and return a count of unique words:

```
$ awk '{print $1}' somefile | sort -u | wc -l
```

This works fine when you execute it on your terminal. You then cut and paste the line into your Tcl program, setting a variable to the number of unique words:

```
set numWords [exec awk '{print $1}' somefile | sort -u | wc -l]
```

Tcl will report an error "can't read '1': no such variable." You might try to fix that error by quoting $1 as \$1, but that causes another error message, "awk: syntax error near line 1." You ask, "What gives? It worked as a shell command but fails under Tcl!"

Tcl's *exec* command executes other programs directly without the use of the shell. Tcl's *exec* goes about collecting arguments, building pipelines, and invoking another program, all according to Tcl syntax rules. A single quote character (') has no special significance, unlike in most user shells. Tcl applies its parsing rules and breaks up the command pipeline into Tcl words. Thus, the *awk* program in *awk*'s first argument is passed as:

```
'{print
```

and not as the desired string:

```
{print $1}
```

as it is passed with a command-line user shell (Bourne shell, C shell, Korn shell, Bash, etc.).

The simple fix is to use Tcl quoting instead of shell quoting! Replace the single quotes (') with Tcl braces:

```
set numWords [exec awk {{print $1}} somefile | sort -u | wc -1 ]
```

Since Tcl strips off one layer of braces during parsing, the first argument to *awk* is now a Tcl quoted string whose value is the correct *awk* program.

Another difference between Tcl's *exec* and typical shell processing is dealing with filename expansion. Most shells expand the wildcard characters * , ?, and [], matching filenames. Each matched filename becomes a separate argument to the program being executed. Tcl's *exec* does not perform filename matching directly, but you can use the *glob* command to match filenames. The only trick to this method is that most programs still need to have each filename as a separate argument. *Glob* command expansion returns a single *word*, the list of filenames matched, as if the resulting value had been enclosed in quotes.

For example, trying to print all C source files might be attempted as:

```
set printRequest [exec lp [glob *.c] ]
```

but this fails, complaining "file not found." The solution is to use the *eval* command, which adds one more round of Tcl command-line expansion. This effectively "unrolls" the filename list into separate word arguments:

```
set printRequest [eval exec lp [glob *.c] ]
```

When Is a Number Not a Number?

Tcl's primary data type is the string, but commands are free to interpret numeric strings as integers and floating-point values. *Expr* and *incr* are such commands; the evaluation mechanism in *expr* is also used for conditional testing in *if, while,* and *for* commands.

Tcl has a few rules for interpreting numbers, some of which are obvious. A string of digits is a decimal integer; with a decimal point or scientific notation, it's a floating-point value. The two often overlooked number specifications are octal (base 8) and hexadecimal (base 16).

Tcl interprets a sequence of digits as an octal integer if it begins with a leading "0". Numbers that begin with a leading "0x" are interpreted as base 16. Thus, "012" is decimal 10 and "0x100" is decimal 256. Sometimes hexadecimal values are easy to spot, since they contain a non-numeric character. Octal numbers are harder to recognize, since the string is composed of all numeric characters.

Unexpected results often arise when octal numbers are used inadvertently in expressions. To illustrate, assume you are writing a procedure to calculate a future date. Tcl's *clock* command can return a date string in the same format as the Unix

---

date program, and you begin by parsing out the day number of the month (we will ignore month and year rollover issues, as well as better possible implementations, for now), as in the following code:

```
set currentTime [clock seconds]
puts [clock format $currentTime]
```

produces the following output:

```
Mon Aug 03 10:05:50  1998
```

followed by:

```
set timedate [clock format $currentTime]
set day [lindex [split $timedate] 2]
puts $day
```

which outputs:

```
03
```

and finally:

```
proc one_week {timedate} {
    return [expr [lindex [split $timedate] 2] + 7 ]
}
```

This procedure runs fine, but breaks a few days later with the message "syntax error in expression '08 + 7'" while executing the *one_week* procedure. Of course, "08" is an invalid octal representation (decimal 8 is 10 octal). Two solutions to this problem are to strip off the leading zero using *string trimleft* or *scan* commands:

```
set day [lindex [split "Sat Aug 08 10:05:50  1998"] 2]
set dec_day1 [string trimleft $day 0]
scan $day %d dec_day2
puts "$day $dec_day1 $dec_day2"
```

This code produces the following output:

```
08 8 8
```

Quoting and More Quoting

Tcl's quoting characters allow special interpretation of the characters they quote. There are also quoting characters for regular expressions used in the *regexp* and *regsub* commands. Most troublesome are the quoting characters that are special to both Tcl and regular expressions.

Regular expression processing with *regexp* and *regsub* makes short work of parsing strings. However, regular expressions can be daunting to read and construct. *Mastering Regular Expressions*, by Jeffrey E.F. Friedl (O'Reilly & Associates) explains regular expressions in detail, including one chapter devoted to Tcl regular expressions.

Care must be taken when constructing regular expressions, keeping in mind that unquoted regular expression strings also make their normal trip through Tcl's parser. Since the backslash ("\") character quotes both Tcl and regular expression characters, it must be doubled for use in regular expressions. In order to match a single backslash character in a regular expression, *four* backslash characters are required.

The following table lists examples of matching certain characters, the regular expression, and the Tcl coding of *regexp*.

Character to Match	Regular Expression	Tcl with Unquoted Argument	Tcl with Quoted Argument
Single character \	\\	regexp \\\\ $s	regexp {\\} $s
Single character [	\[	regexp \\\[$s	regexp {\[} $s
Single character $	\$	regexp \\\$ $s	regexp {\$} $s

Additional quoting gymnastics occur when a Tcl variable is included in the regular expression. It's often useful to build up regular expressions in Tcl variables, then use the final variable as part of the *regexp* or *regsub* command:

```
# find phone numbers 888-555-1212, 888.555.1212, (888) 555-1212
set n {[0-9]}                    ;# re to match a single digit
set n3 $n$n$n                    ;# a group of three digits
set n4 $n$n$n$n                  ;# and four digits
set phone1 "$n3-$n3-$n4"
set phone2 "$n3\\.$n3\\.$n4"
set phone3 "\\($n3\\) ?$n3-$n4"
set allPhones "$phone1|$phone2|$phone3"
regexp $allPhones $teststring
```

The key to remember is that each command makes one trip through Tcl's variable and command expansion *prior* to the command's execution. In the case of *regexp* and *regsub*, another round of command-specific string interpretation is performed.

Write Once, Run Where?

Tcl is a multiplatform language, running on various Unix systems, Microsoft Windows NT/95/98, and Apple Macintosh. Tcl provides a great deal of machine and operating system independence. If writing portable software is your goal, there are a few areas that still need special attention.

Filenames and Pathnames

Filenames and pathnames differ among Unix, Windows, and Macintosh. Fortunately, Tcl is happy to work with Unix-style filenames internally. The *file* command provides help for dealing with filenames when you need to convert between the canonical form and forms required by specific operating systems. You will likely need a native filename if you *exec* programs that require filenames.

On Unix, the *file* command takes two or more file pathname components and joins them with the Tcl canonical path delimiter "/":

```
file join /home tpoindex src tcl style.tcl
```

This code produces the following output:

```
/home/tpoindex/src/tcl/style.tcl
```

On Windows, the *file* command takes a pathname in canonical network form and returns the native pathname:

```
file nativename "/program files/tcl/bin/wish80.exe"
```

This code produces the following output:

```
\program files\tcl\bin\wish.exe
```

The *file* command has many other subcommands to delete, copy, and rename files in an operating system–independent fashion.

End of Line Conventions

Unix, Windows, and Macintosh each have different end of line conventions for text files. In the default state, Tcl is very forgiving in reading files created on a different platform. When writing files to be used on a different system, you should configure the output channel by using the *fconfigure* command.

For example, if you are creating a file on Unix to be used primarily on a Windows system, use the following code:

```
set fd [open outfile w]
fconfigure $fd -translation crlf
puts $fd "hello windows!"
```

Determining Platform Specifics

Tcl includes a preset array of platform-specific information named $tcl_platform. Elements are shown in the following table.

$tcl_platform(machine)	Name of the cpu of the machine
$tcl_platform(byteOrder)	Machine word ordering, "bigEndian" or "littleEndian"
$tcl_platform(os)	Name of the operating system
$tcl_platform(osVersion)	Version of the operating system
$tcl_platform(platform)	Platform name: "unix", "windows", or "macintosh"

This information can be useful in deciding at runtime how to print a file, execute another program, and so forth.

Scanning and Formatting Binary Data

Reading and writing binary data is always system dependent, especially native integer and floating-point values. The *binary* command provides character specifications to scan and format big- and little-endian 16- and 32-bit integers, machine-native single- and double-precision floating-point values, and other formats. The *binary* command uses format specifiers to determine what format data will be packed into, such as S to denote a 16-bit integer in big-endian* order. The format s denotes a 16-bit integer in little-endian order. See the documentation for a complete list of specifiers. Here is a sample use of *binary*:

```
set binaryMsg [binary format SI 3 129]  ;# 16 & 32-bit big endian
    ints
```

If you are scanning or formatting binary data for use by other programs on the same machine type, consult the endian order information in `tcl_platform` to choose the correct binary specification:

```
switch $tcl_platform(byteOrder) {
    littleEndian { set int32 i ; set int16 s }
    bigEndian    { set int32 I ; set int16 S }
}
binary scan $binaryMsg $int16$int32 messageNum messageCode
```

Note that the *binary* command does not have a specification character to scan unsigned integers. Signed integers can be converted to unsigned quantities with a simple expression. Consult the *binary* command manpages for more information.

```
# convert to 16 bit unsigned value
set messageNum [expr ( $messageCode + 0x10000 ) % 0x10000 ]
```

Common Tk Errors

The following problems are frequently reported by users writing Tcl/Tk programs and are easy to correct with a little guidance. This section is not meant to be a complete guide to writing Tcl/Tk, but serves to address a few common situations.

Global Scope for -variable and -textvariable

Many Tk widgets allow you to tie a widget to a Tcl variable so that changes to either the widget or variable are mirrored in the other. This handy feature makes widget data instantly available in Tcl code, without the need to access the widget command:

```
label .tot_rev -text 0 -textvariable totalRevenue
set totalRevenue 263124 ;# updates widget also
```

The most common problem when using *-variable* and *-textvariable* options is forgetting that the variables the options name are referenced as global variables. If

---

* *Endian* refers to how a particular CPU actually stores integer values in memory. Big-endian processors store integers with the most significant bytes first; little-endian processors store integers with the least significant bytes first.

you create widgets inside of a procedure and then access the widget's variable, be sure to define the variable as global.

```
proc mk_totRev {} {
    label .tot_rev -text 0 -textvariable totalRevenue
    pack .tot_rev
    global totalRevenue
    set totalRevenue 23128
}
```

The -command String Must Be a Tcl List

Tk widgets (particularly buttons) often let you specify code to be run when the widget is selected. This code is known as a *callback*. You should put the code in braces, not quotes, to prevent variables from being interpreted until the user selects the widget. This is illustrated in the following example:

```
set count 0
button .b -text "Increment" -command {puts $count; incr count}
pack .b
```

Callback scripts can be of any length, but long scripts tend to get unwieldy when included in the *-command* argument. It is often easier to define your callback script as a procedure and call that procedure in the callback:

```
proc CallBack {} {
    global count
    puts "Current value is: $count"
    incr count
}

set count 0
button .b -text "Increment" -command CallBack
pack .b
```

Use update to Refresh Widgets and for Event Processing

A Tk application runs as an event-driven program. When your program starts, your code builds widgets and defines callbacks until Tcl reaches the "end" of your code. At this point, Tcl has entered an event loop in which user events are processed, calling the callback scripts that you defined as *-command* options for widgets and *bind* commands. The interface is active during event processing, and updates screen widgets accordingly.

If any of your callback scripts perform a significant amount of processing, the interface will appear to be frozen while scripts are executing. One way to prevent a frozen interface is to periodically execute the *update* command, which allows events to be processed. If your intent is to allow widgets to be updated without accepting new user events, use the *idletasks* option. In the following example, the *update* command allows the label widget to update the screen. Without *update*, the program will appear frozen.

```
label .l -text ""
proc count {} {
    for {set c 1;  .l configure -text 0} {$c <= 5} {incr c} {
        update
        after 1000
        .l configure -text $c
    }
}
button .b -text "count to five" -command count
pack .l .b
```

If your program reads and writes to sockets, or via pipes to another program, consider using file events to keep your interface active. Reading from any channel will cause the Tcl interpreter to wait until data is ready before returning. Tcl's *fileevent* command provides callback processing for files and sockets.

Use the Source, Luke!

It has been said many times before—don't reinvent the wheel. This is also true for Tcl. While Tcl was once called "A surprisingly well-kept secret,"* it has always had a large group of enthusiasts writing and contributing software in the open source spirit. Many high-quality, freely available extensions and Tcl programs are available through the Internet Tcl Archive, currently located at Neosoft, Inc.

BLT, Tix, and [incr Widgets] provide many additional Tk widgets, including those to support charts, panned frames, tabbed notebook frames, and combo entry/selections. Sybtcl, Oratcl, and Tclodbc support commercial relational databases. Extended Tcl (TclX) provides access to many Unix system programming interfaces and supports additional commands to manipulate lists, perform file scanning, and provide a Tcl help facility. Expect automates interactions with other programs, and [incr Tcl] adds object-oriented programming features to Tcl.

Many applications written in Tcl/Tk are also available: mail user agents, HTML browsers and editors, calendar programs, and a selection of games are all available in source code for your use and review. Other sources for Tcl software include the Tcl/Tk CD-ROM available from the Tcl Consortium.

---

* Attributed to Brian Kernighan, 1997 Tcl Conference, Boston, MA.

APPENDIX

Tcl Resources

You will find Tcl-related information at literally hundreds of sites on the Internet. This section lists a few of the major resources as well as some of the currently available Tcl books.

Web Sites

Here are some of the major Tcl-related web sites on the Internet. At these sites you'll find the Tcl/Tk software distribution, language extensions, applications, and documentation (including several excellent FAQs). Many of these sites also provide FTP access to their software archives.

General

http://www.scriptics.com
Scriptics site (John Ousterhout's company)

http://www.sunscript.com
The Tcl Project at Sun Microsystems Laboratories

http://www.tclconsortium.org
The Tcl/Tk Consortium

http://www.neosoft.com/tcl
The Neosoft Archive of Tcl/Tk Contributed Software

http://www.tcltk.com
WebNet Technologies Tcl/Tk site

Tcl/Tk Extensions

http://www.tcltk.com/blt	BLT home page
http://expect.nist.gov	Expect home page
http://www.tcltk.com/itcl	[incr Tcl] home page
http://www.tcltk.com/itk	[incr Tk] home page
http://www.nyx.net/~tpoindex	Oratcl home page
http://www.nyx.net/~tpoindex	Sybtcl home page
http://www.megalos.fi/~rnurmi	Tclodbc home page
http://www.neosoft.com/TclX	TclX home page
http://www.xpi.com/tix	Tix home page

Usenet Newsgroups

Usenet is a good resource for keeping informed of Tcl-related announcements and for finding solutions to your problems from other Tcl users.

comp.lang.tcl.announce
    Tcl-related announcements

comp.lang.tcl
    General Tcl discussions

Books

Listed here are some published books on Tcl:

Effective Tcl/Tk Programming, by Michael McLennan and Mark Harrison (Addison-Wesley, 1997).

Exploring Expect, by Don Libes (O'Reilly & Associates, 1994).

Graphical Applications with Tcl and Tk, by Eric Foster Johnson (M&T Books, 1997).

Practical Programming in Tcl and Tk, by Brent Welch (Prentice Hall, 1997).

Tcl and the Tk Toolkit, by John Ousterhout (Addison-Wesley, 1994).

Tcl/Tk for Dummies, by Tim Webster and Alex Francis (IDG Books, 1997).

Tcl/Tk Tools, edited by Mark Harrison (O'Reilly & Associates, 1997).

Mailing Lists

Most of the popular Tcl extensions have electronic mailing lists set up, which are used to send out announcements of new software releases and to allow users and developers to share information. The specific details of how to join the lists are usually spelled out on the home page for the language extension.

Index

Symbols

\ (backslash), 3-4, 422
{ } (curly braces), 3, 413, 417
$ (dollar sign), 3
# (pound sign), 3-4, 414
" (quotation marks), 3
; (semicolon), 4, 416
[ ] (square brackets), xii, 3

A

abs command (TclX), 285
absolute values, 285
acos command (TclX), 286
after command (core Tcl), 16
alarm command (TclX), 286
aliases for variables, 46
anchor position, 53
append command (core Tcl), 17
apropos command (TclX), 286
arc canvas items, 65-66
arc sines, 286
arc tangents, 286
arccosines, 286
arguments, 21-22, 46, 306
array command (core Tcl), 17
array variables, 17
arrays, 13, 418
    accessing vectors as, 383
asin command (TclX), 286
atan command (TclX), 286

atan2 command (TclX), 286
auto_commands command (TclX), 286
auto_execok command (core Tcl), 18
auto_load command (core Tcl), 18
auto_load_file command (TclX), 287
auto_mkindex command (core Tcl), 18
auto_package command (TclX), 287
auto_reset command (core Tcl), 18
automatic commit of SQL queries, 392

B

background processing
    errors during, 18
backslash (\), 3-4, 422
    substitutions, 6-7, 44
balloon messages, 209
barchart command (BLT), 316, 325-350
base 10 logarithm, 305
base containers, 237
beep command (BLT), 317
bell command (Tk), 101
bgerror command (core Tcl), 18
bgexec command (BLT), 317
binary command (core Tcl), 18, 424
binary data, 424
bind command (Tk), 101-106
bindtags command (Tk), 101, 105-106
bitmap canvas items, 66
bitmap command (BLT), 318

functions
Tcl, 140-155
Tk, 158-173
funlock command (TclX), 298

G

geometry management, 113, 271
functions related to, 164
Tk commands for, 51
get Boolean, Tix command for, 273
get integer, Tix command for, 273
gets command (core Tcl), 28
glob command (core Tcl), 11, 28, 420
global command (core Tcl), 28
globbing, 10-11
grab command (Tk), 112
grab stack, 274
graph command (BLT), 325-350
graphics, BLT commands for, 315
grid command (Tk), 113-115
grid widgets, 237, 251
group ID, setting, 289

H

hash mark (#), 3
hash tables, 144
help command (TclX), 298
help system, 286, 298
helpcd command (TclX), 298
helppwd command (TclX), 299
hierbox command (BLT), 350-361
hierbox widget, 352
hints for the Tcl programmer, 411-426
history command (core Tcl), 28
history, Tcl commands for, 14, 28
hlist widgets, 211, 218, 229, 238, 256
host_info command (TclX), 299
hosts, network, 299
Howlett, George A., 314
htext command (BLT), 361-367
hyperbolic
cosines, 291
sines, 310
tangents, 311
hypertext widget windows, 361

hypot command (TclX), 299
hypotenuse functions, 299

I

id command (TclX), 299
idletasks option, 425
if command (core Tcl), 29, 413
image canvas items, 67
image command
Tix, 278-280
Tk, 116-119
image embedding, 94
image items (Tix), 249
image markers, 347
imagetext items (Tix), 249
incr command (core Tcl), 30
[incr Tcl], 193
commands, 194-200
variables, 194
[incr Tk], 201, 203
methods, 202
variables, 202-203
index files, converting to package
libraries, 291
indices, 59, 73, 90, 94, 289
entry, 352
tab, 375
text, 362
info command (core Tcl), 30
infox command (TclX), 301
initialization, functions related to, 165
input widgets, 262
input/output, 22-23, 26, 39, 41, 45,
146, 182
channel identifiers, 11, 20
Tcl commands for, 14
int command (TclX), 302
inter_return command (Expect), 185
interact command (Expect), 185-186
interp command (core Tcl), 31-33
interpreter command (Expect), 186
interpreters, 49, 137, 141, 198
information about, 30
managing, 31
Tcl commands for, 15
intersect command (TclX), 302

procedures, 39, 196, 293, 385
  definitions of, 308, 310
  performance profiling of, 307
processes, 182-183, 188-189
  child, 313
  closing connections to, 181
  creating, 185
  delaying execution of, 311
  IDs, 38, 182
procs, 3
profile command (TclX), 307
profrep command (TclX), 307
pseudorandom integers, 307
pushd command (TclX), 307
puts command (core Tcl), 39
pwd command (core Tcl), 39

Q

quotation marks ("), 3
quoting, 412, 417, 420-422

R

radioboxes, 241
radiobutton command (Tk), 84-86
raise command (Tk), 124
random command (TclX), 307
ranges of characters, 291
read command (core Tcl), 39
read_file command (TclX), 308
readdir command (TclX), 308
rectangle canvas items, 69
recursive_glob command (TclX), 308
regexp command (core Tcl), 40
regsub command (core Tcl), 40
regular expressions, 9-10, 40, 422
remove_nulls command (Expect), 188
rename command (core Tcl), 41
replicate command (TclX), 308
reports, generating, 307
resources about Tcl/Tk, 412, 427-428
return command (core Tcl), 41
root directory, setting, 289
root window, 49-50
round command (TclX), 308
row options, 372

S

saveprocs command (TclX), 308
scale command (Tk), 86-87
scan command (core Tcl), 41
scancontext command (TclX), 308
scanfile command (TclX), 309
scanmatch command (TclX), 309
scheduling execution of commands, 16
scope command ([incr Tcl]), 200
scoped values, 198, 200
screen units, 53
scrollable lists, 238-239
scrollbar command (Tk), 87-89
scrollbar widgets, 51, 55-56, 88
scrollbars, 239
scrolling methods, 88
searching, 287
  lists, 35
searchpath command (TclX), 309
security, 125
seek command (core Tcl), 41
select command (TclX), 309
selecting, 223-226
  filenames, 221-226
  functions related to, 164
  options, 232
  windows, 228, 243
selection command (Tk), 124
semicolon (;), 4, 416
send command
  Expect, 188
  Tk, 49, 125
send_ commands (Expect), 189
sequences, 101-102
  multi-event, 105
set command (core Tcl), 42, 418
shell commands, 419
shell windows, 242
showproc command (TclX), 310
signal command (TclX), 310
sin command (TclX), 310
sines, 310
sinh command (TclX), 310
slave options, 370

X

About the Authors

Paul Raines is a physicist and scientific programmer at Stanford University's Stanford Linear Accelerator Center. He is part of a large collaboration studying CP violation (why charge times parity is not conserved in some particle decays, an arcane research topic that bears on the more understandable question of why there is an excess of matter over antimatter in the universe). He is a huge advocate of scripting languages and has been using Tcl on various projects since 1992. He maintains a freely distributable quick-reference guide for Tcl/Tk, now published as O'Reilly & Associates' *Tcl/Tk Pocket Reference*. When he can get away from the lab, Paul enjoys hiking, bridge, and soccer. He lives in San Mateo, California, with his wife Deborah and her horse and three cats.

Jeff Tranter works as a software designer for a Canadian telecommunications company and has been using Tcl since 1992 on a number of programming projects related to software tools and testing. He is an active user of Linux, a contributor to the Linux Documentation Project, and author of the O'Reilly book *Linux Multimedia Guide*. His hobbies include ham radio, playing guitar, and mountain biking.

Colophon

The bird featured on the cover of *Tck/Tk in a Nutshell* is an ibis. There are over 30 species of these wading birds distributed throughout the world, primarily in the warmer and tropical regions. All ibises have long, narrow, sharply turned-down bills that they use to probe for insects, mollusks, and small crustaceans in mud or dirt. They are strong fliers and swimmers, and most prefer living in the wetlands near fresh or salt water, marshes, and swamps. They are very sociable and gregarious birds who nest in large colonies and travel in flocks. When flying, all members of the flock alternate wing beats with gliding at approximately the same rate.

Fossils indicate that ibises have existed for about 60 million years, and records of human interaction with ibises dates back 5,000 years. In ancient Egypt, the ibis was revered as the embodiment of Thoth, god of wisdom and scribe of the gods. They are frequently depicted in Egyptian hieroglyphics, and cemeteries of mummified ibises have been discovered.

Today, the most widely distributed of all ibis species is the glossy ibis. The glossy ibis is the last species of ibis known to exist in Europe and has spread to Africa, parts of Asia, and the Americas. The most common species in the Americas is the white ibis, which has gradually spread northward and is now found as far north as Maine.

Edie Freedman designed the cover of this book using a 19th-century engraving from the Dover Pictorial Archive. Kathleen Wilson produced the cover layout with QuarkXPress 3.3 using the ITC Garamond font. Whenever possible, our books use RepKover™, a durable and flexible lay-flat binding. If the page count exceeds RepKover's limit, perfect binding is used.

Madeleine Newell was the production editor for this book, and Sheryl Avruch was the production manager. Cindy Kogut of Editorial Ink did the copyedit. Nancy Crumpton wrote the index, and Seth Maislin produced the final version of the index. Nicole Arigo and Nancy Wolfe Kotary provided quality assurance, and Sebastian Banker and Betty Hugh provided production assistance.

The inside layout was designed by Nancy Priest and implemented in gtroff by Lenny Muellner. The text and heading fonts are ITC Garamond Light and Garamond Book. The screen shots that appear in the book were created in Adobe Photoshop 4.0 by Robert Romano. This colophon was written by Clairemarie Fisher O'Leary.

More Titles from O'Reilly

UNIX Tools

Exploring Expect

By Don Libes
1st Edition December 1994
602 pages, ISBN 1-56592-090-2

Written by the author of Expect, this is the first book to explain how this part of the UNIX toolbox can be used to automate Telnet, FTP, passwd, rlogin, and hundreds of other interactive applications. Based on Tcl (Tool Command Language), Expect lets you automate interactive applications that have previously been extremely difficult to handle with any scripting language.

Programming with GNU Software

By Mike Loukides & Andy Oram
1st Edition December 1996
260 pages, ISBN 1-56592-112-7

This book and CD combination is a complete package for programmers who are new to UNIX or who would like to make better use of the system. The tools come from Cygnus Support, Inc., and Cyclic Software, companies that provide support for free software. Contents include GNU Emacs, *gcc*, C and C++ libraries, *gdb*, RCS, and *make*. The book provides an introduction to all these tools for a C programmer.

Applying RCS and SCCS

By Don Bolinger & Tan Bronson
1st Edition September 1995
528 pages, ISBN 1-56592-117-8

Applying RCS and SCCS is a thorough introduction to these two systems, viewed as tools for project management. This book takes the reader from basic source control of a single file, through working with multiple releases of a software project, to coordinating multiple developers. It also presents TCCS, a representative "front-end" that addresses problems RCS and SCCS can't handle alone, such as managing groups of files, developing for multiple platforms, and linking public and private development areas.

Tcl/Tk Tools

By Mark Harrison
1st Edition September 1997
678 pages, Includes CD-ROM
ISBN 1-56592-218-2

One of the greatest strengths of Tcl/Tk is the range of extensions written for it. This book clearly documents the most popular and robust extensions—by the people who created them—and contains information on configuration, debugging, and other important tasks. The CD-ROM includes Tcl/Tk, the extensions, and other tools documented in the text both in source form and as binaries for Solaris and Linux.

Software Portability with imake, 2nd Edition

By Paul DuBois
2nd Edition September 1996
410 pages, ISBN 1-56592-226-3

This Nutshell Handbook®—the only book available on *imake*—is ideal for X and UNIX programmers who want their software to be portable. The second edition covers the current version of the X Window System (X11R6.1), using *imake* for non-UNIX systems such as Windows NT, and some of the quirks about using *imake* under OpenWindows/ Solaris.

Writing GNU Emacs Extensions

By Bob Glickstein
1st Edition April 1997
236 pages, ISBN 1-56592-261-1

This book introduces Emacs Lisp and tells you how to make the editor do whatever you want, whether it's altering the way text scrolls or inventing a whole new "major mode." Topics progress from simple to complex, from lists, symbols, and keyboard commands to syntax tables, macro templates, and error recovery.

UNIX Tools

lex & yacc, 2nd Edition

By John Levine, Tony Mason &
Doug Brown
2nd Edition October 1992
366 pages, ISBN 1-56592-000-7

This book shows programmers how
to use two UNIX utilities, lex and yacc,
in program development. The second
edition contains completely revised
tutorial sections for novice users and
reference sections for advanced users.
This edition is twice the size of the first, has an expanded
index, and covers Bison and Flex.

sed & awk, 2nd Edition

By Dale Dougherty & Arnold Robbins
2nd Edition March 1997
432 pages, ISBN 1-56592-225-5

sed & awk describes two text manipulation
programs that are mainstays of the UNIX
programmer's toolbox. This new edition
covers the sed and awk programs as they
are now mandated by the POSIX standard
and includes discussion of the GNU versions of these programs.

The UNIX CD Bookshelf

By O'Reilly & Associates, Inc.
1st Edition November 1998
444 pages, Includes CD-ROM & book
ISBN 1-56592-406-1

The UNIX CD Bookshelf contains six
books from O'Reilly plus the software
from UNIX Power Tools—all on a
convenient CD-ROM. A bonus hardcopy
book, UNIX in a Nutshell: System V
Edition, is also included. The CD-ROM
contains UNIX in a Nutshell: System V Edition; UNIX Power
Tools, 2nd Edition (with software); Learning the UNIX Operating System, 4th Edition; Learning the vi Editor, 6th Edition; sed
& awk, 2nd Edition; and Learning the Korn Shell.

Managing Projects with make, 2nd Edition

By Andrew Oram & Steve Talbott
2nd Edition October 1991
152 pages, ISBN 0-937175-90-0

make is one of UNIX's greatest
contributions to software development,
and this book is the clearest description
of make ever written. It describes all the
basic features of make and provides
guidelines on meeting the needs of
large, modern projects. Also contains a
description of free products that contain major enhancements
to make.

UNIX Power Tools, 2nd Edition

By Jerry Peek, Tim O'Reilly &
Mike Loukides
2nd Edition August 1997
1120 pages, Includes CD-ROM
ISBN 1-56592-260-3

Loaded with even more practical
advice about almost every
aspect of UNIX, this new
second edition of UNIX Power
Tools addresses the technology
that UNIX users face today. You'll find
increased coverage of POSIX utilities, including GNU versions,
greater bash and tcsh shell coverage, more emphasis on Perl,
and a CD-ROM that contains the best freeware available.

Perl

Perl in a Nutshell

By Stephen Spainhour, Ellen Siever &
Nathan Patwardhan
1st Edition January 1999
674 pages, ISBN 1-56592-286-7

The perfect companion for working
programmers, Perl in a Nutshell is a
comprehensive reference guide to the
world of Perl. It contains everything
you need to know for all but the most
obscure Perl questions.This wealth
of information is packed into an efficient, extraordinarily
usable format.

Perl

The Perl Cookbook

By Tom Christiansen &
Nathan Torkington
1st Edition August 1998
794 pages, ISBN 1-56592-243-3

This collection of problems, solutions, and examples for anyone programming in Perl covers everything from beginner questions to techniques that even the most experienced Perl programmers might learn from. It contains hundreds of Perl "recipes," including recipes for parsing strings, doing matrix multiplication, working with arrays and hashes, and performing complex regular expressions.

Learning Perl, 2nd Edition

By Randal L. Schwartz &
Tom Christiansen
Foreword by Larry Wall
2nd Edition July 1997
302 pages, ISBN 1-56592-284-0

In this update of a bestseller, two leading Perl trainers teach you to use the most universal scripting language in the age of the World Wide Web. Now current for Perl version 5.004, this hands-on tutorial includes a lengthy new chapter on CGI programming, while touching also on the use of library modules, references, and Perl's object-oriented constructs.

Learning Perl on Win32 Systems

By Randal L. Schwartz, Erik Olson &
Tom Christiansen
1st Edition August 1997
306 pages, ISBN 1-56592-324-3

In this carefully paced course, leading Perl trainers and a Windows NT practitioner teach you to program in the language that promises to emerge as the scripting language of choice on NT. Based on the "llama" book, this book features tips for PC users and new, NT-specific examples, along with a foreword by Larry Wall, the creator of Perl, and Dick Hardt, the creator of Perl for Win32.

Mastering Regular Expressions

By Jeffrey E. F. Friedl
1st Edition January 1997
368 pages, ISBN 1-56592-257-3

Regular expressions, a powerful tool for manipulating text and data, are found in scripting languages, editors, programming environments, and pecialized tools. In this book, author Jeffrey Friedl leads you through the steps of crafting a regular expression that gets the job done. He examines a variety of tools and uses them in an extensive array of examples, with a major focus on Perl.

Learning Perl/Tk

By Nancy Walsh
1st Edition January 1999
376 pages, ISBN 1-56592-314-6

This tutorial for Perl/Tk, the extension to Perl for creating graphical user interfaces, shows how to use Perl/Tk to build graphical, event-driven applications for both Windows and UNIX. Rife with illustrations, it teaches how to implement and configure each Perl/Tk graphical element.

Mastering Algorithms with Perl

By Jon Orwant, Jarkko Hietaniemi &
John Macdonald
1st Edition August 1999 (est.)
688 pages (est.), ISBN 1-56592-398-7

There have been dozens of books on programming algorithms, but never before has there been one that uses Perl. Whether you are an amateur programmer or know a wide range of algorithms in other languages, this book will teach you how to carry out traditional programming tasks in a high-powered, efficient, easy-to-maintain manner with Perl. Topics range in complexity from sorting and searching to statistical algorithms, numerical analysis, and encryption.

Perl

Perl Resource Kit—UNIX Edition

By Larry Wall, Nate Patwardhan,
Ellen Siever, David Futato &
Brian Jepson
1st Edition November 1997
1812 pages, ISBN 1-56592-370-7

The *Perl Resource Kit—UNIX Edition*
gives you the most comprehensive
collection of Perl documentation
and commercially enhanced software
tools available today. Developed in association with Larry
Wall, the creator of Perl, it's the definitive Perl distribution
for webmasters, programmers, and system administrators.

The *Perl Resource Kit* provides:

- Over 1800 pages of tutorial and in-depth reference
  documentation for Perl utilities and extensions, in 4
  volumes.
- A CD-ROM containing the complete Perl distribution,
  plus hundreds of freeware Perl extensions and utilities—
  a complete snapshot of the Comprehensive Perl Archive
  Network (CPAN)—as well as new software written by
  Larry Wall just for the Kit.

Perl Software Tools All on One Convenient CD-ROM
Experienced Perl hackers know when to create their own,
and when they can find what they need on CPAN. Now all the
power of CPAN—and more—is at your fingertips. The *Perl
Resource Kit* includes:

- A complete snapshot of CPAN, with an install program for
  Solaris and Linux that ensures that all necessary modules
  are installed together. Also includes an easy-to-use search
  tool and a web-aware interface that allows you to get the
  latest version of each module.
- A new Java/Perl interface that allows programmers to
  write Java classes with Perl implementations. This new
  tool was written specially for the Kit by Larry Wall.

Experience the power of Perl modules in areas such as CGI,
web spidering, database interfaces, managing mail and
USENET news, user interfaces, security, graphics, math and
statistics, and much more.

Programming Perl, 2nd Edition

By Larry Wall, Tom Christiansen &
Randal L. Schwartz
2nd Edition September 1996
670 pages, ISBN 1-56592-149-6

Coauthored by Larry Wall, the
creator of Perl, the second edition
of this authoritative guide contains a
full explanation of Perl version 5.003
features. It covers Perl language and
syntax, functions, library modules,
references, and object-oriented features, and also explores
invocation options, debugging, common mistakes, and much
more.

Perl Resource Kit—Win32 Edition

By Dick Hardt, Erik Olson,
David Futato & Brian Jepson
1st Edition August 1998
1,832 pages
Includes 4 books & CD-ROM
ISBN 1-56592-409-6

The *Perl Resource Kit—Win32
Edition* is an essential tool for Perl
programmers who are expanding their
platform expertise to include Win32 and for Win32 webmasters
and system administrators who have discovered the power and
flexibility of Perl. The Kit contains some of the latest commercial
Win32 Perl software from Dick Hardt's ActiveState company,
along with a collection of hundreds of Perl modules that run
on Win32, and a definitive documentation set from O'Reilly.

Advanced Perl Programming

By Sriram Srinivasan
1st Edition August 1997
434 pages, ISBN 1-56592-220-4

This book covers complex techniques
for managing production-ready Perl
programs and explains methods for
manipulating data and objects that may
have looked like magic before. It gives
you necessary background for dealing
with networks, databases, and GUIs, and includes a discussion of
internals to help you program more efficiently and embed Perl
within C or C within Perl.

In a Nutshell Quick References

How to stay in touch with O'Reilly

1. Visit Our Award-Winning Site

http://www.oreilly.com/

★ "Top 100 Sites on the Web" —*PC Magazine*
★ "Top 5% Web sites" —*Point Communications*
★ "3-Star site" —*The McKinley Group*

Our web site contains a library of comprehensive product information (including book excerpts and tables of contents), downloadable software, background articles, interviews with technology leaders, links to relevant sites, book cover art, and more. File us in your Bookmarks or Hotlist!

2. Join Our Email Mailing Lists

New Product Releases
To receive automatic email with brief descriptions of all new O'Reilly products as they are released, send email to:
listproc@online.oreilly.com
Put the following information in the first line of your message (*not* in the Subject field):
subscribe oreilly-news

O'Reilly Events
If you'd also like us to send information about trade show events, special promotions, and other O'Reilly events, send email to:
listproc@online.oreilly.com
Put the following information in the first line of your message (*not* in the Subject field):
subscribe oreilly-events

3. Get Examples from Our Books via FTP

There are two ways to access an archive of example files from our books:

Regular FTP
- ftp to:
  ftp.oreilly.com
  (login: anonymous
  password: your email address)
- Point your web browser to:
  ftp://ftp.oreilly.com/

FTPMAIL
- Send an email message to:
  ftpmail@online.oreilly.com
  (Write "help" in the message body)

4. Contact Us via Email

order@oreilly.com
To place a book or software order online. Good for North American and international customers.

subscriptions@oreilly.com
To place an order for any of our newsletters or periodicals.

books@oreilly.com
General questions about any of our books.

software@oreilly.com
For general questions and product information about our software. Check out O'Reilly Software Online at **http://software.oreilly.com/** for software and technical support information. Registered O'Reilly software users send your questions to:
website-support@oreilly.com

cs@oreilly.com
For answers to problems regarding your order or our products.

booktech@oreilly.com
For book content technical questions or corrections.

proposals@oreilly.com
To submit new book or software proposals to our editors and product managers.

international@oreilly.com
For information about our international distributors or translation queries. For a list of our distributors outside of North America check out:
http://www.oreilly.com/www/order/country.html

O'Reilly & Associates, Inc.
101 Morris Street, Sebastopol, CA 95472 USA
TEL 707-829-0515 or 800-998-9938
(6am to 5pm PST)
FAX 707-829-0104

International Distributors

UK, EUROPE, MIDDLE EAST AND AFRICA (EXCEPT FRANCE, GERMANY, AUSTRIA, SWITZERLAND, LUXEMBOURG, LIECHTENSTEIN, AND EASTERN EUROPE)

INQUIRIES
O'Reilly UK Limited
4 Castle Street
Farnham
Surrey, GU9 7HS
United Kingdom
Telephone: 44-1252-711776
Fax: 44-1252-734211
Email: josette@oreilly.com

ORDERS
Wiley Distribution Services Ltd.
1 Oldlands Way
Bognor Regis
West Sussex PO22 9SA
United Kingdom
Telephone: 44-1243-779777
Fax: 44-1243-820250
Email: cs-books@wiley.co.uk

FRANCE
ORDERS
GEODIF
61, Bd Saint-Germain
75240 Paris Cedex 05, France
Tel: 33-1-44-41-46-16 (French books)
Tel: 33-1-44-41-11-87 (English books)
Fax: 33-1-44-41-11-44
Email: distribution@eyrolles.com

INQUIRIES
Éditions O'Reilly
18 rue Séguier
75006 Paris, France
Tel: 33-1-40-51-52-30
Fax: 33-1-40-51-52-31
Email: france@editions-oreilly.fr

GERMANY, SWITZERLAND, AUSTRIA, EASTERN EUROPE, LUXEMBOURG, AND LIECHTENSTEIN
INQUIRIES & ORDERS
O'Reilly Verlag
Balthasarstr. 81
D-50670 Köln
Germany
Telephone: 49-221-973160-91
Fax: 49-221-973160-8
Email: anfragen@oreilly.de (inquiries)
Email: order@oreilly.de (orders)

CANADA (FRENCH LANGUAGE BOOKS)
Les Éditions Flammarion ltée
375, Avenue Laurier Ouest
Montréal (Québec) H2V 2K3
Tel: 00-1-514-277-8807
Fax: 00-1-514-278-2085
Email: info@flammarion.qc.ca

HONG KONG
City Discount Subscription Service, Ltd.
Unit D, 3rd Floor, Yan's Tower
27 Wong Chuk Hang Road
Aberdeen, Hong Kong
Tel: 852-2580-3539
Fax: 852-2580-6463
Email: citydis@ppn.com.hk

KOREA
Hanbit Media, Inc.
Sonyoung Bldg. 202
Yeksam-dong 736-36
Kangnam-ku
Seoul, Korea
Tel: 822-554-9610
Fax: 822-556-0363
Email: hant93@chollian.dacom.co.kr

PHILIPPINES
Mutual Books, Inc.
429-D Shaw Boulevard
Mandaluyong City, Metro
Manila, Philippines
Tel: 632-725-7538
Fax: 632-721-3056
Email: mbikikog@mnl.sequel.net

TAIWAN
O'Reilly Taiwan
No. 3, Lane 131
Hang-Chow South Road
Section 1, Taipei, Taiwan
Tel: 886-2-23968990
Fax: 886-2-23968916
Email: benh@oreilly.com

CHINA
O'Reilly Beijing
Room 2410
160, FuXingMenNeiDaJie
XiCheng District
Beijing
China PR 100031
Tel: 86-10-86631006
Fax: 86-10-86631007
Email: frederic@oreilly.com

INDIA
Computer Bookshop (India) Pvt. Ltd.
190 Dr. D.N. Road, Fort
Bombay 400 001 India
Tel: 91-22-207-0989
Fax: 91-22-262-3551
Email: cbsbom@giasbm01.vsnl.net.in

JAPAN
O'Reilly Japan, Inc.
Kiyoshige Building 2F
12-Bancho, Sanei-cho
Shinjuku-ku
Tokyo 160-0008 Japan
Tel: 81-3-3356-5227
Fax: 81-3-3356-5261
Email: japan@oreilly.com

ALL OTHER ASIAN COUNTRIES
O'Reilly & Associates, Inc.
101 Morris Street
Sebastopol, CA 95472 USA
Tel: 707-829-0515
Fax: 707-829-0104
Email: order@oreilly.com

AUSTRALIA
WoodsLane Pty., Ltd.
7/5 Vuko Place
Warriewood NSW 2102
Australia
Tel: 61-2-9970-5111
Fax: 61-2-9970-5002
Email: info@woodslane.com.au

NEW ZEALAND
Woodslane New Zealand, Ltd.
21 Cooks Street (P.O. Box 575)
Waganui, New Zealand
Tel: 64-6-347-6543
Fax: 64-6-345-4840
Email: info@woodslane.com.au

LATIN AMERICA
McGraw-Hill Interamericana
Editores, S.A. de C.V.
Cedro No. 512
Col. Atlampa
06450, Mexico, D.F.
Tel: 52-5-547-6777
Fax: 52-5-547-3336
Email: mcgraw-hill@infosel.net.mx

O'REILLY®

TO ORDER: **800-998-9938** • order@oreilly.com • http://www.oreilly.com/
OUR PRODUCTS ARE AVAILABLE AT A BOOKSTORE OR SOFTWARE STORE NEAR YOU.
FOR INFORMATION: **800-998-9938** • **707-829-0515** • info@oreilly.com